Kemper County Vindicated, and a Peep at Radical Rule in Mississippi

KEMPER COUNTY VINDICATED,

AND

A PEEP AT RADICAL RULE

IN MISSISSIPPI.

By JAMES D LYNCH,

AUTHOR OF THE POEMS, "ROBERT E LEE, OR, HEROES OF THE SOUTH;"
"THE KU-KLUX TRIBUNAL," ETC.

NEW YORK:
E. J. HALE & SON, PUBLISHERS,
No 17 MURRAY STREET.
1879

Entered, according to Act of Congress, in the year 1879, by the people of Kemper County, Mississippi, in the office of the Librarian of Congress, at Washington, D. C.

PREFACE.

The object of this work is to present a true history of the deplorable events that occurred in Kemper County, Mississippi, during the rule of the radical party, and resulting from it, and which have been so persistently and maliciously exaggerated and misrepresented for the purposes of calumny; and to show that, in regard to these events, the people of that county have been more " sinned against than sinning."

In treating of these circumstances, the author has necessarily been led to a view of the whole field of official corruption, which spread itself from the Capitol all round to the borders of the State, and which was extended, planted and cultivated by means of the infamous process called ' reconstruction," which was originated and enforced by the hatred of the then all dominant party that wielded the power of the Federal Government; and from this survey it will be manifest that the terrible state of affairs that existed in Kemper County, and so assiduously ascribed to the depravity of its citizens, was but a prominent outgrowth of that harvest of crime sown by the hand of radicalism all over the State.

The author has not permitted himself to be actuated by

any partisan impulse or personal prejudice. He had no personal acquaintance whatever with the individuals whose characters and careers form the main features of this work; and he has had no ends to subserve in its production save those of justice and truth. In the promotion and vindication of these he has availed himself of every reliable source and means he could command. He has obtained the facts enunciated in this work from the records of the State and of Kemper County, and from the personal statements of witnesses, upon whose knowledge and candor he could implicitly rely; and wherever there were any doubts connected with an act, they have been assigned to the benefit of the parties charged.

He was conscious of the fact that he was dealing with the characters and deeds of those whose voice of defence was forever hushed, and he has turned a deaf ear to every breath of report.

But from the grave comes the voice that brings the greatest terror to vice and the most eloquent admonition to virtue, and to reflecting minds this legend will have significance:

The ancient Egyptians subjected the bodies of their dead to trial and imaginary punishment. For this purpose a solemn tribunal was instituted, before which the dead were brought, and the virtues and vices of the deceased disclosed and weighed, and if the scales were found to dip to the side of vice, the body was sentenced to some desecrating formality; and it is said that this custom was more effective in deterring from crime than the punishment of the living.

The author has opened the graves of the unfortunate victims of these events with a cautious hand and a conscientious motive; and if the disclosure of their career and terrible fate should rescue truth from the shackles of slander, and send a sound of warning to the ear of oppression, his labor in the production of this work will not have been in vain.

JAMES D. LYNCH.

WEST POINT, MISS, *February*, 1879.

KEMPER COUNTY VINDICATED.

CHAPTER I.

At the termination of the war between the North and South, the Southern people promptly submitted to the decision which the sword had rendered against them, and accepted in good faith all the legitimate results of the arbitrament. They immediately and voluntarily abolished the institution of slavery, which, if it was not the chief cause of the war, was the ground upon which were gathered all the elements of the strife; and they endeavored forthwith to fashion their laws and customs in conformity to the exigencies of their situation.

But all their efforts at a speedy resumption of allegiance and loyal relations to the Union were thwarted by a partisan and revengeful process of reconstruction, dictated by a spirit of hate on the part of the North; and its odious terms were imposed upon them by the most humiliating and degrading methods that vengeance could devise.

Their States were stripped of every vestige of sovereignty and remanded to the condition of territories, while the people, in many instances, were disfranchised, and an ignorant and inferior race, their former slaves, were enfranchised and placed over them.

No sooner had the last sulphurous smoke curled up from the field of battle—and before the Southern soldiers, armless and helpless, had reached their homes, where, agreeably to the terms upon which they had surrendered, they expected to find peace, and an untrammelled opportunity of rebuilding their desolated homes, of reclothing their naked families, and replenishing their empty larders—than a howl of vengeance rolled up from every hill and hamlet throughout the North; not from those who had met them on the bloody field, but from the dastard politicians, hypocritical preachers, and canting Puritans; which echoed against the walls of the national capital, and called forth hordes of greedy and vicious adventurers, who swarmed toward the South, and, by the aid and protection of the Union army, became fastened upon the land.

It was now that the Southern people began to feel the hand of the carpet bagger in their pockets, and the heel of the negro upon their necks, while the bayonet of the Federal soldier was pointed at their breasts. They saw their President, with manacled limbs, lying in a loathsome prison, whose only crime was that he had yielded to their wishes and headed their cause. They saw their property, honestly acquired by their own and the sweat of their fathers' brows, and guaranteed to them by the laws and constitution of the land, swept away from them. They saw their lands become barren, and their wives and children reduced to penury and want. It seemed to them, indeed, as if the dark ages were about to hover again over the ruins of civilization, and from these black clouds of wrath came swarms of thieves and robbers, whose advent was as blighting and noxious as the locusts and lice that covered the land of Egypt.

Mississippi, with a negro population largely in the majority, offered a fertile field to the carpet bagger, who came South for the purpose of seizing all the public offices by means of the negro vote, which, on account of the negroes' ignorance and superstition, and consequent jealousy of their newly acquired rights, was easily to be accomplished when once he became familiar with their character and instinct. Yet, it is doubtful whether the carpet bagger, with his ignorance of the negro's nature and characteristics, could have ever succeeded in severing all the relations between him and his former master, and in so completely and bitterly antagonizing him to the white people of the South, had it not been for the aid and co-operation of those exceptional individuals, who were so lost to every sense of honor, patriotism and sectional pride as to ally themselves with such an enemy to their country and such a curse to their people as the carpet bagger. It is true that there were here and there some who, in all other respects, were good citizens, who suffered their old prejudices against the Democratic party to lead them astray; but, granting their honesty of purpose, they were nevertheless the worst foes to their country. They piloted the carpet bagger to the negro heart. Being well versed in every feature and peculiarity of the negro character, they formed the confidential medium through which the jealousy, ignorance and superstition of the one were blended with the cunning and rapacity of the other.

But the causes that, for the most part, produced that class called scalawags, had their origin deep down in the depths of human depravity. In some instances it arose from a spirit of resentment for some political defeat, and in some it sprang from a desire to gratify some old grudge against their neighbors, or from the dictates of that envy so often found nestling in the bosom of inferiority; but the most prolific cause of all was the spirit of cupidity, the desire of plunder and self enrichment, for which the unsettled state of society offered an ample opportunity, but which could be perpetuated only by keeping up a state of public excitement by means of race issues, and by continually fanning the prejudices and hatred existing in the minds of the masses of the Northern people against the white people of the South.

Having thus severed themselves from every claim upon the respect of their fellow citizens, they found a congenial companion in the person of the carpet bagger, who in turn found in them efficient and indispensable tools for his operations. To this combination the radical party owed its existence at the South. It was planted and fostered there by the cupidity of the carpet bagger, the depravity of the scalawag, and the ignorance, jealousy and superstition of the negro, all under the protection and supervision of the military power of the Federal government, which was kept in motion by the enforcement acts of Congress.

Under the rule of the radical party composed of these elements, began a system of official robbery and corruption throughout the South unparalleled in the history of any civilized people, in the endurance of which the patience of the Southern people could only have been sustained by that high sense of honor which characterized their conduct throughout the great struggle, and impelled them to a strict observance of faith in abiding the terms of their surrender. But the clouds that hung over them like a pall grew darker and thicker, until the last ray of hope seemed to be forever hidden from their view, and driven almost to the brink of despair, they seized upon every opportunity of conciliation, for the protection of their property, which they saw continually vanishing beneath the tread of the tax gatherer, whose frequent rounds were necessary to satisfy the multitudinous demands of the State and county officials, many of which were heretofore unknown to their laws.

But the impudence of these exactions added indignity to their spoliation, encouraged by the ever threatening attitude of the Federal government, and the constant mobility of the Federal army, which was kept always in readiness to fly to their aid upon the least cry of rebellion or intimidation they chose to make; the carpet bagger and the scalawag walked the lords of the land, while the filthiest and most degraded negro was taught to believe himself superior to any Southern white man who was not a radical. But the importance and demands of the carpet bagger increased with his success, and, fortunately for the Southern people, caused the birth of jealousy and distrust between him and the scalawag.

While the negroes, growing weary of disappointment and deceptive promises, and seeing themselves gradually thrust aside by the avarice of their white allies, began first to grow lukewarm in politics, and finally to manifest a dis position for the first time to listen to the advice of their former owners, whose interest they saw was closely connected with their own.

Such was the state of affairs in Mississippi at the opening of the campaign of 1875. The white people of this State had made every effort to penetrate the alliance against them; in a spirit of conciliation they had voted for Horace Greeley, a radical, for President of the United States, and they had voted for Dent and James L. Alcorn, both radicals, for governors of their State. But all their efforts were heretofore in vain, and seeing now for the first time even the resemblance of a rift in the cloud that blackened their horizon, they gathered all their strength for a supreme effort to roll back the avalanche of destruction and to stay the tide of ruin that swept over them.

At the beginning of the year 1875 there was scarcely a Democrat in office in the State of Mississippi. Carpet baggers, scalawags and negroes wore every vesture of civil, judicial and political authority in the State. The situation of affairs at this juncture cannot be better and more truthfully described than in the following extract from the minority report of Senators Bayard and McDonald, of the Senatorial Investigating Committee:

"The reconstruction policy of Congress had fully and perfectly forced the institutions of the State of Mississippi into the most entire subjection and conformity with its provisions. What Mississippi was, she was 'the work of reconstruction by Congress.' The will of her people, their tastes, their prejudices, their virtues, and their faults, had been melted and run into a mould fashioned by the will of Congress alone. If her institutions were defective, if they were not conducive to the ends of good government, if they were arranged with an unwise disregard of the condition and wants of the people, that people are no more responsible than the population of France, for they had no voice. Such as she was, the Congress of the United States had made her."

This is very true as to her outward form, but the inner

rottenness that permeated her whole system will probably ever remain inconceivable, save to those who experienced its pollution. But again "Unfortunately, these new and arbitrary political conditions, imposed upon both races by the will of Congress, were disturbed by the presence of a class of unscrupulous, needy and rapacious adventurers, who came down to fill the political offices to which prejudice against the Southern whites on the part of those who held power in the Federal government, and the absolute ignorance and incompetence of the negroes, prevented those whites from being appointed, . . . and by means of low arts the negroes of the State of Mississippi have been banded together in an unthinking mass, under the lead and blind control of a handful of Northern strangers, with here and there a native white man."

They saw the ignorant African and the refuse of the North perched in the seats once occupied only by their purest and most talented citizens, while these same citizens were now in many instances disfranchised and not allowed to raise their voice; while their former slaves, with idiotic grins and clamorous hurrahs, bustled up to the ballot box with a ticket placed in their hands by a foreign or native radical, and which they could not read. Great God! was this to be their constant doom? No; that God who scourged the thieves from the temple, that caused Felix to tremble on the judgment seat, and Pilate to wash his blood-stained hands, would not suffer such a disgrace to be long perpetuated in mockery of every sentiment of humanity.

The great political struggle of 1875 bore upon its crest the issue of life or death to the white people of Mississippi. Their labor system, which depended upon the negro, who alone was inured to the hot suns of her summers, had become entirely worthless, while theft was resorted to as a means of livelihood to such an extent, by the blacks, that the very grass grew uncropped and untrodden on her pastures and commons, while any attempt to convict a criminal was sure to fail before a negro jury.

What people is there on earth who would not have resorted to every legitimate means in their power to remedy such a state of affairs? And yet, because they made a successful effort and redeemed their State from such barbarous rule, the cry of fraud and intimidation was raised throughout the radical party, the army invoked, a remand to military rule threatened, congressional inquisitions inaugurated, the private correspondence of individuals seized and made public, the privacy of domestic relations invaded for the purpose of finding some infringement upon the constitutional amendments or infraction of the reconstruction laws, as an excuse to reinstate the old order of things, which was necessary to maintain the radical party in power.

No sooner had the great change in the condition of things by the success of the Democratic party been inaugurated, than the carpet bagger, his occupation being now gone, fled the haunts of his former vice, and disappeared almost entirely from the Southern States as suddenly as he had made his advent; while the scalawag, possessing less mobility, in many instances, clung to a forlorn hope, and, in 1877, in some counties in the State, made another effort to band the negroes together in their old state of hostility to the whites; and as there was no longer any possibility of obtaining Federal military aid, those who had the boldness to undertake the task, must necessarily resort to other means by which to effect their purpose. What these means were will form a dark feature in the following pages, among which were instigations to riot, by imposing upon the ignorance of the negro, the assassination in some instances of leading Democrats, or some other act that would bring them to the notice of the radical administration; so that if they should fail to be elected by the negro vote to the office to which they aspired, they would be sure to receive some appointment from the hands of the Washington authorities suitable to and commensurate with their services to the party in control of the Federal appointments

The State of Mississippi had been, since the election of 1875, as thoroughly Democratic as it had before that been radical. The negroes had abandoned entirely their hostile attitude to the white people, and had reestablished the most cordial relations with their former owners. The whole State had begun to put on the robes of a new prosperity, laws were promptly and impartially executed without discrimination of race, color or former condition. The feelings of peace and good will reigned supreme throughout the State; and the native citizen who could have the hardihood to attempt to disturb this state of things, and again kindle the fires of discord and of race prejudices, and reinstate the reign of barbarism, must have been a man whose heart was not only callous to every sentiment of virtue, but wanting in every purpose that aims at the welfare of humanity.

Mississippi was the peculiar object of Northern hatred. She had been proscribed as a leading State in the war. The promptness with which she entered the struggle, and the constancy with which she adhered to the Southern cause, had from the first, drawn upon her the most poisoned arrows of vengeance; and no depths of prostration, no degree of degradation, or measure of penance, could in the eyes of the Northern masses atone for the part she acted, or satisfy the insatiable spirit of revenge which the heart of the North harbored against her. A deliberate policy had devoted her to utter ruin, and it was this that dictated the harsh proceedings inaugurated against her citizens, upon the slightest charges, in the Federal courts, under the name of ku klux trials, and it was this proscription that caused her to become so completely under the control of the carpet bagger. They were encouraged by the assurance of receiving military aid whenever needed to protect them in anything they might do. But if there had been no scalawags, if the white people of the South had presented a solid front to the tide of oppressive measures that was rolled upon them, the career of the carpet bagger would have been confined to, and ended with, military occupation.

It was the consciousness of this fact that rendered the scalawag the peculiar object of contempt, which was only modified, sometimes, by old bonds of personal friendship, and in some instances by their respectable connections and antecedents; but they were for the most part individuals who were known to have always lacked most, or all of the virtues that constitute an honorable man or good citizen, which rendered them fit subjects to play the despicable *role* of spies upon every circle of society into which their connections might procure them admission.

But if the carpet bagger lived easily, he died hard. It was to him like the plunge from the Tarpeian rock, to be so suddenly deprived of his crown and emoluments of office; and it is no wonder that he should vent his spleen upon the heads of those who so ruthlessly deprived him of his occupation, and invoke his powers of falsification by which he first deprived the poor negro of his ballot and then of his money. He lets us hear from him occasionally through the infamous slanders and falsehoods which he from time to time still concocts about the Southern people for the purpose of gratifying his revenge and appeasing his ravenous longings for an opportunity of once more thrusting his pilfering fingers into their pockets.

Conspicuous among these is one James M. Wells, formerly a deputy revenue collector in Mississippi.

This individual has written a book entitled the "Chisolm Massacre; or, Home Rule in Mississippi," meaning, of course, a rule in which the amiable carpet bagger does not share, in which he has seen proper to asperse the good people of Kemper County with the vilest slanders, and through them the people of the State of Mississippi, and of the whole South.

It is the main object of this work to reply to the slanders perpetrated by that individual, and to present to the world in behalf of the people of Kemper County and Mississippi, a true statement of the transactions which he has so whiningly and flippantly falsified. Were it not for the gravity and importance of the occurrences upon which he has built his slanderous effusions, and their widespread report, neither the people of Kemper County nor the writer would have any desire to attempt a refutation of charges couched in such shallow terms, clothed in such party colored robes, and whose baseness is so lucidly manifest.

The people of Kemper County bore a full share of the consequences and results of the rule and ruin policy inaugurated by the radical party throughout the State of Mississippi.

This county, prior to the war, had been, in a great measure, exempt from those violent political excitements and personal disturbances which so often shock society in other localities, and especially in many of the Northern States, where labor and railroad riots, often attended by the most heinous crimes, are so rife, and where *spiritualistic* influences, free loverism and "no hell" doctrines produce their diabolical results.

To say that there were no crimes committed, would be to upset all the experience of mankind and deny the frailties of human nature; but it may be positively asserted that the criminal records of this county, prior to and during the war, will compare favorably with those of any other community, notwithstanding its comparison to the "dark and bloody ground" so flippantly made by the craven carpet bagger.

It is a wonder that the descriptive Wells did not invoke the smoke of the burning witches of New England, or the rule of the Kansas squatter, or the burning of the Catholic convents in Boston, to give expression to his slanderous purpose.

But he need not even to have gone beyond the scope of radical rule in the South to have found comparisons sufficiently apt to give the desired vividness to his description, for any comparison to illustrate the deeds of radicalism in the South will be made more manifest by a process of involution—its features are best reflected within itself. There is no extraneous mirror that can do it justice. No sooner had it established itself in all the offices of the county and lodged its elements upon the most degraded, ignorant and vicious portion of its inhabitants, than the Pandora of crime was opened, and a drama begun which for infamy and corruption would puzzle the historian to find a comparison. "*It was then that the multiplied villanies of nature swarmed upon them with unwonted profusion;*" a description of which has been more dispassionately and certainly more truthfully given by an author of far more reliability than could ever blend with the character of a carpet bagger. I refer to the minority report of the Boutwell investigating committee, which contains the following description, and yet it is only true so far as it extends, and only so far as observation can represent experience. It is like the breeze of summer personating the blasts of winter.

"A condition of affairs which would be incredible and utterly intolerant in any of the Northern States, exists in many of the black counties of Mississippi, where the property, intelligence and character of the community is trodden to the earth, insulted and ignored by the most ignorant and sometimes vicious members of the community. Things are of daily occurrence, and were proven almost daily before the committee, which if attempted in the States of Massachusetts, Wisconsin, Minnesota, or indeed, any of the Northern States, would be met by a popular uprising and a speedy overthrow. In such a condition of affairs, the forbearance and self subordination exhibited by the white population demand and should receive the strong sympathy and high respect of every just and well regulated mind."

All this was strictly true of the County of Kemper. It was one of the black counties, and in some respects perhaps the blackest of all. The negroes constituted the majority of the voting population, and they were banded solidly together and arbitrarily controlled by as vicious a set of white men as ever cursed a community. Nor were they carpet baggers. Their reign was too intolerant even for that vice trained class. There were but two Northern radicals in the county. It was HOME RULE and home ruin; yet under the inspiring auspices of the foreign horde that ruled the State and extended the arms of judicial, executive and military protection, and immunity for any crime which they might see proper or deem necessary to commit, in order either to preserve their power, or to gratify their cupidity or revenge.

CHAPTER II.

Mounted on the crested tide of ruin that now rolled its utter waves in lashing billows, over the heads of the people of Kemper County, appeared, in bold relief, a figure which at once became the controlling spirit and the most active agent in this embodiment of villanies, whose hand not only piloted the strokes of vengeance, but fashioned every means of evil that vice could prompt, or an utter disregard for every sentiment of virtue could suggest.

William Wallace Chisolm, whose crimes and their terrible retribution will form the chief import of the following pages, was, it seems, a native of Georgia, but who, for a long time prior to the war and the events about to be described, had been a citizen of Kemper County, Mississippi, and a very obscure citizen. Possessed of neither education nor wealth, he labored under the further misfortune of possessing a disgustingly coarse and profane nature. This he perhaps inherited from his father, who, in addition, was a man of notoriously dissipated habits. At the death of his father, Chisolm came into possession of his little farm, a very dilapidated piece of property in the Southern portion of Kemper County, where he continued to reside.

At this time there lived in the same neighborhood an old man by the name of McRea, who was a very popular man and possessed great political influence over his neighbors. He was an old line whig, and so had been Chisolm's father. This circumstance had created a friendship between them which the old man now extended to the son, and, through his influence, young Chisolm was chosen, in 1858, as justice of the peace. This office, however, was, at that time, of but little importance. The jurisdiction of a justice extended, in criminal matters, only to the trial and punishment of petit misdemeanors and to an investigation and committment in other crimes; in civil cases it extended only to those suits which involved the amount of fifty dollars and less, and in no case could its judgments and executions reach real property; hence the emoluments were small, and few persons who had any aspirations or other means of livelihood could be induced to hold the office.

While in this obscure position and in a secluded corner of the county, young Chisolm had but little opportunity to develop those depraved instincts which afterward rendered him so conspicuous in the annals of infamy. This office he held until 1859, during which time his wife taught school and aided in the support of the family. But when the tocsin of secession sounded, and the tide of revolution swept over the land, Chisolm leaped lustily into the maddened current; he even outswam the tide, helped to clear its channels, and unlike its swelling floods. He made secession speeches, and there are hundreds to-day in Kemper County who well remember the fierce expressions of his thirst for "Yankee blood." This he never denied, yet his pliant biographer, the carpet bagger, J. M. Wells, has the mendacity to say:

"In all these years Judge Chisolm was a pronounced Union man, of whig proclivities, and an uncompromising enemy of the party which precipitated and hurled headlong upon the country the terrible consequences of the rebellion. When the *tide* of secession swept over Mississippi like a devouring *flame*," [He here slightly missed the stereotyped phrase and introduced a new element in his combination of *flood* and *flame*.] "he, with thousands of others like himself, who shuddered at the thought, in an unguarded moment, through *force* and *intimidation*, cast a vote favoring the disruption of the Union—an act which it is known he regretted all the remainder of his life."

So much Wells says of Chisolm. Now let us see what Chisolm says of himself in this respect. In his testimony before the Subcommittee on Privileges and Elections, as to the denial of the elective franchise in the State of Mississippi, at the elections of 1875 and 1876, Washington, D. C., February 13, 1877, on page 715 of the report, he said:

"Question by Mr. Teller: Were you in the Confederate service?

"Chisolm: I was in the service—in the militia some; my sympathies were with the South."

Again, before the Mississippi Investigating Committee, at Jackson, on June 23, 1876, he testified as follows:

Question by Senator Bayard, page 773 of the report: 'Did you perform any military service?

"A. Yes, sir; I was on the post there and picked up the conscripts in De Kalb, and then I was out with the militia one time; I was wherever they called me, but I was particular not to be called very far off if I could avoid it. That has nothing to do with this. My people had all gone to the war. It was not that I didn't believe in the cause of the South and was not interested in it. I voted for secession, though my brothers none of them voted for it. I have several brothers in the county, and they went and fought, but I didn't."

This discrepancy will, at the outset, show the facility of this man, Wells, in the fabrication of falsehood upon which to build his rickety edifice of slander against the people of Kemper County:

> "Like one who having unto Truth,
> Made a sinner of his memory
> To credit his own lie"

By means of this open and avowed devotion to the Southern cause, or rather in consequence of his vehement protestations in this respect, at a time, too, when the minds of the Southern people were distracted by the contemplation of what would be the consequences of the election of Lincoln, and through the influence of John W. Gully, his complicity in whose death formed the culmination of his criminal career, Chisolm was, in 1860, elected judge of the Probate Court of Kemper County. This was a very important position, as that court had exclusive jurisdiction of all matters pertaining to guardians and wards, the settlement of estates and all kindred matters; but the country having been soon involved in a war of national life or death, there was but little business transacted before the court, and his opportunities yet dallied in the future, so that during this time, if his conduct was not unobjectionable, it was, at least, unnoticeable.

At the expiration of his term of office, in 1864, he was again, through the instrumentality of his friend John W. Gully, elected to this same office, which he held until he was forced to resign in 1867; but immediately after the close of the war, his depraved nature being no longer under the restraints of circumstances, he at once connected himself with the radical party, and became its champion and leader in the county. It was now that that extended field of operations was opened to him which he soon strewed with the skeletons of his crimes and misdemeanors.

The first act of this panorama of guilt was performed in the spring of 1867. He was, at that time, as we have seen, judge of the Probate Court of Kemper County—a court which, from the very nature of its functions, was invested by the law with peculiar sanctity; and it presumed their exercise to be robed in the purest vesture of virtue and morality.

This bench had heretofore been occupied by those whose ermine was worn and transmitted without soil, or the least stain of the breath of scandal. But what effect these pure and undefiled precedents and virtuous examples, interwoven with the dignity and sacred obligations of this office, produced upon the official character of this man, may be deduced from the following disgusting details, for full exposition of which the sworn testimony of witnesses, including that of Chisolm himself, is invoked and introduced; and in this connection it may be stated, once for all, that the writer would scorn the idea of charging offences upon any one living or dead that are not warranted by facts of record, or based upon information on which he can implicitly rely; and where their foundation is only circumstantial, he will simply spread the circumstances before the reader, with such observations, on his part, as their nature and import may inspire.

On the termination of the war there were some individuals in Mississippi, as well as in the other States of the South, who, by oaths of uniform and unshaken loyalty to the Union, sought to obtain compensation from the government for property destroyed, or alleged to have been destroyed, by the Federal army.

At this time there lived in Kemper County an aged man, whose name was Perry Moore, and who died on the 8th of February, 1867. The name of this old man, on account of the character he bore of strict integrity and his unpretending deportment, was now selected by Chisolm as a suitable cat's paw with which to accomplish his nefarious purpose of defrauding the United States Government of a large amount of money for the destruction of cotton, concerning which, he forged an affidavit purporting to be that of Perry Moore, who was then dead; and he was only thwarted in the consummation of this fraud through the stanch integrity and alertness of Mr. Geo. L. Welsh, who was at that time probate clerk, a highly respected gentleman, and now the popular sheriff of the county.

It will be observed that Chisolm had gathered well the mantle of probability around his design. He had selected the name of an innocent old man who had lived in an obscure corner of the county, and who had recently died; but subsidiary to this, it was necessary to exercise the caution of keeping these papers from the hands and the eyes of his clerk, who was the legal and usual repository and custodian of all papers connected with this court, and who in this case was required to certify to the signature of the judge in order to give the proper legal effect to the instrument. This could only be obviated by another forgery, which, no doubt, would have been perpetrated had not the clerk, by some means, become cognizant of the spurious affidavit, upon which he demanded it of Chisolm, who immediately gave it up to the clerk, and on being charged by him with the fact, he promptly admitted the forgery; thereupon Mr. Welsh also demanded his resignation, to which he also consented. The following documentary evidence of this infamous transaction speaks for itself:

(Perry Moore was dead when this affidavit was made.)

"THE STATE OF MISSISSIPPI, }
   Kemper County. }

"Before me, W. W. Chisolm, judge of probate, in and for said county, personally came Perry Moore, to me well known as a just and reliable citizen in said county, who after being by me duly sworn according to law, deposes and says that he was with the United States forces under the command of General Sherman, in the County of Lauderdale, in eighteen hundred and sixty-four (1864), in said State of Mississippi, on or about the 20th day of February of said year, on the road leading from Marion Station to Hillsboro, in Scott County, Mississippi; and he, the aforesaid, saw at one White's Gin, on said road, the said United States forces put fire to and burn one hundred and eighty-four (184) bales of lint cotton, belonging to Robert J. Moseby. They, the United States forces, stated, and told me it was by order of General Sherman.

                      "PERRY MOORE.

"Sworn to and subscribed before me, this }
   2d day of February, A. D. 1867. }

                "W. W. CHISOLM,
                        Probate Judge."

THE FRAUD ACKNOWLEDGED.

"I certify that the foregoing is a true copy of the original papers, and that the name subscribed thereto purporting to be the genuine signature of Perry Moore is a base forgery, and so admitted to me by W. W. Chisolm. At the time I arrested the said papers in his hands, said Chisolm was at that time judge of the Probate Court of Kemper County, and I was clerk of said court.

                    "GEO. L. WELSH.

"De Kalb, Miss., September 20, 1867."

CLINCHING THE NAIL.

Affidavit of the Probate Clerk who Detected the Fraud. He Demanded Chisolm's Resignation.

"I, Geo. L. Welsh, a citizen of Kemper County, in the State of Mississippi, state upon honor that the paper purporting to be the affidavit of Perry Moore, as to the burning of one hundred and eighty-four bales of lint cotton by General Sherman's army, in February, 1864, is a forgery so far as the name of Perry Moore is concerned; that I saw and arrested this paper in the hands of W. W. Chisolm, of said county and State, in April, 1867; said Chisolm was then judge, and I was clerk of the probate court of said county; that upon arresting said paper I demanded Chisolm's resignation, and he did resign. The paper accompanying this statement is his original resignation, wholly written and subscribed by himself. I attended his trial before Centre Ridge Lodge, and know that he was expelled as the accompanying publication states. His masonic status is that of an expelled and published mason.

"June, 1870. GEO. L. WELSH."

CHISOLM'S RESIGNATION.

"DE KALB, MISS., *May* 6, 1867.

"HIS EXCELLENCY B. J. HUMPHRIES, JACKSON, MISS.

"*Sir:* I have the honor to this day tender to your excellency my resignation as judge of the probate and county courts in this (Kemper) County, and trust that it will be accepted, to take effect from this date. I have the honor to be, very respectfully,

Your obedient servant,

W. W. CHISOLM."

EXPELLED FROM THE LODGE.

"At a regular communication of Centre Ridge Lodge, No. 150, of Free and Accepted Masons, held July 4, 1868, in Kemper County, Mississippi, W. W. Chisolm, a member of said lodge, having been charged with gross, unmasonic conduct, was tried and unanimously expelled from all the rights and privileges of masonry by said lodge.

"It is ordered by the lodge that the above be published in the Mississippi *Flag*.

"P. S.—All papers friendly to masonry please copy.

"August 17, 1868."

The following is an extract of a letter written by W. W. Chisolm to the Jackson *Clarion*, and dated October 16, 1876:

"Welsh says that Perry Moore was dead before the affidavit in regard to the cotton was made, and that was on the 2d of February, 1867, and yet Jordan Moore made affidavit before this same George L. Welsh that Perry Moore died on or about the 8th day of February, 1867. See how plain a tale will put a lying scoundrel down! By the records of his own court he stands a convicted liar. Need I say more? Now, upon this slanderous charge of Welsh, all the superstructure of persecution against me has been raised. Proving the foundation to be false, what becomes of the edifice?

"This same George L. Welsh says that 'he arrested Perry Moore's affidavit in my hands; that I admitted that it was a forgery; that he demanded my resignation, and I did resign.' I congratulate Welsh in doing what he seldom does —stumbling upon one scrap of truth, for 'I did resign.' But that I did it upon the demand of Welsh, or any one else, is a falsehood too infamous to be coined by any other than his brain—notoriously fruitful in such productions. When I resigned my successor was appointed by my recommendation."

A short time after this a letter, dated October 28, 1876, and written by George L. Welsh, appeared in the same paper, from which the following is extracted:

"At the time I arrested these papers in the hands of W. W. Chisolm, in the early part of April, 1867, I charged upon him that it was a forgery, and he promptly and frankly admitted the truth of the charge. I charged upon him that old Perry Moore was dead and buried long before the papers were fixed up, and he as promptly and frankly admitted the truth of the charge. I charged upon him that the paper, though bearing date February 2, 1867, was only a few days old at the time I arrested it, and that he had dated it inside the old man's life time to 'kiver accounts,' as the saying goes, and this charge he as promptly and candidly admitted.

"I made this charge as to the age of the paper, from the general appearance of the paper and writing, all looking fresh and new."

It has been often said that "It takes a thief to catch a thief," and it may be as truly said that it takes a carpet bagger biographer to endeavor to hide his own and the tracks of his criminal coadjutors; and no doubt the reader will be inspired with the mingled feelings of amusement and disgust at the following effort of Wells in behalf of his martyr and hero. He says: "It is a fact well known in the South, that for several years immediately following the close of the war, and even before that period, speculation in cotton became very common. In these operations vast fortunes were sometimes made, and almost everyone who, by dint of good luck, or what often proved better, a determination to win, could in any way become a party to a 'cotton transaction,' entered upon it with a will equalled only by their cupidity."

The fact will be recognized that the Southern people were even at a loss how to express these infamous operations so eagerly entered into by the hordes of knaves and thieves that teemed upon them at the close of the war, by any other term than that of theft; but this crafty carpet bagger manifests the same aptitude for the name as he did for the substance of the act. He calls it "speculation" and "winning," and attempts to defend his martyr only on the grounds of the universality of the crime. He should have added "among his class."

Before leaving this subject, let us turn again to Chisolm

and see what disposition he himself finally makes of it. In another published letter he says: "Welsh lies to deceive the public when he says I resigned to prevent exposure, and at his demand. The cowardly assassin never opened his dirty mouth to me about resigning from office. I was paid in money every dollar to the full amount of warrants I was entitled to receive from the county for any services as probate judge to the time the office would expire by law. I will always make that kind of a trade, especially when the warrants were only worth twenty-five cents on the dollar. Welsh's friends paid me the money, thinking at the time Welsh would get one of the crowd in office, so as to steal out of estates then in progress of being passed on by the court."

Thus, by his own confession, the crime of bribery was added to that of forgery. But no sooner did he discover his self crimination than the prolific baseness of his nature invoked falsehood to parry the effect of his own written words. When this letter was produced by Mr. Money, upon Chisolm's examination before the Congressional Investigating Committee, in Washington, the latter resorted to the following prevarication and final confession.

Q. By Mr. Money: Did you write that letter? (Handing him the one above.)

Chisolm. No, sir. I did not write it.

Q. Is that your composition?

A. I do not know that it is.

Q. Is this your signature to it?

A. Well, sir. Some time during the canvass over in Le Flore County, I believe.

Q. Let me have a categorical answer. I wish to know if you wrote this letter, and if this is your signature?

A. I do not think I wrote it. I know I did not write it.

Q. Is it a copy of one you wrote?

A. I never wrote either. I never wrote any at all.

Q. By Mr. Teller: What did you mean to ask him— whether that is his signature or not?

Mr. Money: That is one thing.

Chisolm (looking at it): That looks very much like it, with pencil.

Q. I desire you to read it first, and then say if you wrote it?

A. I know I did not write it.

Q. Nor have it written?

A. I know I did not write that letter or have it written.

Q. Did you write anything of this kind?

A. No, sir; nor did I dictate it.

Q. Did you not procure it to be written?

A. I did not.

Mr. Money: I will ask to have some witnesses subpœnaed who will prove the signature.

Chisolm: I acknowledge the signature. I state that I think that is my signature.

By Mr. Teller: Is there any explanation you want to make of this?

A. Yes, sir. In my speech at Greenwood, I stated about this way: In speaking of this fellow, Welsh, and his crowd that was hounding after me after I had left home. I was nominated about a month before I left home, and not a word was breathed about me until I had gone away; and Col. Money went and got some *ante bellum* papers thinking they would keep me out of the canvass. I had to come back home and get papers to reply to that. The charges had all been once answered to Governor Alcorn. Welsh's friends said to me that I ought to resign my office; that I was elected by the white people and took sides with the negroes; and that I ought to resign my office, and insisted on my resigning my office. I stated to them that I did not propose to resign my office. I had been elected for a certain period, and that I was ready to perform the services; and, as any other man who had been hired to do labor, I was entitled to my wages. They came back to me and told me that if I would recommend Mr. Gully for the probate judge's place, they would make my wages good if I would resign. I would not state to them what I would do on that subject at all. I wrote to General Ord, who was then commanding the district, and asked him if he would appoint Judge John McRea, of my town, upon my recommendation. He answered me that he would. They returned back to me, and I told them: "You are making a great fuss about my imposing upon the people, about my being a Radical, and about the Democrats electing me. Now, if you will make good the salary due me up to the time I was elected by the people—I have not failed to do any of the duties of the office—I am perfectly willing to get out of your way." I said that in a speech. They agreed to it. I then asked General Ord to appoint John McRea, and he did.

And thus were treachery and perfidy added to forgery, bribery and perjury.

But it is necessary to return to the forgery.

At the March term, 1868, of the Circuit Court of Kemper County, Jordan Moore, a son, and Addison Ward, a son-in-law, of Perry Moore, and both of whom were perfectly familiar with his handwriting, together with Mr. Welsh, on an examination and thorough inspection of the paper, stated on their oaths to the grand jury that the signature to the affidavit, purporting to have been signed by Perry Moore, was not his signature, and that it was a forgery. Yet this jury failed to find a bill of indictment against the forger. But at the subsequent term of the court, September, 1868, upon the sworn statements of these same witnesses, before a jury characterized by the district attorney as having been more than ordinarily intelligent, a bill of indictment was found and framed against W. W. Chisolm for forgery.

At this time the office of sheriff of Kemper County was held by H. A. Hopper, a Radical, and known friend of Chisolm, and who had been appointed to that position by the military governor of the State. All the county offices were in the hands of the same party, and it is evident that the selection of the grand jury for the March term was made with a view of shielding Chisolm from an indictment for his forgery. This fact is sufficiently disclosed by the character of that jury. And how this jury, under their solemn oaths, could refuse to find a bill of indictment against Chisolm upon the testimony of young Moore, Addison Ward and Geo. L. Welsh, as given herewith, is inscrutable to any view outside of the pale of perjury. They had been gathered for the occasion, and well did they sustain the estimate of baseness which their very selection had placed upon them.

In the appointment of grand jurors for the next term of the court, and in fact, in the election of the board of police, which had the selection of the grand jurors, this same influence was brought to bear, and for the same purpose, yet not with the same success, for the suspicions of the people were now thoroughly aroused, and the district attorney, a gentleman of integrity and sagacity, exerted himself strenuously in the cause of justice. Consequently, at the ensuing term of the court, a grand jury of even unusual intelligence and probity was impanelled, and which, upon the same evidence, found a bill of indictment against Chisolm for forgery. Efforts had also been made to prevent the session of the court. The clerk, doubtless for this purpose, resigned his office at the opening. The records were incomplete, and the papers scattered in confusion. Nevertheless the court appointed a temporary clerk, and the session was effectuated, and as there was no clerk except by temporary appointment, the court ordered the presentments of the grand jury to be placed in the custody of the sheriff for safe keeping. This sheriff, as has been said, was H. A. Hopper, a crony of Chisolm, and what became of the indictment against the latter will be seen hereafter. The following presents the action of the grand jury in reference to the matter under discussion:

SWORN STATEMENT OF THE DISTRICT ATTORNEY.

THE STATE OF MISSISSIPPI, }
   Kemper County. }

Before me, F. M. Poole, clerk of the circuit court, personally appeared Thomas H. Woods, citizen of said county, who having been sworn in due form of law, deposes and says:

First—That at the September term, 1868, of the circuit Court of said county and State, affiant was district attorney for the sixth judicial district (in which said county was embraced), and was present at said term, and attended upon the deliberation of the grand jury, and gave to that body such assistance as by law he was required to do, and with his (affiant's) hand drew the indictments found and preferred by said grand jury at said term of said court.

Second—That among other indictments found by said grand jury, prepared and framed by this affiant, presented in open court at said term of said court, was one substantially charging W. W. Chisolm with falsely and fraudulently and knowingly uttering and publishing a certain paper, purporting to have been signed by one Perry Moore, touching the loss of a large lot of cotton, alleged, in said paper, to have been the property of one Robert J. Moseby, which said cotton was, in said paper, charged to have been destroyed by the army commanded by General Sherman, in the winter of 1863-4.

Third—That upon the adjournment of the court, there being a vacancy in the office of clerk of the circuit court, the furniture, records and papers belonging to that office were, by order of the court, placed in the care and custody of the then sheriff, Mr. H. A. Hopper; that between said September term, 1868, and the next March term, 1869, affiant was informed by said sheriff that his office had been violently opened and entered, and all indictments found at the September term, 1868, stolen and carried off. Since affiant has had no further information touching said indictment or its whereabouts.

Fourth—That the grand jury of the State, at the September term, 1868, was composed of the best men of the County of Kemper, and of men of more than ordinary intelligence and unimpeachable integrity.

Fifth—That, owing to various causes, there has been no

term of the circuit court held in said county since said September term, 1868.

THOMAS H. WOODS.

Sworn to and subscribed before me, } June, 1870.

F. M. POOLE,
Clerk.

[SEAL.]

STATEMENT BY JUDGE FOOTE.

The indictment against W. W. Chisolm, referred to above, was presented by the grand jury of Kemper County when I was the presiding judge. The facts as to the indictment are substantially correct.

H. W. FOOTE.

AFFIDAVITS OF TWO MEMBERS OF THE GRAND JURY.

STATE OF MISSISSIPPI, }
    Kemper County.

Before me, William Ezelle, an acting justice of the peace in and for said county and State, personally appeared, James Haughey and W. B. Locket, who, having been first sworn in due form of law, depose and say, and each and every one of them deposes and says:

First--That they were members of the grand jury for the County of Kemper, in said State, at the September term, 1868, of the circuit court, in the then sixth judicial district, Hon. H. W. Foote being the presiding judge.

Second—That at the September term, 1868, the said grand jury, after patient and thorough examination, found and presented in open court an indictment against W. W. Chisolm, charging said Chisolm, in substance, with the crime of having falsely and knowingly uttered and put in circulation a paper purporting to have been signed by one Perry Moore, touching the alleged burning of a large lot of cotton, said to be the property of one R. J. Moseby, by the army of General Sherman, in the winter of 1863-4.

Third—That, in the finding and presentation of said indictment against said Chisolm, affiants say for themselves and undertake to say for their fellow grand jurors, that the proceeding was had, under the functions of their oaths, as the deliberate conviction of their best judgment; and that no other conclusion upon view of the said papers so charged to have been falsely uttered and published, with the accompanying testimony, laid before said grand jury, could have been arrived at with clear conscience.

JAMES HAUGHEY,
W. B. LOCKET.

Sworn to and subscribed before me, this June 7, 1870.

WILLIAM EZELLE,

[L. S.]   *Justice of Peace, in and for, etc.*

This indictment, thus found by the grand jury and formally presented to the court, and committed by the court to the hands of the sheriff for safe keeping until another clerk of the court could be chosen, suddenly disappeared and ceased to be among the things *in esse*—by whom, when and in what manner will perhaps never be known, except to those who perpetrated the theft, and to Him whose eye alone can penetrate the depths of radical infamy.

Hopper, the radical sheriff in whose custody it was placed, said that his office was forcibly entered, his safe forced open, and the paper stolen, but the writer has this day carefully examined that safe. It is Herring's well known and reliable patent, in perfect condition, and not one mark or trace of a burglarious attempt can be seen on any portion of it; but it seems that this transparent explanation was accepted by the court which, in Kemper County, was perfectly under the control of Chisolm and his clan.

It should be observed, that the term of the court at which this indictment was reported by the sheriff to have been stolen, was the last term prior to the usurpation of the State government by the military authorities, which continued two or three years, during which time the civil courts were suspended, and on the resumption of their functions they were entirely under the control of the radicals; and, consequently, no explanation of that circumstance has been made or required up to this day. There never was any radical district attorney in this district, for the reason that there was no one of that faith to be found in the district capable of filling the position.

Not even a sworn statement or the least trace of this transaction can be found upon the records of the court. So much for the sheriff's explanation. Let us now see what Chisolm says about it.

In his examination before the subcommittee at Washington, February 14, 1877, in answer to the questions of Mr. Money in regard to this matter, he said:

Question by Mr. Money: You are Mr. W. W. Chisolm, who was the Republican candidate for Congress from the third Mississippi district?

A. Yes.

Q. You are the W. W. Chisolm who was expelled from a masonic lodge at Centre Ridge, Kemper County, Mississippi?

A. Yes.

Q. There was submitted in evidence the certificate of H. W. Foote, judge of the circuit court of that county; Thomas H. Woods, the district attorney, and W. B. Locket, the foreman of the grand jury, that one W. W. Chisolm was indicted for perjury and forgery in the circuit court, in 1868. I believe you are that man, are you?

A. I do not know whether I am or not. Nobody ever presented any indictment against me.

Q. Is there any other W. W. Chisolm there?

A. None other.

By Mr. Teller: What about this indictment? Mr. Money asked you whether you were the man or not.

A. Of course we all know a grand jury is a secret body, and I know nothing about what the grand jury did; but I learned from several gentlemen that Mr. Welsh had been before the grand jury to indict me. There was then getting up in that county considerable feeling against me, because

I had taken part in trying to carry the county, and did carry the county, for the constitution.

Q. For Republican measures?

A. For Republican measures. I paid no attention to it particularly. In the fall of 1868 I learned from the papers submitted here (not that any gentleman told me) and from rumor in De Kalb, that there was an indictment found against me. That was directly after the heated canvass, in that county, between myself and the opposition party for the governor and State officers running on the Republican ticket.

Q. Have you ever been arrested about that matter?

A. No man has ever spoken to me about arresting me upon that charge or any other charge.

Q. Have you ever been called before the court?

A. Never. There has never been a charge preferred against me in that county upon which I was ever arrested, except one here a little while ago—a minor offence—and the district attorney had it *nolle prosequied*.

Q. It had nothing to do with this matter?

A. None in the world. I was in the county when the court was in session, and was in the county at the adjournment when it adjourned, and have been in the county all the time.

Q. Is there anything further you wish to say about it?

A. Nothing further.

And here we must leave this man wrapped in the folds of forgery, bribery, robbery and perjury which he drew around him and invoked in the commission of crimes still more heinous. It will be remarked that, according to the affidavit of the district attorney, from various causes, there was no circuit court held in Kemper County, from the finding of this indictment, in September, 1868, until March, 1870, and at that time Chisolm had been appointed the sheriff of the county, and controlled its official affairs with an arbitrary, intimidating and despotic hand, consequently, it is not to be expected that this charge could be again agitated until barred by limitation of law, while he occupied that position, and which he held until just prior to his death.

It was in consequence of this forgery that the first rupture occurred between Chisolm and John W. Gully. Prior to this event, Gully, as has been seen, was a political and personal friend of Chisolm. They were both whigs in politics, and Gully had taken an active part in the official promotions of Chisolm. In fact, it was through his influence that the latter had been twice elected to the office of probate judge; but so soon as Gully became aware, by means of these transactions, of the true character of the man, than he immediately withdrew his patronage from him, and used his utmost endeavors to have these crimes brought to light, and strenuously advocated the vindication of law and justice upon the heads of the guilty parties.

And it was from this moment that Chisolm placed the name of John W. Gully at the head of his "black list," and marked him for the assassin's blow.

It may be proper before leaving these matters to notice the reference made to them by the slanderous carpet bagger Wells. It will be observed that these affidavits of the district attorney and others, in regard to this matter, were all made in September, 1867, and June, 1870, and will be so found on the congressional records in the reports of the investigating committees. That of Welsh, the chancery clerk, was made in September, 1867, and that of the district attorney and jurors, June, 1870. The affidavit of Welsh was made at the time he discovered the forgery, and that of the district attorney and jurors when it was ascertained that the indictment had been stolen from the safe in the sheriff's office. Yet this delectable author, fully partaking of the character of his hero in this respect, has invoked forgery to the aid of slander! He copies these affidavits in his contemptible book, signs the names of the parties, and then, instead of their true date, September, 1867, he affixes that of September, 1876, for the purpose of connecting them with the political campaign of that year; but this is but a compara tively slight feature in his tissue of falsehood, in which he has sought to invade the course of time, and crook the current of events in order to avoid that exposure and refutation of his slanders which the true order and relation of the circumstances would unfold in vivid colors.

During the continuance of radical rule in Mississippi, as long as the appointing power was lodged in the hands of that party, there was no surer method or means by which an appointment could be procured than to possess the ill will of, or to fall into discredit with, the white people; and every effort they would make to detect a criminal or to bring him to punishment was sure to result in the promotion of the party against whom the charges were made. So apparent and invariable was this policy, that no doubt oftentimes crimes were committed by aspirants for the purpose of attracting the attention of those in possession of the appointing power. It was the sibyl's bough, an unfailing "sesame" to open the door to office.

So the reader will not be surprised to hear that at the expiration of Hopper's term of office, in 1869, W. W. Chisolm being then under disabilities for having served as probate judge during the war, John E. Chisolm, his brother, was appointed by the notorious Gov. Ames to the shrievalty of Kemper County, under whom W. W. Chisolm became deputy, and, as he himself says, "ran the office."

It was now that a still wider field was presented for the scope of his villainies, the opportunities of which he began at once to improve.

But there was one man still in his way, whose patriotic vigilance and wide influence might again cause him some trouble in the lawless career which he had now chalked out. This was John W. Gully; and his first act was to wreak his grudge upon that gentleman, and, if possible, to check or impair his scrutiny in public affairs. Here again Wells is permitted to state the case.

He says: "When John E. Chisolm, a brother of Judge Chisolm, became sheriff by appointment of the governor, a warrant, fraudulently obtained (while Gully was sheriff), amounting to two hundred and forty dollars, more or less, was taken by Judge Chisolm, then performing the duties of the office of sheriff for his brother, for taxes due the county. But now that a man of a political faith which they did not indorse had the handling of the public funds, claims of every description presented against the county underwent the most rigid examination by a Democratic board of supervisors; and this warrant offered by Judge Chisolm was rejected by reason of exorbitancy of the account on which it was based, and other gross irregularities.

"One reason assigned for this was, it had been taken by Judge Chisolm at a discount, and that he now sought to turn it over in settlement for taxes at its face.

"The judge called up the man from whom he took the paper, Mr. John A. Manese, who swore that he had been allowed its full value.

"Upon further investigation it was found that the original account itself was a forgery, as it had never been approved by the presiding judge or district attorney. At least, the prosecuting officer, Mr. Thomas H. Woods, declared at the time that the signing of his name to the document was a forgery, and so it was rejected by the board. Judge Chisolm's only recourse then was to sue Gully for the amount, which he did, obtaining a judgment against him accordingly. Gully appealed, and for some error in the declaration, the supreme court remanded the case, where it remained unsettled until Gully's death."

The above rigmarole has been inserted for the purpose of again presenting to the reader the address of Wells in the art of mendacity. And first, Capt. Woods informs the writer that this is wholly false; that he had nothing to do with the warrant; that it was all right, and that his signature to the order of the court, allowing the amount, was genuine and correct; that the reason why the warrant was first rejected was this: that the order for the issuing of the warrant was for an amount due jointly to Gully and Brittain for jail service; and that the clerk, upon this joint order, at the urgent request of the beneficiaries, issued a separate warrant to each for the part of the amount to which he was entitled. Consequently, the minutes showed no order for separate amounts. It was allowed as soon as explained. As to the Democratic board of supervisors referred to, John C. Chisolm was appointed sheriff on the 14th day of September, 1869, as Wells himself says in his book, page 39. And on page 249 he presents the names of the supervisors for this and the succeeding year, and their politics, as follows:

T. N. BETHANY	Republican.
D. McNEIL	Republican.
G. E. PRIDDY	Independent.
WM. EZELLE	Republican.
HOZIE FLORE	Republican.

And thus it will be seen that the board to which he here alludes, and characterizes as intensely Democratic, was composed of one independent and four Republicans. But this facile carpet bagger, as will constantly be seen, finds no difficulty in giving any feature or any complexion to a fact that may be necessary to accomplish or conceal his purpose of slander; and, as it suited him best that this board should be intensely Democratic when examining and rejecting the warrant, so it was necessary that it should be strongly Republican when given its true feature as above. Yet, perhaps Wells forgot that he was uncovering one he to hide another, or he may have thought the distance of two hundred pages of jungled and disconnected assertions would confuse the mind of his readers and hide the truths of his falsehoods, as he had so often succeeded in hiding those of his deeds while participating in these villanies which he now invokes the ingenuity of slander to shift to the shoulders of others.

Again, in regard to this warrant, he says: "One reason assigned for its rejection by the board was, that it was taken by Judge Chisolm at a discount, and that he now sought to turn it over in settlement for taxes at its face." This was certainly an unusual manifestation of regard for honesty by a radical board of supervisors; so much so, as within itself to create grave suspicions of its truth with all who have any knowledge of the general character of their proceedings.

Mr. John A. Manese, the gentleman Wells here refers to, a man of staunch and well known integrity, informs the writer that the statement in regard to him has not the least foundation in fact; and as to the alleged declaration of the district attorney, Capt. Woods, the record shows that he was counsel for Gully in the action instituted by Chisolm on this warrant, having been engaged as such prior to his election as attorney for the district; that in this case, a judgment was obtained in the circuit court against Gully by default, and that the Supreme Court of Mississippi set the judgment aside, when Gully filed his plea in justification of the warrant, and that when Chisolm agreed for it to be settled; for he himself had caused it to be rejected by the radical board in order to harass Gully.

The whole matter was brought before the board of supervisors. The statement of the amount the clerk made at the time the account was allowed, and the statement of Capt. Woods, were all spread before the board, and the account allowed to Chisolm.

FROM THE RECORD.

Proceedings of the board of supervisors, March 13, 1876, E. Edwards, president; R. Griggs, J. C. Carpenter, John R. Davis, T. H. Hampton.

It appears that at the September term, 1867, of the circuit court of Kemper, the officers of said court, the district attorney and the judge, made and allowed to John W. Gully, then sheriff of Kemper County, $188, for payment of guards of the jail of said county, heretofore employed and paid by him; and it further appears that said John W. Gully subsequently indorsed said order to J. A. Manese, and that J. A. Manese paid said order to W. W. Chisolm, then sheriff and tax collector of Kemper County; and it further appears that said guards were employed by said John W. Gully, then sheriff of Kemper County, and paid by him, and that said allowance was properly made to said John W. Gully; but that, owing to some misapprehension on the part of the treasurer of the County of Kemper, any allowance for said order of $188 has hitherto been denied and refused to said W. W. Chisolm, sheriff and tax collector, in his settlements with said treasurer. It is by the board of supervisors now ordered that, on the surrender of said order for $188, by the said W. W. Chisolm, to the clerk of the board of supervisors, said clerk do issue to said W. W. Chisolm a warrant to the treasurer of the County of Kemper for $188, to be paid in any funds that may be in said treasury, in due time.

Yet Wells says this matter remained unsettled up to the time of Gully's death, and he was killed on the 26th of April, 1877.

Here looms up another peak in this carpet bagger's mountain of mendacity.

And again he says: "That for three years following that of 1855, this man (Gully) collected a sum of money due from the county to the Mobile & Ohio Railroad Company, amounting to $3,000, and which up to the year 1870, at least, had not been given to that corporation, while the receipts for the money paid to Gully can be seen to-day" (1877).

How about the matter that day (1877)? Why did he not say, and why did not the Mobile & Ohio Railroad Company bring suit on Gully's bond?

Simply because there was no occasion for it, and the whole thing is the product of a slanderer's brain.

THE ACRE TAX.

One of the most infamous acts of the radical legislature of Kemper County was the order commanding a special tax to be levied upon Land; in regard to which Wells is again permitted to make his statement. He says: "Before the administration of John E. Chisolm, under the supervision of a Democratic board of supervisors, a tax was levied upon the county, which was known as the 'acre tax,' and against which there appeared, at the time of the levy, no special objection; but when Judge Chisolm undertook to collect the tax there went up a terrible cry against the law, which was characterized as a great 'radical steal.'"

And the writer will add that if he does not show it to to have been a "radical steal" indeed, he will readily admit the forfeiture of all claim to the confidence of the reader.

It will have been observed that John E. Chisolm was appointed and entered upon the duties of the shrievalty on the 14th day of October, 1869. And we have seen from Wells' own showing (page 249), that the police board of Kemper County during the year 1869 was entirely Republican—four radicals and one so called independent—it being the identical board mentioned heretofore, and which rejected the warrant.

The following order establishing this tax is copied from the minutes of the board of police of Kemper County, November term, 1869:

"Ordered by the board, that a special tax be levied of one cent per acre on lands worth one dollar and under; over one and under three, two cents per acre; and all over three dollars three cents per acre, for repairing bridges, building bridges, repairing court house and jail.

T. N. BETHANY,
President.

So it will be seen that this infamous tax was ordered by board, called *Democratic* by Wells, of which every member save one was an avowed and active radical, and mere puppets and pimps of W. W. Chisolm, who was at that time the radical high priest of the county, deputy sheriff, and, as he says, "running the office and collecting the taxes."

But we will here let him speak for himself. Before the

Congressional Investigating Committee, at Washington, February 14, 1877, page 757, Chisolm says: "There was a tax levied in 1869, by a *Democratic* board of supervisors of the county, for county purposes, levied upon land—upon the acres of land—one cent given in upon land at such a price, two cents upon land given at another price, and three cents upon land given in at the highest price."

Q. Per acre ?

A. Yes. The tax books were turned over to me, or rather to my brother. I was doing the collecting and was running the office. It was before my disabilities were removed, and a number of gentlemen asked me what I thought about the levy. I told them that it was not my business to decide any legal question; it was simply a matter for them to enjoin the sheriff about, or else to pay the tax; that the board of supervisors left no discretion with me. I had to collect the tax, or else I had to be enjoined. A majority of the land holders of the county enjoined the sheriff from collecting the tax. Some paid the one, two or three cent tax rather than enjoin. That tax was paid over to the county treasurer, and I got his receipt for it. I never heard any man make any complaint about it, except Squire Mills, who was a kind of crazy man down there. He paid the tax, and then commenced a lawsuit against me for not paying it back to him. It was my duty, under the law, to pay it to the county treasurer, and I did pay it to the county treasurer. Mr. Mills commenced suit against the treasurer, and the circuit and supreme courts both decided that I had done right in the premises."

The reader will readily observe that, notwithstanding this false and flimsy explanation of this matter, it was a premeditated and well conceived swindle.

In regard to this matter the following circumstance has been related to the writer by Mr. J. W. Maury, of Wahalak, who was afterward the Democratic candidate for sheriff in opposition to Chisolm. Mr. Maury says:

"My special tax, levied under that order of the county board of supervisors, was $150, and when I paid my other taxes I told the sheriff, W. W. Chisolm, that I was unwilling to pay that part known as the 'acre tax,' until the injunction which had been sued out by some of the citizens had been decided. He told me I had better pay it, that the injunction amounted to nothing, and that damages and costs would be the result. He, however, promised me that if the injunction was not dissolved, that he would refund my money. After it was decided that the tax was illegal, I called on him for it. He told me he had paid it over to the county treasurer. I then applied to Capt. B. F. Rush, Chisolm's deputy, who kept the books of the treasurer, Powel Chaney, and he said Chisolm had not paid a dollar to the treasurer. Rush proclaimed this publicly. At that time he was somewhat at variance with Chisolm, but they were soon united again by the cohesive power of public plunder, and Rush again became silent in the matter."

This tax was levied by a radical board of supervisors or police, as it was then called. Chisolm proceeded at once to collect it, notwithstanding the strenuous and steady opposition of the people to the measure from its very incipiency. Some of the people enjoined him. This simply afforded him the desired excuse for *not* collecting a large part that he *did* collect. He turned over a portion of it, however, to the treasurer, a radical and pimp of Chisolm's, and a very ignorant man, and took his receipt. He afterward, in consummation of his prearranged swindle, returned to the treasurer and demanded the money back, upon the ground that he had wrongfully turned it over to him. The obsequious treasurer gave him back the money, without demanding in return the receipt he had given for it, and that was the last that was ever seen of the "acre tax" money —a tax that fell hard upon the poor planters of Kemper County, in order to meet which, in addition to other burdens, they were compelled in many instances to deprive themselves and their wives and children of the actual necessaries of life, and in many instances their lands became forfeited to the State or fell into the hands of tax brokers, mostly radicals and scalawags, the only persons who had the money or the heart to purchase them. And the reader will discover in these transactions and their results, some of the causes of that popular exasperation which culminated in an uprising, limited it is true, but no less indicative in its nature, and terrible in its conclusion.

Yet the people of Kemper County, in common with the whole State, for a long time patiently bore these burdens, and strove, as it were, against the clinched fist of fate. They saw their property passing from them, in many instances their wives and little ones turned out doors—all the consequence of official cupidity and theft; and what was worse, this state of affairs seemed to be perpetual, with a negro radical majority banded together in a solid phalanx against the property interest, and individually subservient in every respect and capacity to their thieving and lawless leaders, for whose acts there appeared no remedy. If relief was sought in the courts, there were the corrupt radical judges and negro juries to repel the effort. If they appealed to the legislature of the State by respectful and humble petition, it was spurned by this same element, and the color line drawn in the halls of legislation, where stood on one side a motley horde of negroes and New England rowdies, and on the other a handful of white men representing the property interest and intelligence of the State.

But let us return to the chain of events in Kemper County. In November, 1869, James L. Alcorn, radical, was elected by the negroes and New Englanders, governor of Mississippi; and soon after his accession to that office, he appointed W. W. Chisolm sheriff of Kemper County— a man, as we have seen, whose character was already gangrened with infamy, and whose tongue and hands were festered with perjury, bribery and theft, and to which were now soon to be added the bloody stains of murder and assassination.

CHAPTER III.

No sooner had Chisolm got well in hand the reins of the shrievalty, and through it the control of the political machinery of the county, than he commenced the formation of his "black list," and for the execution of which he began at once to gather around him such individuals as, from their character and disposition, seemed best suited to his purposes. With this view he made Ben Rush his deputy.

This man had made a gallant soldier in the Confederate army, and, consequently, had heretofore stood fair in the community, though always known as a man easily urged to desperation, and ready for any enterprise attended by the chances of emolument or excitement, and was, therefore, a proper person for Chisolm to present his bait to. Impelled, also, by the further reason that Rush was a personal enemy to John W. Gully, he immediately appointed him as his deputy.

Gully and Rush had formerly been associated in business, and had fallen out about some business transaction. But it was sufficient for Chisolm's purposes that a feud existed, and, as might be expected from the developments already made of his character, it was not long before he contrived a difficulty between them, in hopes, no doubt, that Rush would kill Gully, and rid him of that surveillance and restraint which, through his influence, the latter exercised over his official acts.

The first, however, of these persistent attempts to get rid of Gully occurred in 1869. One John McRea, a very dissipated man, had been appointed by the military authorities of the Federal government to succeed Chisolm in the office of probate judge, and afterward to that of circuit judge, without any qualification for either office, save that of being a radical and having the support of Chisolm, who had already inaugurated his career by reporting to the military authorities the prominent Democrats of the county and all who were obnoxious to his purposes or objective to his fears.

As Wells has attempted to array this occurrence, also, in artificial colors, I shall let him describe it, in language purporting to be that of a sister of McRea, whom he represents as now living in Kemper County, and from whom he quotes as follows:

"It has often been denied that politics had anything to do with the frequent killing of Republicans in Kemper County, but I am certain it had in the case of Judge John McRea. It is true there was a family feud between the McReas and Gullys that dated back to the fall of 1848; and as the Gullys bragged they never forgave, so did the McReas. They had been on speaking terms for years before the death of Judge McRea, but nothing more; the hate was still there, and was only fanned into a fierce flame in the bosom of the Gullys by the sons of the McReas rising in life and displaying talent which the Gullys never possessed.

"Judge McRea was a lawyer of ability. When the war broke out he went as a private soldier, and rose to the rank of adjutant of his regiment. He remained in the army until the summer of 1864, when he came home, and said his conscience would not permit of his continuing in a cause which he abhorred.

"He was the first white person in Kemper to declare himself a Republican, which was in the year 1867. John W. Gully was then sheriff, and from that time commenced to insult and persecute the judge.

"McRea was appointed probate judge by Gen. Ord, and afterward circuit judge by Gen. Ames. McRea and Chisolm began to recommend men to office whom they knew had been loyal. This gave an additional offence to the Gullys, as they knew they would have to go out, for they had formerly controlled all the offices of the county.

"John Gully had had a habit of blustering and scaring people out of his way. He tried it several times with

Judge McRea, but found it would not work, and concluded to use buckshot.

"In February, 1869, as Judge McRea was leaving the court house in company with the district attorney and his (McRea's) father, an old, gray headed man, Gully came walking down the street, singing a vulgar song, evidently for the purpose of insulting Judge McRea. McRea stopped, and told his father and the district attorney to stay there until he could 'see that man,' meaning Gully. Gully had his pistol in his hand, and Judge McRea had his in his sheath. As McRea advanced Gully backed, neither speaking a word until he reached his own store door, when he reached out a double barrelled gun, dropping his pistol. McRea's father had followed, and was just behind the judge. When Gully raised his gun McRea said, 'You are not coming it right, sir,' when Gully fired. McRea kept advancing, and Gully fired the other barrel. Then McRea said, 'Now I'll get you!' and rushed forward.

"Both barrels of Gully's gun took effect in McRea's face and breast. When Gully fired the last barrel he ran into his store and shut the door after him, and in through the store into the back room and shut that door. By the time McRea got to the door he was so blinded with blood that he could see nothing. He pushed the door open and fired every round of his pistol in the store, playing sad havoc with dry goods, but failing to hit Gully. But Gully's gun happened to be loaded with squirrel shot."

Now, if this statement of Wells be true, taken with all its attempted garnishments and its contradictions, the writer, as a lawyer, will undertake to say, that there could not be a plainer case of an assault with intent to kill found in all the volumes of the law, than was this affair on the part of McRea.

He sees a man, with whom he is not friendly, walking innocently down the street, singing a cheerful song indicative of good will toward all the world. He tells his companions to wait until he can "see that man." He draws his pistol and advances upon his intended victim, who, unarmed, and at the mercy of his foe, or, as Wells has it, armed and drawn, walks backward to his store, seeks refuge in his castle, vigorously pursued by his armed assailant, finds a shot gun there loaded with small shot, turns on his pursuer while in the door of his house, and fires once, twice. Yet his bloodthirsty foe still advances. Still he retreats into an inner room, when his determined pursuer and deadly assailant bombards his house to drive him from the sanctity of his sacred retreat. The shot were small; were in truth what are called bird shot, and in three days McRea is again on the street. The reader is now, perhaps, prepared for his arrest and trial for an assault with intent to kill; but he will be disappointed. The whole machinery of the county was now in the hands of the radicals, and if McRea had killed John W. Gully, the law could not have reached him through the dense mass of corruption that lay between him and its vindicatory arm. "The case," says Wells, "was never presented to the grand jury until after McRea's death, and *then no indictment was found.*"

The following statement of Capt. Woods, who witnessed the affair, may be relied upon:

"Early one morning I was sitting with John W. Gully on the door steps of his store. McRea came up muttering to himself, with his eyes fixed on Gully. I then observed that McRea was intoxicated. I got up and took hold of McRea and endeavored to carry him away, and succeeded in getting him to walk with me a short distance. On looking back I saw Gully with a gun which he had procured from some place beyond his store, and was returning with it in the direction of his store. I motioned him back with my hand. At this time McRea also saw Gully, and, with his pistol in his hand, which he had drawn when he first came up to where Gully and I were sitting, attempted to advance upon Gully. I tried to restrain him from going, but he would not permit me to do so. I then said: 'Well, go then.' I walked aside, as I knew, or rather expected, what was about to transpire, and I did not wish to see it.

I then saw McRea's father for the first time approach and endeavor to persuade his son off. Immediately after this I heard the firing, and I saw McRea, with bloody face, advancing toward Gully's store, and firing his pistol into the store."

McRea was but slightly wounded on this occasion. He died not many months after with consumption,—a disease of which, as the writer is informed, nearly every member of his family has died. Yet, Wells says, the bird shot peppering brought it on.

So much for this attempt to assassinate Gully, and its failure, and the ludicrous effort of Wells to render it subservient to his purpose, like "a slave, whose gall coins slander like a mint."

Let us now return to the operations of Chisolm, and his man Rush. We have already seen the very apparent purpose for which he was inducted into the office of deputy sheriff under Chisolm, and the personal feud existing between him and Gully, without any further prosecution on the part of the latter, save such as the carrier tongue of mischief communicated to and fro between them, in pursuance of the purpose to be wrought. Some time during the month of August, 1870, Rush sent Gully word that he would attack him on sight. Gully knew very well what this meant, and he was not a man to hide himself under such circumstances. Yet, it will be observed, that in all the difficulties which his Democratic prominence incurred, and which radical vengeance devised, in not a single instance has he been shown to be the aggressor.

His place of business was in De Kalb, but his residence was about two miles distant, to which he repaired every evening; and, on the evening he received the foregoing message, he started home at his usual hour in company with his brother Sam Gully and a Dr. Smith, but took the precaution to take his gun along. The other two were unarmed; and as the three rode along the street leading in the direction of Gully's residence, and just as they were passing the last storehouse of the village, Rush, who had been waiting for Gully, suddenly approached them with his gun raised in his hand, and cocked, calling upon Gully to stop, that he wished to settle with him then and there; and while he was in the act of discharging its contents at John Gully, Sam Gully rushed between them and seized Rush's gun by the muzzle, which exploded at the same time, shooting Sam Gully in the thigh. John Gully, who, in the meantime, had rode beyond the corner a few steps off, now turned as soon as he saw his brother shot, and fired two shots at Rush, one of which took effect, and Rush fell to the ground. Gully then immediately turned his attention to his wounded brother, who was mortally wounded, the arteries of his leg having been torn away. He lingered but a few hours and died.

This was the second open attempt to assassinate the devoted Gully. A man deliberately sends him a message to prepare for death, waylays him, rushes upon him with cocked gun from a covert alley, while he is quietly seeking the bosom of his family, and in an avowed assault with intent to kill, slays an unarmed and innocent man who is attempting to parry the deadly muzzle aimed at the heart of his brother!

I ask the lawyer reader if this was not murder, by every principle, precept and precedent of law? Yet Rush was brought to trial and acquitted by a court, sheriff, clerk and jury, all prepared and packed for the occasion.

The crime of murder is defined as follows under the laws of Mississippi. Revised code, sec. 2,628. Code of 1857, art. 165, page 600. "The killing of a human being without the authority of law, by any means, or in any manner, shall be murder in the following cases: When done with the deliberate design to effect the death of the person killed, or any human being.

"When done in the commission of an act eminently dangerous to others, and evincing a depraved heart, regardless of human life, although without any premeditated design to effect the death of any particular individual.

"When done without any design to effect death, by any

person engaged in the commission of the crime of rape, burglary, arson, or robbery, or in an attempt to commit such felonies."

The crime of manslaughter is described as follows: Revised code of Mississippi, 1857 and 1871, art. 179, page 601: "The killing of a human being, without malice, by the act, procurement, or culpable negligence of another, while such other is engaged in the perpetration of any felony, except rape, burglary, arson, or robbery, or while such other is attempting to commit any felony besides such as are above enumerated and excepted, shall be deemed manslaughter; or the killing of a human being, without malice, by the act, procurement or culpable negligence of another while such other is engaged in the perpetration of any crime or misdemeanor not amounting to felony, or in the attempt to perpetrate any crime or misdemeanor, in cases where such killing would be murder at common law, shall be deemed manslaughter."

The reader will readily perceive under which description the offence just described falls.

The act was done with a deliberate and avowed design of effecting the death of a human being, although other than the victim. And there was no attempt to deny these circumstances on the trial; and notwithstanding the difficulty at that time of obtaining an indictment of any character against a radical, the district attorney succeeded in procuring the following bill for manslaughter to be found against Rush:

CIRCUIT COURT.

STATE OF MISSISSIPPI, }
   Kemper County.   }   *November Term*, 1870.

The grand jurors of the State of Mississippi, elected, empanelled, sworn and charged to "inquire in and for the body of the County of Kemper," upon their oath present that B. F. Rush, lately, to wit: On the third day of September, 1870, in the County of Kemper aforesaid, in and upon one S. K. Gully, unlawfully and feloniously an assault did make, and him, the said S. K. Gully, then and there, did unlawfully and feloniously kill and slay.

The cause, after numerous continuances, at the instance of the defendant, came on for trial at the March term of the court, 1873. As we have seen, the whole judicial machinery at this time was in the hands of the radical party; consequently, the whole trial was looked upon as a mere mockery of law, and no disappointment or surprise was occasioned by the result. And it is merely for the purpose of showing the bent of the proceedings, the impossibility at this time of bringing any radical to punishment in the County of Kemper, that these records are introduced.

The following charges were asked for on the part of the State and refused by the court: " If the jury shall believe from the evidence that Rush, the defendant, entertained no malice toward S. K. Gully, and even had no quarrel or contest with him at the time Gully is alleged to have been killed, and that he accidentally killed Gully in doing or attempting to do any felony or misdemeanor, yet he is guilty as charged, and the jury ought so to find." Whar. Criminal Law, vol. 2, page 934.

"If the jury shall believe from the evidence that Rush, the defendant, entered into the conflict in which Gully lost his life, armed with a deadly weapon, not intending to use it, but only resorted to it in the heat of conflict, whereby Gully's death ensued, then he is guilty of manslaughter, and the jury ought so to find." Green v. State, Morris' State cases, 785. The following charges were given by the court for the defendant:

" That, before the jury in this case can find a verdict of guilty against the defendant, B. F. Rush, they must be satisfied from the evidence before them, beyond any reasonable doubt, that the defendant, B. F. Rush, did intentionally, unlawfully and feloniously kill and slay S. K. Gully, as charged in the indictment.

" That, though the jury may believe from the evidence before them, that the defendant, B. F. Rush, shot S. K. Gully, yet they cannot find him guilty, unless they further believe from the evidence, beyond any reasonable doubt, that said B. F. Rush voluntarily killed S. K. Gully intentionally, unlawfully and feloniously."

The next charge is the same, with this addition: "That is to say, without any sufficient cause or reason, or provocation for such act."

"That, if the jury believe from the evidence, that while the defendant, B. F. Rush, was crossing the street and going toward his house, he was spoken to, and hailed or halted by said S. K. Gully, or by either of the parties with said S. K. Gully, namely, John W. Gully or S. K. Smith, and that stopping or turning about, in obedience to such summons, he, the said B. F. Rush, was approached by S. K. Gully in a manner not friendly or amicable; and a colloquy between them ensued, during which a pistol was shown, or exhibited, or fired at B. F. Rush, the said defendant, by the said deceased or by either of the other parties; then and in that event, said B. F. Rush had a right to defend himself, and if in so defending himself he killed S. K. Gully, then such killing was justifiable or excusable.

"That, if the jury believe from the evidence that S. K. Gully rode up to said Rush and seized the barrel of his gun, or took hold of his gun, or tried to take it away from him, and that the defendent tried to retain and keep the gun, and that, therefore, a struggle ensued for the possession of the gun between S. K. Gully and B. F. Rush, and that in this struggle the gun went off and shot and killed S. K. Gully, then the defendant is not guilty."

"That, if the jury believe from the evidence that there were hostile relations between the defendant, B. F. Rush, and John W. Gully, a brother of S. K. Gully, the deceased, then the defendant had a right to prepare to defend, and to defend himself, from any attack, or apprehended attack on him, by said John W. Gully, and to arm himself accordingly; and if the said John W. Gully, and S. K. Gully and S. K. Smith approached the defendant, Rush, and if the said S. K. Gully went up to said defendant, Rush, while the said John W. Gully took his position on the opposite side of the street, with his gun in his hands and within shooting distance of said Rush, then said defendant had a right to prepare to defend himself and to stand on his rights of self defence, and to repel force by force, even to the extent of disabling or killing his adversaries."

These were the charges given by the court to the jury as law in this case, and the verdict of the jury was as follows:

The State of Mississippi
v.
Benjamin F. Rush.

Charged with Manslaughter in the Killing of Samuel K. Gully.

This day came the State of Mississippi, by Thomas H. Woods, Esq., who prosecutes for and in behalf of the State of Mississippi; and came also the defendant, Benjamin F. Rush, who pleaded not guilty to the charge made and preferred against him in and by said indictment. And thereupon came a jury of good and lawful men, to wit, J. C. Carpenter and eleven others, who, upon their oaths do say: "We, the jury, find the defendant not guilty. And it is therefore considered by the court, that said defendant, Benjamin F. Rush, be discharged, and go hence without day, and that he do have and receive of and from said State of Mississippi his cost in this cause expended, and that his sureties on his recognizance be and they are hereby discharged and exonerated therefrom." Marked, "Order entered on the minutes of the court."

It will be observed that Rush and his counsel never once denied his killing of Sam Gully during the trial. Rush confessed, both in and out of court, that he killed him, but declared that he was not after Sam, but after John.

But this reckless and criminal killing an innocent man, who was endeavoring to prevent bloodshed, was rather too much for our carpet bagger Wells. He says, in his book, page 12: "The evidence elicited before the grand jury was to the effect that a shot from Rush's gun, at the time, could not have inflicted the wound that caused Gully's death. Notwithstanding this fact, an indictment was found, but it is believed to this day, by all who have gone into an impartial investigation of the subject, that John Gully, in shooting at Rush, accidentally shot and killed his own brother."

It is indeed strange that this "*impartial investigation*" was not made on the trial of the case, by Rush or his counsel, and the resulting fact brought out in the pleadings; for, in any other age, in any other country, and before any other court of justice, it surely would have saved him from the gallows.

Soon after Rush recovered from his wounds he charged a young man, named Williams, living in De Kalb, with disturbing his domestic relations, upon which the young man fled to his father's residence, a few miles distant; but Rush gathered up his clan and followed him. They attacked the house, but young Williams fought with such desperation, wounding several of the party, one of whom was a negro and another H. A. Hopper, the ex-sheriff of the county, and the one from whose office was stolen the indictment against Chisolm, that the Williams residence has since that time been known by the martial name of Fort Williams.

On the night of the attack upon the Williams residence, Rush was accompanied by H. A. Hopper, ex-sheriff; John Hill, Chisolm's deputy; George Jack, a negro; and the old Scotchman, McClelland, whose name will again appear in a prominent *role* in this work. The manner of attack was as follows, as related in substance by the father of Williams, who now resides a few miles from De Kalb:

"About midnight, a negro, named George Jack, presented himself at the door of the Williams residence with an anonymous note, addressed to young Williams, and purporting to be a summons requiring him to be at De Kalb, without failure, early on the following morning. A brother of Williams, on reading this note, asked the negro what it meant, and what he came there for, at the same time advancing to the door. At this moment Rush, who was standing just outside of the door with a gun in his hand, cried out, "Close up!" when immediately the report of a gun was heard on the other side and in rear of the house. Young Williams then seized a gun and took his position at a window, whence he fired at some one just beyond the fence of the back yard. At this the firing became general around the house. Several shots directed at the flash of Williams's gun entered the window at which he was standing. In the meantime his sister rushed to the door, and made a narrow escape, thirteen buckshot having entered the facing of the door within a few inches of her person. At the second or third shot fired by young Williams, some one cried out with an expression of pain, upon which the assailants retired."

The result was that two of the attacking party were wounded; and fearing the consequences of the assault, on the next morning, Rush, together with Chisolm and his deputy, Hill, appeared before J. C. Carpenter, a justice of the peace, and by affidavit applied for a warrant to arrest Williams, and desired that it should be antedated, so that it might appear to have been issued on the day preceding and prior to the attack. The purpose of this was to obtain some pretence for the assault. This being refused by Carpenter, they applied to another justice of the peace in another beat, who granted the warrant, and antedated it as desired. Chisolm then summoned a posse and proceeded to arrest Williams and another young man, who was alleged to have been present aiding and abetting Williams, during the night of the attack, in offering resistance to process of law in the hands of the deputy sheriff. Young Williams could only escape the vengeance of his persecutors by flying to Texas. The following is Chisolm's sworn testimony in regard to this affair before the congressional committee:

"I will say that I never have summoned anybody but Democrats to help me arrest anybody. I summoned some

Democrats to help me arrest a man out there who had shot a deputy sheriff of mine, and they went very cheerfully with me; but there was a clamor raised against them by this same crowd of men, and the next day we came very near having a general riot in our town on account of it. The deputy sheriff was shot while trying to arrest a man in my county, who had insulted a lady of our town, and when he came back slightly wounded, I raised a posse, all Democrats but one, and went after him, but we never found him. When we came back it was very late at night, and news was brought to the men with me before they got to town, that Mr. Gully, Dr. Fox, and other men in the town had said that they hoped they would get their damned heads shot off for going with such a man as me, a damned radical, to arrest a gentleman. The next day a boy came running to my house, and said that I had better go down in town, that there was going to be a general fight. When I got there I found four or five young men who went with me there, with their double barrelled guns, and other men who were in sympathy with them. I asked them what was the matter. They said they did not intend to let any man say they were a G—d damned set of low down scoundrels, for going to do what they conceived to be their duty, to execute the law.

"Q. Who was it that was making a fuss with them?

"A. Gully and Dr. Fox were the leaders of the crowd. I told them that we must have quiet and peace there, but that if anybody had insulted them, and had done any wrong to them, 'I will fight, notwithstanding I am sheriff. I am not sheriff enough to have you run over us all.' When Dr. Fox saw that I was in town, and a big crowd coming around me, a man brought me a double barrelled shot gun. Fox put his head out of the den they stayed in, and said: 'It is a damned infernal lie! None of us said anything about you, or any of those men who went with you yesterday; and these boys are getting a stir up in this town for nothing.' Said I: 'Fox, while I have my own opinion as to what you said, come out here and declare that pubhely and all will be right.' He came out and said: 'The man who said I said anything about you, or the men who went with you yesterday, tells a damned infernal lie.' Said I, 'Boys, that is satisfactory. It does not make any difference now as to what anybody may tell you, they may go to him now.' And then Gully wrote a note stating that he had not said anything about it."

Here we have, according to his own sworn statement, a sheriff, the peace officer of the county, encouraging a pending affray, and heading a threatened riot. The individuals who composed this so called posse, to whom he alludes, and characterizes as being all Democrats save one, and belonging to the first families in the town, were as follows:

John Hel, a radical, mentioned before as the desperado whom Chisolm imported and made deputy sheriff to intimidate, if not to assassinate, John W. Gully; Charles Rosenbaum, a former deputy of his, and a radical; J. M. Roberts, a radical, and crony of Chisolm; Henry Bohannan, a radical; J. L. Grace and A. M. McClelland, radicals; Ben Rush, a radical, and former deputy sheriff under Chisolm, the man who killed Sam Gully, and who had publicly charged his own wife with discreditable intimacy with young Williams; and Tom J. Hampton, who was the only Democrat among them, and who was inveigled into the mob under the impression that it was a lawful posse, and that his summons was a duty which he could not avoid.

As to the scene which Chisolm so glowingly depicts under oath, as occurring in the streets of De Kalb, in which he, as sheriff, with double barrelled gun in hand, headed these men, all likewise armed, and promenaded the streets to the intimidation and terror of Gully and Fox, the writer has been able to find no confirmation of it whatever. Yet, be this as it may, the allegation itself, so audaciously and boastfully made, shows the character of the man, and forms another link in the chain of lawlessness that marked his course on all occasions, and stamped every feature of his career.

It is certain that neither John W. Gully or Dr. Fox, to

whom he alludes, ever manifested any disposition to cringe to Chisolm under any circumstances, or to shirk any personal responsibility which he might see proper to saddle upon them, save so far as to avoid, if possible, the difficulties into which he constantly sought to involve them.

Not long after this occurrence, an attempt was made at night to shoot Rush while entering his gate. The shot proceeded from a gun in the hands of some person concealed behind the corner of an old church, about forty yards distant. Chisolm seized upon this circumstance as the means of producing another collision between Rush and John W. Gully. Before the Joint Select Committee of Congress, in 1871, appointed for the purpose of gathering up outrages throughout the South with which to feed the enforcement acts, and to perpetuate military rule for the benefit of the radical party in the South, Chisolm testified in reference to this affair as follows. In answer to a question as to what he knew about the matter, he said:

"I was the first man who got to Rush after he was shot; was at the court house when I heard the shots. We were trying to secure a person at the time Captain Rush left the court house. I had seen a great deal of maneuvering going on among men who I regarded as very bad men in the community. Just at dark I told Captain Rush that I thought he had better look out, that I thought there was going to be another raid in the county; that I saw some maneuvering going on that I did not like.

"Q. You said you discovered some suspicious movements then, that day?

"A. Yes, sir; and I had informed Rush and three others there, that evening, that there was something wrong going on; that the men who concocted bloody schemes before were concocting them again, and I requested three different men to have their guns ready for a night's fight, if it was found necessary to make it. These movements consisted mainly of seeing a number of men collected in the back of Gully's store—a gentleman there whom I think every man in the county regards as one who does not care anything about having the law executed. There were several men there from out in the country, two of them brothers of this man Gully, and several other suspicious characters. There was one other man in town whom I did not know at all.

"Q. Why did you suspect these men of hostility toward Rush?

"A. I suspected them of hostility toward any man who was opposed to lawlessness, and rioting, and doing things illegal and wrong in the county; more especially to Rush, because he and they were not friendly, as these parties are not friendly to any man who does not agree with them in politics."

Whatever may be the truth or falsity of these statements, it is plain that Chisolm seems never to be barren of the disposition to cast obloquy and imputation upon John W. Gully, and never forgetful of an opportunity of, in some way, connecting him with every discreditable occurrence.

The preceding testimony of Chisolm will, I am sure, readily suggest the spirit that actuated the testifier. The character of his suspicions, and the reasons he assigns for their existence, bear the stamp of absurdity and the color of purpose upon their face.

There is not now, nor has there ever been, the least scintilla of evidence to connect any of the Gullys with this act. It is certain that John W. Gully had nothing to do with it; his character forbids such a supposition; he was not a man to attack his enemy in the dark. This feature of his character is vouched for by all who knew him; and if any suspicion rested upon the younger Gullys, it had no other foundation than the plausibility arising from a sufficient cause. The innocent blood of a brother, uncle and father will, like that of Abel of old, continue to cry from the ground in a voice that cannot fail to reach the dullest ear and the most callous heart of humanity, and if sentiment proves superior to vengeance, it is because reason is more powerful than rage. But we must leave this detestable act wrapped in the clouds of mystery, which none but the perpetrator and the eye of Heaven can penetrate.

During the period we are now traversing, that is 1870 and 1871, the star of Mississippi that had blazed so brightly upon the escutcheons of both the Union and the Confederacy was obscured by the glitter of the military epaulet, her mantle of sovereignty was trailed in the dust, and her political vesture was parted between the soldier, the negro and the carpet bagger.

It was during this time that a military force was stationed at Lauderdale, on the Mobile & Ohio Railroad, close to Kemper County, and the reader will now, perhaps, be prepared for an era of quietude in that county, but it is only necessary to refer again to the book of J. M. Wells to have our hopes and expectations again dashed to the ground. He says: "From late in 1869 to 1871 — less than two years—some thirty-five negroes were known to have been killed by the ku-klux; while whippings took place almost nightly."

If this be true, and there be no limitation upon the trial of military offenders, I would respectfully call the attention of the President of the United States and that of the general of the army to the fact, and would respectfully suggest that the officers in command of this Lauderdale garrison be at once placed upon trial and cashiered or shot for such grave, aggravated and high handed dereliction of duty, as to allow thirty-five negroes to be killed by the ku-klux under their very noses, while their records and reports show but one, a single instance of a citizen of Kemper County having been tried for negro killing.

John E. Chisolm, brother of W. W., was at this time the sheriff and peace officer of the county, while W. W. Chisolm was his deputy, and was, as he testified before the investigating committee, "running the office." There should certainly be some severe penalty in waiting for officers who, upon the word of a crony, are thus shown to have been guilty of such culpable misfeasance and nonfeasance.

But here Wells again comes to the rescue. He says: "By the untiring perseverance of Judge Chisolm and a few associates, the military were enabled to raid heavily and more successfully upon the klan, and numbers of them were arrested, while others fled for safety and sought new fields of glory in more hospitable climes. Many of the men apprehended, says Judge Chisolm in his testimony, told by whom they had been encouraged to perform these acts of lawlessness. Foremost among the names given in this connection were those of John W. Gully and Dr. Fox."

Notwithstanding all this bugaboo of thirty-five human beings having been launched into eternity in a shorter space than two years, by the hand of the masked assassin, the writer after the most diligent inquiry and assiduous investigation has been unable to discover the least trace of these events. He is writing this work at De Kalb, the county seat of Kemper County, where he has all the records of the courts at his command, and constant access to the people in all parts of the county. He has inquired of men of all classes and politics, and the universal and invariable characterization of Wells' ku-klux story is, that it is utterly false and without the least foundation either in fact or rumor. The writer has been able to discover but two instances of negro killing in Kemper County during the period assigned by Wells to such a holocaust of blood; and one of these was the killing of Miles Hampton, a few miles from De Kalb, who was accidentally killed, having been mistaken in the night for another negro who had committed a heinous offence, and his killing was attended by circumstances somewhat similar to the attack made by the Chisolm clan upon young Williams, which has been referred to.

Captain Thomas Woods, who, during this time was district attorney, informs the writer that all this is most maliciously false, that there were but few killings in the county during this period, and they were, in nearly every case, the result of the misrule inaugurated by the radicals.

I will trace Wells once more through the dreary wilds of his imaginary murders of this period, and then discard his bloody fictions and concocted reports as no less wearisome and disgusting to the writer than he feels assured they will be to the reader.

It is said that on one occasion when Hercules was attending his herds among the mountains of Thrace, they began to disappear one by one in a mysterious manner. Hercules endeavored to track them, and by that means to ascertain the direction in which they had wandered or had been driven off; and yet he could find no trace of an off going track. He discovered, it is true, a suspicious looking cave, but then the tracks were all leading away from it. But he finally discovered that this cave was the abode of the thief, and that the latter had carried off the stolen cattle by the tail, in order to prevent their being tracked. In this same manner Wells has endeavored to parry attention from any opening in his mountain of mendacity. He has drawn all his falsehoods after him by the tail. His chapter of crimes in Kemper County finds no support in the records of the courts, nor in the knowledge of the oldest inhabitants of the county.

> "Yet, whether true or basest lie,
> His party must have food or die."

The following proceedings before the military commission, held at Lauderdale, in the winter and spring of 1870, will give a pretty good idea of the quality of the food used, and the manner of its preparation: In this connection Wells quotes from the testimony of R. C. Powers, once New England governor of Mississippi, and which he invokes as utterly unimpeachable, when it is well known in Mississippi, where he now resides, that during the whole radical career in this State, in which he was a prominent actor, Powers fully and unreservedly participated in every scheme, of whatever nature, calculated to advance the interest of his party or himself; and that he, in unison and complicity with all others of his party in Mississippi, looked to the process of the "outrage mill" as an unfailing source of support, and his conduct has never warranted his veracity being deemed any more indubitable than that of his political associates.

And here, it may not be improper to relate a circumstance that occurred at De Kalb during a political canvass in which this same Powers was playing a conspicuous part. It was while W. W. Chisolm was sheriff of Kemper County. Powers was making a speech, represented to have been extremely violent and incendiary in its character, in which he was taking occasion to tell the negroes that the Democrats had and would continue to steal from them everything they made; that that was a common complaint and a universal fact; whereupon John W. Gully, who was present, said to Powers that if that assertion was based upon negro testimony, then negro testimony should be as available on one side as on the other, and that he had it from good authority that the negroes on his (Powers') place had refused to pay their taxes on the ground that he (Powers) had robbed them of everything they made, and that he ought to pay their taxes.

This interruption was made in a mild and respectful manner; when W. W. Chisolm, who was then sheriff, and a candidate for re-election, ran out of the court house and up to the speaker's stand, with his pistol in his hand, exclaiming, "By G—d, John Gully shan't talk to Governor Powers in that way," and seeing a negro with a gun standing by, he placed his hand on his shoulder, saying, "That is right, old fellow, stand up to us, and should they kill me, by G—d, don't you let any one of them escape! I have got ten thousand dollars saved for my wife, and, by G—d, I would just as soon die as not!" This circumstance has been related to the writer, and vouched for by many of the most respectable men in the county, who were present at the time.

But I will leave this question of veracity with Wells Powers, and the officers of the following commission, the proceedings of which are introduced here for the further reason that the writer deems them worthy of perpetuation as a memento of radical infamy. The cases tried before this commission are the same, of which Wells manufactures some of his most "terrible killings."

HEADQUARTERS FOURTH MILITARY DISTRICT,
DEPARTMENT OF MISSISSIPPI,
JACKSON, MISSISSIPPI, *September* 14, 1869.

SPECIAL ORDERS
No. 198.
EXTRACT.

I. A military commission is hereby appointed to meet at the post of Lauderdale, Mississippi, at 10 o'clock a. m., on the 17th instant, or as soon thereafter as practicable, for the trial of such prisoners as may be properly brought before it.

DETAIL FOR THE COMMISSION.

1. Captain J. F. Randlett, U. S. army.
2. First Lieutenant W. H. Vinal, Sixteenth Infantry.
3. Brevet Major G. Van Blucher, U. S. army.
4. First Lieutenant E. C. Gaskill, U. S. army.
5. First Lieutenant William Quinton, U. S. army.
6. Brevet Major Placidus Ord, U. S. army.
7. First Lieutenant J. S. Appleton, U. S. army.

First Lieutenant William J. Daws, *Judge Advocate*.

The commission will sit without regard to hours.

By command of

BREVET MAJOR GENERAL AMES.

(Signed.) WILLIAM ATWOOD,
Aide-de-camp, Acting Assistant Adjutant General.

By subsequent special orders, the following members have been relieved: Captain J. F. Randlett, Brevet Major Placidus Ord, First Lieutenant William H. Vinal.

HEADQUARTERS FOURTH MILITARY DISTRICT,
DEPARTMENT OF MISSISSIPPI,
JACKSON, MISSISSIPPI, *October* 7, 1869.

SPECIAL ORDERS
No. 217.
EXTRACT.

II. Captain Reuben Robbins is hereby relieved from duty at the post of Vicksburg, Mississippi, and detailed as a member of the military commission instituted at Lauderdale, Mississippi, by special orders No. 198, paragraph II., current series, from these headquarters.

By command of

BREVET MAJOR GENERAL AMES.

(Signed.) WILLIAM ATWOOD,

Aide-de-camp, Acting Assistant Adjutant General.

A true copy,

WILLIAM DAWS,

First Lieutenant U. S. Army.

Charges and specifications preferred against Dick Evans, Riley Hickerbotham, James Fulton, Harvey Brown, John Lovine, Amos Humphries, Thomas Kuntz and Michael Kuntz, citizens.

CHARGE FIRST—MURDER.

Specification.—In this, that Dick Evans, Riley Hickerbotham, James Fulton, Harvey Brown, John Lovine, Amos Humphries, Thomas Kuntz and Michael Kuntz, citizens of Winston County, in the State of Mississippi, conspiring with other evil disposed persons heretofore, to wit: On or about the sixteenth day of June, in the year of our Lord one thousand eight hundred and sixty-nine, in said County of Winston, State of Mississippi, did make an assault upon one Alexander Triplett, otherwise called Alexander Duncan. They, the said Dick Evans, Riley Hickerbotham, James Fulton, Harvey Brown, John Lovine, Amos Humphries, Thomas Kuntz and Michael Kuntz, did then and there, feloniously, wilfully, and of their malice aforethought, kill and murder.

CHARGE SECOND—ASSAULT WITH INTENT TO KILL.

Specification.—In this, that they, Dick Evans, Riley Hickerbotham, James Fulton, Harvey Brown, John Lovine, Amos Humphries, Thomas Kuntz and Michael Kuntz, citizens of Winston County, in the State of Mississippi, conspiring with other evil disposed persons heretofore, to wit: On or about the sixteenth day of June, in the year of our Lord one thousand eight hundred and sixty-nine, in said County of Winston, State of Mississippi, did feloniously and with malice aforethought, make an assault with intent to kill upon three persons, to wit: Alexander Triplett, otherwise called Alexander Duncan, Alexander Triplett and Lizzie Triplett, of said county and State.

CHARGE THIRD—ASSAULT AND BATTERY.

Specification.—In this, that they, Dick Evans, Riley Hickerbotham, James Fulton, Harvey Brown, John Lovine, Amos Humphries, Thomas Kuntz and Michael Kuntz, citizens of Winston County, in the State of Mississippi, conspiring with other evil disposed persons heretofore, to wit: On or about the sixteenth day of June, in the year of our Lord one thousand eight hundred and sixty-nine, in said County of Winston, State of Mississippi, did then and there feloniously assault and beat Alexander Triplett, otherwise called Alexander Duncan, Alexander Triplett and Lizzie Triplett, of said county and State.

CHARGE FOURTH—RIOT.

Specification.—In this, that they, Dick Evans, Riley Hickerbotham, James Fulton, Harvey Brown, John Lovine, Amos Humphries, Thomas Kuntz and Michael Kuntz, citizens of Winston County, State of Mississippi, conspiring with other evil disposed persons, did on or about the sixteenth day of June, one thousand eight hundred and sixty-nine, in said County of Winston, and State of Mississippi, feloniously, maliciously and with evil intent, disturb the peace of the inhabitants, by destroying private property, to wit: portions of the dwellings of Alexander Triplett and others, injuring and abusing three persons, to wit: the bodies of Alexander Triplett, otherwise called Alexander Duncan, Alexander Triplett and Lizzie Triplett, and by such violent and turbulent conduct, rendering it unsafe for well disposed persons to remain in said County and State.

(Signed.)   JAMES F. RANDLETT,

          Captain U. S. A.

Then comes a long line of witnesses, and from the number of Duncans and Tripletts among them, it would seem that they were mostly for the prosecution, and yet these men were all acquitted and released after all the stern formalities of the military code had been thoroughly exercised upon them.

But what will Wells do about the fact, that there was no Gully in this case? He thought, perhaps, that he had gotten beyond the reach of the truth when he misnamed some of the parties in this case, and transferred it from 1869 to 1871. But in the book written by that individual, neither years, nor months, nor days, nor facts, nor falsehoods, are assigned any particular significance, only when they suit the occasion. He evidently deemed anachronism and incoherency the most potent allies of falsehood, as being the best calculated to conceal his impossibilities and absurdities.

The writer is assured by the then officers of the county that Wells never once examined the records of their offices, and that no one can be found in the county of whom he made any inquiry, other than the members of the Chisolm clan.

And his geography, too, is as mendacious as his chronology and nomenclature, and adds additional falsehood to his facts, as the following extract from his book will show. He says:

"The immediate occasion of this visit of the klan to the plantation of ex-Governor Powers, was as follows: Matt Duncan, the colored man whom they sought to kill that night, some two years before had reported to the military, at Camp Lauderdale, the murder of a little brother of his by the same crowd of men. This boy Matt's brother — was taken from his cabin, *drawn and quartered,* and his mangled body thrown into the *Talladega* swamp. Matt's offence was that he had reported this 'little act of pleasantry' to the authorities." It is evident from this, that Wells had heard of the English crime of high treason, and from it invoked to his aid an expression that for generations has had no practical significance under the English law, yet it has the sound of horror, and that was sufficient for his purpose. Again, it is believed, that there is not in the State of Mississippi, a river, creek, bottom, or swamp that bears the name "Talladega." There is a town and small stream by that name in the northern part of the State of Alabama, hundreds of miles from the alleged scene, but none in Mississippi. The very name was unknown to the Indians who inhabited its forests, and the writer, after thorough inquiry, has found this story to have been fashioned by the same mould that has given formation to most of the " terrible killings " of Wells. It would be inconceivable how any one could read the following narrative, so obnoxious to paternal experience and to every sentiment of humanity, without the mingled feelings of scorn and indignation for the author of the concoction. He says:

"George Evans, the young man killed," on this visit of the klan to the plantation of ex-Governor Powers, "had been raised in the county, and was well known by everybody. Two of his brothers were arrested by the military previous to this, charged with killing a freedman. Evans' body was buried secretly, on his father's place, early the next morning, and the report was circulated that he had died suddenly of cholera morbus. His father said that his death was caused from eating too many oysters and sardines the night before. The kind of which he partook was unhealthy, no doubt."

Such a ruthless invasion of the most sacred precincts of human relations for the purpose of giving color to slander will certainly excite the feelings of disdain in every upright heart and well regulated mind. As might well be presupposed, this man, George Evans, as the writer has been reliably informed, and whose family still resides in the county of Winston, was not killed, but is at this day living in the State of Texas, whither he fled to escape the persecution of his radical enemies; and his death, like the killing, drawing, quartering, and exposure of the scattered limbs of the boy in the Talladega swamp, has no foundation save in the mind of Wells and his historical *chaperons*.

But he proceeds from this to point the unfailing moral of his tales, whether their scene lies in Kemper, Winston, or any other county, or in the swamps of Alabama. He says:

"During all these years of outlawry, unequalled in the history of barbarous tribes anywhere on the earth, according to the sworn testimony of Judge Chisolm, the headquarters of the klan for Kemper County were at the grocery store of John W. Gully."

The shades of this man, like the ghost of Hamlet, will never down in his pathway, but, by some mysterious influence, seems to constantly penetrate the line of his slanderous narratives, until his pricked conscience seems to seek strength for new fabrications in a fresh attack upon the devoted Gully, which but adds confirmation to the adage that " A guilty conscience needs no accuser."

And yet, during all these years of outlawry, unequalled in the history of barbarous tribes anywhere upon the earth, according to the testimony of Judge Chisolm, this same Judge Chisolm was the sheriff and peace officer of the County of Kemper, had a military force to back him stationed on the very borders of the county. Why were they not arrested and brought to trial? And, if guilty, why were they not punished?

Wells is not lacking for a solution. He says: "James Watts and A. G. Ellis, two sycophantic and hypocritical lawyers, were their legal advisers, when, at the same time, they were under pay of Judge Chisolm and his friends for the transaction of legitimate business."

The writer is well acquainted with Captain James Watts, and he has known A. G. Ellis from his boyhood up to his death. They were both gentlemen, and good lawyers, and their sympathies were warm for their oppressed and persecuted countrymen, and in what respect and to whom they were playing the part of the characters assigned them, was not capable of definition even by this skilled defamer. If he means that they were playing the part of sycophancy to Chisolm, or ever engaged their services to aid him in any of his alleged "legitimate" schemes of villainy, the writer will undertake to say in their behalf that such intimation is but another stalk in his broad field of prevarication.

Again, he says: "Thomas W. Adams, a white man, having been a clerk in the Republican constitutional convention, which met in Jackson, in the winter of 1868, had thus incurred the wrath of Fox and the Gullys, and, accordingly, was carried from his house at night and whipped. While undergoing the tortures of the lash, Adams was told by the klan that their object was to teach him to take the whip like a 'nigger,' as he had been associated with the niggers' in the 'radical' convention. Adams knew and recognized many of the men engaged in this affair, gave their names to the military, and they fled the country.'

Now, Adams, who is now living not far from De Kalb, in Kemper County, denies this whole statement, and says that it has not the least foundation in fact, nor did he even hear of these circumstances until he was told of the representations made by Wells.

The history of this man Adams, which the writer has ascertained to be beyond all question, is this, and it shows the kind of material selected: An old man, living in Lauderdale County, had a negro daughter, whom he openly recognized as such. She was his slave, and he hired or bribed this man Adams to marry her. Adams, about the commencement of the war, applied to George L. Welsh, then Probate clerk of Kemper County, for license to marry the negro girl. Welsh, notwithstanding that there is no law in Mississippi forbidding miscegeny, but it has been only declared to be void between a white person and negro,

took upon himself the responsibility of refusing to issue the license. Whereupon Adams went away from the county, carrying the negro with him. He was heard from no more until after the war, when he returned with his negro wife to Kemper County, where he is still residing with her.

These are the facts in this case, and it may not be improper to observe, that had Adams met with the punishment he is alleged to have received, it is questionable whether it would have been unmerited; at least it may be asserted that there are many communities other than Southern where such a penalty would have been inflicted; yet Adams, to-day, in this *terrible* county, revels, unmolested, with his dusky consort in the shocking bonds of miscegeny.

Another circumstance seized upon by Wells to point his usual moral of aspersion upon the Gullys, occurred prior to these occurrences, but order of time seems to have no place with him. It is as follows: A young man, named Jones, who had killed his stepfather in Alabama, and who had fled from justice, arrived at the house of Sloke Gully entirely destitute and seeking for employment. He remained there during the night, and on the next morning, while he was negotiating with Mr. Gully in regard to his services, a posse of men from Alabama, who were pursuing him, and had secured the services of Hal Dawson, a resident of Kemper County, in the capacity of a guide, suddenly made their appearance at the gate. So soon as Jones saw them he recognized them, as they were his relatives, and immediately comprehending their object, he ran out through a back way, and made good his escape to a neighboring forest. The men pursued him, but after a fruitless search, continuing several hours, they returned to the house and informed Mr. Gully of the circumstances, of which he had learned nothing from Jones. These men gave up the pursuit and left the neighborhood. There was not a shot fired, and Jones was no more seen or heard of until sometime after the war it became known that he was living with some other relatives in Alabama, where he now resides.

And yet of this simple circumstance, the indefatigable Wells has concocted the following unreasonable story: "That Jones who was sitting at Gully's table fled and was pursued by Dawson and Gully to the forest, where several shots were heard. In a few minutes Gully and Dawson returned, stating that they had been unable to overtake the object of their pursuit. A few weeks thereafter some ladies, when out walking, discovered the body of the murdered boy in the creek which runs near the place from whence the firing was heard," and that, in the meantime Mr. Mardis, an uncle of the boy, living in Kemper County, "supposing his nephew had gone back to Alabama, said nothing of the matter until one day, some months afterwards, when in De Kalb he was accosted by John W. Gully, then sheriff, who told Mardis that he had better 'go slow,' adding at the same time, 'that is catching before hanging, and you can't prove who killed young Jones.'"

The reader will not be slow to observe how plainly the above representation bears the marks of falsehood on its face, and the writer has ascertained beyond question that all these circumstances are purely fabrications, in which it has been plainly seen Wells is never deficient, especially when there is any possibility of connecting a Gully with his tragical inventions.

Again, says Wells: "It was before this time that Etna, a colored woman, was taken out by some unknown parties, tied to a tree and whipped to death. Her body was found there on the following day, in a perfectly nude state."

The truth of this matter is that a negro woman by that name, who was in a delicate situation, was whipped by some one, and that she in all probability died from its effects, but it is at the same time well known by those living in the vicinity, that this woman had caused a scandal to be circulated in respect to the families of some radicals who lived in the neighborhood, and, there being no other assignable cause for the act, it is believed to this day by the citizens that it was the work of some of these parties. As to her

Again: "About the same time, a colored man named Moses McDade was found dead in the road. He had been shot by some parties unknown."

It is known that he was shot by another negro who ran off, and has never been heard of since; the jury of inquest impannelled by the negro coroner, who now lives in De Kalb, so stated in their return to the court.

Again: "A Baptist minister by the name of Henry White was present at the lynching and hanging of a negro for some alleged offence during the war, and lent material aid in the performance of the murderous act. He afterwards asserted that he was ready, and more than willing to engage at any time in an undertaking of the kind when his *pastoral* duties would not interfere."

If Wells obtained the least scintilla of truth upon which to build this story, it is more than the writer has been able to do, notwithstanding that he has had access to every source of information, has conversed with and made inquiries about these matters of all classes of persons of all colors and all politics; yet he finds that even the voice of report itself is silent concerning them.

Thus it will be seen that Wells has no regard as to the subjects of his slander. He tears open the graves of the *living* and the dead, enters the sacred precincts of domestic relations, invades the very sanctity of religion, and leaves his stains upon the altars of the Most High.

> "Yes, 'tis slander,
> Whose edge is sharper than the sword, whose tongue
> Outvenoms all the worms of Nile, whose breath
> Rides on the posting winds and doth belie
> All corners of the world, kings, queens and States,
> Maids, matrons, yea the secrets of the grave,
> This viperous slander enters."

Again: "In the spring of 1865, James Johnson, a white man, was waylaid when going from his home in the southwestern beat to De Kalb, shot and instantly killed. Johnson had been a merchant and highly respected."

He had also been a conscript officer in the Confederate service, and was at the time of the surrender, and it was and is fully believed by his friends and by all who were acquainted with him and the circumstances of his death, that he was killed by some one of the so called Union men or deserters, who afterwards became a conspicuous and fundamental element of the radical party, and the active adherents of the clan that produced all the subsequent troubles in Kemper County.

In the following instance, related by Wells, he has lit upon some ground of truth. John Edwards had killed a man by the name of Eakins. The father of young Edwards and his uncle, Jack Edwards, applied to and engaged the services of a young lawyer named Simms, in the defence. These three started out together in apparently perfect friendship, to some distant point, whether on business connected with the defence of young Edwards or not, the writer has not been able to ascertain. However, while riding along, a dispute arose between Jack Edwards and Simms, which resulted in a fight and the death of Simms. It was supposed that all three of them were drunk. The parties made their escape and were never brought to trial. They were both dissipated men and desperate when drunk.

"Soon after this," says Wells, "a man named Tyson assaulted Mr. Spear with a hoe, while in a field at work. Spear was thus slain and his head beaten to a jelly." A gentleman who was a witness to this affair, has just stated to the writer the following facts regarding this matter: That Tyson was the keeper of a livery stable in De Kalb prior to the war, and that Spear went to the stable in an intoxicated condition and began to abuse Tyson, who made every effort to rid himself of Spear, but on the latter persisting in his efforts to get into a difficulty with Tyson, his patience finally became exhausted, and picking up a hoe lying near at hand, he struck Spear on the head with it, without any further intention than that of chastising him and repelling the assault. Spear having been struck on a tender portion of his head, died from the effects of the blow.

After this, one of the Spears had a difficulty with a man by the name of Goins. It was simply a drunken brawl, and in the warmth of the fight Spears stabbed Goins with a small knife, from the effects of which he died. A nephew of this Goins then attacked and killed Spear at his wagon camp, and then fled from the country.

These circumstances all occurred long previously to the war, and at long intervals, and are of no more importance and no more indicative of a depraved state of society than similar ones to be found in the history of almost every community.

But if in the relating of these events, Wells has here and there left a track in the path of truth, he has left no trace along her highway in his description of the following case: He says: "At Blackwater, in Kemper County, George Alexander, a brother-in-law of one Phil Gully—whose character and name will be more fully discussed hereafter, had some words with Ben Caraway. They subsequently made friends, shook hands and separated; and from all civilized or savage usages of which we have any account, one might suppose that further danger of assault by either party was at an end. But not so in Kemper County. Caraway was a blacksmith, and went to work in his shop, little thinking of danger, when Alexander walked stealthily in, stepped up behind him, and at a single blow with a heavy piece of wood, struck him dead. For this murder, an unusual occurrence in cases of this kind, Alexander was arrested, placed under guard, and that night it is said Phil Gully procured his escape. Gully, on being asked if it would not have been better had Alexander been tried before leaving, replied that he thought not; he had taken counsel of Judy Hamon—then a practicing lawyer, and Hamon had told him that if tried, Alexander would certainly be hanged."

The truth is, that Caraway was no blacksmith; nor was it his shop at which they met. Alexander and Caraway had previously to this had a difficulty, and on the occasion of the killing they met by accident at a smith's shop, in the neighborhood, belonging to a man by the name of Buchee.

The quarrel was renewed, and Caraway seized a sledge hammer and made an attack on Alexander, and would no doubt have killed him but that the latter anticipated the blow by knocking Caraway down with a billet of wood, from the effects of which he died. Alexander was arrested, placed under bond, gave bail, made his appearance at the bar of the court at the time to which the recognizance was returnable, when, as the record shows, there was a continuance obtained by the State. And at the next term of the court he was fairly tried and acquitted upon the plea and proof of self defence.

ALEXANDER KILLED CARAWAY ON AUGUST 1, 1858.

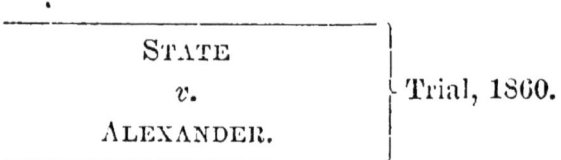

State
v.
Alexander.

Trial, 1860.

The following is an extract from the final record in this case: "This day came the district attorney, who prosecutes for the State, and also came the defendant, into court, who, having been arraigned in open court on a former day of this term of the court, and pleaded 'not guilty' in manner and form as charged in the indictment, and for his trial puts himself upon the country; and the district attorney, on behalf of the State, doth the like. And therefore, came a jury of good and lawful men, summoned for the purpose of trying this case, and chosen as well by defendant's counsel as by the State, from the number summoned according to law as aforesaid, to wit: A. L. McKaskill, D. D. Briggs, R. C. Mobley, E. Fost, E. McDonald, J. C. Dale, A. M. White, W. D. King, William Fulton, Levi Johnson, P. H. Hampton and M. Hunnicutt, who were duly sworn and impanelled according to law and the evidence, well and truly to try the issue in this cause, joined by the State of Mississippi and the defendant, and true verdict to render ac-

argument, as well for as against the said defendant, returned to their room in charge of James L. Hudnall and Alfred White, officers and bailiffs of the court, specially sworn in open court to take charge of said jurors, and after considering, rendered their verdict in court in the following words: 'We, the jury, find the defendant not guilty.' It is therefore considered by the court that the defendant go hence without day, and that the State of Mississippi pay the costs herein expended, for which execution may issue." To which is appended the usual certificate of the clerk of the court. This case is one of Wells's escapes alleged by him to have been procured by the Gullys.

Charles Robinson, whom Wells represents as having been staked to the ground, was a school teacher in Neshoba county, and on one occasion severely whipped a little girl, one of his pupils. The chastisement was inflicted with so much cruelty that it naturally and rightfully aroused the indignation of the parents and brothers of the girl, and they went to Robinson's school house and took him out with the intention of whipping him in turn; but upon his making suitable apologies and satisfactory explanations of the matter, he was released without injury. But the reports in regard to this circumstance injured his school to such an extent, that Robinson left the neighborhood.

After the war, and during radical rule in Mississippi, it was almost impossible in many neighborhoods to raise any stock whatever, and utterly out of the question for fruit or melons to ripen in the garden or orchard. This was peculiarly the case in the greater part of Kemper County. And it was during this time, and under these circumstances, that Thomas Burton, living near Narketa, while watching his melon patch by night, shot at some one in the act of carrying away his melons; but no one was hurt, and no one ever knew who the thief was.

Yet, out of this simple circumstance, Wells has concocted a wonderful story of Burton shooting a negro woman and child, and even some other person, none of which has any foundation in fact. Burton was a man of exemplary character; was an elder in the church, and of unquestionable piety; and he has not a single neighbor who would not raise his hand in horror at the idea of his being guilty of murder and assassination.

There were during all this time but two negroes, one named Peden and one Miles Hampton, who were killed in Kemper County by unknown persons, and only one whipped, whose name was Henry Greer. And the author has been this moment informed by Hon. George Woods, a Northern man, who was the State's attorney for this district from the year 1846 to 1854, and who is now chancellor of the seventh Mississippi district, that during all this time there were but few cases of killing in the county of Kemper. That it was comparatively free from occurrences of this nature, and its criminal docket remarkably light. And another district attorney, who served from 1866 to 1870, says that there are but few of the killings referred to by Wells, of which he has any knowledge, or ever heard of before.

How Wells obtained his information can only be solved by the supposition that he obtained none at all. He certainly never looked at the records of the county; and although he was here in De Kalb, pretending to be waiting on the Chisolm family, he talked with no one but the clan. He walked along the street, and no one paid any attention to him; and the writer has not found a single person who formed his acquaintance, or of whom he asked a single question. And it is apparent that he obtained only such insight into affairs as was sufficient to afford suggestions for his concoctions. I would like to dismiss him entirely, and will do so, at least, for awhile, and return to the career of W. W. Chisolm.

In the fall of 1869, as has been before mentioned, W. W. Chisolm was appointed sheriff of Kemper County by J. F. Alcorn, who had just been elected, by the negroes and New Englanders, governor of Mississippi. In this position he saw his field of operations still expanded, and his opportunities for wreaking his vengeance more frequent and decisive. And one of his first overt acts was, as might be expected, directed against the Gullys, as they seemed to be at this time the only obstacles to his unbridled career.

A man by the name of Higgins had a fight with and killed another by the name of Floyd. Higgins was promptly arrested by the friends of the deceased, and as there was no sufficient jail at that time at De Kalb, he was sent to Macon, the county seat of the adjoining County of Noxubee, where he remained in jail until his trial. When brought back for trial, there still being no safe jail, he was, as a matter of course, intrusted to the hands of the sheriff and his officers.

The friends of Floyd moved the court to have a guard placed over the prisoner, alleging that Chisolm would certainly permit an escape, for the reason that Floyd was a relative of the Gullys. The judge refused to order the guard, upon the ground that it was the duty of the sheriff to summon sufficient strength to guard his prisoner. Instead of that, however, he was sent down to the residence of Ben Rush, who was Chisolm's deputy, and there a horse was furnished him belonging to the old Scotchman, McClellan (who will hereafter form a conspicuous figure in this work), upon which the prisoner Higgins made his escape, aided, abetted and promoted by Chisolm, the sheriff of the county, and his deputy Rush, and for no other reason than that the person whom he had killed was a friend and relative of the Gullys.

It may not be improper, in this place, to revert to the personal character of this man, Chisolm, and his family, whose names have been flaunted in the face of the world as synonyms of virtue and purity. In regard to the ancestors of Chisolm, who were Georgians, the writer has been able to learn but little. He has, however, been informed by a gentleman who was raised in the same neighborhood, who was a school mate of Chisolm, and who is now one of the most distinguished physicians in Mississippi, that the Chisolm family were low and obscure; and as to the noble family of Mann's, whose pedigree Wells has traced upon the early oaks of the forests of Florida through the wars of the Spanish settlements, and upon the walls of Moro Castle, all their mighty deeds and heroic patriotism culminates in the character of John W. Mann, the father of Mrs. Chisolm, who, as the writer has been informed by a gentleman who knew him well, and who now holds a distinguished position in the judiciary department of Mississippi, was a man of low, mean instincts, and a perfect and worthless sot, ignorant and degraded in mind and morals.

It is with regret that the writer feels the necessity of condescending to notice the character of obscure individuals, especially of those who took no part directly in the transactions which form the main features of this work, but as the Chisolm biographer, Wells, endeavors to set up a false character of the members of this family for the purpose of drawing false and invidious comparisons, and of giving plausibility to his false statements, it is deemed proper to introduce, at least one circumstance—one fact beyond all question—as an exposition of the true character of a family from which Wells draws the following inspiration:

"Whether the theory is correct or not, it is one of the inherent elements of human conjecture to credit and foster the belief that the strong characteristics which may, in any way, distinguish the conduct of individuals, are sure to mark and mould, in some degree, the fortunes of their lineal posterity. Perhaps the bold and venturesome spirit which characterized the lives of their family in generations past, has had its influence in shaping the remarkable life and character of Emily Mann Chisolm." Of the *bold* and *adventurous* spirit alluded to, we have only the vague statement of Wells; but there is one adventure of a member of this family that bears the most solemn stamp that humanity has ever invented for the perpetuation of truth. Before the time of her marriage Mrs. Emily Chisolm was residing with her uncle, Hiram Mann, in the town of Louisville, the county seat of Winston County, Mississippi, and concerning the character of this Mann, I have been furnished with the following certified transcript from the records of that county:

THE STATE OF MISSISSIPPI, } *Circuit Court, March Term,*
  Winston County   }   *A. D.* 1861.

The grand jurors of the State of Mississippi, elected, impanelled, sworn and charged to inquire for the body of the county of Winston, upon their oaths present, that Hiram Mann and Michael Burns, late of said county, on the 23d day of March, A. D. 1861, in the county aforesaid, one chicken (commonly called a hen) of the value of one dollar, of the goods and chattels of one W. L. Baker, then and there in the possession of said W. L. Baker being found, did then and there feloniously take, steal and carry away, against the peace and dignity of the State of Mississippi.

S. M. MEEK,
District Attorney.

THE STATE OF MISSISSIPPI, }
  Winston County.   }

I, R. M. Hight, clerk of the circuit court of said county and State, do hereby certify that the above and foregoing is a true and correct copy of the indictment of the State of Mississippi *v.* Hiram Mann and Michael Burns, as appears on file in my office.

Given under my hand and seal of office, at Louisville, Mississippi, this the 20th day of July, 1878.

R. M. HIGHT,
Circuit Clerk.

From this true bill it will be seen that what comfort this biographer can derive from the connubial honors of his hero becomes itself an INHERENT ELEMENT OF CONJECTURE. Perhaps the pliability of this *adventurous spirit* renders it capable of varied manifestations.[*]

---

[*] Before Hiram Mann could be arrested upon this indictment he suddenly sold out his business, which was the keeping of a small grocery, and left the county

Thus it will be seen that if there were any peculiarly virtuous proclivities attached to the disposition of any member of this family, it was certainly not the gift of inheritance. W. W. Chisolm was, both by birthright and by nature, a man of exceedingly coarse and profane manners, of a brutal aspect and overbearing disposition toward the object of his enmity. He possessed in a high degree that savage ambition to rule which delights in strewing its pathway with monumental marks of the ruin of all opposition. He was a man of implacable hatred and perfectly unscrupulous as to the methods of gratifying his love of revenge, or the means of accomplishing his purposes.

The writer is reliably informed that, while probate judge, Chisolm frequently and habitually indulged, on the bench, in the most profane, vulgar and obscene language. A gentleman who was probate clerk states to the author that almost every decision or judicial observation of any length was sure to be welded with " By G—d!" and " Damn it!" while such expressions formed so large a part of his ordinary conversation as to render him disgusting to every person of refinement. But the writer need not adduce any other evidence as to this trait of his character than his own language of record.

These and similar expressions were frequently used by him in his testimony before the Senatorial Investigating Committee, at Jackson, Mississippi, June, 1876, greatly, no doubt, to the disgust of the grave senators who composed that committee.

To this testimony, with its manifestations, admissions and evasions, the writer will have more than one occasion to refer in the progress of the following pages.

No sooner had this man become the sheriff of the county, than he determined upon its control in every respect, and those who were the least obnoxious to his plans were first reported to the military authorities as being members of the ku-klux-klan.

There is no denying the fact that there was a secret organization pretty generally entered into by the young men of most of the Southern States immediately after the war, and the necessity for such an organization was as apparent as the fact of its existence.

In many communities, and in some counties in Mississippi, there were ten blacks to one white person, ten negroes with savage instincts and brutal passions to one white man; and the former, just emerged from the *quarters* of slavery, were incited to acts of revenge upon the families of their former masters by the teachings of adventurers and vagabonds, whom they were taught to regard as the authors of their emancipation. Consequently, a state of affairs was soon established in which neither life, virtue nor property could find safety but from the fear of a sudden and mysterious retribution.

It was this necessity that first gave rise to what has been known as the ku-klux-klan. That its operations were afterward perverted, and that it in many instances was transformed into a political machine, does not by any means criminate its origin or mar the incalculable good which it was producing as the champion of virtue.

The ku-klux mask will take its place in history by the side of the lance of chivalry, and it was the very mystery of its proceedings that rendered it so effective in the suppression of crime. But its tendency to become political in its nature, and a means of taking private revenge, was reprehensible; and that it assumed this character in some instances in Kemper County, as well as in other places, is not to be denied. In consequence of this several negroes were killed, or supposed to have been killed, by members of the klan in the State of Mississippi.

But no sooner did the necessities which provoked the formation of the associations known as ku-klux-klans disappear, than the organizations themselves ceased to exist. They were the product of the fears engendered by the dangers which, after the war, enveloped Southern society, and penetrated to the very homes and nurseries of virtue and innocence. These dangers were much aggravated by the presence of a few white men of degraded character, who being as it were, to the manner born, could do more to excite and inflame the naturally unbridled passions of the ignorant and bestial negro than all the influences of the carpet baggers and soldiers combined, at the mere suggestion of whose wishes he would not hesitate to violate every law of God and man.

This association was a great obstruction in the way of the carpet bagger and scalawag. They abhorred it, and pursued it with the utmost vigor and vengeance. This pursuit, however, was confined to the path of slanderous and exaggerated reports to the authorities of the Federal government. And the radical party, which was now in possession of this, was sadly in need of reported outrages to enable it to adopt, and put in execution, the enforcement acts by which it hoped to acquire an indefinite lease of power. Consequently, the ears of the Northern people were ever open, and the army ever obedient, to the call for active aid against the hated klan.

It was in this way that Chisolm first endeavored to get rid of his enemies in Kemper County, and to stifle the voice of all opposition to his diabolical career. It was well known that it was through his instrumentality that a military garrison was stationed on the borders of Kemper County, at Lauderdale, and through his instrumentality that many innocent citizens were dragged from their homes and subjected to the rigors of a military trial, but one of whom was convicted or found guilty of any offence. This conduct on the part of Chisolm was doubtless the origin of that hostility against him afterward, so unanimously manifested in the county.

The proceedings of some of these trials have already been given in full. There was one poor fellow, however, who was sent by the military authorities to Little Rock, Arkansas, where he was kept closely confined for two years, when a requisition was obtained from the governor for him, and it was then found that there was not the slightest legal charge against him. And when this plan had failed —when it was found impossible to procure the imprisonment of his enemies in some distant military prison, or to drive them from the county by military raids—Chisolm began to assemble around him what he usually styled "his crowd." These were chiefly Hopper, Gilmer, Rush, Hill-Rosenbaum, and the old Scotchman, McClellan; and to which number may be added the name of Walter Riley. The parts enacted by Hopper, Hill, Rush and Rosenbaum, have already been partially given in connection with the killing of Sam Gully, the safe robbery and the assault on Williams.

CHAPTER IV.

At the fall election in 1870, Alabama was redeemed from radical rule, and no sooner had the Democracy become triumphant in that State, and the consequent dispersion of the carpet baggers had taken place, than the border counties of Mississippi were the recipients of a large accession of negro population. The towns especially became places of refuge for hundreds of vagabonds and fugitives from justice. Among these Meridian seemed to be a favorite resort for this class of persons. At that period the authorities of the town were radicals, and generally of the very worst character. William Sturgis, the mayor, was a Northern man, who consorted with negroes to such an extent as to cause him to lose the respect of even many of his own class. He collected around him the most malignant characters of the two races, and fanned the flames of race prejudice and partisan animosity, until he had succeeded in producing a bitter feeling between the two races, at least on the part of the negroes. And he never lost an opportunity of manifesting in his official capacity his own bitterness against the native white people.

Among his clan was a man named Price, also a Northern man, and a teacher of a negro school. He came from Alabama, where he had officiated as a leader of the loyal leagues, and having acquired great influence over the negroes, he persuaded many of them to leave the farms on which they had contracted to labor, in Alabama, and go to Meridian. This was for the purpose of promoting his political schemes, and in this he had the full sympathy of the mayor, who desired an increase of the negro population for like purposes. This man was the high priest of the religious features of radicalism.

During this state of affairs, and in the spring of 1871, a negro from Alabama, named Adam Kennard, went to Meridian and endeavored to carry back some negroes who had abandoned the contracts made with their employers. To effect this, it is said that he represented himself to be a deputy sheriff. While operating among the negroes in pursuance of his mission, he was taken one night from the house in which he was lodging, and severely whipped by Price and others. He had known Price well in Alabama, and promptly recognized him as the chief party to this transaction, although he was disguised. The other parties were all negroes, with whom he was unacquainted. The next morning Kennard made complaint to the justice of the peace, and lodged an affidavit against Price for a violation of the statute of Mississippi, enacted for the punishment of persons wearing disguises or perpetrating any crime in disguise. His back bore the marks of a severe castigation.

Upon this affidavit Price was arrested and placed under a bond of $200, to make his appearance for examination, before the same magistrate, on the ensuing Friday. On that day Kennard returned from Alabama, bringing with him some fifteen or twenty white men, and two colored witnesses to attend this trial of Price. These men announced that they had come with Kennard and the two negro witnesses, for the purpose of protecting them and of enabling them to testify; that they were afraid the negroes of Meridian would mob them in consequence of their appearing as witnesses against Price. So exasperated were the feelings of the negroes on account of the arrest of Price, that the counsel for both the prosecution and defence, in common with the whites generally, became alarmed lest serious difficulties between the two races might arise from his trial, and they mutually agreed that the case should be postponed until the excitement subsided; consequently, the case was continued one week, and the original bond of $200 for the appearance of Price was increased to the sum of $800, for his appearance on the day to which his case had been continued. At the next trial, an important witness being absent, the cause, at the request of the prosecution, was continued the second time, until the following week.

In the meantime Price, who associated entirely with the negroes and had great influence over them, continued to fan the flames of prejudice, and to stir up feelings of animosity on their part against the whites. His chief friend and coadjutor in this matter was a negro named Warren Tyler, a most malignant character, and who now became the constant attendant and companion of Price. These two promenaded the streets together, and openly declared that if Price was sent to jail on his approaching trial, there would be shooting at once in the court room; and Price requested his attorneys to be on their guard and keep out of the way, as he did not wish to hurt them. The counsel to whom this warning was given conveyed it to the opposite counsel.

So general was the feeling of alarm in consequence of the threats and conduct of these parties and the grum appearance of the negroes generally, that some of the leading Republicans advised Price to leave the town and forfeit his bond, and this he did; but it was also understood between the counsel that if he did so, no further proceedings should be had in the matter. In pursuance of this understanding, which, however, did not embrace the court, on the trial day of the cause Price failed to appear, but not so with his friend, Warren Tyler. He came insolently into court, armed with pistols and with a club axe in his hand. He had also attended all the other occasions on which the case had been continued, and seemed to take extraordinary interest in the conduct and issue of the proceedings. The negroes were very much incensed at the idea of Price leaving under these circumstances, and low mutters of dissatisfaction and vague threats were heard from suspicious and grum looking groups collected in various portions of the town.

The mayor of the town too, William Sturgis, did not attempt to conceal his displeasure at the loss of his friend, Price. He continued assiduously and by every means in his power to fan the fires of discontent, until he had succeeded in arousing the most bitter feelings on the part of the blacks. He then applied to the governor for Federal troops to be quartered in the town. The troops were sent, which had the effect of increasing the dangerous state of feeling between the races.

Upon this, a petition was signed by a large number of citizens, including many leading Republicans, and dictated in the interest of peace and the welfare of the community, requesting Sturgis to resign the mayoralty. This he positively and petulantly refused to do. The petitioners then asked the governor to remove him from office in order to preserve peace.

At this Sturgis became very much enraged, and sent several leading negro politicians and personal friends to Jackson to see the governor and counteract the movement for his removal. In this they succeeded.

The governor spurned the petition, and the negroes who had, in the interest of Sturgis, thwarted the efforts of the citizens, returned to Meridian on Friday preceding the riot, bringing with them from Jackson, J. Aaron Moore, the notorious negro representative from that county and town in the legislature, who left his seat in order to participate in the triumph on the part of the mayor and his negro allies.

On the next day, Saturday the 4th of March, they called a negro meeting, which was largely attended, and from the early morning until the sun was low down the sky, the angry tones of their speakers resounded from the court house, while the whoops and howls of the excited audience fell with ominous forebodings upon the ears of the alarmed citizens. These speeches were said to be highly inflammatory and incendiary in their character, particularly those of J. Aaron Moore, Warren Tyler and William Dennis, *alias* Clopton, the import of whose speeches was that the negroes should immediately arm and protect themselves against the outrages perpetrated upon them, and which they characterized in terms most inflammatory to the negro mind.

Aaron Moore, in his speech, declared that Sodom and Gomorrah had been destroyed by fire, and if they did not mind, Meridian would be burned up likewise. It was testified before the committee of investigation, appointed by the citizens, that Warren Tyler declared in his speech, among other inflammatory expressions, that the negroes must stand by each other, and adopt the policy of the Indians—when one was killed, they must kill in retaliation. Many remarks of a similar character were made during the meeting.

Among other circumstances which they invoked to instil a spirit of violence in the bosom of their audience was the recent conduct of some white men from Alabama. These men, who came over with the negro Kennard, to attend the trial of Price, had immediately, on their arrival at Meridian, arrested two or three negroes whom they recognized as criminals, who had committed larcenies and other crimes in Alabama, and who were fugitives from justice. These they bound and sent back to Alabama. Whether they did so upon the ground of continued pursuit is not known. If not, their arrest, without authority or requisition, was in violation of law, and highly reprehensible. Be that as it may, it gave these vicious negro leaders and their white allies additional grounds upon which to found their incendiary appeals. This meeting continued until near sunset, and when it then adjourned, the negroes marched out upon the streets in military order, and with drums and fifes sounding, paraded through the town armed with pistols and swords buckled around their bodies. This hostile display continued until dark, when, suddenly, amid the din of their angry tramp, and breaking squads, was heard the cry of "Fire!"

The alarm, which seems not to have been altogether unexpected, soon spread throughout the little city, and soon the flames were seen issuing from a little wooden building adjoining the store house of Sturgis, the mayor, which soon involved the building.

The white people hurried up from all parts of the town and made every effort to stay the conflagration, but it was noticeable that but few of the blacks could be induced to lend a helping hand, which was very much at variance with their known conduct on former occasions of this character, when they had cheerfully rendered the most efficient aid. And what was even more suspicious, as to the origin and purpose of this fire, some of the white people, while on their way to the scene, and some, while engaged in endeavoring to extinguish the flames, were fired upon by unknown persons concealed beyond the lurid glare of the flames. And no sooner had the alarm of fire been given, than some of the leading negro politicians took every possible step to prevent the negroes from rendering any assistance. Among them Billy Dennis, *alias* Clopton, played a conspicuous *role*. He placed himself in front of those blacks who seemed disposed to help, exclaiming, with bitter oaths, that it was a white man's fire, and it was their property; let it burn. They have ruled here long enough. That if they wanted war, let them have it; that now was as good a time as any.

And then, after the block had been consumed, and the fire had been arrested, he was heard to address a crowd of negroes who were standing on the street: "Why in the hell don't you go and get your arms; something to shoot with? What in the hell are you standing here for? I have no secrets to keep. What I have to say I say openly and above board." He then turned away, several of the crowd following him, and began to fire his pistol, which he did four or five times, exclaiming at the same time that, "If the G-d d——d white people wanted war, let them come out! We are as ready now as we will ever be."

It is stated that there was a meeting of the Loyal League Club that night, and that the bell tapped at the same time that the cry of "Fire!" was raised. So abusive and riotous was Clopton's conduct in endeavoring to incite the negroes to violence, and to prevent their assistance in the effort to extinguish the flames, that the sheriff finally ordered him to be arrested.

During all this time large bodies of armed negroes were gutting different parts of the town, and when asked the meaning of this demonstration, they promptly answered that they were going to fight the white people if they wanted to fight, and, in the meantime, frequent and numerous reports of fire arms were heard in all parts of the town. The conflagration was not arrested until one whole block or square of the town was destroyed.

On Monday morning the white people held a meeting to consult as to what measures were best to be taken to insure the safety of the town, to prevent any further hostile demonstrations on the part of the blacks, and if possible, to allay the bitter feeling engendered by the teachings of Sturgis and Price.

They appointed a committee of safety, the duty of which was to consult and co-operate with the officers of the county in the preservation of peace, to act under the orders of the sheriff, or to furnish him with reliable and discreet men to aid him in re-establishing a state of security. They also appointed a committee to wait on Governor Alcorn, and ask the removal of Sturgis and other officers of the town and county, whom they recognized as instigators of these difficulties, and they also appointed another committee to investigate the causes and origin of the fire.

This committee proceeded to summon witnesses and take the testimony of persons of all politics and every color. As the result of a thorough investigation, they reported in substance: That the testimony all tended to cast the gravest suspicions upon the mayor, William Sturgis; that they were of the belief, and the testimony justified and forced the opinion, that he had procured the destruction of his own property in order to reap the insurance, and with a desire to destroy the town, so as, for political effect, to cast odium upon the Democrats.

Be this as it may, on the night after the appointing of this committee of investigation, Sturgis fled from the city, and to which he has never returned. But prior to his leaving the town, and on this same day, Monday, March 6, 1871, Aaron Moore, Billy Dennis *alias* Clopton, and Warren Tyler, who had been arrested on the night of the fire, were brought to trial before Judge Bramlette, of the magistrate's court, charged with riotous conduct and incendiary language.

During this trial, Sturgis occupied a seat adjacent to Warren Tyler, and, to all appearances, seemed to be advising and counseling with him. He seemed to take peculiar interest in the trial; he wrote questions in a blank book, and handed the book to Tyler, who, in examining the witness (for he managed his own case), would refer to this book when asking questions. From all this, and from the fact of his retiring with Tyler at the time the latter returned into court armed, it may very properly be inferred that he furnished Tyler with the pistol with which he killed Judge Bramlette. These prisoners had all been promptly disarmed by the sheriff, and entered the court room in that state, but while the trial was going on, Sturgis (the mayor), together with Aaron Moore and Warren Tyler, suddenly left the court room, which was unusual for prisoners to do unless accompanied by the sheriff or other officer, and on their return it was observed, by many who testified to the fact, that Tyler wore a pistol on his person. This man was placed upon trial first, and during its progress James A. Brantley was placed upon the stand as witness on the part of the State, and in his testimony he stated the language of a conversation that had taken place between him and Tyler.

On finishing his testimony, and while in the act of retiring from the stand, immediately in front of Tyler, the latter arose from his seat, and, addressing Brantley in a defiant and insulting manner, ordered him to remain on the stand, as he intended to introduce a witness to impeach his testimony. Upon this Brantley picked up a stick belonging to the sheriff or marshal, and which was lying on the table before him, but the marshal took hold of him and wrenched the stick from his hands, still holding him. In the meantime Tyler moved toward the door, with his hand on his pistol, on reaching which, he turned, drew, and taking deliberate aim, shot Judge Bramlette through the head

PLAN OF COURT ROOM FLOOR, MERIDIAN, MISS.

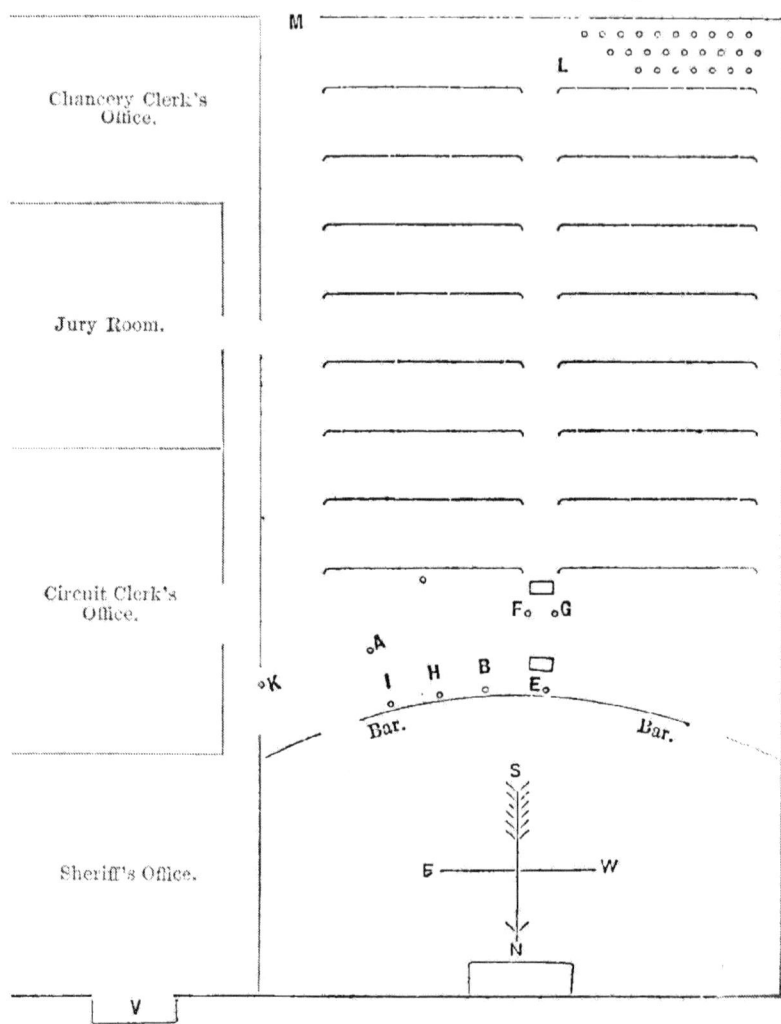

A   Tyler's seat before he left the court room.
B   Tyler's seat after his return to the court room.
E   Seat of Justice Bramlette.
F   Seat of the city marshal.
G   Position of witness Brantley.
H   Seat of J. Aaron Moore.
I   Seat of Billy Dennis, *alias* Clopton.
K   Position of Tyler when he shot Judge Bramlette.
L   Colored people standing.
M   Main entrance to the court room.

while on the bench, and then running through the sheriff's office, jumped from a veranda into the street, and as he ran across the street some one on the veranda from which he had leaped fired at and wounded him in the back. He was pursued and killed in a house across the street, in which he had taken refuge. This fatal shot fired by Tyler was followed by a volley in the court room by which several other persons were shot down, among them Bill Dennis, *alias* Clopton, who was soon afterward dragged out upon the veranda by some unknown persons and tossed over on the sidewalk. He was taken up by order of the sheriff and carried back to his office, where, during the night, the wretch's throat was inhumanly cut by persons who overpowered the deputy sheriff in charge of the office. During the night three other negroes were arrested and placed in the sheriff's office. One of them had been wounded in the afternoon. These three men were taken out during the night by unknown parties, and were found dead on the next morning in a pine thicket on the edge of the town. There was a great mystery connected with these acts: notwithstanding that the citizens, who were indignant and horrified at these circumstances, made every effort to ascertain the actors, they have never, to this day, succeeded in arriving at any satisfactory solution.

The general supposition and belief is that the perpetrators of these horrible deeds were strangers, and that there was no person residing in Meridian who took any part in the transaction, or had any knowledge either of the persons who committed the acts or of the causes that prompted them.

During the night there were other acts performed at which the citizens were indignant. Among these was the burning of the negro Baptist church, and also the burning of Aaron Moore's house. It is contended that if this burning had been done by citizens of Meridian, that it would have been the Methodist church, as that was generally known to be the church of Aaron Moore and Price, and

Baptist church was known to be conducted in a much more orderly manner. This Methodist church had long been the seat of the loyal league, and the place where the negroes held all of their political meetings, while the Baptist church had no associations connected with it at all calculated to render it offensive to the citizens. The burning of Moore's house, no doubt, was done by persons goaded by disappointment in their search for Aaron Moore, against whom the citizens were now greatly enraged, and who had adroitly made his escape from the court house during the confusion occasioned by the killing of Judge Bramlette.

This officer, though a radical, was held in esteem by the white people, because of his inoffensive disposition, and his apparent desire to do justice to all parties before his court, and because he kept himself aloof from the company of Sturgis and Price and their negro associates. It may be remarked also that Sturgis was at personal enmity with Bramlette, and he had succeeded in stirring up the negroes against him to such an extent that there was great complaint among them that Bramlette was siding too much with the white people. Sturgis had attempted, or at least threatened, to have Bramlette removed. And Judge Bramlette remarked, on the morning of the trial of these men, that he felt a reluctancy in sitting on the case, as he was aware that they had ill feeling toward him, and that he knew them, particularly Warren Tyler, to be bad men.

He stated before the trial, that he had attempted to advise Tyler to go on peacefully and quietly, and to try to get along well with everybody, and not stir up any strife between the races; that Tyler became angry with him for it, and said that the next white man who advised him to do any such thing, he would slap in the mouth. Judge Bramlette remarked, before he went up there to hold court, that he did not like to do it, because Tyler was to be there, and that he (Tyler) was mad with him. The result justified the premonitions of the unfortunate man.

In regard to the character of this man Sturgis, the

Hon. Robert Leachman, circuit judge of the sixth judicial district, a Republican and a resident of Meridian, and before whom a full investigation was had of the whole matter, testifies himself as follows: "Mr. Sturgis was the cause of the trouble to a great extent. I have advised him frequently to run the machine more moderately, and not to foment the feeling between the whites and blacks. Had he been a moderate man and a good adviser, this affair never would have occurred. He had not lost the confidence of the colored people. I do not think there were any politics in this thing. I think that it arose out of the mere course of things. The white people believed that Sturgis was fomenting the disturbance."

The truth is, that this terrible affair was but another instance of the result of radical rule in Mississippi, the fruit of official power lodged in corrupt and venal hands to be prostituted to personal and political purposes.

We will dismiss the painful subject after reverting to the version of this matter given by the carpet bagger Wells. In the face of all testimony elicited before a radical judge, and a radical committee appointed by a radical and carpet bag legislature, that individual, in referring to this matter, has the temerity to indulge in the following eulogy on the character of this partisan, degraded and infamous mayor, and that, too, without the least premise or foundation. He says:

"It will be remembered that Sturgis was a good mayor, and in the thorough and important discharge of every duty pertaining to his office, the best the town has ever had before or since. This fact, perhaps, was the cause of greater hostility toward him than anything else; for, in the matter of making arrests, and in the treatment of all parties who came or were brought before him in his official capacity, he made no distinction on account of color or previous condition. But his integrity was so great, and his administration so thorough, that he had many friends and admirers, even among his greatest political enemies; and came to his assistance by the way of remonstrating with the mob, and promising that if his life was spared, he should leave the town and the State for all coming time. These terms were finally agreed upon, and under the escort of one hundred men, headed by R. L. Henderson, a brave and good citizen, he was taken to the train and permitted to depart."

I will likewise dismiss this ludicrous encomium as a fitting rear guard to the troop of villanies that form the character of William Sturgis, once mayor of Meridian. It may be remarked that the petition for the removal of this man, tendered to the governor by the committee of safety, organized on the day of the riot, was favorably received, and Governor Alcorn promptly removed Sturgis and the other town officers.

These events transpired more than seven years since, and from that time to the present, not a breath of disturbance has ruffled the political calm. Upon the departure of Sturgis, the terrible elements he had gathered around him were dispersed, and kindly feelings began to assume their natural sway between the races, which have been mutually fostered until now. It is almost inconceivable that such horrible scenes could ever have occurred in this quiet and prosperous little city. Yet, it has taken long years to redress the grievances inflicted so long, and with such a high hand, by the corrupt radical officials of the town and county, in addition to the common cloud cast over all by the maladministration of the State government.

CHAPTER V.

John P. Gilmer, whose career will form a striking feature in the almost unparalleled panorama of crime, which will be hereafter unfolded in these pages, was, it seems, a native of Heard County, Georgia. He possessed a mind utterly destitute of every sentiment of virtue, and even of humanity itself, when its exercise was at all calculated to thwart his plans or restrain the gratification of his cupidity or revenge; and, being conscious that his character deserved the hatred and contempt of every white man and woman, his ferocious spirit was constantly irritated by the stings of depravity and guilt. Yet his biographer, Wells, says "that he moved in the first circles of the society where he lived." If there ever was or is a first circle of white society in any Southern community in which this individual did or could have moved, it surely must have been the lowest as well as the *first* circle. And to allege that he ever had any standing in respectable society either at Scooba or De Kalb, *where he lived*, would, in the mouth of truth, be indeed humiliating to many residents of those hamlets. But if Wells considers mulattoes and mongrels the identifying elements of his *first circles* of society, then, perhaps, he could claim both for himself and Gilmer the social status which he has assigned to the latter.

Human life was of no consequence in the eyes of this man when in conflict with the gratification of his brutal passions. So manifest and so well known was his disposition in this respect, that the writer has often heard the expression used by men of the most moderate views and calmest judgment, that "Gilmer would no more mind killing a man than he would a dog, in order to effect his purpose."

Being imbued with every sentiment and qualification requisite for the performance of the part he was destined to play in the dark drama, he never shirked any *role* that was assigned him.

These characteristics were soon discovered by Chisolm, who appeared to possess, in an eminent degree, a capacity for making such a selection of his allies as best suited his designs. And, consequently, no sooner was he appointed sheriff, in 1869, than he made Gilmer his deputy, who now took up his abode at Chisolm's residence, which, from this time, became the headquarters of the clan that wrote the names of its victims in letters of blood along the highways and unfrequented paths of the assassin.

About this time occurred the first act of this drama of assassination on which the curtain will be raised in the proper order of the scenes.

Joshua H. Ball was the name of a young man who had been born and raised in the western part of Kemper County. His parents were poor but highly respected, and young Ball early manifested a warmth of heart and vigor of character that gained him many friends in his youth. This boy at an early age became an orphan, and was thrown entirely upon his own resources for a livelihood. But his manly bearing, frankness and industry, had attracted the notice of Mr. Phil Gully, then sheriff of the county, and he at once offered young Ball a home, and gave him employment about his farm. Here he followed the ploughshare until the war came on, when young Ball, impelled by his ardent nature, was one of the first young men of this county who exchanged the plough handle for the sword. He enlisted for the war, and was known and esteemed by his comrades as a high toned, brave and honorable boy.

That he was a model of a soldier is fully attested by many living comrades in the County of Kemper. At the close of the war, young Ball, with the memory of the lost cause engraved deep in his heart, returned to his old home, where he soon married a young lady of more than ordinary attraction and traits of character, but like himself, poor. And it was now that young Ball again found himself buffeting the billows of poverty, and his " noble rage" was chilled by the penury that spread universally over the South, and drove many a promising young man from the quiet attics of his paternal roof to the dens of dissipation.

Young Ball soon became a victim to strong drink, which, kindling all the natural fires of his nature, rendered him, while under its influence, peculiarly prone to scenes of excitement, and liable to rush into difficulties. Yet he was beloved by his friends as a man of great natural amiability of character.

He was a most uncompromising Democrat, and, on that account, early incurred the hostility of the Chisolm clan. He was one of the first men whom Chisolm reported to the military authorities as a ku-klux, and upon which Ball was arrested and carried before a military commission at Lauderdale Springs, where, although there was no sufficient evidence against him, or any, other than his open and outspoken opinions, through the unrelenting persecution and powerful influence of Chisolm and his "crowd" with the military authorities, Ball was subjected to imprisonment and to treatment of great rigor. He finally, however, escaped from the hands of his enemies and returned to his home. He was well known to be a man of true courage, and to possess but little of the spirit of the braggadocio.

Soon after his escape from the military authorities, he accidently met Chisolm in the road, amidst a swamp. They were alone, and Ball being fully apprised of the heartless author of his troubles, attacked Chisolm, charging him with having reported him to the military, and expressing his intention of having satisfaction then and there. Chisolm, with all his braggart bullyism, quailed before the solitary eye of the man whom he had so grossly injured. He denied that he ever reported Ball, and was suffered to pass, in a crouching manner, without the intended chastisement which he, no doubt, fully merited.

From this time Chisolm was afraid of Ball. Ball himself frequently narrated the above incident. And that it was true to the letter would be readily vouched by all who were familiar with the characters of the two men. And that Chisolm had a hand either directly or indirectly in the death of Ball, is certainly not incompatible with the circumstances of that event, but, on the other hand, forms with them a suspicious congruity. These were as follows:

Not long after the meeting in the swamp, and at the still hour of midnight, while Ball was in his bed asleep with his wife, a crowd of armed men surrounded his house, and with shots and savage yells, closed in on all sides upon their startled and helpless victim. So soon as Ball became fully aroused from his slumbers, and aware of his situation, leaping from his window, he attempted to make good his escape to a neighboring thicket; but his alert assassins discovered his retreat, and he was shot and mortally wounded, from the effects of which he died in a few days, but not until he had made his family and attendants fully understand who were the murderers—the vague shadows of whom left their dim outlines upon his glazed eyes. His dying declarations made to his wife and others now living in Kemper County, left no doubt as to the identification of the murderers, for

> "The tongues of dying men enforce attention.
> When words are scarce, they are rarely spent in vain.
> They breathe the truth who breathe their words in pain."

He said, in substance: "That, at first, he thought his assailants were Federal soldiers who had come to arrest him again, and he determined to make his escape if possible, and ran down a short hill into a dense thicket of small pines, but when the murderers discovered his retreat they pursued him, at the same time crying out, 'Here he goes, head him,' upon which he recognized the voice of Bill Clark and other negroes; and not fearing that he would be hurt by them, he turned and walked back up the hill facing them, and when he had approached within a short distance, Clark cried out: 'Turn loose! Turn loose!' and immediately he and George Cole, both negroes, fired, Clark's shot taking effect in his shoulder, breast and bowels."

Upon the faith of these dying declarations, and the attending circumstances, two negroes, named respectively Bill Clark and Julius Griffin—Geo. Cole having made his escape—were arrested and placed in the hands of W. W. Chisolm, who was then sheriff of Kemper County.

But it was not unnoticed by many that the death and burial of poor Ball, which, otherwise, seemed to awaken universal sorrow, alarm and indignation throughout the county, seemed to cast a feature of peculiar placidness over the countenances of the Chisolm clan.

And yet the slanderer Wells had stuck his tarnishing moral even at the point of this blunt circumstance. He alleges that this killing occurred near Phil Gully's house, and that Chisolm's friends, at that time, as to-day, assert that Phil Gully planned Ball's murder, and every other murder committed by the clan.

The impudence that could have suggested such an imputation is almost inconceivable; that Phil Gully, whose charity had for years afforded this poor orphan a home, who had raised him with all the tenderness of paternal affection, and which was reciprocated by this boy to the extent of filial devotion, should have "planned his murder" by a crowd of armed negroes, at the dead hour of midnight, while asleep in the arms of a fond wife, and for no assignable reason, is so preposterous that it cannot fail to excite the feelings of indignation and scorn in the mind of every reasonable man, and surely will have the further effect of bringing the suspicion of guilt upon the heads of those whom its concoction was intended to shield.

But let us see to whom the facts also guide the finger of suspicion. These two negroes were arrested upon the affidavit of Phil Gully, grounded upon the dying declarations of Ball. One of them, Bill Clark, who, as Ball declared, fired the fatal shot, was soon permitted by Chisolm to make good his escape, and was heard of no more. The other, Julius Griffin, against whom there was no positive testimony, arising from the declarations of Ball, was retained in custody, and finally brought to trial and acquitted. Thereupon W. W. Chisolm established this negro in a confection business in the village of De Kalb. The negro, it is said, had not a dollar, and it is also said that Chisolm helped to pay his fees to his attorneys. He furthermore gave him a residence on the back portion of his lot, on which stood his office, in De Kalb.

Surely, the permitting of the escape of the negro upon whom the murder was fixed by the dying declarations of the murdered man, and the sudden unmeasured patronage bestowed upon the other, whose defence he had aided, while sheriff and peace officer of the county, viewed in connection with the affair in the swamp, would justify Chisolm's biographer in making some effort to parry the arrows of suspicion from the head of his martyr! but the misfortune in the matter lies in the effort to shift it to the shoulders of a Gully.

The weight of prejudice which he has sought to heap upon the shoulders of this family leaves little room, apparently, for the lodgement of anything else. And even at this time it began to be evident that no crime committed upon a Gully, or the friend of a Gully, could obtain any retributive response from the law in Kemper County.

Rush, who had murdered Sam Gully, had been acquitted even of manslaughter by a jury of negroes, whom Chisolm had evidently procured to be packed for the purpose. Higgins, who had killed Floyd, the cousin of Phil Gully, had been permitted to make his escape upon the horse of the old Scotchman, prepared for him.

McRea had gone to his final account without having experienced a possibility of a bill being found against him for his deadly assault upon John W. Gully, and now a negro who had killed young Ball, the foster child of Philip Gully, was permitted to escape, and another, charged with the same crime, taken under the protecting eyes of the peace officer of the county.

The negro, Julius Griffin, declared while in jail, that if he was hurt for this matter, Chisolm was not the man he promised to be.

It seems to have been the constant aim of Chisolm to impress the infinity of his influence, and the vastness of his power in all the government of the State, upon the minds of the negroes. This he succeeded in accomplishing to such an extent that the negroes of Kemper County believed him to be imbued with power sufficient to accomplish anything he wished. They looked upon him as being but little less than a god.

It was this dazzling appearance of potency which he knew so well how to exhibit on all occasions, and to the best advantage, that enabled him to wield, without a foreign or native rival, the most despotic control in his county of all the radical leaders and officials in the State.

The following circumstance is an instance of the manifestation of his influence: On the 16th day of May, 1871, while Chisolm was sheriff, one W. R. Bethany, a constable of the county, and a radical, proceeded to the residence of his sister, one Sarah Sellers, in his official capacity, to levy upon some property, in pursuance of a writ of execution against this woman or her property, and there lived with her at this time, and in her employment a negro, by the name of George Sansum, with whom it was thought she lived in illicit relations.

This negro shot and killed Bethany from a window of the house of this woman, as he was entering the gate with his writ. The negro was tried before a jury, composed of seven negroes and five white men, and was fairly and properly convicted of murder. There was no palliating circumstance whatever, and the court passed sentence of death upon the prisoner. Whereupon Chisolm, with no other purpose than to give to the negroes a fresh exhibition of his power, sent up to Adelbert Ames, then governor of Mississippi, first a petition for the commutation of the sentence of death to that of imprisonment for life in the State penitentiary. Upon obtaining the object of this petition, he sent up another asking for a full pardon of Sansum, which he likewise procured. And through his further efforts and influence Sansum was taken into the private employment of the governor, either as body servant or body guard, which position he held up to the time Ames fled the State.

There had been no feelings of unfriendliness between Chisolm and the Bethanys, and no relations other than political between him and the negro. His purpose in the matter was very apparent, and it is not to be wondered at that the negroes of Kemper followed him with a blind devotion akin almost to adoration.

In this instance they saw him first snatch one of their number from the gallows, to which he had been sentenced with all the sanctity and formalities of law, and place him safe and sound in the penitentiary. They next saw him, in quick succession, take him out of the penitentiary, whose doors had apparently closed on him for life, and place him in uniform and in waiting at the doors of the governor's palace, where his striped trousers were exchanged for the gaudy livery of a governor's waitman.

But if he was enabled to present to their wondering eyes such exhibitions of his influence at the State capitol, its manifestations were no less striking in Kemper County, where they saw men charged with the highest crimes, and of which they knew them to be guilty, go scot free at the smack of Chisolm's fingers; and finally, they began to see, what to them was still more striking, the mangled bodies of those who opposed his course lying in the highways riddled with the bullets of the assassin.

The exercise of this unlimited control over the minds of the negroes, to the ruin of the whites, seemed to be the culmination of his ambition.

Under these circumstances it is not surprising to find that he held the entire negro ballot in his hands. Nor is it a wonder that the ends of public justice were invariably defeated whenever it was the wish of this man that they should be. In reference to this feature of his career his biographer indulges in the following remarks:

"Guided by the firm hand and unconquerable will of one man, the County of Kemper, for a succession of years, has stood the tide of hatred engendered by secession and nursed by the overthrow of the 'divine institution,' and

rights under the law, and that stronghold of 'radicalism' become an object of special attention by the white line Democracy all over the State."

It may be observed that, as that author can never finish one of his killings without the ghost of a Gully, so he cannot allege a political fact without the use of such stereotyped expressions as "tide of hatred," "secession nursed," "divine institution," "white line Democracy," "intimidation," "fraud," "violence;" and it is difficult to see for what purpose he so flippantly flaunts these phrases, other than that of concealing under the wings of abuse the falsity of his statements.

But if Wells endeavors to hide the tracks of his mendacity, like the thief who stole the oxen of Hercules, so did Chisolm and his "crowd" strive to leave no tracks of their villanies upon the official tablets of the county.

The author has not been able to discover any final record of the courts of Kemper County, covering a period of five years, extending from the fall of 1866 to the fall of 1871.

During this time there were two persons who filled the position of clerk of the circuit court. One, who was a carpet bagger, was appointed by the military authorities; the other, who was also a radical, was appointed by Ames.

In regard to final records, the General Code of Mississippi contained the following requirement, article 21, page 481: Within three months after the final determination of any suit, or, if an appeal or writ of error shall have been taken, then within three months after receiving a certificate of the affirmance of the judgment, the clerk shall enter, in well bound books to be kept for the purpose, a full and complete record of all the proceedings in such suit; and, on failure to do so, such clerk, on such failure being notified to the court, may be fined twenty dollars for each case in which he shall have failed to make up such final record, and he shall also be liable in damages to any party injured.

Yet, notwithstanding this severely sanctioned provision of the statute, the author has not been able to find a single final record of the court over the signature of either of these clerks during the whole time of their respective services, which covered a space of five years.

But, when it is taken into consideration that, during this time, the judge, sheriff, and every other officer of the county were members of the same party and clan, such malfeasance need not occasion any surprise.

All this was well known to the members of the bar who practised in this court, and to others, but they felt and knew that it would be utterly useless to bring the matter up.

They saw so many crimes passed by without the possibility of punishment, that they had no heart to become prosecutors or informers in what seemed comparatively innocent matters; besides, there was naturally a disposition to avoid the useless aggravation of those who possessed the power of doing them so much injury.

In the summer of 1870, John P. Gilmer, whose character has already been partially delineated, began his career with his participation in the killing of Hal Dawson, at Scooba. Dawson was quite a youth, just entering the threshold of manhood. He was born and reared in the County of Kemper, and only a few miles from Scooba. He was of a good family; on his mother's side he was descended from the Winstons, of Alabama, of which family Governor J. Anthony Winston was a prominent representative, and the uncle of Dawson. He was also a relative of Governor Pettuce, of Mississippi. On his father's side he was connected with some of the best families of Kemper County.

His father was for many years one of the most prominent and highly respected physicians in the county.

Young Dawson was of a warm and vehement disposition, and was much beloved by his friends. He had but one fault, and one very common with young men of his ardent temperament. He had a year or two previous to his death fallen into the habit of indulging occasionally too much in strong drink, yet his natural good nature asserted itself even while his mind was clouded with the fumes of liquor, and whatever wildness or imprudence of speech or action he might indulge, while intoxicated, there was no one who had any fears that he would commit any crime.

It was on one of these well known blustering but innocent occasions that he met with a foul death.

There was in Scooba, at this time, a man by the name of Davis, who was a member of the Board of Registration, which was then holding its session in the back room of Gilmer's store. Davis was likewise a native of the county, and had known Dawson from boyhood, and on the occasion in question, Dawson, being under the influence of liquor, and in one of his harmless blusterings against the radicals, went down the street to Gilmer's store, saying to some persons whom he passed that he wanted to see the registrar, Davis.

On arriving at the door, Gilmer walked out upon the steps, and asked him if he wished to see him, and if he had anything against him. Dawson replied, "No; I have nothing against you, Gilmer. I want to see Davis." Upon this Gilmer stepped out upon the street, remarking to Dawson: "There he is in there; see him if you wish." Dawson then entered the door, at the same time having his hand on his pistol. No sooner had he entered when Davis, who was standing behind the counter a few feet to the right of the door with a double barrel gun in his hand, fired at Dawson, the contents of the gun—a load of buckshot—passing through his body. Dawson immediately sank upon his knees in a dying condition and rested his head upon the steps. Then Gilmer, who was standing some ten or fifteen feet distant, deliberately advanced, and placing his pistol against the head of the dying man, shot two balls through it.

These facts were obtained from eye witnesses, one of whom is a very intelligent lady, an old friend of the writer and the wife of a popular and promising young lawyer of De Kalb. This lady happened to be sitting in a buggy in full view of the scene, and her description of it may be relied upon with gospel certainty.

Gilmer and Davis were both arrested immediately by the town constable, but by some means procured themselves to be carried to De Kalb, instead of before the town authorities of Scooba or the magistrate of that beat. The object of this was to reach the hands of their friend Chisolm, then sheriff of the county, in which they were certain to fare in every respect to their advantage.

This act of carrying criminals to a distant beat to be tried, far away from the evidences of their guilt, was such a shocking violation of law, and so apparent an attempt to baffle the pursuit of justice, that on the next day several citizens of Scooba proceeded to De Kalb and demanded that the prisoners be returned to Scooba and tried before the investigating court of the mayor of the town, or the justice of the beat. But the criminals and their friends well knew that if this was done, that they would be committed to jail without bail to await the action of the grand jury, as the crime with which they were charged, and the attending circumstances, would, under the existing law, render the offence unbailable. Besides, the mayor of Scooba and the justice of the beat, although the latter was a radical, were not men likely to turn a totally deaf ear to law and justice.

To this demand of the citizens, the sheriff, W. W. Chisolm, positively refused compliance, alleging that as they were in his hands he had the right to retain and protect them. Upon this they were brought before a radical justice court at De Kalb, distant from and out of the reach of much of the evidence of their guilt. Yet, notwithstanding the influence of their friend Chisolm, and its active exercise in their behalf, they were put under bonds of $3,000 each to appear and answer to any indictment that might be presented against them in this matter, at the next term of the circuit court of the county. This bond was procured for them by Chisolm, and they were released. But it became evident long before the meeting of the circuit court, and the impanelling of the grand jury for that term, that a jury would be assembled whose selection had been made for the purpose of preventing the finding of a bill of indictment against Gilmer and Davis. This could be easily effected, inasmuch as the members of the board of police for the years 1869 and 1870 were all radicals, and mere puppets of the sheriff, Chisolm. Upon this board devolved the duty of selecting the grand jurors for the ensuing term of the court.

The following are the names of the jurors thus chosen for this occasion, together with the well known politics of each:

THOS. W. ADAMS	Radical.
JAS. A. BURTON	Democrat.
PETER E. SPINKS	Democrat.
WILLIAM DEES	Democrat.
T. H. MORTON	Democrat.
J. J. TINSLEY	Democrat.
J. C. CARPENTER	Democrat.
C. P. CHANEY	Radical.
GEO. ROBINSON	Radical.
THOS. ORR	Radical.
HENRY GREER	Radical.
JAMES WELSH	Radical.
KIRSCH WELSH	Radical.
CHAS. NICHOLS	Radical.
HENRY RUMSEY	Radical.

Thus it will be seen that this grand jury was composed of nine radicals, and, as the author is informed, the very worst in the county, and six Democrats.

This jury refused to indict either of the parties to this diabolical murder.

It is plain that whatever justification or palliation might have been adduced on the part of Davis, there was not the slightest excuse for the conduct of Gilmer. He had met Dawson at his door, and, in an insulting manner and attitude, challenged him with the inquiry: "Do you wish to see me? Have you anything against me?" "No," replied Dawson; "I have nothing against you," and in three minutes after he advances upon Dawson, after he had fallen to the ground in a dying condition, and placing the muzzle of the pistol against the head of the dying man, shoots two bullets through his brain, and the people of Kemper county had the mortification and the patience to see this horrible crime pass by unpunished and unreproved!

Nor was this all. Their fears were also aroused as to who would be the next unavenged victim of such lawless impunity, and it is no wonder that it occasioned throughout the county a feeling of intense indignation as well as alarm.

It will be proper, perhaps, to mention, in this connection, the fact that young Dawson was a near relative of Judge Dillard, who was a prominent and influential citizen of the adjoining County of Sumter, in the State of Alabama, which fact, if borne in mind, will explain other circumstances mentioned hereafter.

The hostile feeling produced against the clan, as it now plainly manifested itself to be, in the minds of the people of Kemper, the patience they exercised, and the impudent indifference with which these men viewed their bloody work, may be gathered from the admissions and evasions of Gilmer, in his testimony before the committee of Congress, to inquire about the free exercise of the elective franchise in Mississippi, at Washington, in January, 1877.

Q. By Mr. Money—About 1875, what was the condition of political affairs in your county? In whose hands was the county at that time, and who was responsible for the condition of things there—I mean up to the election in 1875?

A. The county officers were Republicans.

Q. And they had succeeded in keeping the county in a lawful state all the time?

A. There was no outbreak or anything of the sort.

Q. The laws were strictly complied with and enforced?

A. As much so as in other counties in the State.

Q. Did you not kill a man at Scooba that year?

A. No, sir.

Q. Did you in 1876?

A. No, sir.

Q. In 1874?

A. No, sir.

Q. Did you ever kill a man at Scooba?

A. I presume I know what you are driving at.

Q. That is what I want to get at.

A. It was in 1871.

Q. The county was then in the hands of the Republicans and Judge Chisolm was the sheriff?

A. Yes, sir.

Q. Were you ever indicted for that killing?

A. No, sir. There have been some twelve or fifteen grand juries since, both of Democrats and Republicans.

Q. You were never indicted?

A. No, sir.

Q. Did not a great deal of bitter feeling arise out of the circumstance of that killing, on the part of the white people, toward you and toward Judge Chisolm, entirely independent of politics?

A. I do not see why there should be any feeling against Judge Chisolm. There was a feeling as between me and some of this party's relations, and I did not speak with most of them.

Q. Was not that extensively used against you in the county? Was there not a great deal of feeling gotten up against you and against Judge Chisolm, who was held responsible for the management of the affairs of that county, he being the sheriff?

A. I do not know whether that was the cause of it or not. A good many Democrats told me this party ought to have been killed, and that I was justifiable in doing it, and that if I would go with the Democratic party it would be all right.

Q. Give me the name of some Democrat who told you that.

A. I dislike to give you the name of any man who would tell me that the party ought to have been killed.

Q. I do not want you to give that, but give the name of a Democrat who said that if you would go with the Democrats it would be all right.

A. I do not know that I can exactly recall any particular name just now—I might if you would give me a little time to think over it. But there may have been a hundred who told me so.

Q. And you cannot recollect one of the hundred?

A. Perhaps I can if it is necessary.

Q. I should like to have the names if you can give them. Take time and think of it.

A. Well, sir, I do not believe there is a Democrat in Scooba but what has talked to me and told me if I would go with the Democratic party it would be all right.

Q. I mean on account of this killing. That is what we are talking about.

A. Perhaps I do not understand your question.

Q. I ask you if a great deal of this bitterness, which you complain of toward yourself and Judge Chisolm, did not arise out of the killing of a Mr. Dawson by you at Scooba, and your protection by Judge Chisolm, who was sheriff of the county at that time, and the fact that there was no indictment found against you at all?

A. No, sir; I do not think any such feeling exists, from the very fact that the Democrats have had the grand jury their own way ever since, and I have not been indicted, and from the fact that we are mighty friendly in our business relations.

Q. Have the Democrats had possession of the grand jury since 1871?

A. They have it now.

Q. Is it true that they have had it since that time?

A. No, sir; but they have had the last two grand juries.

Q. This last year?

A Yes, sir.

Q. Is not that offence barred by the statute of limitations?

A. I hardly think so; I do not think murder is barred.

Q. It was murder then, was it?

A. If it could be made out murder; I do not know what kind of an indictment they might get; they might make it murder, or they might make it manslaughter; I do not think any capital offence of that kind is barred.

Q. But the statute itself wiped out the offence. The fact was that that county was in the hands of Republicans, and under the administration of Judge Chisolm, and you were not indicted for this offence—call it murder, manslaughter, or whatever you please?

A. Yes, sir; so far as county officers are concerned; the board of supervisors in Mississippi appoint the grand jury.

It would be difficult to surpass the indifference and nonchalance manifested in this testimony, but not at all difficult to draw from it the true character of the witness. The statute referred to by Mr. Money is as follows:

An act to amend the rules of practice and procedure in criminal cases in this State.

SECTION 8. *Be it further enacted*, That all prosecutions for criminal offences heretofore committed, shall be commenced within two years after the commission thereof, and not after:

Provided, This section shall not apply to any case in which the offender shall have fled from the State.

SECTION 9. *Be it further enacted*, That in all cases where any person has heretofore given bail or security on recognizance for the appearance of any other person, whether said bail bonds are now pending in the several courts to which they are made returnable, or whether such bonds have been forfeited, and proceedings thereon have been instituted, such bonds are hereby declared to be void and of no effect, and such proceedings are hereby suspended, and the same ordered to be dismissed.

Approved April 5, 1872.

This infamous act, done in contravention of all the teachings of the common law, and in repugnance to all juridical experience, was given effect from its passage on the above date, and continued in operation until the fall of 1875, when it was expressly repealed. It was but one of the many legislative devices enacted by the carpet bag and negro legislators of Mississippi to shield official corruption, and to afford that immunity for crime so pleasing to the great body of the radical party in the South. Under the operations of this act, if any one was detected in the perpetration of any crime whatever, it was only necessary to fly to the swamps or step over the State line, remain away for the space of two years, and the offence would become *non esse* in law.

The killing of Dawson was such a shock to every sense of humanity, and created such a general feeling of exasperation, which was aggravated by the fact that Gilmer and Davis had been taken away for the purpose of thwarting the course of justice, that on the night following the murder, and while the mangled body of the butchered man lay in sight of his friends, a mob gathered in the streets of Scooba, broke into Gilmer's store and destroyed a large portion of his goods.

This conduct was wholly and in the highest degree reprehensible, and nothing less than the high state of excitement, and the ample cause for that, could prevent it from being criminal as well as disgraceful. And the parties who did this act were evidently of the same sober opinion, for no sooner had their feelings cooled down than they offered to pay, and did pay to Gilmer more than he had lost.

It may be remarked that this attack upon his store was made when it was first known that Gilmer had been carried off to De Kalb, and which they well knew was done for the purpose of placing him under the protection of Chisolm, and they, by this time, had learned well what that protection meant.

This circumstance of the killing of Dawson fully developed the true character of Gilmer, and at once cemented that cord of fellowship, and pledge of faith and co-operation, ever afterward so cordially maintained between him and Chisolm. Gilmer from this time became one of the chief actors on the stage. But as Chisolm desired no partner, or partition of the functions of the high priesthood of the county, which he now held and enjoyed *in solido*, it was thought best for Gilmer to go to the legislature.

At this time a man by the name of Gambril held the office of State senator from this district. Gambril was a native of Ohio, but had emigrated to Mississippi when quite a young man, and engaged in teaching school, and like all of his class and nativity, at that time, he was received with the greatest kindness by the Southern people. While, in many instances, the former were busily engaged in sowing the seeds of corruption and insurrection among their slaves, Gambril succeeded in obtaining quite a flourishing school, and finally married in a Southern family, and when the war came on he was the father of several children.

He continued to conduct his school until the passage of the conscript act, when, not having a sufficient number of scholars to procure his exemption from military duty under the law, he was, like all other unexempted able bodied men, forced into the Confederate army by the officers of the conscript bureau.

At this time W. W. Chisolm was the chief conscript officer in Kemper County, and in the exercise of his duties as such, was never known to show any mercy to the victims of his authority. And here it may be remarked, that at no time during the first years of the war was there any obstacle to prevent any Northern man, or alien enemy, from removing himself and family out of the Confederacy; and if Gambril was a Union man and an alien enemy, he had ample opportunity of taking himself away. But he remained teaching his little school until Lieutenant Chisolm seized upon him and hurried him off into the army.

There were many Northern men in the South at the beginning of the war who were similarly situated, and who, be it said to their honor, adhered steadfastly to those who had ministered, with unsparing hand, to them in their adversity. Not so, however, with Gambril. In the uniform of a Southern soldier, he deserted at the first opportunity and went over to the enemy, with whom he remained until the close of the war, when he skulked back, without molestation, to the bosom of his family, of whom he was unworthy.

This was the man whom the radicals of Kemper had selected to represent them in the State senate—a man who had, years ago, come South, clad in the rags of poverty, homeless and friendless, had feasted upon the hospitality of the Southern people; had been received into the bosom of their families; entrusted with the training of their young; joined in marriage with one of their fair daughters, and yet, when they became involved in a war of political, social and national life or death, he deserted the wife who had placed all her trust in him; abandoned the children she had given him; deserted the friends of his youth; and on the first opportunity passed over to their enemies, and accepted an office in their ranks. And yet all this is counted as merit by the thieves and villains who composed the most of the white element of the radical party in the South.

It is said that the Spartans took great pains to instruct their youth in the art of cunning and deceit; and that adroitness, particularly in theft, was by them considered meritorious. Yet to steal so unskilfully as to be detected was a great disgrace. And it seems that the moral teachings of the Southern radicals were of a somewhat similar nature.

It made no difference what crime they committed, just so they could procure, by any means, immunity from punishment, they were sure to receive the applause of their associates at the South and their allies at the North. No harm to break faith with, deceive and steal from a Southern white man, *alias* a rebel, was a doctrine early advo-

party, and constantly thundered into the ears of the negroes. Although Gambril was capable of abandoning his family, and deserting to the enemy of the country in which they resided, and of which they were natives, yet he seems to have been a man of but little vigor and force of character. Hence it seems that he was never gathered affectionately into the folds of the Chisolm clan.

His villanous conduct during the war had caused him to be elected State senator; but apart from his lack of spirit, Chisolm, no doubt, from his own experience, thought that a man who had before so basely deserted his friends and family, was worthy of but little reliance. Be this as it may, the event of his death, which occurred in 1871, opened the way for the advancement of Gilmer.

The circumstances of the killing of Gambril were as follows: It seems that he had two or three daughters grown, or about grown, and that one night a negro entered their apartment. An old negro woman, who was sleeping in the room saw the negro, gave the alarm, and told Gambril who she took it to be. The negro suspected was named Flander Jones. Gambril attacked this negro, and an altercation occurred between them. The negro then went off and procured a pistol, at the same time telling another negro that he intended to kill Gambril with it. They met again, and another fight took place, in which the negro shot and killed Gambril.

Chisolm was at this time sheriff and peace officer of the county, yet none of the parties were ever arrested. It was a radical personal quarrel, and as the white people had but little respect for Gambril, they left the whole matter to be settled by the party which had entire control of the county, and it was settled in this way: Gambril was buried; his murderer went unmolested, and Gilmer was put in his place as State senator. Although there was no proof to that effect, yet the conduct of Chisolm in this matter caused grave suspicions to rest upon him in regard to it.

The whole matter was soon hushed up; and the indiference manifested in regard to it by the members of the clan, caused many to believe that his death was procured for the purpose of making way for Gilmer; but it is evident that this conjecture arose solely from the mysterious conduct of the leading radicals in regard to it, for the author has been able to find no other ground on which the implication of Chisolm could be surmised. It is certain, however, that the opportunity for promoting Gilmer was at least the attainment of his wishes in that respect. This was apparent to all who observed his manners on the occasion.

It may be observed that at the time of the killing of Gambril, Gilmer was an avowed candidate for the office held by the former, and it was positively understood and arranged by Chisholm and his clan that Gilmer should succeed him in the senatorship. But there was necessarily some difficulty in the way of accomplishing this object, to surmount which it was necessary to act with vigor.

Gilmer was a new comer in the county, and had but recently declared his political status. In fact, it seems that the prospect of this office mainly determined his career; and his accession to the ranks of the clan, after the killing of Dawson, promised too much importance to justify the omission of any endeavor to secure his co-operation with the party.

But Gambril was an old citizen, and possessed, in the eyes of the negro, all the qualifications and antecedents requisite for the position. He was a Northern man; had deserted to the enemy during the war; and having forfeited the respect of his old friends, he had placed himself upon a level with the negro, and was a strong advocate of political, if not social, equality. This gave him great popularity with a majority of the voters of the county, as the negroes were largely in the ascendency; and it could not be overlooked that the chances of Gilmer, under these circumstances, in a fair race with him, were bad.

This was the state of affairs in the radical camp at the death of Gambril; and these circumstances, connected with the mysteries attending his death, were well calculated to create the pretty general belief that his life was sacrificed to the promotion of Gilmer, and that his death had been deliberately procured for that purpose.

This event removed every obstacle in Gilmer's path to the State capital, where his career was hinged upon the issue of race, and the worst features of the radical party. His history in the State senate is inseparable from anything that was obnoxious to the white people and tax payers of the State. Apart from this, no striking feature marked his course, save that of his repairing to Vicksburg, and becoming, while yet senator, the deputy sheriff of the notorious Peter Crosby, in 1875. His own testimony, in regard to this matter, before the committee at Washington, page 506, is here introduced:

Q. You stated that your place of residence is Kemper county. How did you happen to be in Vicksburg, as deputy sheriff, in 1875?

A. I will tell you how I happened to be there; I carpet bagged over there. That county was a very large county, and it had a larger population than any other county in the State. It was a county that might, perhaps, wield considerable influence in the politics of the State.

Q. You say you carpet bagged over there. State to the committee what they are to understand by your carpet bagging there. What do you mean by carpet bagging?

A. I mean that any man who leaves his own county and goes into another county and holds office, if he is a Republican, is called a carpet bagger by the Democrats. I was only using the term they apply.

Q. That they apply to persons who hold office?

A. Yes, sir.

Q. State how you came to be employed there as deputy sheriff?

A. There had been great trouble the year previous in Warren County. There was great excitement all over the State, and reports of some two or three riots, and the killing of a great many Republicans and colored men. The sheriff had been forced to resign his office, and every effort was made that could possibly be made——

Question by Mr. Money: Is this of your own knowledge, or did you hear it?

A. I know that the trouble occurred; I did not see it, but anybody who lives in Mississippi knows it.

Q. You are stating what you got from newspapers and such sources of information?

A. It was my knowledge that the sheriff did not have a bond and could not make one, and he made arrangements through some of my friends by which I was to make his bond. I thought it was a great outrage that a large and influential county, a county that had, at least, four or five thousand Republican majority, should be handed over to the Democrats simply by cheating the Republican officials, or either defeating them from making their bonds when they were elected to positions. I felt that it was a fight being made on account of their being Republicans, and not against them upon any other ground. On that account I volunteered to go over there and make Crosby's bond.

Q. To make the bond and run the office?

A. Yes, sir.

Q. You went over there and accepted the position of deputy sheriff, did you not?

A. Yes, sir.

Q. You were sworn in as such?

A. I think so.

Q. At that time were you not a member of the State senate from the counties of Kemper, Neshoba and Noxubee?

A. I resigned my senatorship.

Q. At what time did you resign?

A. About the time I went over there.

Q. Can you recollect the date of your resignation?

A. I will not be positive; it is on file at Jackson.

Q. But it is not on file here. I want to know the date of your resignation?

A. I will not be positive, but I resigned some time

Q. Do you not know positively that you did not?

A. I think I resigned when I first went there.

Q. Do you not know that you were holding both offices at once?

By Mr Pease: Do you consider the deputy shrievalty an office?

Mr. Money: I will waive that point; but I want to prove the fact that the witness was a senator when he went over there and took that office.

Q. You say you went over there to give the bond and run the office?

A. Yes, sir.

Q. And at that time you were a senator in the legislature of the State?

A. Yes, sir; at the time I went over there I was a senator. I do not know what time I resigned. I resigned when I was there, but I do not know when it was.

Q. Was not the sheriff of that county, Peter Crosby, shot at some time?

A. Yes, sir.

Q. Was he shot while you were his deputy?

A. No, sir; I was not his deputy.

Q. How long had you ceased to be his deputy when he was shot?

A. Two or three days.

Q. Did Crosby ever charge you with doing that shooting?

A. Yes, sir.

Q. And he dismissed you then from the office of deputy?

A. I was dismissed before he was shot.

Q. Why did you leave the place, or why were you dismissed? I do not know how you got out of it.

A. The deputy's office?

Q. Yes, sir. You ceased to be Crosby's deputy, for what reason?

A. We did not agree. He did not give me any reason for the dismissal at all.

Upon this charge Gilmer was arrested and acquitted. But the writer is informed by gentlemen of undoubted veracity that on his return to Scooba he frequently confessed that he did shoot Peter Crosby, and for the reason that the latter had dismissed him from the deputy shrievalty, when he had aided in making Crosby's bond, and that if his pistol had been all right, the result of the affair would have been different.

Soon after the shooting of Crosby, Gilmer returned to Scooba, and resumed his mercantile operations, and made large purchases of goods on credit, which he sold recklessly, or divided among his friends, in such a manner as to arouse the suspicions of his creditors; and very soon four indictments were lodged against him in the criminal court of the City of St. Louis, Missouri, charging him with having obtained goods by fraud and under false pretences. Upon these indictments the governor of Missouri made requisition for Gilmer, and he was arrested and delivered to the authorities of that State. He was carried to St. Louis, and was required to enter into recognizance for his appearance at the proper trial term of the city court, or go to jail.

In this dilemma Chisolm went promptly to his rescue, and succeeded in making the necessary bonds, which aggregated the sum of twenty-four hundred dollars. This he did, it is said, by depositing the amount with Gilmer's sureties. Chisolm immediately returned to Kemper after this arrangement had been effected, but Gilmer did not return until several days after, for which he assigned as the reason that some letters of information in regard to his conduct and character had been sent from De Kalb to his prosecutors in St. Louis, of which he suspicioned John W. Gully to be the author, and that he remained there for the purpose of ascertaining that fact. But it was, and is still believed by many, that he was hunting up the negro Walter Riley, who had fled from justice several years before, and was at this time living at some place in the State of Tennessee, well known to Chisolm and his clan.

Be this as it may, it is true that Riley returned to Kemper County soon after, but as this circumstance forms an important link in the chain of events to which we will have occasion to revert more fully hereafter, its discussion will be reserved till then.

These indictments were pending, and the recognizance was in force at the time of Gilmer's death, which occurred not long after this. Upon Chisolm's return, he declared repeatedly, in reference to the letters referred to, that if Gilmer should ascertain the author it would be bad for the latter, and that both Gilmer and himself were satisfied that Gully wrote them. A short time prior to these events an incident occurred in the streets of De Kalb, which will conduce to a fuller development of the character of Gilmer and the disposition he cherished towards Gully, and which, when combined, may lead to an insight into that chain of mysterious circumstances which culminated in the terrible tragedies that followed.

On the occasion referred to, John Gully was sitting quietly on the lower steps of a store in the front street of De Kalb, when Gilmer procured a wheelbarrow, and proceeding down the street with it, rolled it deliberately against the legs of Gully, at the same time placing his hand on his pistol, which he finally drew and cocked, and holding it in one hand, continued to push the wheelbarrow against Gully with the other and with his stomach, which he applied to the round connecting the handles of the implement. Gully was entirely unarmed, and well knowing the desperate character of his assailant, made no resistance and said nothing. Finally Gilmer said to him, "By God, you know what I mean! I mean, that you are a damned rascal, and that you have to get out of my way!" "I'll do it," said Gully, and, rising, he went immediately to his store and procured a gun, with which he returned to his position on the steps.

In the meantime, Gilmer had been arrested and carried into the court house yard, just across the street—not, however, until he had primed and fired off his pistol—

where for hours he strove with the utmost desperation to escape from the officers and return to the assault. For this conduct he was fined by the radical judge one dollar and the costs. And thus the fist of impunity was again shaken in the face of the Gullys and the whole community.

Of all these glaring manifestations of immunity for every degree of crime, the people of Kemper County were not, nor could they be, unobservant or oblivious. Their minds became deeply impressed with a general feeling of insecurity that finally resulted in something akin to desperation.

They saw themselves in the midst of a semi-barbarous race, of brutal instincts and strong race prejudices, inflamed with avowed hostility to them, and whose passions were continually fanned by men who seemed to have no sympathy with any class of Southern white society, or any respect for the laws of God or man. They saw the scales of justice swinging in the hands of the assassin and the thief, and their laws administered by outlaws.

Such a state of affairs was well calculated to excite first their fears and indignation, and then a spirit of self defence; and these combined to urge the adoption of every measure that promised them relief.

Such was the state of affairs in Mississippi at the beginning of the year 1875, and which had existed for seven long years, with a constant tendency to, if possible, a still worse condition.

CHAPTER VI.

Among the worst of the avenues of corruption that permeated every department of the State and county governments of Mississippi during radical rule, and one which afforded, perhaps, the most ample opportunities for plunder, was the public school system, every feature of which seems to have been fashioned with a view to its prostitution to purposes of iniquity, and every position connected with it seems to have offered a bid to corruption.

At the period which we are now discussing, the State superintendent of education was a negro of the most vicious character, and the example set by the chief seems to have been followed, as a fixed policy, by every subordinate in the entire system. Of which a better description cannot be given, perhaps, than that set forth in the testimony of the Hon. J. A. Campbell, at that time one of the judges of the supreme court of the State, before the Mississippi investigating committee at Jackson, on June 21, 1876. It will be observed that at this time the State government had passed into the hands of the Democratic party and the native white people.

Q. By Senator Bayard: Who is the present superintendent of the schools?

A. T. S Gathwright.

Q. Who is he?

A. He has been a devoted teacher for many years.

Q. A man of education?

A. Yes, sir. I will add that he is thoroughly imbued with the spirit of maintaining the schools without regard to race, color or previous condition of servitude.

Q. Who preceded him?

A. A man by the name of Cardozo, a colored individual.

Q. How did he get out of office, and how long did he hold his office?

A. He must have held it about two years.

Q. What office had he held prior to that?

A. He had been circuit clerk of Warren County, I believe.

Q. Do you know whether, as circuit clerk, he had been charged with forgery of warrants?

A. Yes, sir. He had been charged and indicted.

Q. Were those indictments found before or after his election as superintendent?

A. Prior, I think. I know he was charged with being a forger, a thief and a felon—all that sort of thing. I know the disposition on the part of the Republicans to shake him off, as being unable to carry such a weight.

Q. Notwithstanding this charge and this reputation, he was elected State superintendent of education?

A. Yes, sir; he was.

Q. What was his course in that office?

A. Well, I only speak from reputation. It was bad. I can speak from some knowledge of one transaction. I am president of the board of trustees of the normal school of Tougaloo. I am president of the board of trustees of the State department of that normal school. This man, Cardozo, as State superintendent of education, was *ex officio* member of that board. Prior to that, however, I would not associate with him, even officially, or in any way. Cardozo was, as stated, a member of that board, and he was treasurer of the board, and he drew from the State treasury the full appropriation by the State for the maintenance of its department in that university, or normal school, and he accounted for about twenty-two hundred dollars, and the balance of it he has never accounted for; and the trustees have recently instituted a suit, or ordered it to be instituted, against Cardozo, or the sureties on Cardozo's bond, in Warren County, to recover for his deficit in that appropriation. He drew the money from the treasury, and paid over twenty-two hundred dollars, and the balance he put in his pocket, I suppose.

A. Forty-five hundred dollars, I think, and accounted for twenty-two hundred dollars, I think—I am not certain that I am accurate in the figures—and suit has lately been instituted, or ordered to be, against him. Martin Casey is one on the bond, but says his name is a forgery. Mrs. Williams is the other one, and her signature will probably be invalidated, as she will undoubtedly claim that she signed it in view of this name being upon it, relying upon it.

Q. You have stated that you would not associate, officially or otherwise, with Cardozo. State your reasons for that.

A. His character is most infamous, according to reputation.

Q. Do you know under what indictments he rests at present?

A. No, sir; I cannot say I know. I have understood there were sixteen indictments against him.

Q. For what crimes?

A. For forging, I think, county certificates, county warrants—embezzlement, perhaps. I am not sure as to that.

Q. How was he gotten out of office?

A. He was impeached by the House of Representatives of the legislature of Mississippi.

Q. And tried by the senate?

A. No; he resigned, I believe. I do not think he was tried. I think he resigned under impeachment; that is my impression.

Q. In your school system, what part and authority has the board of supervisors?

A. The board of supervisors, composed of five men, is the county school board of education.

Q. Does the board levy a school tax?

A Yes, sir; it is allowed to levy an additional sum for the payment of teachers; also, a school house fund, as it is called

Q. Are those levies discretionary with the board?

A. They are, within certain limits—which is two per cent., or two mills on the dollar, I should have said.

Q. Who composed the board in Madison County after the election of 1873?

A. Five negroes.

Q. Were any of them educated men?

A. No, sir.

Q. Do you know whether any of these five negroes were able to read and write?

A. My information is that one of them could sign his name, after a fashion.

Q. And it was to that board the control of education in that county was submitted?

A. Yes, sir; they levy the county taxes for education, and other purposes.

Q. Could any one of that board calculate the rate of assessment estimates upon sums of money?

A. I have no idea they could. I do not know from personal knowledge, but, from information, I do not think there was any one of them that could make any sort of computation. Not one of them was familiar with the simple rules of arithmetic.

It may be remarked that Madison County was the home of Judge Campbell, and the same state of the school system which he has described as existing in his county, was common in all the black counties of Mississippi, or counties in which the negro voters were in the majority, with the addition that the intermixture and participation of carpet baggers found in some of them, but added a still more dangerous and corrupt element than ignorance to the control of the moral and educational training of the people.

It had been the early aim of the radical party to force social equality upon the Southern people through the instrumentality of the public school system, and the first constitution prepared for the people of Mississippi, under the reconstruction acts of Congress, embodied a feature requiring the whites to mingle with the negroes in the public schools of the State, or submit to the unjust alternative of contributing from their scanty substance a heavy tax to maintain a costly system of public schools, in the advantages of which they did not participate.

Never was there a more arbitrary and humiliating condition imposed upon a people, than this of being compelled either to accept the terms of having their children trained and educated upon a social footing with the negro, or on the other hand to become vassals to the effort to make him their superior.

It was this provision that early and naturally excited the opposition of the white people to any contribution to the education of the negro, who paid no taxes himself comparatively worthy of consideration.

With the destruction of slavery, they had become woefully impoverished. Their lands were almost valueless. Their personal property, too, had been swept away by the tide of war, and they thought that these consequences were sufficiently onerous without being forced to contribute their slender means of support to educate their former slaves. But when the burden was rendered humiliating and insulting, it, indeed, became insupportable.

It was this that provoked the strenuous efforts on the part of the white people of Mississippi, which resulted in the defeat of the constitution fashioned for them by Congress, in 1868.

Nor did this feature of mixed schools enlist the sympathies of the negroes themselves. Their own sense of inferiority led many of them to oppose the scheme; consequently they voted largely with the whites against this constitution. This proscription policy of the radical party was prompted by a desire to perpetuate its power, even at the cost of producing a state of social anarchy and mongrelism, or a war of races, in the South.

But when these objectionable clauses had been severed, and the constitution was resubmitted to the people, it was adopted by a large majority, and the system providing for separate schools for the whites and blacks would no longer have met with any serious opposition, had it not been for its gross and outrageous mismanagement. It still proved under radical rule to be a prolific field for the growth of every species of corruption, which, if it did not in a measure revive the spirit of opposition to the entire institution, produced, at least, a general feeling of apathy and indifference in regard to it.

Four mills on the dollar were levied by the legislature of 1871, and two mills additional by the county boards of education, which, for the most part, were composed of illiterate negroes, as in Madison County, or by a mixture of these and the more vicious white radicals; while the county superintendents were mostly adventurers from the Northern States, who proved in almost every instance to be defaulters, who had no sympathy for the white people, and whose habits for the most part were so dissolute and degraded that they were not admitted into the society or even to the acquaintance of those, the education of whose children they were presumed by law to supervise.

In the County of Lowndes, there was a small school district containing but two schools, one for the use of each color. The negro school was taught in a house on the plantation of Mr. James Sykes. This house he had caused to be built prior to the war for a negro church, and it had always been devoted to that purpose, and was being so used at the time of the following occurrence. An arbitrary demand was made of him for this building by the superintendent of education or school board, to which he replied that the building was being used by the negroes as a church, and that if they, the negroes, desired to have a school there, he had no objection. Upon this the school was established.

Some time afterwards, Mr. Sykes, on looking over the records of the county, was surprised to find that the county school authorities had made a charge of about one hundred and seventy dollars for the rent of this house. They had also assessed seventy-five dollars for a stove, fifty dollars for repairs, fifteen dollars or twenty dollars for benches, and about seventy-five dollars for fuel, and that for this small school district with only two schools, the aggregate amount of three thousand eight hundred dollars had been charged. In regard to this, Mr. Sykes, in his sworn statement before the ku-klux committee, says:

"This was my own house. I made no charge for rent, nor did I receive any, and there was no fuel used but my own, for which I charged nothing. There was an appropriation made for the repairs of the house which was never received. They appointed me to do it; the work was never performed, and I never made application for, or received, any pay. They had, themselves, pocketed these pretended appropriations, and it was the same way with nearly the whole sum of three thousand eight hundred dollars charged upon the record."

This instance is mentioned as a specimen of innumerable transactions of a similar character attending the conduct and management of the public schools in various counties of the State.

So abounding in opportunities for official theft was this field that every dollar that could be was thrown into it. As an instance of this. In the County of Kemper there was a special fund raised for the purpose of erecting a jail, of which the county was much in need, amounting to about twenty-five hundred dollars. This fund had been raised by a special tax, authorized and limited in its appropriation by the following clause of the State constitution: Art. 12, Sec. 16, "No county shall be denied the right to raise, by special tax, money sufficient to pay for the building and repairing of court houses, jails, bridges, and other necessary conveniences for the people of the county; and money thus collected shall never be appropriated for any other purpose: *provided*, the tax thus levied shall be a certain per cent. on all tax levied by the State."

It will be seen from the above that the money raised by such special tax was expressly restricted in its use to the purpose for which it was levied, yet Chisolm and Gilmer cast their longing eyes on this Kemper County jail fund, and the consequence was that Gilmer procured the passage of the following act of the legislature in regard to it, while he was senator from this district:

An Act to authorize the Board of Supervisors of Kemper County to loan certain funds belonging to said county.

Whereas, The board of supervisors of Kemper County did, at the August term of their meeting, A. D. 1873, levy a tax of two and a half mills on the dollar on the taxable property of said county, for the purpose of erecting a jail in said county; and

Whereas, The said board of supervisors have not made any order for the building of said jail, and said funds so derived from said tax are lying idle and profitless to the county; therefore,

SEC. 1. *Be it enacted by the Legislature of the State of Mississippi*, That the board of supervisors of Kemper County be, and they are hereby authorized and directed, by an order spread upon their minutes at a regular term of their court, to loan the money derived, or to be derived from the levy for jail purposes, to the school fund of said county, to be paid back and returned to the treasurer of said county whenever the same may be needed for the purpose for which the same was collected; and said board shall, at their next meeting, cause said funds to be disbursed as follows:

First.—To the payment of all outstanding warrants, issued for the salary of the county superintendent of education, prior to a passage of an act entitled an act to amend the laws of the State, in relation to public education, approved April 17, 1873.

Second.—To the payment of warrants, issued in said county, in favor of the common school fund.

Third.—To the payment of the outstanding teachers' warrants of said county.

SEC. 2. *Be it further enacted*, That this act take effect and be in force from and after its passage.

Approved February 28, 1874.

Chisolm, who was then sheriff of the county, and Gilmer, it is said, prior to the passage of this act, in the very face of the above constitutional provisions, had bought up and procured a large amount of the class of warrants designated, at merely nominal prices, and so soon as the act was passed they presented those warrants and absorbed the whole amount of the pretended loan.

They had determined to obtain this money, and no official oaths or constitutional barriers could prevent the consummation of their plans to effect their purpose; and thus was the County of Kemper robbed of more than two thousand dollars by means of a conspiracy between its officers. The county superintendent of education who issued the warrants, the board of county supervisors who passed upon them, and the treasurer who redeemed them, were all radicals and tools of Chisolm; while Gilmer, whose seat in the legislature seems to have been prepared for him especially for such purposes, was his accomplice and active abettor in dragging this money within the precincts of the school system, where it could be thus fraudulently appropriated.

Such were some of the workings of the public school system in the South, the most stupendous humbug and most gigantic swindle ever perpetrated and fastened upon the shoulders of a people.

Prior to the war there was no general public school system in Mississippi. There were but few persons unable to pay the ordinary tuition, and the people preferred employing their own teachers, and where there was any need of aid, special provisions afforded aid that was necessary; consequently, the proceeds of the sales of the public lands, turned over to the State for school purposes, as its quota, by the general government, was loaned out for the purpose of aiding internal improvements, and if any portion of this fund has been lost, or is now in anywise a desperate condition, it is not the fault of those who had its management prior to the war, but the result of the general destruction of property and the widespread impoverishment of the people occasioned by it. But the fact that these funds, denominated respectively the seminary fund, the sixteenth section fund, and the Chickasaw school fund, whether secure or not at this time, were for the most part beyond the reach of the fingers of the carpet bagger, was sufficient to call forth from them a howl of disappointment, indignation and rage. Hence, we find one of them, H. R. Pease, concluding his report as State school superintendent to the legislature, in 1872, with the following wail:

"I am of the opinion that when full and complete returns are made of the amount of loss of the sixteenth section school funds alone, to say nothing of the seminary fund and the Chickasaw fund, will exceed one million of dollars absolutely squandered and irretrievably lost."

Whether the above allegation has any foundation in fact, or not, it is a lesson of experience, that had these funds found their way into the hands of Pease and his successor, Cardozo, there could be no doubt as to what would have been their disposition.

Nothwithstanding this onerous tax of four mills, levied by the legislature of Mississippi, for the support of the public schools, and the additional levy of two mills made by the county board of education, the schools were required by law to be kept open but four months in the year, and for the accomplishing of this short scholastic period there was maintained perpetually the most costly organization of officers. There was the State superintendent of education, with a large annual salary. There was a State board of education, whose officers were maintained in the capital of the State; then there were the county boards of education, and the county superintendents, who kept their costly furnished offices at the different county seats, and whose salaries for their four months' pretended supervision reached, in some instances, as high as two thousand dollars. All these, gathered under the clouds of ignorance, or the banner of defalcation, will present a horde of parasites never before fastened upon the body politic of any people.

Such was the state of the public school system of Mississippi under radical rule. When, in 1874, the Democratic party became possessed of the State government, one of its first efforts was to reform the school system. The onerous tax was abolished, and in its stead was substituted the proceeds arising from the sale of the sixteenth section lands, all proceeds of lands forfeited to the State for non-payment of taxes, the net proceeds of all fines and forfeitures, and all money accruing to the State from the sale of licenses to retail vinous and spiritous liquors, which aggregated much more even than the former burdensome taxation on the valuation of property. The schools were required by law to be maintained five months in the year, and longer, if the money arising from the above mentioned sources should be more than sufficient for the period designated. All poll taxes were appropriated to the "teachers' fund," and the supervisors of counties, and the mayor and aldermen of towns of more than two thousand inhabitants, were required to levy a tax upon the taxable property of the county or town "sufficient for school house purposes, the superintendent's salary, and any deficit in the teachers' fund that may arise."

The salaries of the county superintendents were reduced by law, in every instance, to one fourth of their former amount. In addition to this, the sum of fifty-seven thousand dollars of United States bonds, in the State treasury, which had arisen from an investment of State funds, was ordered to be appropriated to school purposes, and devoted to immediate use. The renting of offices for the superintendents, practised by the radical party, the purchasing of furniture for the same, and the furnishing of stationery, etc., were all promptly abolished, and the great benefits derived from these changes began at once to be manifested in the greatly improved condition and enhanced efficiency of the public schools, which, to-day, rests upon as solid a foundation as in any State in the Union.

But although the harness of the school system, as inaugurated by the radical party in Mississippi, fitted easily upon the shoulders of the thief, it was not the only department of the State or county governments gangrened with infamy and corruption.

The boards of supervisors, which constituted the legislatures of the counties, as well as the county boards of education, were, during the years of radical rule, composed, in large part, of the most ignorant and vicious men that ever participated in the government of any people. Their offices were political soup houses to which every vagabond in the counties looked for support, and their sessions were occasions of party largesses, where corrupt contracts were dispensed with lavish hand—conclaves of conspiracy, where all manner of schemes were concocted in secrecy to wrench money from the white people, and to promote the interest of the radical party in all its features.

We have already noticed the composition of the board of supervisors of Madison County with the observation that the same description would apply to the boards of many other counties in the State.

In Issaquena County the negro board had established but one white school, while there were a great many negro schools in operation there. Under this state of things the white people preferred a petition through an old gentleman named Smith, to the board of supervisors, asking for the establishment of another white school, and at the county seat. Smith appeared before the board in a very respectful manner, tendered his petition, when the following scene occurred, as related by T. M. Miller, Esq., a lawyer, and at the time the attorney for the board. He says: "I had been attorney for the board for quite a length of time. These negroes had appointed me unanimously, and I resigned my position on account of their reckless management, and on account of the refusal of the board to hear the whites in regard to schools, and so on. Right there, at Mayerville, there was a great demand for a white school. There were, I suppose, some thirty or forty pupils, and they had no school house. They had to employ a teacher, and they got a room wherever they could to teach in; and the people brought the matter to the attention of the board several times, and earnestly requested them to have a school house erected there. The board finally went through the pretense of posting a notice for bidders. The law provides that the contract shall be let out to the lowest bidder, and bids were offered by good mechanics to build a school house at a much less cost than they had been paying for negro school houses in various parts of the county, and they rejected the bids on the ground of extravagance. Old Mayor Smith came up there, and requested them politely to have the notice renewed. He was very anxious about this school house, and it was the wish of the whole community. It was opposed by a negro named Gross. This man, Gross, was very offensive to Mr. Smith, and ordered him to sit down; he didn't want to hear him, and finally drove him away in disgust and despair. I was present at the time and I left the board in disgust. The white people paid nearly all the taxes of the county, and they had but one school, which was kept in the basement of a church which they rented, and this school was ten or twelve miles from the one they sought to have established."

It would be useless to attempt to bring within the province of this work all the glaring instances of crime and malfeasance committed by the boards of supervisors in the various counties of Mississippi during radical rule in the State. Such a detail would itself compose a volume, but I will subjoin one other instance which occurred within the knowledge of the writer.

In 1872, the legislature created a new county, to which it gave the name of Colfax, but which was subsequently changed to that of Clay. This county was formed of portions of Monroe, Lowndes and Oktibbeha, and the board of supervisors of the new county was authorized to elect some person to transcribe from those counties the records which pertained respectively to the portions severed from them. For this purpose the county superintendent of education, a carpet bagger, named Rugg, was elected by the board, the president of which was a negro named Henry Hardy, who, that same year, had entered into a written contract with the author to perform labor on his farm, and had moved thither with his family, but, on receiving what he conceived to be a better bargain, suddenly moved away, in violation and total disregard of his obligations. This negro, while president of the board, together with another member of the board, named Frank Strong, was indicted for forgery and bribery, and upon the trial of Strong, Rugg testified that he had paid to Hardy and Strong each the sum of twenty-five dollars for their votes in selecting him to transcribe the records.

Yet, notwithstanding this direct and positive testimony, the jury, composed of negroes, and one or two white men, returned a verdict of not guilty. So flagrant was this outrage upon justice, that Judge Orr, a Republican, but the most talented judge in the State, denounced the jury from the bench, and ordered their names to be enrolled on the records of the court as men incompetent and unworthy to sit on the jury, and instructed the sheriff never again to introduce one of those men as a juryman while he occupied the bench.

The trial took place at night, but, in the meantime, Rugg, becoming apprised of the consequences to himself of his confession, fled during the night, and on the trial of Hardy, the following morning was *non inventus*, nor has he been heard of in those parts since. Hardy was, as a matter of course, discharged, there being no other evidence against him, and he continued to officiate as president of the board of supervisors until the spring of 1876—two years afterward. It may be added that the successor of Rugg, as superintendent of this county, one J. T. Harrington, was a man of the blackest character, and had been indicted for horse stealing. This man continued to serve as superintendent until the Democratic party came into power.

The board of supervisors, as thus constituted, formed

the legislative and executive power of the county. They levied taxes, selected the jurors, grand and petit, supervised the education of the children, and had control of the treasury of the county.

And as to the selection of the jurors, it may be readily conjectured from what class of citizens they were generally chosen. The following statement, made by Garnett Andrews, Esq., a lawyer of Yazoo County, in regard to the condition of affairs wrought there by this vicious machinery, was applicable to a wide extent in the State.

"One of the most serious grievances, which I have myself seen, was the administration of justice. I was more familiar with that than anything else. Under the laws of the State the grand jurors are appointed by the board of supervisors. These boards of supervisors are composed of five individuals, one elected from each district in the county. The county is divided into five supervisors' districts. Among other duties, they have the selection of the grand jurors. Each member selects so many, and, as a general rule, these grand jurors amounted to little or nothing at all. There were a few white men put upon them for appearance sake, sometimes very intelligent men—but the majority of them were always composed of negroes, and generally very ignorant negroes, and it was almost impossible to get a radical indicted for anything. They could do what they pleased. I once tried to get a county treasurer, who had been elected by the radicals, indicted for embezzlement. He had appropriated $3,000 of the school fund, which I afterward recovered by suit. I tried to have him indicted for this, but could not succeed. They would not indict him. And this was a general thing."

Another instance of the arrogant conduct of this negro supervisor, Gross, toward the white people, was as follows: "A man by the name of Woolfock had obtained the signatures of seventy citizens and tax payers of the county to a respectful petition to the board of supervisors, asking leave for Woolfock to place a gate across the public road at his plantation, the high water preventing him at that time from fencing his place. This petition was preferred to the board by Wm. S. Farrish, as attorney for the petitioner; and upon his asking permission of the board to read the petition, this man, Gross, ordered him, in the most peremptory manner, to take his seat. Farrish replied that he had a right, he thought, as an attorney, to read his petition, and to be heard. Gross replied, "No, sir; you will not be heard; and, furthermore, if you don't take your seat you will be fined for contempt of this board." He refused to even hear the petition read, the object of which was simply to obtain permission for a citizen to place a gate temporarily across the public road, which would save him several miles of fencing through an inundated swamp, and protect his crops until the water subsided, and he could haul his rails from the bottom.

"In regard to petit juries, it was still worse. The law provides that they shall be selected in the following manner: The tax assessor each year shall return into the circuit clerk's office a list of all qualified taxpayers of proper age, or of all persons qualified for jury duty. Originally, when this list was returned, the names were all put into a box, marked and numbered, and the tax assessor was required, annually, to make amended returns, reporting such persons as had moved out of the county, and those who had moved into it, and the jury box would then be revised by him and the circuit clerk, and, perhaps, the sheriff. I observed for years, and we could not remedy it, that the juries were composed almost entirely of negroes of the most ignorant sort, and they carried the race feeling with them into the jury room. If there was any sort of question between a white man and negro, in which there was any feeling, it was impossible for the white man to get justice. I have known some very outrageous cases of this sort: one in which a negro went into the store of a white man. His wife waited in the store. He was armed, and he assaulted and cursed her in the most shocking and abominable manner. The negro was indicted, tried by one of these juries and acquitted, upon the clearest evidence of a wanton attack and assault upon the woman. These are mere instances of what universally occurred. Not one of these jurors in five hundred could read or write. They invariably slept while we were arguing the cases to them. It was the most disheartening thing in the world. They would sleep during the entire argument, then go out and promptly render their verdicts. You could not do anything with them unless you would repeat to them ribald jokes, or something of that sort. You could arouse their attention in no other way. There was a class of them, or ring, that hung around the court house as professional jurors, and, as witnesses, they thought it their duty, generally, to swear for the side that summoned them."

An instance of this kind is related by Judge Shackleford, a Republican. It occurred in Washington County. There was an Irishman by the name of Kelly indicted for murder, and after all the evidence had been elicited in the case, the district attorney and the counsel for the defence came to an agreement to submit the case. The district attorney stated to the jury that he would be satisfied with a verdict of manslaughter, or a verdict of guilty, as charged in the indictment, coupled with a sentence to the penitentiary for life. This had been agreed to by the counsel for the defence, yet the jury went out, and to the utter surprise of every one, brought in a verdict of "not guilty," and the court could do nothing more than to discharge both prisoner and jury.

The justice courts of Mississippi have jurisdiction in all matters where the amount in controversy does not exceed $150, and they have an extended jurisdiction in criminal matters. They may punish for assault and battery, petty larceny, affrays and riots, all disturbances of the peace, and they have a general committing power in all cases. It will be seen that this extent of jurisdiction renders them the most important courts in the State. Yet these courts were often presided over by the most ignorant and vicious of the negro population, and so illiterate as to be wholly unable to read intelligently any law whatever, or to comprehend a legal argument.

The following description of a negro justice, given under oath by Robert Powell, Esq., a lawyer of Madison County, before the Mississippi investigating committee, may be received as pretty generally applicable to those of other counties:

Q. By Senator Bayard: Had you any justices of the peace who were colored?

A. Yes, sir.

Q. Do you know their condition as to illiteracy?

A. This year we have one in the county that can write his name. Last year, however, I don't think there was a colored justice in the county who could write his name. I know several of them personally. The way they kept their dockets was to get some friendly neighbor to write them up just before the grand jury met, to present to them. They report but few fines. I think one of them reported about five dollars.

Q. When the docket was written were they able to read it?

A. No, sir.

Q. Were these justices of whom you have spoken able to fill up the writs they issued, to sign them, or know what they contained?

A. No, sir.

Q. Did they sign these writs by a mark, or get some one to write their names to them?

A. They signed them by a mark.

Q. Have you seen them so signed?

A. I have.

But, if the offices of supervisor and justice of the peace, were, in many counties, as we have seen, filled almost entirely by ignorant and vicious negroes, the judges of the higher courts, appointed by Governor Ames, from the carpet bag or scalawag element, were in many instances but little less infamous. The chancellors especially, for the most part, were as motley and incompetent a set as ever polluted the seats of justice. In fact, it was difficult for a person of strict integrity, under this administration, to hold the position, and whenever one proved himself to be above partisan influences when on the bench, he was promptly removed. This was the case in regard to Chancellors Peyton and Drennan. The former had been appointed to the bench by Governor Alcorn, and was removed by Governor Ames, because he refused to make certain rulings and decrees in conformity to the wishes of the governor in the case of The University of Mississippi, et al. v. The Vicksburg and Nashville Railroad et al.

For the purpose of making this chancellor subservient to his will in this matter, Governor Ames approached the father of the chancellor, Hon. E. G. Peyton, who was then chief justice of the State of Mississippi, and endeavored to persuade him to exercise such influence over his son as would induce him to frame his decisions in accordance with his will. This infamous proposition the chief justice spurned with scorn and indignation, and, although a Republican, was ever afterwards bitterly hostile to Ames and his administration.

The circumstances of the removal of Chancellor Drennan, of the twelfth chancery district of Mississippi, were as follows: A radical candidate for sheriff in Yazoo County by the name of Morgan, and a henchman of the governor, had shot and killed his rival for the same office, under very aggravated circumstances. Morgan was tried and refused bail by the justice court.

At that time the statute forbade a justice of the peace or any judge granting bail to any person charged with a capital crime where the proof of guilt was positive or the presumption great. Morgan sued out a writ of habeas corpus before the chancellor, who, upon hearing, refused also to grant bail, and remanded Morgan to jail. Upon this he received from Governor Ames an order of removal.

In both of these instances the action of the governor was evidently in pursuance of a purpose to control and render the judiciary of the State entirely subservient to his will, and that, too, by methods in violation of the constitution of the State, and contrary to all the provisions of law, made as safeguards to the integrity of the judiciary.

The constitution of the State of Mississippi provides that the chancellors be appointed by the governor of the State, with the advice and consent of the senate; but Governor Ames, in order to dispense with this trammel upon his purposes, declined to make the nominations to the senate, as required by law, and made the appointments after the adjournment of the legislature by virtue of his authority to fill vacancies in vacation. The character of some of these appointments is here given.

He appointed as chancellor of the eighth chancery district, a man by the name of J. D. Barton, who was not only totally incompetent to discharge the duties of the office, but had been publicly charged with the crime of forgery. Of this Governor Ames was informed upon high authority. Among his informants was J. M. Stone, the present governor of Mississippi, who then resided in the same county with Barton. Yet Ames refused to believe it, or, at least, cared nothing for it, and appointed Barton as chancellor; but when at the next session of the legislature, his appointment came before the senate for confirmation, the charges were investigated, and the proof of guilt was conclusive. Yet Ames refused to withdraw his nomination until he was told by his friends that it was impossible to get the senate to confirm the appointment.

In some cases he appointed men to be chancellors who were not members of the bar; in these instances the persons were promised the appointment as a reward for some services rendered, or to be rendered, to the governor, and they would then pretend to read law for a short time, and get their licenses, which would be followed immediately by their commission as judges of the chancery courts.

There were some of them who had never practised. A man by the name of Cullins was appointed in Marshall County, who had been a sort of physician, but had never read a law book. He was a State senator, received his appointment while at Jackson, went home, managed to procure license, and immediately took his seat upon the chancery bench.

These licenses to practice law were quite easy to obtain, the custom was to make application to the court through motion made by some member of the bar. A committee of two or three members would then be appointed by the court for the purpose of examination; this committee and the candidate would then withdraw to a corner of the court room, talk to the applicant a little about law, then go in and report favorably, and license would be granted at once.

The whole thing of admission to the bar in Mississippi, since the war, has been a mere matter of form and a farce. The writer himself has known young men admitted to practice in the courts of the State who, elsewhere, would not have been considered competent for an efficient clerk in a law office. Hence, even their admission to the bar afforded no recommendation to Ames' appointees.

As chancellor of the ninth district he appointed a man named L. C. Abbott, who was not a lawyer, either by reading or practice. He had never practised law, or written a bill, though he is said to have been a conscientious man and tried to do the best he could, so far as a man could be conscientious, who would attempt to occupy such a position under such circumstances. He had been admitted to the bar only a few days prior to his appointment, and with the distinct understanding that his admission to practice should be followed by a commission to act as chancellor.

In the thirteenth district he appointed William Breck, who was said to be wholly unworthy and incompetent to discharge the high duties of the office of chancellor. He was a man of little or no knowledge of the law, or experience in its practice, and he had also been publicly charged and reported to the governor as having defrauded and swindled, as assignee of the estate of one Green, of Madison

County, the creditors of said estate, and as having been a party to certain illegal and fraudulent contracts let out by the board of supervisors of Madison County, while he was the president of the board.

It may be observed here that the chancery courts of Mississippi have full common law chancery and equity jurisdiction, without limitation as to the amount in controversy, and when the suit is once properly brought, and the circumstances arrayed so as to give jurisdiction to the particular court, its writs run throughout the entire State.

They have control of the estates of minors, and the dower of widows, and the partition of estates, and they have the power of granting all remedial writs, such as the writ of habeas corpus, injunctions, *ne exeat*, etc.

Waiving all questions of honesty of purpose, or leaving them to the judgment of the reader, I will mention here an instance or two of the manner in which these powers were sometimes exercised by these chancellors: In 1875, a large number of the citizens of Oktibbeha County sued out an injunction against the collection of a railroad tax in that county. The sheriff of the county, by whom the tax was to be collected, was a Republican, and a contractor with the authorities of the railroad, and was, therefore, a participant in the advantages of collecting this tax. This tax was to go to him under a contract for work on the railroad. A bill of injunction was prepared and filed by the Hon. J. W. C. Watson, on behalf of the taxpayers, and the sheriff being the principal defendant, the process was placed in the hands of the coroner, as provided by law in such cases. The fiat for the injunction was obtained in the name of some ten or twelve taxpayers, from Chancellor Frazee. The sheriff, upon this, applied to and obtained a fiat of injunction from Chancellor Sullivan, enjoining the coroner from serving the original or prior writ.

Upon the strength of this novel injunction, some ten or twelve other taxpayers came forward and having caused the first bill to be dismissed, filed another bill, praying for the injunction of the sheriff in behalf of themselves and the other tax payers of the county. This was likewise very properly granted by Chancellor Frazee, who lived some distance away in the County of Chickasaw. The fiat came back and was placed in the hands of the clerk to issue; but he was dilatory in his action. In a day or two after, Chancellor Frazee proceeded to Starkville, the county seat of Oktibbeha, and stopped at the residence of the sheriff. The next morning he went to the clerk's office and dissolved the injunction he had granted to all the tax payers in the county, save the ten or twelve whose names were especially mentioned in the bill.

Thus this chancellor, without notice to the opposite parties, and upon his own motion, without even a petition for that purpose, virtually dissolved an injunction, and required the clerk to issue an amended process, declaring that the injunction was to be operative only as to the persons especially named in the bill—some ten or twelve persons, out of, perhaps, three or four thousand.

It is unnecessary to add, that these proceedings were altogether irregular, to say the least, and not at all in accordance with usage, if not in positive violation of law.

It is plain that this whole transaction was prompted by partisan considerations, for its very anomaly is too glaring to be attributed to ignorance, while the purpose was too manifest to be confined within the province of mistaken duty.

Another instance of this character, and one that occurred within the knowledge of the writer, will suffice for the purpose of showing the character of the men whom Governor Ames lifted to the chancery bench of Mississippi. The writer had occasion to act as counsel in a suit before Austin Pollard, chancellor of the seventh district. On rendering his decree, he appointed the clerk of his court, one H. H. Harrington, as commissioner to compute the amount involved in the decree. The clerk made out an exorbitant bill of costs, besides falling into an error of a considerable sum in computing the amount covered by the judgment. The counsel made a motion to have the computation cor rected. The chancellor positively refused to entertain the motion. Upon this the clerk was arrested on a charge of extortion, and brought to trial before the mayor of West Point. The chancellor came in with him and attended the trial. The clerk was found guilty. The next morning the chancellor opened his court, and on his own motion, without the knowledge of the parties, revised the bill of costs, making it even larger than that for which his clerk had been found guilty of extortion. This same clerk was subsequently tried and convicted of forgery and altering the records, and was sentenced to the penitentiary, but succeeded, through means of some technicalities, in having the judgment reversed by the supreme court.

What may have been the notion of right and justice these men entertained, the writer does not pretend to define; but it is certain that such conduct is utterly incompatible with that purity which the teachings of chancery jurisprudence and the sacred functions of that court would lead us to expect.

The clerks of the circuit and chancery courts during this period were extremely ignorant and unreliable; many of them could not write or read, but depended entirely upon some deputy who could, but who was generally, if possible, more untrustworthy than themselves.

The sheriff of De Soto County for four years, was an illiterate, ignorant negro. He had no conception of the duties of his office, and, in fact, did not pretend to discharge them. The business was all done by his deputies, who were generally irresponsible persons. And while the functions of the circuit judges do not require a higher order of talent for the purposes of justice than those of the chancellors, they, at least, are more open to view, and incompetency in their exercise is more readily detected, which, perhaps, made them more cautious; yet, with one or two exceptions, the entire judiciary of the State, during this time, lacked the confidence and respect of both the bar and the people, for there was but little certainty as to whether right or wrong would triumph in any cause in law or equity. They saw the whole judicial machinery ramified with corruption, permeated with vice, and clogged with ignorance.

During this era of crime and misgovernment there was no field more prolific of villainy than the office of the shrievalty. The sheriffs were, ex-officio, the tax gatherers of the counties, many of them notoriously defaulted, while others, no less vicious, managed, by engaging the co-operation of the auditors of public accounts, in concealing the tracks of their crimes, under color of their office and under cover of political fraternity, extorted, at pleasure, the hard earnings of the negro, whose ignorance and credulity toward his white allies rendered him a tame subject for their exactions.

The sheriff of Noxubee County, in 1875, one W. M. Conner, was reported to the governor as a defaulter, holding twenty-two thousand dollars of public money which he refused to pay over to the county, and yet, on account of the partisan services of this individual, Governor Ames refused to remove him from office.

The sheriff of Colfax, now Clay County, was indicted for malfeasance in office, was tried and convicted, and a judgment of fine and removal from office passed upon him. This judgment was affirmed by the supreme court, and, within two hours after the affirmation of the judgment, Governor Ames reappointed him to the shrievalty of the same county. And it was by his direction and aid that the notorious Peter Crosby returned to Vicksburg and attempted to take possession, by force, of the sheriff's office of Warren County, which he had voluntarily abandoned, and which caused a conflict between the races, in which many lives were lost. But, as we will have occasion to recur to these events hereafter in taking a special view of Governor Ames and his conduct during the canvass of 1875, we will defer any particular notice of them until then.

It was in reference to this determined attempt to reinstate Crosby that, on being warned of the hazard attending it, and the terrible consequences likely to ensue, the governor declared that "the blood of the martyrs was the seed of the church," and that "the killing of twenty-five or thirty negroes would result beneficially to the Republican party."

Th euse of these expressions was testified to by Major Allyn, at that time the commander of the Federal military forces in Mississippi, and intimate in both his official and personal relations with the governor; and on another occasion, when there were a number of negro politicians assembled at the governor's mansion, for the purpose of discussing the right of the negro Crosby to be reinstated in his office, and the manner in which that object should be accomplished, some one present intimated that, if that attempt should be made, as Governor Ames urged that it should be, there would be bloodshed. Upon this, the Governor declared, in substance and effect, that he and other white men had faced bullets to free the colored people, and now, if they were not willing to fight for their rights and to maintain their freedom, they were unworthy of it.

In consequence of such expressions and the active aid he promised, on the morning of the 7th of December, 1874, a large body of armed negroes appeared before the city of Vicksburg, with the avowed intention of capturing the city and reinstating Peter Crosby in the office of the sheriff of Warren County. The citizens flew to arms in defence of their homes, and marched out to meet the besiegers. A bloody conflict ensued, in which many lives were lost, and the negroes were totally defeated and dispersed.

On this occasion the people of Mississippi had the mortification of seeing their governor instigating and abetting the negroes in a war of rapine and savage butchery upon the white people of the State; and that the attempt proved a failure was owing to the prompt manner in which the whites accepted the gage of battle.

Being thus baffled in his efforts to produce a war of races, as he declared, for the benefit of the radical party, he now sought to avail himself of the opportunity, at least, of invoking the presence of the United States military forces, and called lustily upon the President of the United States for troops to quell what he characterized as a rebellion on the part of the white people of the State.

The call was answered by the authorities of the Federal government, who were ever ready to seize upon every circumstance calculated to fan the embers of hate in the minds of the Northern people, and to further partisan purposes. Troops were sent to Vicksburg, and through their instrumentality the negro, Peter Crosby, who had now become extremely obnoxious to the people, was reinstated, and the sheriff of their choice, A. J. Flanigan, forcibly ejected by the armed forces of the United States. The governor, so far, was triumphant, and no doubt felt that hereafter his schemes would meet with no further opposition, and that his acts would henceforth be beyond any question or efforts of redress by the white people of Mississippi.

He now began to gather around him the most vicious men of his party that could be found in the State, and who were thoroughly imbued with his spirit of hostility to the whites, and entirely subservient to his vengeful desires.

The following is the record of three of the governor's confidential admirers and bosom friends: Raymond was editor of the Jackson *Pilot*, a paper conducted entirely in the interest of Ames, and in obsequious advocacy of his policy. He was also the State printer, for which he was paid the enormous sum of eighty thousand dollars per annum, when the work could have been procured for less than one fourth of that sum. Yet this man, with this princely salary, placed his printing office in charge of another, it is said, at a salary of eighteen hundred dollars in currency per annum, and accepted for himself a clerkship in the office of the State Treasurer, at a salary of fifteen hundred dollars in State warrants, worth seventy-five cents on the dollar. This was done in order to handle the funds of the State, and cash the warrants, which he purchased at a heavy discount. A. R. Howe, ex-congressman and ex-treasurer of Panola County, was another. He had obtained unlawfully from the negro board of supervisors of that county about five thousand dollars, of which amount he swindled the county. The third, and last, that it is deemed necessary to mention here, was one A. T. Morgan, of Yazoo County. This man had married a negro woman, and, it is said, that when State senator he offered to sell his vote on the printing bill to Raymond for two thousand dollars, but Raymond said he bought it for nine hundred dollars. He is the same individual that murdered his rival or opponent for the office of sheriff, and in which case the governor appointed a chancellor especially for the purpose of granting him bail.

He secretly, and without any competition or public bidding, conferred the contracts for the convict labor of the penitentiary upon two of his partisan and personal favorites—namely, one O. C. French and one C. S. Jobes—who were partners in the transaction, upon terms most unfavorable to the State, and upon conditions precedent that they should render to him certain partisan and personal services for the advantages he had thus bestowed upon them, to the great detriment of the interest of the State, and to the increased penance of the unfortunate inmates of the State prison themselves.

Proving more and more violent in his feelings toward the white people of Mississippi, his mind was constantly irritated by a consciousness of the scorn he merited on their part, and his whole policy seemed now to be shaped by a desire and fixed purpose to degrade the sovereignty of the State, and to bring its constitution and laws into contempt. He never suffered an opportunity of humiliating the people to pass unavailed. All his appointments, removals and reinstatements seemed to be subordinated to that purpose and design. He even assumed to appoint and commission justices of the peace and constables, in contravention of the laws, and in violation of the constitution of the State. This he attempted in the County of Washington. He corruptly approved the bond of one M. L. Holland, who had been appointed State treasurer by him.

This bond, as required by law, was to consist of an obligation made to the State to the amount of eighty thousand dollars, with three or more good freehold sureties, whose solvency and responsibility for that amount should be established by their oaths that they were worth the penalty conditioned and nominated in the bond over and above their just debts, legal liabilities and exemptions in freehold estate, and to be approved by the governor before the candidate could be inducted into office.

Notwithstanding these positive requirements, Governor Ames approved the bond of Holland, regardless of the fact that his sureties had not made the oath of solvency and responsibility as required, and notwithstanding a prompt admonition from the attorney general of the State, his constitutional adviser, that he had examined the bond and found it to be insufficient, and not in the due form of law, and that the said Holland had no right to exercise the functions of the office of State treasurer until his bond was perfected. In the face of all this, Governor Ames thrust this man, thus irresponsibly qualified, into the treasurer's office, and gave force and validity to all of his acts in the same manner as if he had been duly qualified.

Nor was his pardoning power exercised in a less partisan manner, or less in derogation of justice. Indeed, so notorious and arbitrary was his conduct in this respect that the vilest criminals, provided they were his political adherents, looked with no unfounded hopes for this boon, which he dispensed with such lavish hand.

The following is an instance of this character: One Alexander Smith had been tried and convicted in the Circuit Court of Chickasaw County of a heinous crime committed upon the person of a little girl under ten years of age; for this crime he had been sentenced to the penitentiary of the State for life. There was no question as to the guilt of this criminal; no technicality of law violated on the trial, and no grounds for an appeal. The proof was positive and incontrovertible, and the sentence was reached by and through the regular channels and due forms of law. Smith was placed in the penitentiary for the term of his natural life, but soon after this he came into possession of a large sum of money, which was immediately put in operation to procure his reprieve. One Frederick Parsons and one William Noonan were well known partisans and personal friends of the governor. To them he at once applied for mediation. He gave to Parsons the sum of twenty-eight hundred dollars, and to Noonan the sum of two hundred, for their respective services in his behalf.

These men at once set to work to effect the object for which they were hired. They procured the signatures of parties living in remote parts of the State, who had never even heard of the case, to a petition to the governor for the pardon of Smith.

On that petition, neither the name of the circuit judge, before whom the trial had taken place, nor that of the district attorney, nor any other member of the court, or of the jury appeared, nor, in fact, the name of any one connected with the trial; yet upon the strength of this petition thus obtained, the governor tendered his pardon to Smith, and he was enlarged and restored to all his rights and privileges, while dyed all over with the black stains of unatoned and unmitigated guilt.

This liberal exercise of the pardoning power, which was dictated by no humane considerations, but purely for partisan purposes, as the character of its recipients shows, was carried to such an extent as not only to interfere with the course of public justice throughout the State, but it was a charter of immunity for the commission of crime. According to his report of pardons and commutations of sentence, made to the legislature on January 17, 1876, it will be seen that Governor Ames pardoned thirty-seven, and the negro lieutenant governor, while acting governor, thirty-two convicts during the single year of 1875.

Thus were sixty-nine convicted felons turned loose at once upon society, and most of them devoid of any mitigating circumstance to justify a pardon. By reference to this same report, it will be seen that these reprieves were for the most part based upon the recommendation of parties who were particular personal or political friends of the governor.

The immunity from the legal consequences of crime thus occasioned and approved by the chief executive of the State did not fail to bear its fruits. It promoted a disposition of lawlessness, for which the governor himself was, in a great measure, responsible. It encouraged and prompted his partisans to the perpetration of any villainy which might redound to their personal or political advantage, and the contagion once promoted by the examples of the highest officers of the State government continued to spread until the whole machinery was gangrened with corruption, at which even the stomach of Northern Republicans became nauseated to such an extent as to call forth such observations as the following from a leading Republican paper, the Philadelphia *Press:*

"The administration of Governor Ames, a carpet bagger and political adventurer, has done much to disorganize society and teach general contempt for all authority in Mississippi. The disorder is palpably the result of a corrupt and powerless government, that has taught its ignorant negro dependents that they were above the law in a struggle with the whites, and they have made the common mistake of taking their leaders at their word."

During this time the legislature of Mississippi could not be more appropriately characterized than by the apt denomination of "black and tan." It was composed almost entirely of ignorant negroes and Northern political adventurers, happily called carpet baggers! These legislators, having little or no property interest in the State, manifested on every occasion the most bitter feelings against the white people who owned all the property and paid all the taxes. Indeed, the legislature was constantly actuated by the worst spirit of communism, and the desire and intention to so tax the property of the whites as to force them to suffer its confiscation or abandonment, was in many instances open and avowed.

In this the cupidity of the carpet bagger and the race prejudice of the negro found apparently an indissoluble bond of union, and a common incentive to every act antagonistic to the property holders and tax payers. Consequently the taxes during this period were utterly insupportable, and had they continued to exist much longer would evidently have soon produced universally the very effect for which they were imposed.

The people of Mississippi found themselves impoverished to an unexampled degree by the result of the war. The productive property of the State consisted entirely in land and negro slaves, and with the loss of the latter the former became almost worthless, as the negro, naturally indolent, manifested in the early days of his freedom the determination to labor only so much as might be required to supply himself with the necessaries of life, and this disposition continues to this day to be a marked feature of his character.

The white people of Mississippi, driven to these terrible straits, sought by every means in their power to find some palliation of these onerous and oppressive measures. They had offered, as has been before mentioned, every description of compromise, but yet without avail. It was now determined to offer a petition to this infamous legislature for even a partial redress of their sore grievances.

For this purpose, a convention of the tax payers of the State met at the capitol in the City of Jackson, in the month of December, 1874. It was composed of solid property holders from all portions of the State, without reference to political party. It adopted an address to the legislature setting forth their grievances, petitioned for their redress, and designated the remedies they desired to be applied for that purpose. They represented the general poverty of the people and the depressed value of every kind of property, which rendered it impossible for them to pay the enormous rate of taxation to which they were subjected. They compared these rates with those of former days, when the country was abounding in wealth. That, since the reorganization of the State upon a basis resulting from the war, which had deprived them of nine-tenths of their property, the people had grown constantly poorer, and the means of support harder and harder to be procured, while their spirits were even burdened with dread lest the very shelter should be torn away from over the heads of their wives and little ones.

That in addition to their poverty, there were necessarily many burdens to be borne by the Southern people unknown to them in more prosperous times, such as their part of the public debt of the general government, the great expense of the public school system, and the increased price of necessary commodities, and to this might be added the wilful waste and extravagance of public officers, and the heavy local burdens that fall upon the inhabitants of cities and towns. For the remedy of these evils, they asked for *economy* on the part of the party in control of the State government.

They showed the rapid and continued increase of the taxation imposed upon them, which had been continually augmented and raised from a State tax of ten cents on one dollar in 1869, to fourteen times as much in 1874, and that the county levies, in many instances, were increased in a still greater ratio, while the people were much poorer at the latter period than at the former, and that this tax was even greater, from the fact that the assessed value of their property was greatly in excess of its market value, and thus, while their property declined in value, and the people became poorer, their burdens of taxation were continually increased.

That notwithstanding these extravagant tax levies, the public debt during all these years had increased annually on an average of over six hundred and sixty-eight thousand dollars, a sum which, if economically administered, would itself defray all the expenses of the State government.

That proportional results had, in many instances, attended the operations of the boards of county supervisors, whose malfeasances and extravagancies had saddled the counties with ruinous debts. That these facts, whether regarded as the result of misgovernment, or as proof of the unprosperous condition of the people, arising from other causes, were alike painful to contemplate.

That the general failure of crops during that year contributed to place the taxes still further beyond their power of reach. That all the crops raised in the State during that year, if sold at their market value, would not pay the cost of production and their enormous taxes; and that in consequence of this, in many parts of the State, the people were on the very borders of famine, and that these sufferings fell heaviest upon the poor, who formed a very large majority of the citizens: and they then asked, if in this condition of things, the few officials of the State, who were the mere servants of the people, ought to be allowed to grow fat and rich, while the people were suffering for the common necessaries of life.

They asked that a system of rigorous economy be established; that the salaries of public officers, of every grade, be reduced to a scale commensurate with the extreme poverty of the people and the product of all other labor, and that the number of officers be reduced to the smallest number adequate to the performance of the necessary functions of the government.

They enumerated the following particulars, to which they suggested the application of economy: First, the public printing—which they represented to have cost the State, prior to the year 1861, but eight thousand dollars per annum, and that subsequently to the year 1870 it had cost annually an average of more than seventy three thousand dollars, and which could not be attributed to any extra amount of labor in this department, for that, in the State of Georgia, where like conditions exist, the cost of public printing, during the years 1872 and 1873, did not average more than ten thousand dollars per annum, thereby showing that the cost of public printing in Mississippi, for those two years, was eight times that of Georgia for the same period. The remedy suggested and asked for this evil, was a diminution in the size of the public journals and reports, the omission of all useless and superfluous matter, and a reduction of the price of printing, and that the same matter be paid for but once.

They represented, also, the injustice of what was known as the district printing bill, and which required that certain newspapers be designated in each district as the only bearers of public notices, by means of which the people were forced to contribute to the maintenance of a partisan press, and to bestow their patronage on persons who were obnoxious to them, besides the inconvenience and futility of such notices being made in papers often at a distance, and with little circulation.

They suggested a reduction in the number of circuit judges and chancellors, which they represented as having been increased as to circuit judges, without sufficient reason, from ten to thirteen, and which ten circuit judges performed, without complaint, all the duties of the thirteen, in addition to all the duties now performed by the twenty chancellors, and that the litigation before the thirteen circuit judges and the twenty chancellors was far less than it was before the ten judges who formerly performed all these duties. They called attention to the increased expenses of the legislature, and to the number of sinecure offices that had been introduced in connection with it.

They showed that the salaries of the governor and lieutenant governor were far larger than those paid by other States of like population, and they asked that the salaries of the treasurer, auditor, secretary of state, and attorney general, and all other State officers be fixed at the amounts they were prior to the war. That the fees of the sheriffs and clerks of the courts were too high, and, besides, were often greatly augmented by exorbitant and illegal charges.

They also enumerated, as fit subjects for the application of economy, jail fees and the cost for the support of prisoners; the salaries of the inspectors of the penitentiary; the trustees of the insane, deaf and dumb and blind asylums, and the appropriations to the State universities.

They complained of the unjust discrimination made in maintaining a few favored students at these universities in exclusion of other children of the State at large.

They also complained of the extravagant rates of taxation for public school purposes, and the reckless appropriations made for them, which they showed amounted to the sum of six hundred and seventy-five thousand dollars annually.

They suggested that the office of commissioner of immigration be abolished as utterly useless and sinecural, and recommended that the salaries of school superintendents be saved by combining the duties of that office with those of the sheriff; and they requested that the salaries of teachers of common public schools be reduced to the smallest amount sufficient to secure the services of competent teachers. They recommended amendments to the constitution, fixing biennial sessions of the legislature, and prohibiting special legislation. They alleged that a large portion of the time of the legislature was consumed in the consideration of bills of that character, and by means of which the reports and pamphlets of acts were rendered voluminous and expensive, when general laws would attain the same ends. They called especial attention to the powers and abuses of the boards of county supervisors, which they characterized as the most important courts of the State.

They represented these boards as being composed generally of very ignorant and untrustworthy persons, who, for the most part, were under the influence of the sheriffs and clerks of the courts, to whom they made extravagant allowances, and, as a remedy for these evils, they recommended that the law be repealed which allowed them pay for their services. In that event, they believed that while no one would seek the office, the people could always find a sufficient number of good men who would perform its duties. And finally, they asked for more time within which to pay the taxes for the preceding year.

Such are the most prominent and important features of this remarkable document—remarkable for the history it contains, and the disclosures it makes of the true "inwardness" of the terrible state of affairs existing at that time in Mississippi, and also for the calm and statesmanlike manner in which the facts are set forth, and it is a pity that it was intended for such unworthy hearers.

To this calm, lucid and respectful petition and appeal of the tax payers of the State the legislature made no response. Those of its members who were sufficiently intelligent to comprehend it were, no doubt, galled by the unpalatable facts which it brought so lucidly to their view, while on the ears of the illiterate negroes of that body it fell with the hollow thud of inanition, and was spurned with all the insolence of power clad ignorance and African arrogance.

It had no other effect upon the legislature than to still further excite the prejudices and inflame the passions of the negro members and their Northern allies, and to cause them to draw the color line across the benches of the capitol. Legislation became even more partisan and hostile to the white people and property holders of the State. Yet there were a few leading white Republicans who saw in the shocking disclosures made by this remarkable paper the first cloud caps of that storm which a year later swept over the State, and completely revolutionized its politics, driving from power the ignorance and corruption that preyed upon its vitals.

In the utter failure of this noble effort to redress or abate their intolerable grievances the tax payers saw the necessity of girding themselves for the only alternative that could save them from utter ruin—which was the overthrow of the radical party in the State. To this end they now resolved to devote every energy, make every sacrifice and invoke every legitimate means in their power. This movement, with its results, was the keystone of their sucess in 1875. Its effect was to awaken a general feeling of indignation, to cement the sympathies of the people, and to concentrate their efforts, while, at the same time, it tended to paralyze the radical party, by enlisting the sympathies of some of its more respectable members, and causing alarm and confusion to others. The negro citizens had begun to feel the effects of the existing ruinous rates of taxation. They were often, in consequence of their extreme ignorance, made to pay their taxes two or three times in the same year by unprincipled tax collectors, and it was upon this subject that they, for the first time, began to lend a listening ear to the remonstrances and overtures of the whites.

Nor did the effects of this appeal stop within the borders of Mississippi—it thundered against the walls of Congress, and grated upon the ears of the national leaders of the party.

It was then that Geo. C. McKee, a radical representative in Congress from Mississippi, wrote from his desk in the national capital a letter, of which the following is an extract: " I would beg you to bear in mind that there is no fear of cutting too deep. The evil is too enormous. The petition and appeal of the tax payers' convention should be heeded. It is about the ablest paper I have seen in Mississippi for years. Of course, I do not subscribe to each and every one of its sentiments. I do not suppose there was a single member of the convention who did. But in its general tenor it is correct, and I hope our legislature will not allow themselves to be scared off from what is right by any outcry of partisanship. Let not the action of the tax payers' convention at Jackson be identified with the action of the tax payers' league at Vicksburg. The 'petition and appeal' are singularly and carefully non-partisan. Although I doubt not that a large majority of the members of that convention are working and plotting for the overthrow of the Republican party, yet, when the people meet as citizens, and present to the people's legislature well founded grievances, it is no answer to their complaints to say that most of the convention were Democrats. When a party governs for the party alone, and not for the people, it has no business to govern at all. And this tax paying is not so much a question of partisan feeling as of pocket book feeling." For the benefit of those who may desire to study carefully this most extraordinary document that ever emanated from a free people, or was ever preferred to the legislature of a free government, it is presented in full in the appendix to this work. For the lessons it teaches deserve to be learned and treasured.

Upon the principles set forth in this petition, involving issues upon which hinged the question of life or death to the white people of Mississippi, both parties began, in the early part of the year 1875, to gather up all their strength for the conflict. And it was now for the first time that a ray of hope pierced the dark clouds that had so long, like a pall of death, enveloped the political skies. For ten long and gloomy years the negroes and the radical party had possessed full sway over the destinies of the State, while every obstacle to its mad control and its furious career of vengeance, corruption and ruin had hitherto been ruthlessly battered down by the military power of the Federal government. The Democratic party, seemingly in a hopeless minority, could but stand aside with a feeble and scorned protest against the outrages of the dominant and all powerful faction which controlled every department of the Federal and State governments. Yet, that feeble voice that continued to emit its ominous tones, almost unheard amid the wild din of vengeance and corruption, in behalf of justice and peace, was soon to be echoed by half a million majority of the American people, and by nearly fifty thousand majority in the State of Mississippi, while the fall of radicalism in the State was but another verification of the adage, that "*Vis consili expers sua mole ruit*" (power without intelligence falls of its own weight), and the principles which were so long spurned have become the key note of American politics. Surely, "Truth crushed to earth will rise again."

Never was there a political party that had such full power, that had such full control of all of its elements, and so imbedded in every feature of the national and State governments as the radical party. It had completely hedged itself with apparently impregnable barriers, within which it had gathered every means of support, every aliment that could conduce to its own perpetuity. It gathered its tribute with an arbitrary hand from every source, and it drowned the voice of opposition with the beat of the drum and the clangor of the national arms.

It had made and unmade sovereign States at will. It had enacted laws in derogation of the Federal constitution for the sole purpose of perpetuating its power. It had even mutilated, nullified and defaced that constitution for the same purpose. And if this policy obtained in the national legislature, and it was thus prostituted, it did not lack imitation in the State governments. In Mississippi everything had been done in furtherance of the same policy.

The legislature had created numerous new counties for the sake of increasing radical representation. It had passed bills of apportionment of representation of the most unjust character. Formerly, in Mississippi, every county was entitled to at least one representative in the legislature. By these bills ten counties in the State were deprived of separate representation because of their Democratic and white majority, and consolidated with others so as to give an aggregate preponderance to the negro vote, and by that means secure a radical negro representation. It had extended a personal control over the various offices of the counties. Many of the members were the sheriffs of the counties they represented. Some were county treasurers, and some were also members of the boards of county supervisors.

Subsidiary to this, much of the time of the legislature was spent in enacting special laws and in the entertainment of private bills—all for the purpose of enhancing the personal influence of the members.

Yet in all this panoply of power, integrity and intelligence, the only ingredients that can give stability to power in any free government, were utterly wanting, and notwithstanding that it indeed appeared an appalling undertaking to those who sought its overthrow, yet, considering the mass of corruption that pervaded the whole system, and the absurd variance it worked with the very laws of nature, and every sentiment of enlightened humanity, it appears a matter of wonder that it should have existed so long.

That a political party, in a free government, and founded upon ignorance, fostered by hatred, nourished by corruption, and pursuing an aggressive hostility to a people that have no superior, should be able to long rule that people through the instrumentality of an inferior and degraded race, will appear to posterity a fact almost too absurd for conception. The white people of Mississippi, in common with their fellow citizens of the South, were willing to abide with patience the decrees of fate so long as those decrees were compatible with the preservation of their manhood and honor, of which their conduct through the great struggle justified them in expecting no invasion. And it must be confessed that it is painful to acknowledge, and even to contemplate, that the spirit manifested by the dominant section showed such a marked difference in sentiment between the two sections as to engender apprehensions in regard to the continuity of that concord so necessary for the promotion of the general welfare of all classes and conditions of a people with such diversity of interests as is exhibited throughout the vast domain of the Union.

CHAPTER VII.

The whole system of reconstruction adopted and enforced by the radical party upon Mississippi was a network of the most odious terms and degrading conditions, the history of which belongs, for the most part, in common to all the Southern States.

In 1867, the State was reduced to the condition of a military province. Federal garrisons were stationed at all prominent points, and over these was placed in command one of the most blinded, benighted and bitter partisans that could be found among the officers of the army. This was Adelbert Ames, of the State of Maine.

The career of this man, who, by virtue of this appointment, became a kind of military governor, was characterized at once by an utter disregard to the rights and feelings of the white people of the State. He paid no attention whatever to their laws any further than it suited his views and purposes to have them enforced. He endeavored by every means in his power to degrade them. He declared himself to be the champion of the negro race in all its arrogant claims, and even prompted them to more unreasonable demands. He declared that he had a mission to perform in the interest of the negroes, and avowed the union of his fortune with theirs

It was under the auspices of his supremacy as military governor, that a convention was convoked at the State capitol in 1868, to frame a new constitution for the State. This constitution embraced many features of the most odious character; and it is evident that the convention that framed it was actuated solely by a view to party exigencies, and a desire to place the State perpetually in radical harness. While many white citizens of the State, the best and most prominent, were disfranchised by this constitution, it conferred unlimited franchise upon the negro race, and it so apportioned the representation in the legislature, by inexpedient combinations of constituencies, as to give, as they hoped, permanent ascendency to the negroes, who were largely in the majority. Thus, at a time when the State had scarcely emerged from the clouds of a war by which it had been utterly prostrated; when it was on the very borders of bankruptcy; when every source of public revenue seemed to be dried up, and the citizens were reduced to straits that involved a life and death struggle for existence, this convention sought to saddle the State with a constitution that turned the whole machinery of government over to the most ignorant, degraded and vicious portion of the population, who were utterly incapable of conducting it, or even of comprehending its functions. At this juncture it is not surprising that the capital and intelligence of the State took the alarm, while every sentiment of pride and patriotism received such a shock as to cause intelligent men to look aghast at the gloomy prospect with mingled feelings of dread and indignation.

By this constitution the revenues of the State were to be placed under the control of those who bore no part of the burdens of taxation, while those who bore the heaviest portion were shorn of their political rights. It required no profound reflection, or far reaching sight, to discover the germs of violence and ruin engrafted into this remarkable charta of government. Its disfranchising features presented to the negro, on whom the power of voting had already been conferred by the military authorities, the alternative of voting against the adoption of this form of government, which placed them above the whites, or by voting for it, to exhibit the spectacle of exercising their lately acquired rights to deprive others of the same rights.

Under these circumstances it is not surprising that the white people made an ardent canvass for the rejection of this constitution, and the arguments they made for this purpose did not fail to make an impression upon the minds of the negroes. They had not at that time been so completely alienated from their natural affection for their former owners by the teachings of radicalism as to turn a

They saw men in whom they had confidence doing all in their power to defeat the constitution, and they had not yet arrived at that state of arrogance which afterwards prompted them to claim superiority. There were, as has been said, some features in this constitution peculiarly offensive to the white people, one of which was that by which the whites and blacks were mingled in the common schools. This measure, while it was extremely odious to the whites, did not enlist the sympathies of the blacks. They saw at once the unnatural state of affairs it would produce, and they recoiled from the consequences which they well knew would attend its practice.

To counteract all these considerations that operated so forcibly upon the fears and the confidence of the negroes those who favored the adoption of the constitution told them that it was the wish of the Federal government, to which they owed their emancipation, that they should vote for the constitution ; and that not to vote for it, would be a grave offense to their only friends, and would jeopard their newly acquired rights. That the Southern whites were their political enemies, whose advice, if followed, would lead to the loss of all their privileges and remand them to slavery.

This occasion was the beginning of the operations of the Northern adventurers who had already flocked Southward in the wake of the Federal garrisons. Notwithstanding these influences, the large majority voted with the whites against the adoption of this constitution, the spirit of which was proscription, and its embodiment a standing declaration of war between the races.

That it was alone the proscriptive features of this proscribed policy of government that created such antagonism to its adoption, is shown by the fact that when it was afterwards shorn of its principally objectionable features and resubmitted to the people, it was adopted by a very large majority.

But it is a remarkable fact that upon its rejection at its first submittal, the men through whose instrumentality it was framed, charged that its defeat was procured by fraud and intimidation. They appealed to Congress, and to the President of the United States, to set aside the verdict of the people, and impose this constitution upon them, regardless of its rejection by so large a popular majority.

But the Federal government, not yet habituated to usurpation or inured to party exigencies, declined to interfere. Yet, the disfranchisement of many leading citizens of the State was effected by an act of Congress prohibiting any one from holding office except those who could take a certain oath, which it was impossible for any true Southern man to do.

This gave the military governor the pretext for causing the vacation of any office he chose, for removing any officer not in political accord with him, and substituting in their stead his personal and partisan friends; and of this power and opportunity he availed himself, to the fullest extent, in order to pave the way for his advancement to the United States Senate. At this juncture the white people, seeing no chance to have a governor chosen from the citizens of the State, who would be at all in sympathy with them, and in order to mollify the hostility of the general government, nominated for that office Judge Louis Dent, of Washington, a brother-in-law of the President of the United States.

This, indeed, was to them a humiliating alternative. It was very humiliating to realize the impossibility of placing a true Mississippian in her governor's mansion, and very mortifying to be compelled to import a stranger for that purpose; but such were the exigencies under which they labored that they were willing for the time to sacrifice or subordinate their personal feelings to the public good.

In this canvass James L. Alcorn was the candidate of the radical party, into the ranks of which, through the policy of the military government, and the instrumentality of the carpet baggers, the negroes had now been marshalled in a solid mass. Alcorn was a citizen of the State, but one whose conduct had rendered him entirely untrustworthy and obnoxious to the white people.

The election of Alcorn was effected by the active inter'erence of the district military commander. General Ames ittended in person the convention of negroes and carpet jaggers that nominated his friend, and when called upon 'or a speech, he made the following laconic harangue: "You have my sympathy, and shall have my support." This, by reason of his uniform and the military power he had already so prominently displayed, exercised very great control over the sentiments and conduct of the negroes.

In the interest of Alcorn, he sent United States troops to various parts of the State. He caused leading Democrats to be arrested and thrown into prison, and by this means controlled and determined the election in accordance with his wishes. While he was military Governor of Mississippi he ruled with hatred in his heart, and a rod of iron in his hand. His proscriptions were wholesale, and as systematic and inexorable as those of Marius and Sylla. The best men and the truest patriots seemed to incur his special dislike, and were expelled from office without cause. If they stood at all in the way of his ambitious schemes, or in the way of office seeking adventurers, it was sufficient to evoke an order for their expulsion.

Nor were his persecutions less notorious than his proscriptions. Citizens were frequently arrested for their political opinions, and dragged from their homes by armed solliers of the United States, without warrant, and often without knowledge of the offence with which they were charged, kept under a military guard, often in chains, carried to places remote from the scenes of the offences alleged against them, and tried before military commissions created for the purpose to convict.

In such cases the writ of habeas corpus was the only remedy to which the citizen could look for relief. But Ames was not to be baffled in his persecutions by any ancient right or form of law.

He determined at once to forestall any effort to avail themselves of the operation of this time honored writ. Military law, combined with the dictates of his own arbitrary will, was to be, indeed, the supreme law of the land; and to tear away every barrier to his cruel and cowardly persecutions, he issued the following despotic

MILITARY ORDER:

"*To commanders of posts of Grenada, Corinth, Jackson, Lauderdale and Vicksburg.*

"The commanding general, Adelbert Ames, directs that you do not obey in future any writ of habeas corpus issued by the United States district or circuit courts, nor any order made by such courts for the release of prisoners in your custody. Should such order be served on you, you will report the fact by telegraph."

That this order was in violation of that clause of the constitution of the United States, which guarantees to every citizen under arrest the right of judicial inquiry into the cause of his imprisonment, is beyond all question. Nor can it be claimed that any such power was conferred upon military commanders by the reconstruction acts. But the constitution had no bounds for the party then in power. And this partisan tool of the Washington authorities, was left to the free exercise of his own vicious will, in oppressing and torturing a people whom, from the bottom of his heart, he despised and regarded as worthy only to be ruled and robbed by adventurers from the North. It was left for Ames thus to annul this sacred right, a right held heretofore to be inalienable in every common law country, and which has existed from the days of Runnamede.

Governor Ames persistently and disdainfully spurned all kindly relations with the white people of Mississippi. He desired none but the affections of the negro, and with him alone he desired to unite his fortunes; and while he was continually fanning the flames of prejudice against himself, his vanity even suggested to his imagination the spectacle of Mississippians cringing before him with the offers of corrupt overtures. He stated on oath, before the Boutwell committee, that he was satisfied he had been approached from time to time by the leading white people with flattering offers of honor and office if he would put on the garb of Democracy; but this assertion was fully refuted and its falsehood fully exposed at the time by the Democratic press of the State.

In answer to a question of Senator Bayard, he said:

"It is a notorious fact that in that party—and I don't hesitate to say that I imagine I have been approached from time to time by the opposition with most flattering offers held forth that, should I change my coat and become a tool of others, I might receive any honor that I might demand."

Q. Will you state the names of any leading members of the opposition who have made this proposition to you?

A. Not unless it is essentially necessary.

Q. You have stated the fact, and I merely ask you to give you an opportunity to state them if you choose.

A. I say, with reference to that, that any proposition of that kind would not be made in writing, but in a way that the person whose name I might give might evade it, or give another interpretation of it. But, as I stated originally, I imagine that I have been approached, and I have no question in my own mind on that point.

Q. Can you give the name of any person of the opposition party to you in Mississippi, who made such offers to you as you have described?

A. I think I can; but I prefer not to do so unless the committee require it.

Q. Do you know their names, or the names of any one or more?

A. The events referred to occurred a number of years since. I think I would be able to name the persons, or certainly to ascertain their names without any difficulty.

Q. From whom would you ascertain them?

A. The charge was publicly made in a Republican paper, called the *Leader*, in 1870 or 1871, and I think never denied by the opposition press?

Q. Were the parties named, who made you the offer, in that paper?

A. I do not remember.

It is true that such a charge did appear in that paper, but it was promptly challenged by the leading Democratic papers of the State, and proof was demanded. The reply of the *Leader* was that the proposition had emanated from Democratic members of the legislature, who would soon be called upon to elect a United States senator. Upon this a disclaimer was made and published by every Democratic member, in which each one, separately and singly, denied positively that any such proposition had ever been made or thought of.

No reaffirmation of, or attempt to substantiate this charge, was ever made. This, together with the reluctancy and manifest inability of Governor Ames to designate the authors of the proposition, is well calculated of itself to breed grave suspicions as to the existence of any such fact. The administration of Alcorn was impressed with the same features that characterized that of his military predecessor. The active interference of General Ames in the canvass had enabled him to triumph at the election, and it now became a prominent object on the part of Governor Alcorn to consummate the compact by which Ames was to be placed in the United States senate. Thus, owing to the circumstances which have already been mentioned, was easily accomplished. And in 1870, Adelbert Ames, a citizen of Maine, and an officer in the United States army, took his seat in the United States Congress as senator from the State of Mississippi. He was military governor at the time of his being chosen to the senate, and it is said that he certified to his own election. Alcorn succeeded Ames as governor under the new constitution.

During his career in the United State senate, his course was marked by an utter indifference and disregard to the interests and rights of the State he pretended to represent. He was ever ready to give credence and import to any slander which the carpet baggers, and often more degraded native radicals, might concoct and perpetrate upon the white people of the State, and invariably voted for every measure of persecution which their bitterest enemies introduced to congress. Not once was he known to assume the attitude of their champion or defender. In short, his course in congress is too well known to require any lengthy commentary. Suffice it to say that his senatorship was simply a burlesque upon a Republican form of government.

At the expiration of his term in the senate, in 1873, he returned to Mississippi and entered the canvass as a candidate for governor against Alcorn, in consequence of which a rupture occurred between these two radical lights, which eventually caused an incurable split in their party.

Criminations and recriminations of a bitter character were now bandied between them and their respective adherents. In this contest Ames had a decided advantage. He was sustained by the worst element of the party. The carpet baggers flocked to his standard and marshalled the negroes in a solid phalanx under his banner. He was, in consequence, elected by a large majority, and with the opening of the year 1874, he began his notorious career as governor of Mississippi, or rather as governor of the negroes and the few white adventurers who had alone elected him to the position; for from the native white people he sought no support, either before or after he entered upon the office of governor, but his whole conduct manifested a desire to repel any sympathy on their part with his administration. To show that the white people were actuated by the sentiment "*principia non homines*," it may be adduced, that at this election, they, as the least of two evils, accepted and sustained Alcorn, whom they had spurned in his race with Dent. While they had but little confidence in Alcorn, they saw, in the administration of Ames, a prolific crop of the bitter fruits they had already tasted under his military rule.

The mutual denunciations indulged in by the two wings of the radical party during their canvass, did not cease upon the election of Ames. He entered upon his office as governor of the State, confronted by the opposition of the native white people and the hostility of a portion of his own party, whom he had alienated. This breach in his party continued to widen during the progress of his administration.

The two wings now assumed the name respectively of the Ames and the Alcorn wing. In reference to this opposition to his administration by leading members of his own party, Ames made the following statement before the Boutwell committee, in answer to Senator Bayard:

Q. Without going into the fact of the cause of their opposition to you, was there, or was there not, in Mississippi, in the year 1875, a violent and vigorous opposition to you and your administration in the ranks of the Republican party?

A. I say violent—but not powerful—not numerous.

Q. Did not Mr. Pease, the ex-senator, publicly denounce your administration?

A. He did.

Q. Did not Mr. Alcorn, the present senator, denounce your administration constantly?

A. He did.

Q. Have they not constantly charged you in public with making an effort to array the races, one against the other?

A. I am not aware that Mr. Pease ever did; Senator Alcorn has always made that charge; I do not think Mr. Pease ever made that charge; at least, it never attracted my attention.

Q. Are you aware of Mr. Pease's publication in regard to your administration?

A. I never read it, but I know that he did make such charges.

The following is an extract of the publication referred to, and it is inserted for the reason that it emanated from a leading Republican of the day, and one who was intimately acquainted with the workings of Ames' administration. This statement was published in the New York *Tribune* of October 12, 1875:

"I regret to say that in several localities in the State of Mississippi a deplorable condition of affairs exist. Indeed, among the people throughout the State there is a most lamentable want of confidence in the State government. The colored people distrust the power of the State under Governor Ames, and the whites generally question his disposition to administer the government so as to afford protection to life and property and maintain domestic tranquility, for which governments are instituted. As to his motive, I do not undertake to explain; but the fact is, he has, unfortunately, pursued a policy calculated to create distrust, and he has caused the white population, who represent the intelligence and wealth of the State—the true, essential element upon which the maintenance of good government depends—to believe that he has been, and is now, attempting to create an open antagonism between the races, and to plunge the State into a condition of revolution and domestic violence such as will necessitate martial law, and thereby advance his personal political schemes. * * *

"I was going to say that, notwithstanding the excitement incident to partisan strife and the race prejudices, which have been wrought up by the extremists on both sides, the majority of the people, regardless of race or political affiliations, deprecate violence, and are ready to assist the properly constituted authorities in preserving peace. I have no war to make on Governor Ames personally. He is deader now than Hector; but he hopes, by the means he is pursuing, to secure a legislature that will send him to the United States senate.

"To reach the senate was his ulterior purpose in becoming governor. All his appointments are made upon the condition that his appointees shall support him for the Senate. The preservation of the Republican party in Mississippi depends upon an honest administration of the laws of the State, and it will go under unless the remedy for all our troubles is within political integrity, exact justice and honest dealing. Federal interference is not needed or wanted. The use of force would do more harm than good.

Nine tenths of the white population are opposed to him. They want good men to come into office to work a reform in existing abuses."

Upon this same subject, J. S. Morris, Esq., formerly attorney general of the State, and a leading radical, addressed a letter to the chairman of the Republican State executive committee, and bearing date September 8, 1874, in which he said:

"The evils which have for some time past afflicted all classes of our people, are attributable, in a large degree, to the desertion by high Republican officials of the principles of the party, to wilful and flagrant violations of the constitution which they are sworn to support. These are well known to every intelligent man in the State, and will be universally discussed, exposed and punished in the next election."

Thus, with the leading men and most intelligent portion of his own party, whom his misgovernment had alienated from his administration, arrayed against him, and bearing upon his shoulders the terrible load of hatred he had wilfully engendered on the part of the white people, and which he had on all occasions sought to aggravate and inflame, the position of Governor Ames in the beginning of the year 1875 was by no means enviable.

Amid this universal discontent of all classes of the people, and the restless distrust of him and his administration, pervading the whole State, he saw no other means of effecting his ambitious purposes than that of force and intimidation—the exercise of the military power of the general government in co-operation and alliance with his armed partisans. And it is questionable, from the general tenor of his conduct, whether he ever desired to accomplish his political schemes in any other manner. His sole wish seemed to be to ride into the United States senate upon the crest of violence and the palanquin of military rule.

He was charged publicly by ex-Senator Pease, Senator Alcorn, ex-Attorney General Morris, and Attorney General Harris, all leading radicals, with using the executive power of the State for the purpose of securing his election to the United States senate, and to this end it is evident that he had prostituted every function of the gubernatorial power. He had, for this purpose, and in scorn of the intelligence of the State, *united his fortunes with the negroes, whom he believed to be in the majority.*

Although utterly unlearned in the science of civil jurisprudence, he avoided even the acquaintance of the most learned and intelligent citizens, and, in fact, all who could have imparted an air of respectable polity to his administration, and surrounded himself with the most reckless and vicious adventurers, who were entirely obsequious to his wishes. Conscious of having no claim to the respect of the white people, and without the least effort to obtain it, he determined to defy their opposition.

The end of all his methods to consummate his intrigues and accomplish his designs was the sword. He declared that he regarded all opposition to his administration as a "race issue," and avowed his intention of using all his power, personal, political and official, in behalf of the negroes, who were now as thoroughly enslaved to his will and to that of his obsequious tools, with whom he had filled the various offices of the State, as they ever were to the most arbitrary owners.

Yet there were many of the most intelligent of this race who were by no means blind to the disastrous consequences of such a course on the part of the governor Hence, about this time, ex-United States Senator Revels addressed a letter to the President of the United States, the following extracts from which it is deemed not impertinent to introduce in this connection. He says:

"The great masses of the white people have abandoned their hostility to the general government and Republican principles, and to-day accept as a fact that all men are born free and equal, and I believe are ready to guarantee to my people every right and privilege guaranteed to an American citizen. The bitterness and hate created by the late civil strife has, in my opinion, been obliterated in this

State, except, perhaps, in some localities, and would have long since been entirely obliterated, were it not for some unprincipled men who would keep alive the bitterness of the past, and inculcate a hatred between the races, in order that they may aggrandize themselves by office and its emoluments, to control my people, the effect of which is to degrade them.   *   *   *   *   *   *

"If the State administration had adhered to Republican principles, advanced patriotic measures, appointed only honest and competent men to office, and sought to restore confidence between the races, bloodshed would have been unknown, peace would have prevailed, Federal interference been unthought of; harmony, friendship and mutual confidence would have taken the place of the bayonet."

It is hard to conceive of a more terrible responsibility than that lodged by these charges upon the shoulders of the governor, but that he was utterly indifferent to both the circumstances and the consequences of his course, may be gathered from the pertinacity with which he held to it. He was alike deaf to the voice of warning and expostulation, and his short career was like an angry tornado that sweeps onward in its maddening course, strewing its path with ruin, until stayed by its own exhaustion.

Perhaps the most infamous act of the Ames administration, and which drew upon it the fiercest opposition of the more intelligent and honest members of his party, was what is called the Pearl River navigation scheme, which was an act of the legislature, approved by Ames, in regard to the State lands.

The general government had given to the State of Mississippi certain lands for educational purposes, and for the improvement of navigation, etc. The opportunity which this donation afforded for swindling the State had been seized upon by a ring, composed of the editor of the *Pilot*, the official radical paper, and Warner, French, Sullivan, O. S. Lee, adjutant to the governor, and others of his warm partisan and personal friends.

These men proposed to the legislature that if it would

give them these lands, comprising one hundred and twenty thousand acres, that they would open the navigation of Pearl River. The legislature made the grants as requested, and the governor approved them without taking the proper bonds for the performance of the service. These men sent O. S. Lee, the governor's adjutant, to Chicago, to find a purchaser. He soon returned, bringing with him a man named Baldwin, to whom the lands were sold by these men, while not a chunk was ever removed from the river, nor has the State received any other equivalent.

Whether the fraud and other invalidating elements of this transaction will support the principle of *caveat emptor*, or otherwise restore these lands to the State, has never, to the knowledge of the writer, been tested. Surely there should be some way to annul such an outrageous swindle.

In such a state of affairs, it became evident that the Democratic party, composed of the wealth and intelligence of the State, was disposed to combine with the discontented elements of the opposition for a strenuous effort to gain control of the State government.

This alliance was promoted by many natural features which it convoked. It was an alliance between labor and capital, the employer and employé, both of which had suffered alike from the corrupt administration of government. It was also an alliance between natives of the same soil; men who had been reared together from infancy, and whose natural affection and mutual faith had been disrupted by base devices. It was an alliance of mutual interests for the protection of mutual rights and the promotion of mutual prosperity. The radical party had arrayed the negro in a groundless and unnatural state of political hostility against his former owner.

Therefore, it is not surprising, that when the barriers of deceit and prejudice, and the race hedges that had heretofore impenetrably fenced in the radical party were once broken through, that the negroes should have flocked by thousands to the standard of their natural allies. To defeat this event was an object to which Governor Ames directed his efforts early in the year.

For this purpose he procured the passage of a bill by the legislature, in the spring of 1875, called the Gatling gun bill; so named because the purchase by the governor of four Gatling guns was authorized by its provisions. This bill empowered the commander in chief to organize, from the enrolled militia, two regiments of ten companies each, and to purchase four or more Gatling guns, and organize a corps of select officers and men from the infantry to send with these guns. It may be observed that these guns were regarded as peculiarly terrible and destructive.

To effect the purpose of this bill, there was an appropriation of sixty thousand dollars, of which five thousand dollars were limited to the purchase of supplies and munitions of war, equipments, etc. After this five thousand dollars had been drawn and expended for the purposes for which it was designated, the tax payers obtained an injunction from the chief justice of the State.

This injunction was based upon the condition coupled with this appropriation, that it should not be drawn unless the militia be called into active service. The writ prevented the expenditure of the money for the purpose intended, and it is to the timely interference of this mandate from the chief justice that the people of Mississippi to day owe their narrow escape from the horrors of a race war that would have drenched the State in blood. Notwithstanding that the military preparations of the governor were paralyzed by this circumstance, they had produced a dangerous state of feeling—they had inflamed the passions of the negroes, and excited the indignation and fears of the white people. His plans, up to this time, had met with no serious opposition; in fact, they had succeeded but too well, and the state of affairs they had produced caused at last a sense of alarm to seize upon even the mind of Governor Ames himself. He had been, as already stated, baffled in his efforts to secure the co-operation of the Federal army. As early as the 25th of May, as if preparing for hostilities, he had addressed a letter to the secretary of war, in which he applied for a statement of arms and other military stores that had been issued to the State since 1860, and the amounts of the apportionment for the different years. This was for the purpose of ascertaining what quantity of arms and munitions he might depend upon obtaining from the general government, in advance of the formation of his companies.

Again, on the 2d of June, 1875, he wrote to the chief of the United States ordnance department, making application for a price list of ordnance and ordnance stores, also for a book of forms in use in the department. On the first day of May of the same year, an order was issued from headquarters, State of Mississippi, adjutant general's office, in which was announced the officers of the Mississippi State tooops, as follows:

"Brigadier General Albert G. Parker, of Holmes County, aide-de-camp; Lieutenant Colonel James J. Spellman, of Madison County, aide-de-camp; Lieutenant Colonel Omar S. Lee, of Holmes County, aide-de-camp. [This man afterward proved a defaulter for a large amount, and fled the State.] Brigadier General Wm. Gray, of Washington County; General Brown, colonel, first regiment of infantry; Alexander Warner, of Madison County, major general, State militia." These men were all radicals, and three of them, Spellman, Gray and Brown, were negroes. Warner was also chairman of the State Republican executive committee.

There was no Democrat appointed to any office in the military service of the State. It is not deemed necessary to set forth a full list of all Governor Ames' military appointments made during the spring of 1875, preceding the election; but it will be sufficient to observe that they were numerous enough for an army of great magnitude. Coupled with these preparations, were constant threats on the part of Governor Ames, to bring United States troops into the State. It was necessary for the existence of his party that the political unity of the negroes should be preserved, and that they should be solidly massed in the radical ranks. To do this, it was necessary to retain them under the impression that he was supported by the Federal authorities, and would be sustained by the military power of the general government; for the great body of the negroes had but little relish for the idea of entering alone into an armed contest with the whites.

These demonstrations produced the very state of feeling the governor desired. From what has already been adduced, it will not be a matter of surprise that the campaign of 1875, in Mississippi, was conducted by both parties with a feeling of bitterness extending to all parts of the State, and which, being thus aggravated and intensified by the conduct of the governor, soon assumed an alarming aspect. That individual seemed to cherish the idea that the white people over whom he ruled had no rights not subject to military authority, or which could be exercised in antagonism to his own personal interest and the interest of the radical party. The "race issues," which he so promptly recognized and promoted, would, he hoped, produce results which would afford him a pretext for invoking the aid of the United States army in pursuance of his purpose to control the election—to crush out all opposition to radical rule, and to his own ambitious scheme of riding into the United States Senate on the necks of the negroes of Mississippi. Nor did he wait for the self presentation of such pretext, but sent the very functions of his office to fish for them throughout the borders of the State.

Accordingly, on the 24th of September, 1875, he sent the following circular letter to each of the sheriffs of the State, most, or all of whom were candidates for re-election:

"SIR: I am directed by his excellency the governor to inquire if any militia organizations are needed in your county to assist the civil officers? Are there any threats from the opposition that, in your judgment, will be carried into effect; and, if so, will it be possible to hold a quiet and peaceable election?

"A. S. PACKER,
Adjutant General."

The assurance implied in these questions, being the surest method of fixing beyond doubt the re-election of these sheriffs, as a matter of course suggested to them the reply desired; and wherever there were any doubts in this respect, those doubts either gave rise to false reports or to actual efforts on the part of the peace officers of the counties to stir up something as a pretext for the sending of troops into their respective counties. Thus were the very precincts of peace invaded by the governor, and the very fountains of order corrupted that they might contribute to the tide of strife, with which it seems he wished to see the whole State inundated. It is not likely that these sheriffs, with such influences bearing upon them, would fail to avail themselves of this proffered opportunity of rendering their tenure of office secure. Hence we find them replying to the governor in one general strain, the key note of which was "riot and intimidation" in their counties; and, in some instances, as in the case of the sheriff of Monroe, as stated by Ames himself, we find them smuggling arms and ammunition, supplied them by the governor, into their counties.

The negroes were thus informed that they would be supplied with arms, and receive armed protection against the whites from the State and Federal authorities, in any act they might perpetrate in furtherance of the general scheme of carrying the State by violence. And this idea of protection and immunity extended to their individual conduct; they became, in many instances, intolerably arrogant and impudent.

Nothing could more plainly indicate the disposition and purpose of Governor Ames than this unsolicited offer of aid to the sheriffs. The very questions he puts to them preclude any idea of his having received any unfavorable reports from them of the condition of affairs in their counties. It was a spontaneous suggestion evidently intended to apprise them of the means he had adopted to effectuate his plans of controlling the election at all hazards, and, if possible, to place society in such a state as to render the white people forever powerless and terrified by the presence of an armed negro militia. In other words, it seems from the course which he pursued and the means he adopted, that it was his desire and intention, if possible, to Africanize the entire State of Mississippi.

This policy and conduct of the governor was soon productive of its natural and expected fruits. The negroes assumed, day by day, a more threatening attitude, and in many of the negro counties the white men grew pale and haggard with alarm and anguish. In many instances they became sick from constant watching and loss of sleep. Their pillows were haunted with apparitions of the assassin. They lived in constant dread and expectation, not knowing on what night, or what hour of the night, they and their wives and children might be butchered, and their homes consumed by the torch of the incendiary.

Such was the universal state of feeling among the white people in many localities of the State. Yet, notwithstanding these influences, there were, even at this time, a few well disposed negroes here and there who deprecated this state of things, and manifested a feeling of kindness toward their former owners, but in almost every instance of this character they were threatened with death, beaten and silenced by their own race.

In Yazoo County, a negro member of the legislature of the State, named Patterson, paid a negro fifty dollars to take the life of another, who voted with the Democrats. For this Patterson was hung by the friends of the murdered man, who were all negroes, and his procurement of the death of the negro Democrat was confessed by the negro who committed the deed, while occurrences of whipping and threatening for this cause were frequent throughout the State.

The first serious public outgrowth of this state of affairs was also in Yazoo County. The sheriff of that county, one A. F. Morgan, a white man, had, as has been before stated, married a mulatto woman, and, as a matter of course, was an autocrat among the negroes. He had lso murdered a radical rival for the office of sheriff, and ad, in many respects, rendered himself peculiarly obnoxious to the white people. He was a stanch personal and partisan friend of the governor, and was ever ready to serve his wishes, upon the least intimation of their character.

The government of this county was completely in the hands of the worst elements of the radical party, so that it was utterly impossible to bring Morgan to justice for any act that he might commit.

As has been stated, a chancellor, Drennan, had been removed from office by the governor, because, in the exercise of his judicial discretion and his judgment of the law, he had refused to allow bail to this man for the murder of Hilliard, his opponent for the office of sheriff. The white people, believing him to have been guilty of an outrageous murder, were anxious that he should be brought to trial, and law and justice vindicated; but the negroes became furious in his behalf, and made the most terrible threats in regard to the people and town of Yazoo City, if he should be brought to punishment. This was more than a year prior to the event of which I shall presently speak, and the bad feeling engendered by this circumstance continued to grow, and was encouraged by Morgan on his triumphant return from the Hinds County jail, where he had been placed for safe keeping, to the sheriff's office of Yazoo County.

No indictment against him was found until the State passed into the hands of the Democratic party, when he immediately became a fugitive from justice.

That he was guilty of murder was found by Chancellor Drennan, when, after a hearing extending through five days, he refused to grant him bail; but he was a bitter partisan, had married a negro woman, and all these efforts to bring him to justice inflamed the animosity of the negroes against the whites. No sooner had the campaign of 1875 opened, than this man began to ply all his arts in inflaming their minds and instilling the lessons dictated from the mansion of the governor. So violent had he become in his harangues that it was deemed expedient on the part of some white men to attend his meetings, and if possible, to check to some extent by their presence his inflammatory discourses.

For this purpose they were present at a negro meeting in Yazoo City, on the night of the 1st of September, 1875. At this assembly there were about a dozen white Democrats in attendance. Morgan was the speaker of the occasion, and while engaged in one of his usual incendiary diatribes, a Democratic negro in the audience arose and asked him some question, upon which the negroes became very excited and indignant, and such expressions as "Knock him down!" "Put him out!" etc., were heard throughout the hall, which they doubtless would have carried into effect, if nothing more, had not the white gentlemen present offered him protection, which resulted in a general firing of pistols in the room, in which Mitchell, a white man, was killed, and Foote, a negro, was wounded.

Morgan fled from the room and proceeded to Jackson, where he sought protection and aid from his friend the governor. Upon which the governor threatened, and in fact began preparations, to send Morgan back under a military escort of negroes.

This step greatly exasperated the white people of the county, and they began in turn to make preparations to prevent the advent of such an expedition into their county.

A few days after this, on the 4th of September, a riot of a more serious character occurred at the little town of Clinton.

Inspired and inflamed by these events and the attitude of the governor, and by the inflammatory speeches of the radical orators of both colors, a feeling of intense excitement and animosity against the whites existed on the part of the negroes at the capital of the State and in the

directly felt; and while this cauldron of excitement was at its fullest ebullition, a negro barbecue and political meeting was announced to take place at the town of Clinton, on the 4th day of September, 1875. Clinton is in the County of Hines; the county containing the State capitol. To this barbecue and speaking dense masses of negroes, mostly armed and in military order, flocked from the surrounding country. The number was estimated by many eye witnesses as being not less than twenty-five hundred men, women and children, of which more than twelve hundred were men, of whom a large number bore arms of some description. A general invitation had been extended to all persons to attend this meeting, at which, as had been announced, there was to be a joint discussion between members of the two political parties. According to this understanding, there were some sixty or seventy white men in attendance. Of these, some twenty or thirty, perhaps, wore pistols on their persons. Not more than half of them, however, participated in the fight. All that is known, to any degree of certainty, about the inception of the riot that occurred on this occasion, is that it originated in a personal altercation between a white man and a negro. This happened amid the dense throng of negroes that enveloped the speaker's stand. It seems that this white man attempted to avoid the difficulty, and retreated from his dangerous and helpless position in the dense crowd, and reached a small party of whites who were standing about a hundred yards from the stand, whither he was pursued by the negro and his friends. This party consisted at first of four or five persons, but on the assault on the white man being renewed, it was increased to about a dozen white men, who were soon, however, separated into groups of two or three by the pressure of the dense masses of negroes who immediately gathered around them. At this time the cry of "A fight!" "A fight!" was heard, and immediately such exclamations as "Come on!" "Rally!" "Kill the white men!" were heard in every direction. Upon this the drums were beaten, and dense masses of negroes with knives, pistols and clubs, rushed upon the little party of whites, who still endeavored to retreat, and had succeeded in making their way a short distance to a small ravine, at the same time asking the negroes to stand back and keep the peace, and saying that they desired no difficulty; but at this juncture their retreat was cut off by the advance of another dense mass of negroes who bore down upon them in front, at the same time crying, "Kill them!" "Damn them!" "Kill them!" There were now eleven white men surrounded by, perhaps, five hundred armed negroes, all clamoring for their blood. The whites made every effort to escape and avoid bloodshed. They pleaded for peace, but they were now pressed almost to suffocation by the dense crowd of negroes. At this time an unfortunate circumstance gave the desired signal for the attack. A pistol in the hands of one of the white men, being struck by some one jostling against him, was discharged into the ground at his feet; a negro then shot a white man named Wharton. Upon this the firing became general, the whites using their arms vigorously. Two negroes were killed and four or five wounded, when the crowd in front of the whites began to break and retreat. The whites also began to leave the grounds in small squads and in different directions. At this some negro cried out, "Don't let a white man get away!" The negroes then rallied and pursued the whites in every direction. Two young white men, Sively and Thompson, were overtaken, killed, and their bodies horribly mutilated.

One Charles Chilton, a white man, who had reached his home immediately, on the road, a short distance from the speaking grounds, was shot and killed while in the act of assisting some negro women and children to enter his yard to escape being run over by the dense troop of negro horsemen who were dashing wildly up the road. A Captain White was captured, shot, stabbed and beaten and left for dead by the road side, while several other white men were wounded in the fight or in attempting to leave the grounds.

Such, in substance, was the origin, so far as known, and the result of the riot at Clinton, Mississippi, on the 4th of September, 1875, as concurred in by all of those persons whose testimony was taken before the mayor of Clinton, within a few days after the events occurred. That the negroes were anticipating and desired a fight, and went to Clinton that day prepared for it, is a conclusion that can scarcely be avoided by any calm and passionless view.

It is stated by many gentlemen who were present that the negroes seemed from the first, and throughout the day, unusually disrespectful toward the whites, and frequently rubbed against them in a boisterous manner, as if they were seeking to provoke a difficulty, and at the same time remarking that they intended to have their way there that day. It is quite evident that the negroes, who were armed, went to Clinton that day with the intention of attacking the whites, and that they made a quarrel between a white man and a negro the pretext and signal for the slaughter. Upon the heel of these events the wildest and most horrifying rumors flew through the country. It was reported that the negroes were gathering for the destruction of the town and a general slaughter of the whites. The citizens were horrified with the events that had already taken place, and even more so at the yet more terrible scene, which their just fears pictured upon their imaginations. They called aloud for their fellow citizens to bring them relief and save their town from ruin, and their wives and children from destruction. A prompt and speedy response came up from all directions, and before the bright sun of the Sabbath morn had again peeped at the scenes of the previous day, five hundred white men, with glistening arms, were gathered in the streets of Clinton for the protection of the town. During the great excitement that followed this massacre, which continued for several days, there were some seven or eight negroes killed in the vicinity, who were known to have been leaders in this riot or chief actors in the murders. This was the work of the friends and relations of the murdered men.

Yet, notwithstanding this scene of turbulence and bloodshed, in which more than a thousand negroes either directly or indirectly participated, on Monday morning, two days after, the town of Clinton and the surrounding country were as quiet as if the soil had never been bathed but with the balmy dews of heaven. All was quiet and peace restored.

Another riot occurred not long after this at Friar's Point, in Coahoma County, which was inaugurated by the negroes, and originated in the party schism between the adherents of Governor Ames and Senator Alcorn. On this occasion three or four hundred armed negroes approached the town for the avowed purpose of destroying it. They were promptly met by the Alcorn party, headed by Senator Alcorn himself, and in the conflict that ensued two white men and nine negroes were killed. The Democrats had no share in this matter. These riots are all traceable directly to the policy of the governor, and were the natural results of the teachings of his partisans, and to the feeling which his own conduct aggravated and inspired.

Prior to these events, a disturbance took place at Vicksburg, but it seems to have been unpremeditated and of no political importance. In this affray, which occurred on the 5th of July, a man by the name of Hill, the same who had figured so notoriously in Kemper County, was wounded. This man was there befriending Cardozo, the negro superintendent of education, who was engaged in a difficulty with a white man, from which the riot originated. These riots created alarming rumors throughout the State, and greatly added to the flames of animosity between the two parties and the two races. There was no prosecution or legal investigation of these riots set on foot by the civil authorities of the State. Governor Ames had but one remedy he desired to apply, and that was the bayonet. There is nothing to show that he exercised any of the civil functions and powers of his office to suppress these disorders, or to pacify the spirit from which they originated; but in conformity with his ideas of government, he promptly applied to the President of the United States for protection, but as he failed to establish such a condition of affairs as could justify General Grant in sending United States troops to his aid, the application was refused; not, however, from any returning respect for constitutional government on the part of the President and his advisers, but owing, as he said, to the repugnance on the part of a majority of the people of the United States to the further interference of the general government in the affairs of a State. Yet, at his suggestion, the attorney general sent a man in a rather nondescript capacity to the capital of Mississippi.

This man, whose name was Chase, acted as a kind of spy of the Federal government, with power to investigate the police condition of the State of Mississippi, and to control matters, by constant threats to introduce Federal troops in the State, should he find it necessary to do so.

In the meantime the rebuff he had received from the Federal authorities, and the resolute and manly attitude of the white people, entirely disconcerted the military plans of Governor Ames; consequently, he intimated to the Democratic leaders of the State, through this man Chase, his willingness to enter into an arrangement with them in regard to the conduct of the election. This intimation met with a cordial reception, and, accordingly, a committee of gentlemen waited on the governor, and represented to him the terrible state of affairs; the great danger of a race conflict; the determination of the white people to defend their rights; to protect themselves, their families and their property to the utmost of their ability; but that they deprecated such a necessity, and begged the governor to disband his militia, and to put a stop to armed negroes marching to and fro through the country, as that alone could possibly preserve the peace between the races.

They stated to him in substance that it was these military and intimidating movements on his part, which were the sole cause of the excited state of public feeling; that his calling out, and arming the militia, their marching through the country with fixed bayonets and with drums beating, and his reported intention of invading the county of Yazoo, attended by all the circumstances of war, had produced an intense feeling of indignation among the white citizens, and that all these demonstrations were attributed to political purposes on his part. They assured him that the people would not tolerate this flourishing of bayonets all over the country, and that if it was not discontinued it would surely result in a collision between the races; that the best way of settling matters was for him to disband his troops, and accept the pledges of the best citizens and most influential gentlemen of the State that peace and quiet should be maintained. Upon this, the governor proposed to disband his militia with their arms in their hands. This was objected to, upon the ground that the retention of their arms by the negroes might still be the source of serious disturbances. The governor then agreed that the troops should be disbanded and their arms deposited with the commander of the United States troops stationed at Jackson.

This agreement gave general relief to the people of the State, and at once re established the reign of peace. This failure to procure Federal troops to garrison the counties, and this sudden fall, as they considered it, from his lofty military pretentions, caused a great reaction to take place in the minds of the negroes, and a great change in their conduct towards the white people. They at once began to listen to their arguments and to flock to the Democratic clubs. Their ardor and race animosities gave place to a disposition, *for the first time*, to cultivate terms of friendship with the white people, and to vote with them in their efforts to obtain a respectable administration of the State government. Yet no sooner was the result of the election known than the cry of "fraud and intimidation" was raised by the radical party throughout the land. The leading radicals of the State, carpet baggers, whose occupation was now gone, flocked to Washington and poured their slanderous tales into the ears of Congress, and the congressional investigating committees were at once set on foot to visit the State, drag to the light of day the dark crimes represented to have been committed, and to exhibit the monster of intimidation to the eyes of an execrating world; and yet the testimony taken before these investigating committees was so damaging to radical rule in Mississippi, that their reports were not suffered to be published till after the presidential election of 1876. Before the subject of the general State canvass is dismissed, it may be proper to insert the following address of the State executive committee of the Democratic party, for the purpose of showing the principles which controlled the canvass on the part of the white people:

HEADQUARTERS DEMOCRATIC AND
CONSERVATIVE STATE EXECUTIVE COMMITTEE,
JACKSON, MISS., *Sept* 29, 1875.

To the People of Mississippi:

Recent occurrences in the State render it proper that we should address you in reference to the conduct of the present canvass.

An unexpected conflict was brought on at Clinton, on the 4th instant, by the fault of the members of the Republican party. In that conflict several citizens of the State were brutally murdered, and their lifeless bodies inhumanly mutilated. In a day or two, sooner than could have been anticipated, considering the circumstances of brutality and outrage attending the conflict in the beginning, quiet and order were restored. The governor of the State has made this disturbance a pretext for calling on the President for the use of the national army to suppress what he was pleased to term "domestic violence." To prevent the disgrace which would fall upon the people of this State by the representations made by the governor, that disorder prevailed here which could not be suppressed by the local authorities, many good citizens in various parts of the State, though seeing no necessity for the military power, voluntarily organized themselves into companies and tendered their assistance, should it be needed to preserve order and enforce the laws. These offers, though made in good faith, and in a most respectful manner, were not, in any instance, accepted, but were uniformly treated with contempt. It is a subject of congratulation, and of just pride to the people of the State, that cursed as we are with rulers, alien to us in sympathy and interest, and utterly impotent to perform any good function of government, and with ability only to commit mischief, that we have been able to preserve order and to hold society together.

In fact, we can safely say, that in no part of the Union does there prevail a more perfect peace, or a greater respect for law, or a greater desire to preserve order, than in Mississippi, and this is well known to the State executive, if he knows anything of the disposition of the people over whom he rules. Under these circumstances, we can regard the present efforts of the chief magistrate of the State to put into active service the militia, and thus, in a time of profound peace, to organize a standing army in violation of the Constitution of the United States, and of this State, in no other light than as a deliberate attempt to incite disturbances, so that there may be an imaginary insurrection which he may suppress in blood.

We deem it our duty to warn you against these machinations of the chief magistrate of the State, and to urge you not to be betrayed in a moment of passion and just resentment into acts of violence not necessary for self defence. The governor, in his efforts to blacken the fair name of the State, and to procure Federal troops, which he hoped to use for the advancement of his personal fortunes, telegraphed to the attorney general of the United States that the race feeling was so strong, that it was believed that the organizing of a militia of colored men would develop a war of races extending even beyond the limits of the State, and that the organization of whites alone would be ineffectual. Notwithstanding he entertains these views, he has steadily refused the proffered aid before alluded to, and is now proceeding to organize, as we are informed, a regiment of each race, and to muster them into active service. There can be no other reason for this than a wish on the part of the chief magistrate of the State to incite that war which he said would be produced, and to bring about disorder and confusion. For it is well known to all of you that there has not been the slightest disorder, not the pretence of a riot or insurrection since the disturbance at Clinton, nor has there been any obstruction to the execution of the laws at any time, except such as may exist in the incompetency and wilful neglect of Republican officials to discharge their duties. That there is crime in the State is true; but there is not more than exists in our sister States, and there is nothing that looks like insurrection, or an attempt on the part of our people to obstruct the enforcement of the laws.

The horrible misrule of the present State government has, very naturally, produced an intense interest among all classes of our people in the result of the pending election. It is right, and an auspicious omen, that this interest is so deep and so universal. We would not have you to abate one jot or tittle of the earnest zeal and determination you have hitherto manifested to rescue our State from the corrupt horde of adventurers and their ignorant allies who, by sowing distrust between the races, seized the government of the State for selfish and unworthy ends, and who have so administered it that, but for the conservative love of law and order of our people, we would now be in a state of anarchy. We would rather urge you to work with a still greater zeal and with a more untiring energy, until the redemption of the State is secured beyond all doubt.

We are glad to be able to assure you that victory is so certain that it cannot be lost, except by our own mismanagement or failure to carry on the contest to the end, in the same spirit that has characterized it up to the present time.

In every part of the State our friends are organized and thoroughly alive to the importance of the contest. Everywhere on our side there is union, harmony, activity and confidence. Our adversaries, on the contrary, are divided, demoralized and dispirited, and their rank and file are kept together only by the desperation of their leaders, who seem determined to retain their ill gotten and ill used power at any cost to the people of the State.

Be patient, yet firm and determined. Let every true son of Mississippi act as if the fortunes of the day depended on his individual exertions. If there be, in any quarter, strife and rivalries among our friends, let them cease. Let every consideration of self and personal advancement be buried out of sight. Let us all be animated by the one sentiment that there can be no higher duty to discharge than to work faithfully to secure the redemption of our beloved State, unless, perhaps, it be to use nobly the victory, when it is won, for the common and equal good of all her people and to the injury of none.

J. Z. GEORGE, *Chairman*,
I. A. P. CAMPBELL,
U. M. YOUNG,
THOMAS B. SYKES,
H. M. STREET,
JOHN A. BINFORD,
W. H. H. TYSON,
H. H. CHALMERS,
L. B. CHRISMAN,
E. C WALTHALL,
A. T. ROANE,
I D. VERTNER,
W. A. PERCY,
E. RICHARDSON

On the 24th of September, 1875, the following secret circular was sent by the chairman of the Republican State executive committee, addressed to the sheriffs, chancellors and circuit judges of the State, who had jointly the appointment of the registrars of election:

"DEAR SIR: You are aware that during the present canvass and in the coming election, while the opposition are using every means to defeat the Republican party, we are forced to the necessity of employing every lawful advantage our position gives us. Not the least of these is the matter of registration, and the proper performance of the duties of registrars.

"It is apprehended that many Republicans have already been prevented from registering by threats and intimidation. It is, therefore, of the greatest importance that the majority of the board of registrars should be composed of men not only true and faithful, but who will also have the courage and firmness to discharge their duties fearlessly, especially in canvassing the vote and making up the returns. With this view, we earnestly ask you to examine the list of your appointments critically, and satisfy yourself fully as to the character of each man, and make such changes as, in your judgment, will promote the free and full expression of the people at the ballot box. We take the privilege of addressing this circular letter to all the judges and chancellors throughout the State, because it has been suggested to us that there are some professed Republican registrars who are incompetent, unworthy and of doubtful fidelity.

"A. WARNER, *Chairman.*"

It surely requires no close examination of this document to disclose its import and purpose. The circuit judges, chancellors and sheriffs of the several counties, jointly appointed the board of registrars; that is, the circuit judge, chancellor and sheriff respectively appointed a registrar for the county. These registrars, in their turn, appointed the inspectors of election, and supervised and canvassed the votes and made up the returns, and, in fact, controlled the whole machinery of the elective franchise in their respective counties. Such were the organization and power of the officers whose adaptation of character to the *duties* required is so strenuously demanded by the chairman of the Republican State executive committee. What these "*lawful advantages*" were, in an honest and impartial performance of their sworn duty, to the party which possessed the appointment, is not readily discernible. But they are further required to be "not only true and faithful," but to have sufficient courage to meet whatever requisition may be made upon them in the interest of their party, "especially in canvassing the vote and making up the returns."

It is hard to conceive of language more suggestive of the *rôle* expected of these election officers, by the chief of the party, than this last phrase.

To lock themselves up in a secure and retired room, with

the boxes, and then peaceably and leisurely count the ballots, certainly does not seem to require any high degree of courage; but, in the face of their oaths, to make and utter a false list of the votes, surely requires attributes which none but an unscrupulous partisan could denominate courage.

But it seems that the chairman was apprehensive that there might be some registrars appointed who would not possess a sufficiency of the "courage" for the purpose in question. He had been informed that some were "incompetent, unworthy, and of doubtful fidelity," and he desires the *honorable* and grave and dignified judges and chancellors of the State to lay aside their sanctified ermine and patrol the counties in search of registrars who might have the *courage, worth and fidelity* to use every advantage their position conferred; in short, who would make up the returns favorable to their party at all events.

CHAPTER VIII.

Let us now return from our peep at the general condition of affairs in the State to the conduct of the campaigns in Kemper County. The feeling of distrust and alarm which we have found existing almost universally in Mississippi at this time, was greatly increased in this county by the lawless and violent conduct of Chisolm and Gilmer. There was a general and peculiar interest felt in every canvass in this county, not on account of any special importance they possessed, but in consequence of the high handed career these men had long pursued in the county, and of which I have treated in previous chapters only of the most criminal and diabolical features.

It will be necessary now to advert more especially to their political despotism and partisan outlawry, which led to the complete overthrow of all law and justice in the county, and produced an era of alarm and distrust well nigh bordering on desperation.

They had the whole negro population of the county, which exceeded that of the whites, completely under their control, and were, in fact, the arbiters of life and death throughout the county.

From the time that Chisolm was appointed sheriff, in 1870, he had been the acknowledged leader of the radical party in Kemper County. He was looked upon by the ignorant negroes, whom he controlled with despotic hand, as the fountain of all law and the medium of all power—county, State and Federal, civil and military. They voted in every instance for whomsoever he designated for office.

The first canvass in which Gilmer threw his black heart into the radical scale was that of 1872, in which he was a candidate for the State senate, to which aspiration his diabolical part in the murder of Dawson, as has been already stated, promoted him.

No sooner had he entered the canvass than, hand in hand

with Chisolm, he began his infamous career. Indeed, so joint and inseparable became the careers of these two men from this time, that it would be difficult to treat of their conduct singly. Prior to this time Chisolm, as he himself testified, caused a great many of the leading citizens of the county to be arrested by the military authorities. This fact has already been alluded to in a former chapter. He had, besides this, and after the cessation of military rule in the State, while sheriff, reported many citizens to the grand juries of the Federal court. This was done to procure, if possible, their imprisonment and removal from the county, or such a conviction as would either work their disfranchisement or afford grounds for challenging their votes at the polls.

In consummation of their plans to intimidate all disaffected negroes, and to prevent the white people from voting, Chisolm and Gilmer procured United States troops to be sent to Scooba on the day of the election, who surrounded the polls with fixed bayonets, and appeared ready to do their bidding.

On this occasion it is said that Gilmer took his position in a middle door leading to the poll room, and examined the ticket of every negro that approached, and whenever he found one with a Democratic ballot in his hand he seized and tore it up, at the same time forcing the negro to pass in with a radical ticket, which he substituted in place of the Democratic. He also challenged all the white men who had been indicted chiefly upon his information and that of Chisolm in the United States court, and on their pleading "No conviction," he would reply that there soon would be, and that they consequently could not vote; and thus, with such impudence hurled in their face, and the bayonets of the Federal troops pointed at their breasts, they were but too glad to make their escape from the scene, retire to their homes and there contemplate these glorious features of the "best government," etc.

Perhaps the most cruel and outrageous instance of this kind occurred at De Kalb. An aged gentleman, who lived

a short distance in the country, named McClelland, a man of the most peaceable and innocent character, came in to the polls bringing with him several negro men whom he employed on his farm. This old man went to the polls with his negro employees, and all voted the Democratic ticket. When the lieutenant in charge of the Federal troops, named Shelby, saw these negroes vote the Democratic ticket, he, without the slightest provocation, kicked the old man out of the court house, where the election was being held, in a most shameful and brutal manner. When the people saw the poll box in the hands of Federal soldiers, ready to do the bidding of Chisolm, who stood over it with observant eye as the arbiter of the very right of franchise, and men beaten because their negro employees voted with them, they, as a matter of course, felt that it was an intolerable humiliation, to remedy which no effort in their power should be spared.

Nor was there any remedy or redress to be found for these outrages—surely none to be had by a recourse to the courts of law. They, too, were controlled by these same men. The law was in their hands, and its vindicatory arm was never raised, save in its maddened strokes against the objects of their personal or political vengeance. In any cause of virtue the courts were dumb.

During this same canvass, Chisolm, in a speech at Scooba, told the negroes to stand firm for their rights, and if they could not obtain them otherwise, to go for the white people in their homes. Mr. J. W. Maury, a highly respected and reliable gentleman, who was the opposing candidate for sheriff, on hearing of this expression, afterward took occasion to ask Chisolm, while making a public speech at De Kalb in this same canvass, if it was true that he gave such counsel to the negroes at Scooba; when Chisolm, drawing himself up, replied with much emphasis, " Yes, by G-d ; I did !"

At this same meeting one Kellis, a radical, was making a speech, in which he denounced Dr. Saunders, the Democratic candidate for the legislature, as a habitual drunkard, upon which John W. Gully, who was present, with many other Democrats, replied in a very mild manner that Kellis erred ; that he knew Dr. Saunders well, and that he did not get drunk on all occasions as asserted. Upon this, Chisolm rushed up to the speakers' stand in a very boisterous and angry manner, seized a double barrelled gun, and exclaimed, " John Gully, you damned old scoundrel, if you can't keep your mouth shut, leave the court house!" At this the Chisolm clan made a rush toward Gully and gathered pressingly around him. Mr. Maury, the opposing candidate for sheriff, then remonstrated with Chisolm and his crowd, telling them that Gully meant nothing, and that he had only told the truth in defending the personal character of a friend. By this means he succeeded in allaying the excitement of Chisolm and his partisans, who, for this trivial offence, had assumed an attitude toward Gully which even threatened instant death. Mr. Maury, then, by pre-arrangement, arose in reply, and after contradicting and refuting the slanderous assertions made in regard to the Democratic candidates and the white people generally, demanded of Chisolm what he had those guns concealed behind the judge's stand for; to which Chisolm replied that John Gully had that morning brought some guns to town hidden beneath his shawl, which was known to be entirely false, and so proclaimed by Mr. Maury. Soon after this, Chisolm announced that he would speak on a certain day in the village of Wahalak. News of this was dispersed far and wide among the blacks, accompanied, as usual, by such instructions as Chisolm deemed necessary to the consummation of his plans; and accordingly, on that day the negroes poured into the village from every direction, in a boisterous and threatening manner, and prominent among these hostile demonstrations was a wagon load of shot guns, all loaded, which was stationed near the speakers' stand. In addition to this, the negroes, as they arrived upon the grounds, were formed into line, placed under the command of a very desperate individual named David, and regularly drilled.

Before the speaking began these guns were distributed among the negroes, who immediately gathered around the stand with them in their hands. After Chisolm had finished a very inflammatory harangue, Mr. Maury arose in reply, and contradicted some assertions that Chisolm had made. Upon this there was a general uprising of the negroes, and every gun was cocked and pointed toward the stand. Captain James Jenkins, a highly esteemed citizen, called on Chisolm for an explanation of all this bristling and flourish of arms. To which Chisolm replied that he had taken these precautions through fear that he might be mobbed; and yet there was scarcely a single pocket pistol even worn by the whites in attendance that day. It is said, moreover, that Chisolm's speech on this occasion was extremely bitter and incendiary. It seems that he had but one speech, which he used on all occasions, and which he toned to suit the circumstances. It seems that this ghost of assassination—which no doubt had its origin in the throes of conscience—often haunted him, and was often invoked as a pretext for conduct, the purpose of which was too apparent for so flimsy an attribution as the aggressive character of his fears.

On one occasion there was a small squad of men, said to have come from Alabama, who were, on some errand or other, passing through the county, and had camped overnight on the outskirts of the village of De Kalb, in a grove near Chisolm's residence. In the early morning they were discovered by a negro boy, and their presence reported to Chisolm. As to what followed I will let him state upon his oath, as testified before the ku-klux committee, page 250. He says: "I met this boy at the gate, and I saw that he was very much excited. He said: 'Judge, there are twenty-five or thirty men over there after you.' Said I: 'What in the devil are they after me for?' He said: 'I do not know what they are after you for.' I said: 'Where are they?' Said he: 'They are gone on in the direction of De Kalb.' Said I: 'Hezzy, you go by and tell Joe and Tom and April to get their guns and come up town just as quick as they can.'"

Q. Who were they?

A. They were colored men living on my place.

It will be observed that at this very time Chisolm was the sheriff of Kemper County, and we have him here arming four negroes who were living on his place, and pursuing a squad of strangers for the purpose, evidently, of creating a disturbance.

But the climax of this story yet remains to be told.

Q. Were these men mounted?

A. They were all on horseback. They halted at Gully's store, and got a gallon of whiskey, and then left town. I got up a crowd of fifteen men, white and colored, and followed them to the Alabama line—to Painville, in Kemper County.

Q. Was that over the line?

A. Yes, sir. I followed them over the line and waked up a grocery man, as I supposed they would stop there to get a drink.

Q. When did you get to Painville?

A. About an hour before day, Sunday morning.

Q. Did you overtake them?

A. I did not see one of them. I stopped where they got dinner, and saw where they had killed a great many chickens and dogs, and one thing and another in the road.

This invasion of the State of Alabama by the sheriff of Kemper County, Mississippi, with an armed posse of negroes and white radicals was, perhaps, without parallel in the American States, and could only spring from a state of affairs whose counterpart would be sought in vain on this continent, save in the lawless provinces of Mexico. This expedition was no doubt intended to spite and intimidate the friends and relatives of young Dawson, who resided in that part of Alabama, and who, as has been said, manifested great indignation at the barbarity and impunity with which the murder of that unfortunate man had been attended. Some of these visited Kemper County immediately after that occurrence, and made every effort in

The open aid which Chisolm afforded his friend Gilmer in this matter, and his strenuous exercise of his influence as sheriff and partisan leader of the county, to shield him from the strokes of justice, had very much enraged the friends of Dawson against him. They well knew that it was his influence that prevented an indictment or even a committal of Gilmer and Davis for this crime.

It was in consequence of this that some severe articles appeared in the *Mercury* (a newspaper published at Meridian), written by Judge Dillard, an uncle of Dawson, charging him with defeating the ends of public justice, to which very acrimonious and insulting replies were written and published by Chisolm.

This correspondence resulted in a personal altercation in the streets of Meridian, in which Chisolm shot Dillard, under the following circumstances. It seems that neither had ever seen the other before, and by accident they met that day. Without deeming it necessary to set forth the full particulars of this circumstance, which is of no general importance, save so far as it elucidates the character of Chisolm, and to show that the account given of it by his fulsome biographer, Wells, is utterly false. For this purpose I will rely upon the reader being satisfied with Chisolm's own sworn statement in regard to it. He says (Boutwell report, page 772): 'I was returning from Jackson, and stopped over at Meridian on business, and me and Dillard met in Judge Ham's office, who knew the bitter correspondence that had passed between us, and knew our feelings toward each other. I did not know Dillard myself at all; didn't know the man; never had seen him before that morning; and a big man came in, and they all seemed to be greatly excited, and I was dumbfounded myself. Judge Ham said, 'Judge Chisolm, walk into Judge Fewel's office, and let us talk this matter over,' and when I got in there, he said, 'That is Dillard.' Says I, 'Hell! is that Dillard?' and I started to walk out, and he says, 'Come back into the office; Judge Dillard is a very bad man; he is a desperate man, and he is drunk to-day, and I would advise you now to try to avoid meeting him at all, if you can.' Says I, 'Fewel, this is one of the days I don't feel like fighting at all; I ain't got any fight in me to-day.' He said, 'I don't think you do want a difficulty with anybody.' Says I, 'I don't.' In passing along the street, I went into the People's Savings Bank, to make some deposit of money, and to take the receipts of the cashier, and me and him was talking, and he asked me where I was going, and I told him I was going down to Judge Love's; I had promised to pay some money for a man in that county, and I walked down the street, and I saw Love and the man Dillard about twenty steps before me. I saw that there was nothing for me to do but to walk right on, and I went on and spoke to Judge Love, and shook hands with him, and he says, 'Allow me to introduce you to Judge Dillard; I remarked that we didn't talk, and Dillard then commenced abusing me with his pistol in his hand, and mine was not out; my hands were loose. I stayed there and took it until I got a chance to cross the street, and then I fixed myself and came back, and we met on half way ground, and I shot him. I mean by 'fixing myself' to have my pistol like his was."

This description of the shooting of Dillard not only shows the character of Chisolm, but gives the lie to the representation made of it by J. M. Wells. If that individual desired the truth, why did he not refer to this sworn description of Chisolm himself? But the features of the narrative did not suit the purposes of this slanderer, and so he preferred drawing upon his own imagination for a justification of his hero—which that hero himself did not attempt, or perhaps even desire. As a matter of course, Chisolm stated this matter to the senatorial committee in a manner most favorable to himself. From whom did Wells obtain his version of the affair? for it is entirely different from the representation of it which Chisolm made under oath. It is certain that the sworn words of the dead man contradict his vicarious biographer in this, as well as in many other instances, which have already been, or will be, noticed in this work.

For this attempt on the life of Dillard, Chisolm was placed under recognizance for his appearance, and at the circuit court was indicted and brought to trial at the second term, before Wm. M. Hancock, a radical and partisan friend of Chisolm. Therefore, it will not be a matter of surprise, from what we have already seen of the rulings of this class of judges, and the prejudices of negro juries, that he was acquitted.

It may be observed, however, that Dillard had the magnanimity to forbear the exercise of any influence in the prosecution.

This circumstance formed another ground for Chisolm to base his apprehensions of danger from the dreaded Alabamians. Judge Dillard was a prominent citizen of the adjoining County of Sumter, in that State, and was, as has been before observed, an uncle of Hal Dawson. The conscious guilt in the killing of this man had, as we have seen, caused both Chisolm and Gilmer to entertain lively suspicions of all Alabamians. And these suspicions were intensified by the circumstance of the shooting of Dillard. Henceforth the grim spectre of an Alabamian seems to have forever haunted their minds, and formed a favorite analogy for the constant association of the name of John W. Gully. So apt was Chisolm in this respect, that in his examination before the ku-klux investigating committee, the fact was noticed and observed by Mr. Blair, in the following colloquy with Chisolm:

Q. Who is this man Gully?

A. He is a great big Southern bully.

Q. You have had some quarrel with him, have you not?

A. Oh, yes, sir; certainly I have.

Q. I thought so, from the way you brought him in on all occasions. What have you quarrelled about?

A. Well, he is regarded as the leader of the crowd that comes to my town. Mr. Taliaferro told me that he was the president of the shebang—the high priest of the concern in my county.

Q. Is that what you and he quarrelled about particularly?

A. I never knew anything else for us to quarrel about.

Q. Was it not about some matters of a note, or a forgery matter?

A. No, sir; that had nothing to do with it; we were quarrelling before that came up; we had had one or two rows before that thing ever came up.

Q. That only made it worse?

A. I suppose so, but I do not know that it did; it did not amount to anything that I know of. There never has been the scratch of a pen against me in the county, if that is what you want to get at, and there has been everything, from rape down, against him.

Q. What was this allegation that he made about you?

A. He made a charge against me there, after we had split, that I was trying to fix up, to get some government cotton.

Q. From whom?

A. From the government.

Q. How did he say you were trying to do that?

A. He said that the man who was on the affidavit never made the affidavit. He never said that, however, until after the man died, you understand.

Q. Was that all he said?

A. The God of Israel only knows what he said. I do not know anything about that. That is what I heard him say. I know the courts never bothered me about it. There is nothing on God's green earth against me in the courts or anywhere else, that I know of, except what Gully says.

Q. I thought you and he were somewhat acrimonious?

A. Yes; that did not start the thing at all; we were out before that, and he thought he would take that start of me to break me down.

Q. Generally, he is a pretty bad man, is he not?

A. Well, I think the people think so, both Democrats and Republicans; that is my opinion about that. I think they regard him as a very bad man. He has some money yet, because he does not pay his debts, and lives in a palatial house, and all his property is in the name of his son.

I suppose that is very easy to do in this country; but I only refer to him (there are other men there besides him) is the head centre of the concern. That is why I referred to him; not because I care anything more about him than I do about any other little man in the county, because he is a very small man here; I only refer to him because other men told me that he is the head centre of the concern there.

It may be observed here that John W. Gully, at this time, was the recognized leader of the Democratic party of the county. Ardent, enthusiastic, bold and outspoken by nature, he labored with untiring zeal in the interest of his party, and was the trusted leader and representative of the intelligence and property interest of the county, while Chisolm occupied a like position in the radical party, and that their respective spheres should have engendered unfriendly feeling between them is not at all wonderful. Chisolm had always considered Gully, as he calls it, the *head centre* of the Democracy of the county, and his most powerful opponent. To get rid of him, or to destroy his influence, had from the first been his most ardent aim. He had reported him to the military authorities as a ku-klux, and that having failed, he was charged with the crime to which he alludes in his testimony. For this he was arrested and carried before a military tribunal. The woman who was alleged to be the victim of this crime went before the clerk of the court, and made an affidavit that it was false. Yet Chisolm and his clan were not to be baffled in their purpose. She was carried to the military camp and there coaxed and induced to retract her oath of denial. Her former affidavit was considered a nullity, and full force and effect was given to her subsequent and forced accusation. Yet Gully succeeded not only in tracing the original charge to its malicious source, but proved by incontrovertible testimony the impossibility of the act at the time alleged. So clear was his proof of innocence, and so plainly was it the work of malice, that he was again triumphantly and honorably acquitted, and thus once more escaped the meshes of his inveterate foes. But if Gully was thus fortunate in refuting the charge of illicit love, it was not the case with Chisolm. It is a notorious fact in De Kalb and in Kemper County that he dressed a negro woman and quartered her in one room of his law office, and on one occasion, it is said, Mrs. Chisolm repaired to this room, pistol in hand, and was only prevented by her husband from killing her dusky rival and quenching in blood his illicit flame.

During the year 1874, an act was passed by the legislature of Mississippi, requiring the county boards of supervisors to summon before them all delinquent taxpayers of their respective counties, to show cause why they had not paid their taxes, and to suffer such pains and penalties as might be imposed upon them for their delinquency. Under that law Mrs. Hull, a widow lady, and sister to John W. Gully, was summoned as a delinquent, although her brother had promptly paid her taxes, for which he held the receipt of the sheriff, W. W. Chisolm. On the day appointed for the appearance of Mrs. Hull before the board of supervisors, Gully presented himself with the receipt, and upon his remarking the fact that he had it, Chisolm became furious, and there, in the court room, and in the presence of the board, began to indulge in the most profane and insulting language, directed to Gully. Upon this, Gully observed to the board that he thought it hard that he could not appear before them to attend to business without being insulted by the sheriff. At this Chisolm immediately retired to his office, which was an adjoining room, and soon reappeared with his pistol in his hand. Gully simply called the attention of the board to this, when the president told him that he could retire, and that they would send for him when needed. When the case was reached, the clerk of the board was ordered to notify Gully, upon which Chisolm, with an oath, said that he himself would summon him, and at once proceeded to Gully's store, and on his notification to Gully, which he made in a very imperious manner, the latter remarked that he had already insulted him about this matter, as he had done on almost every occasion that he visited the court house on business, and that it must not be repeated. Chisolm then went to his house, which was but a short distance away, and got his double barrel gun, came back, fired it off, and reloaded it, then placing it against and behind the corner of the next house to Gully's store, promenaded for some time back and forth in front of the store. In the meantime, he had summoned his clan, several of whom seized their guns and repaired to the court house. Gully, well knowing their designs, took every precaution to avoid the difficulty, and, quietly walking over and presenting the receipt, returned to his store. This circumstance was witnessed by many of the most reliable citizens, who were satisfied that Chisolm was then seeking an opportunity to kill, or have Gully killed, as his conduct was otherwise inexplicable.

During this same year, the legislature passed an act imposing a privilege tax upon all merchants, bankers, lawyers, keepers of livery stables, and all transient venders, and others. This tax ranged from two to five hundred dollars per capita, and was collected by Chisolm, as sheriff and tax collector for the year 1870. Yet, in the report of the State auditor for that year, the amount of the revenue from this tax is summed and expressed for every county in Mississippi, except Kemper, in reference to which the auditor tersely adds, "No privilege tax collected in Kemper." Yet there is, perhaps, not a single person in the county, belonging to one of the classes designated as subject to this tax, but would on oath declare that he paid it to Chisolm, or his deputy, and for which many still have his receipt.

These facts are corroborated by a radical who was at that time one of the officers of the county, and who stated to the writer that he had a personal altercation with Chisolm for remonstrating with him about his conduct in this respect. But a sufficiency of these disgusting circumstances have been enumerated to serve the purpose for which they are adduced, namely, to depict the true character of the man, and with an expression of disdain, and a feeling of relief, the writer dismisses the subject.

It now becomes necessary, in order of time, to advert to an incident which, no doubt, had its origin, like many other crimes committed in the county about this time, in the inspiration drawn from the immunity afforded by the radical authorities. Of this circumstance, the carpet bag biographer, Wells, has manufactured quite a supply of food for his mendacity. To again show his aptitude and proficiency in this respect, it will be necessary to quote his statement. He says: " In the month of October, 1874, some one, in the night time, entered the room of a daughter of George Calvert, who lives in the southwest beat of Kemper County. The young lady awoke in great alarm, and just in time, as she believed, to see some one, whom she did not recognize, run through the doorway and escape before the family were aroused.

"Suspicion of this grave offence centred upon one of two negroes living on the place, but no evidence whatever, and no circumstance tending to strengthen this suspicion, was ever obtained, farther than, the boy was not found at home that night. His own explanation of his absence was that he had been out, as he had often done before, to witness a fox hunt in which some gentlemen were engaged not far away. Notwithstanding this, he was taken into custody, without process of warrant, or any legal arrest, and carried to De Kalb, when the deputy sheriff, Charlie Rosenbaum, very properly refused to take the prisoner, save only in the manner and form prescribed by law."

After a careful examination of the facts, and from his knowledge of them, obtained from the officers and eye witnesses of the proceedings in this case, the writer is prepared to say, that there is not one iota of truth in the above account. The young lady fully recognized her assailant, whose name was Perry Greenlea, and the negro was duly arrested and tried before a justice of the peace of the county. The evidence of guilt was positive, and he was found guilty, and was sent under a regular and lawful *mittimus* to the sheriff of the county. The deputy sheriff, although a radical, did not refuse to receive the prisoner upon any such grounds as those alleged, but he was returned to the custody of the justice and his constable, for the reason that the jail of the county had become so decayed that it was totally unsafe as a prison, and he was refused by the sheriff or his deputy with a request that he be sent to the jail of an adjoining county, as provided for in such cases by the statutes of the State. When this action of the sheriff was known, and the negro brought back to the neighborhood, a crowd of both black and white gathered, and took the negro from the hands of the constable and hung him, just as they would have done under similar circumstances in perhaps any other county and neighborhood. In consequence of this visitation of justice, long a rare thing in any form under radical rule in the county, the negroes became greatly enraged, and their movements and sulky deportment showed but too plainly that they had something serious in view. Finally, a negro, named Wash. Smith, informed Mr. Harbour, a gentleman residing in the neighborhood, that, headed by a negro school teacher, named Brown, they were endeavoring to get up an insurrection, for the avowed purpose of killing all the whites, and that they were making violent threats of wreaking summary vengeance upon the perpetrators of the hanging of Greenlea. On learning this, Captain J. L. Spinks, who was then a justice of the peace, and now the popular representative of Kemper County in the legislature of the State, visited the negro who gave this information, for the purpose of interviewing him more closely concerning it. The negro seemed very much alarmed, and proposed to make an affidavit before the justice in regard to the truth of his statements, which he did. He stated that the plan was for the negroes to assemble with arms and proceed to the neighborhood of the hanging, carrying with them the negro coroner, who was also a waiting boy of Chisolm, under the pretence of holding an inquisition, and that a note written by Brown had been sent among the negroes apprising them of the movement. He charged four negroes in the neighborhood with being the instigators and leaders of the scheme. These were immediately arrested, and

Moses Griffin, one of the four accused, confessed the conspiracy. They were brought to trial before the justice and two of them were convicted. Griffin, having turned State's evidence, was released, and was simply placed under bonds to keep the peace.

The news of the information of Smith, and the confession of Griffin had, in the meantime, spread through the county, and even into the counties adjacent, and the minds of men being prepared by experience for the reception of such reports, their fears were aroused to the highest degree, so that on the day of the trial of these negroes, quite a large crowd of citizens had gathered there from the surrounding country. Prior to this, however, as Chisolm was the high priest of the radical party, and exercised full control over the county, a correspondence had been entered into with him in regard to the matter, for the purpose of securing his co-operation in the interest of peace. To this end, Mr. A. P. Davis was sent to him as the bearer of the expression of the wishes of the people, upon which Chisolm promptly wrote and sent a note by Davis to one of the leading negroes, ordering him to desist from his hostile demonstrations. But on the assembling of the citizens at the trial, and when the whole truth was laid open by the testimony, the matter was deemed to be of so serious a nature, that it was thought best to come to some more definite understanding with Chisolm, in order to allay the fears of the people, and, if possible, to obtain some satisfactory guarantee against any future attempts of this character, and, he being the sheriff and peace officer of the county, as well as the recognized leader of the negroes, it was considered important that he should visit the neighborhood, as his presence would, it was thought, have a soothing and assuring effect. In pursuance of this, they now dispatched two gentlemen of the neighborhood, Archy McMahon and J. E. Driver, to invite Chisolm to come there. He, with some excuse, declined going, but gave these men every assurance that he would use his influence in the interest of peace. Upon the return of these envoys, at the request of the citizens generally, the following note was written and sent to Chisolm. Two of the signers of this letter were justices of the peace, and the other a member of the county board of supervisors. The note and its purport speaks for itself; and it may be observed, that the writer is informed by one of its authors that its having been written on a grange letter head was purely accidental, and that neither its import or inditement had any connection or relation whatever with that association.

"MOUNT PLEASANT GRANGE,
No. 230
"J. R. DAVIS, Master.   J. L. SPINKS, Sec.
"MOSCOW, MISS., *October* 1, 1874.
"JUDGE W. W. CHISOLM, DE KALB, MISS.

"DEAR SIR: We have been requested, by at least some two hundred persons, now assembled at J. L. Spinks', Esq., to inform you that we are proud of the conversation you had with Archy McMahon and A. P. Davis in regard to the excitement now in our beat about the negroes rising in arms against the whites. We have additional evidence to substantiate our fears. We have arrested several negroes, and the proof is positive against them. We do not intend to do anything in violation of the law or anything without reflection. We intend to defend ourselves, if the negroes come upon us as they threaten to do. We insist on your immediate presence at J. L. Spinks', Esq., to-day, just as soon as you can possibly come. We assure you that you will be treated as a gentleman, and hope that you will not fail to come.

"Respectfully, your friends,
ADAM CALVERT,
J. L. SPINKS,
JOHN R. DAVIS."

Of this innocent and commendable proceeding of some of the best citizens of the county, the carpet bagger, Wells, indulges in the following dissertation, which, in view of the facts, is as ludicrous as it is contemptible. He says: "It was believed by the leaders of this affair, that an opportunity was now presented for carrying out a long cherished desire—that of murdering Judge Chisolm, and making it appear as the voluntary act of the whole community." * * "The admonition of friends saved Judge Chisolm's life on this occasion, as that which follows will clearly prove: David Calvert, a brother of Adam Calvert, who married a sister of Judge Chisolm, afterward told his wife's family that he was cognizant of the note being carried to his brother in law on the occasion of the 'negro hanging' near the house of Justice Spinks; that he knew the object for which it was delivered, and to thwart the purpose of the men who sent it, and prevent the shedding of innocent blood, he himself despatched a man with a message to warn Judge Chisolm of the danger which awaited his arrival at the scene of the riot. With no further evidence than the statement of an individual to prove a conspiracy like this, there might be found room for questioning its existence, but, fortunately, whatever evidence may be needed to dispel every doubt in the matter is at hand, and will be found in the letter which follows:

"RIO, MISSISSIPPI, *September——.*

"JUDGE W. W. CHISOLM.

"SIR: I believe there is a plan on foot to assassinate you. This belief is founded upon an assertion that I heard one William Pearse make, in the presence of four respectable ladies. He said that you would be taken out of De Kalb before next Sunday night, and meet with the same fate that the negro did who was hung on last Saturday, near here. Other remarks, similar to this, have been repeated to me by your friends, which I will not take time to mention now. There was an armed force of from fifty to one hundred men met at the grave of the hanged negro, on Monday, to prevent the holding of an inquest. Your friends in this neighborhood think you would do well to be on your guard. My light is dim, and I don't see well at night. I will close by saying that I hope you will be on your guard. The hanging of the negro was an outrage of the blackest character.

"Your friend, as ever,
S. S. WINDHAM."

"P. S.—The excitement in the neighborhood is great."

"The above," says Wells, "was written and sent to Judge Chisolm by a special messenger. Mr. Windham, its author, was an honest and kind hearted man, although a Democrat, and a brother-in-law of Adam Calvert. His opportunities for knowing the facts were the very best, and his statement in writing over his own signature will hardly be doubted. The fact that he is now dead, and out of the way of all harm, accounts for his name being given here."

Now let us for a moment notice the contradictions and falsehoods that glare upon the very face of this statement. In the first place, Wells has already been quoted as alleging that the assault upon this lady, and the hanging of the negro, Perry Greenlea, took place in the month of October, 1874; yet it will be observed that the reported warning was dated September.—(Wells, Chisolm massacre, pages 102 and 107.) Again, he says: "The leaders of this affray" (meaning, of course, the two justices and the supervisor who extended the invitation to Chisolm to come to the neighborhood) "sought to murder Chisolm and make it appear that it was the work of the whole community;" and yet he makes his man, Windham, say that there were a hundred men there. Again, Wells, after stating a fact purported to be alleged by one David Calvert, suddenly admits that "there might be found room for doubting its existence," and in his preparation for the introduction of the letter, he premises its assured truthfulness and ponderous weight with such vehemence that the reader is doubtlessly surprised that Windham should confess, in the second sentence, that his story was "founded upon" what he heard one Pearse say. And Wells closes his comments upon this letter with the magnanimous peroration, that the fact that this man Windham was dead, and beyond the reach of harm, accounted for his name being given. Perhaps it did not occur to him in what terrible jeopardy he had left David Calvert, the brother-in-law of Chisolm, who was not dead, whose family secrets and confidential communications he had so ruthlessly divulged; but it seems, unfortunately, that Wells cannot make his blanket cover all his bed—when he pulls it to one side he exposes another. It is remarkably strange that Chisolm, in his two examinations at Washington, before the congressional committees, in which he took so much pains to recount and picture every semblance of spite or threats against him, should have been so perfectly silent in regard to this terrible conspiracy. Perhaps it can be accounted for on the ground that John W. Gully had no connection with it.

As to this man, Windham, for whose veracity Wells so gushingly vouches, it is well known in Kemper County that he was a disreputable radical—who went about officiating as chairman of negro night meetings, and was expelled from the masonic lodge for defrauding it. But the date of this letter being a month anterior to the events to which its contents relate, engenders grave suspicion that it was either a forgery, or was written subsequently, for a purpose foreign to its import. But I will not follow Wells any further in this matter. I will leave him to the contemplation of the reader, while he branches off into his usual encomium upon the merits of the unfortunate Miss Chisolm, which he almost invariably does after every flight of invective and spasm of ku-klux delineation. It is a great pity that the task of preserving the memory of this young lady has not fallen into the hands of one with more discretion and sense of propriety than to make it a hobby to pass from one slander to another, and to so mingle it with political events as to leave it in doubt as to which was the more bitter partisan, she or her father. The writer is prepared to give her a more amiable character, and to treat her memory with a more delicate consideration than to constantly use it as an interjacent theme between murders and assassinations, with which she had not the slightest connection. The memory of pure and virtuous Southern women is not accustomed to such treatment, and the conspicuous *rôle* assigned her by Wells is no doubt a prominent feature of his slanders.

CHAPTER IX.

At the beginning of the year 1875, John W. Gully and W. W. Chisolm were, as has been stated, the chairmen of the county executive committees of their respective parties. The Republican ticket for the canvass of that year, in Kemper County, was composed of the following names:

For the State Senate	JOHN P. GILMER.
For Representative ...	MOSES G. HALFORD.
County Assessor	MOSES MCDADE.
County Treasurer . .	HEZZY JACK (colored).

The harmony of the canvass, on the part of the radicals, was disrupted early in the campaign, in consequence of the nomination of the negro, Jack. H. A. Hopper, the then treasurer of the county, desired re-election, and upon his defeat before the convention, publicly charged, in a speech, that Hezzy's candidacy against him had been corruptly procured, to which Hezzy promptly gave the lie. This caused a flourish of pistols among the parties and their friends at the time; which, however, resulted in nothing serious; but threats of revenge were continued to be made by Hopper, which caused Hezzy to be on his guard, and to go constantly armed until a short time afterward, when he was engaged in conversation with some gentlemen in the court house yard. Hopper came along, and with his hand on his pistol, attempted to seize hold of Hezzy, and fired two shots at him without effect. At this Hezzy leaped back, then drew his pistol, and fired two shots at Hopper, one of which took effect in his face. Hezzy then ran away, and the affair ended. They were both indicted for assault with intent to kill, and tried, and both were acquitted

This negro, Hezzy Jack, had long been, and was at the time, a waitman of Chisolm, and was completely under his influence. He was, otherwise, by no means a bad negro, and would have been more acceptable, without this influence, to the white people than any one on the ticket.

It was he who informed J. W. Gully of the threats that Ben Rush had made against him, and warned him of his danger.

This difficulty had the effect of impairing the influence of the Chisolm clan over the negroes, and rendering the minds of the latter more accessible to the overtures of the Democrats, and was worth more to them than all the intimidation that existed even in the imagination of Wells and his class.

The state of affairs in Kemper County at this period is truly beyond the conception of those not familiar with it. The same condition of general corruption, which has been described as prevailing throughout the State under radical rule, existed with multiplied aggravation in Kemper County. The radical government had here become intensely unpopular, and had engendered personal feuds and bitter political and race animosities. The negroes had a voting majority of about three hundred in the county. They were entirely under the control of Chisolm and his clan, and voted solidly on the radical side, while the white people were as solidly Democratic, with the exception of the Chisolm clique. This small clique controlled the entire machinery of the county. It numbered among its members all the county officers, the judges and registrars of election, except one registrar at each precinct, and through this combination Chisolm ruled the county as despotically as a satrap of Persia.

He had ruled the county as its sheriff for seven years preceding the election of 1875, while the other offices were filled by the men whom he told the negroes to nominate. It was too much power to be possessed by any one man be he ever so just.

As sheriff, he had the selection of petit jurors, and a board of supervisors, chosen at his dictation, selected the grand jurors, and he sent whomsoever he wished to the legislature of the State, and filled all the offices of the county with his personal friends. Indeed, it may be said that the very life of every man, woman and child in the County of Kemper hung upon the smack of his finger, so great was his influence over the negroes and his white adherents.

The Republican candidate for representative, Moses G. Halford, was a man of but little force of character, and a fit subject to become the tool of Chisolm. For this reason he was placed upon the ticket. McDade, the candidate for county assessor, was of a similar character, and Chisolm had his name placed on the radical ticket for a like reason, for otherwise it is impossible to perceive what merit or quality either of these individuals possessed to entitle them to promotion, even in the radical ranks.

The candidate for county treasurer, Hezzy Jack, was a negro, totally ignorant and illiterate, who was unfamiliar with a figure in arithmetic or with a letter in the alphabet. Surely not a very suitable person to conduct the financial affairs of a county! but the more ignorant and incompetent these officers, the more absolute would be the rule of Chisolm.

During the seven years of radical rule, the indebtedness of the county had been increased to an extent bordering on bankruptcy. It was said to be the most indebted county in the State, and yet the rate of taxation was nearly forty dollars on the one thousand, while the property was arbitrarily assessed at an excessive value, and a debt of twenty-seven thousand dollars was contracted for the employment of teachers; for the greater number of log cabins used for school purposes were erected by private enterprise and contributions.

So burdensome were the taxes, and so utterly impossible was it for the people in their extreme poverty to meet them, that more than one hundred thousand acres of land were seized by the State for taxes, as no purchasers could be found, even at the profitable percentage guaranteed to them should the lands be redeemed. During all this time the poverty stricken people beheld Chisolm and his friends growing rich. It is said that when he entered the office of sheriff he was too poor to purchase a horse, and when he left it he was worth fifty thousand dollars; yet he was an extravagant man, but he possessed at least one good quality—the quality of liberality. He would rob the county without compunction and lend money to his personal and political friends without the least prospect of regaining it.

He is also said to have been liberal in his contributions to the churches and other eleemosynary objects. But this liberality evidently proceeded more from a spirit of vanity than from the promptings of any virtuous sentiment, for he was apparently utterly destitute of religion and of any refined moral sentiment. He was coarse, vulgar and profane in the extreme, which rendered him truly disgusting to all gentlemen of refinement.

As an instance of this, United States Senator Bayard, who was one of the senatorial investigating committee, in a letter to the writer says: "I send you Chisolm's testimony, which will show him to have been a violent and disorderly man. I remember his personal appearance, his production of his pistol in the committee room, and the general impression he made upon me of being an outlaw; so that when I heard of his shocking death I was not much astonished, although I could not but be horrified with its details."

Here we have a true impression of Chisolm's character, made upon one who never saw or heard of him before, but whose tutored observation and knowledge of human nature enabled him to form at once a correct opinion of his character. No doubt the other grave senators, who composed that committee, were no less disgusted than Senator Bayard, and with the same candor, would express themselves in a similar manner.

Chisolm took especial delight, on all occasions, in flaunting his ill acquired prosperity in the face of the people whose losses furnished his ill gotten gains, while any attempt on the part of the people to investigate and expose the financial condition of the county was met by insult and even danger to life. To such an extent was this the case, that many of the best citizens of the county refrained from visiting the court house, unless they were compelled to do so on business.

To throw off this intolerable yoke, became now the one ruling passion of the people, and they determined to make one supreme effort, and to employ every legitimate means to this end, while the radical leaders were as equally determined to maintain themselves in power at all hazards.

Under these circumstances the campaign of 1875 was inaugurated, and it was conducted with all the vehemence and vigor of desperation. The radicals sought in every way to stop the ears of the negroes against the arguments of the Democratic speakers, and to prevent them from listening to their speeches. For this purpose every method of inflaming their minds and kindling the prejudices of race was resorted to; every old cry, by which the party had heretofore been so successful, was raised with lusty voice. They predicted to them the utter ruin of their race if the Democracy should come into power; invoked all the memories of the past, and painted in gloomy colors the return to slavery as an inevitable consequence of Democratic success. From long habitual political associations with the negroes, they well understood their fears, were perfectly acquainted with their weaknesses, and knew well how to take advantage of their ignorance. Subsidiary to this, the party whip was raised over them with keen lash, social ostracism for party defection was promoted and encouraged among them, excommunication from the church was urged to be enforced, and even personal violence incited against all who should vote the Democratic ticket. Yet, notwithstanding all these potent influences, there was, early in the canvass, a notable disposition on the part of many of the negroes to cut themselves loose from these men. This feeling was particularly enhanced by the failure to obtain Federal military presence, and to gratify their peculiar fondness for military parade and display.

This characteristic and disappointment was availed of by the Democrats, who procured drums and fifes and bands of music, with which they traversed the county, and which they freely employed at their meetings. Flags were thrown to the breeze and innocent displays invented. This did not fail of its purpose. The negroes were first attracted and then gradually began to lend a listening ear to the Democratic speakers. This having been accomplished, it was no longer difficult to make them understand the true situation and to comprehend the fact that their own and the interests of the white people were one and the same. This done, they flocked by hundreds to the Democratic standard. The county was thoroughly canvassed by the candidates of both parties, and many political meetings were held.

At these meetings the Democratic speakers would offer to divide time with the Republican, but this was almost invariably declined by the latter. The chief arguments used by the Democratic speakers to induce the negroes to change their political affiliations were the incompetency and corruption of the radical officials, the high and ruinous rate of taxation, and the general depression of all business, which kept them, as well as the white people, in extreme poverty.

They showed them what they might expect under a competent and honest administration of the affairs of the county, and this they promised should be the result of the success of the Democratic party. They also gave them to understand that there could never be any state of amity, good will and mutuality between the two races, which was so necessary to their mutual prosperity, so long as the negroes continued to foist such corrupt men in office. These arguments were not such as the radical candidates desired or were competent to meet; their hobbies were the old issues of race, and the designs of the whites upon the liberties and rights of the negroes. They appealed to their worst passions, and pointed at the great social gulf between the two races, which they endeavored to convince them to be the result of an invasion, or a withholding of their just rights.

Another argument was that they were indebted to the radical party for their freedom; that General Grant had fought for them, and was the great champion of their rights, and that it was his desire that all of them should vote the radical ticket; that all who did not so vote would be abandoned by him to the white people to be put back into slavery, or be treated in any way they might see proper.

These arguments, however ridiculous, were yet an improvement, as respected the credulity of the negro, upon the old *forty acres and a mule* doctrine, and the like, which were for a long time so effective. They had been so often deceived by these promises that they now no longer paid any attention to them, and the radical leaders found themselves at a loss to invent some new talisman to work upon their imaginations. Military support had failed them, and in their desperation they resorted to every possible device as a substitute. It had always been the custom heretofore for the negroes to march to the election precincts and up to the polls after the manner of soldiers, armed with clubs and sticks, some of them with old swords and pieces of scythe blades. In this way they would take possession of the polls, and the white men would be compelled to give way to them, and wait for them to get through before they could vote. This way of rushing them to the polls in a body and in military parade was resorted to by the radical leaders to prevent any of them from being approached by the white people for the purpose of influencing their votes; and in like manner they heretofore attended their political meetings, except that on these occasions many of them carried their shot guns in addition to their swords and staves.

The canvass of 1875 in Kemper County was conducted, on the part of the radical party, chiefly by Chisolm and Gilmer. They did the speaking. Chisolm, by his long continuation in the office of the shrievalty and his rapid accumulation of money, had managed to have quite a number of small farmers indebted to him, upon whose property he held trust deeds. These he promptly notified that they must either vote for him or come to a settlement, or the trust deeds would be enforced. By this means he compelled a few Democrats to either vote for him, or stay away from the polls, to which he triumphantly alludes in his testimony at Washington. As that testimony not only develops further his character, but gives an insight into the conduct of this campaign on the part of the radicals, it is here quoted.

Report of the senatorial committee, page 756.

Question by the chairman: The object of this committee is to ascertain how the canvass was conducted, especially with reference to whether there were any acts of intimidation; and this committee would like to have you state fully, in your own way, what occurred under your own observation in Kemper County.

A. The canvass in that county was, I thought, very warm, and there was a good deal of excitement attending my meetings. I don't know anything about the meetings of the opposite party, except what was in my own town. I attended one or two of those. The canvass opened in the county at Black Water, so far as the Republican party was concerned. I made an appointment to make a speech at Black Water, and Judge Bell, a candidate for the legislature, asked me to divide time with him. I told him I would, of course. There were some colored men came to me in a few days, and told me that I had better not go to Black Water; that they swore that I should not speak there. Old Billy Bailor, a prominent colored man, came to me and told me that if I went to Black Water I would not be apt to come back home; that the Key boys and the Hudnalls and the Hodges, and McClelland and D. V. McWhorton, down to Black Water, said that I should not make a speech there—such a speech as I had been accustomed to make. I saw Judge Bell a few days after that, and says I, "Judge, I don't want any trouble, you know. In the first place, I am not able to fight a regiment of men, and if there was going to be any speaking down there, I wanted just to take my own course in this thing. I am perfectly willing to divide time with you, but I don't want to go down there and have any trouble with these men." He said that he thought it was a mistake, and that he would try to control that thing. I got several of my friends, white Republicans, fifteen or twenty, all Southern men, and most of them Confederate soldiers, some of them the first men that ever left the county and went into the army, to go with me to Black Water. We met a large crowd of white men and some freedmen there, and Judge Bell made a speech, and I replied to him.

In my speech there were a good many questions asked me. I had been notified previously how a fight was to be started by questioning me. An old man, Dorset White, was to ask me some questions, and they thought I would fire up and say something very severe to him, and then they would open on me. When he asked me some questions I replied to him that Judge Bell and me were making the canvass, and that I didn't think I ought to be interrupted, and Judge Bell told him to stop. * * *

Q. By Mr. Bayard—Were the questions disrespectful or improper to be put?

A. Well, if I am not mistaken, one of the questions was to know why I hadn't had all the school warrants paid. That was a disrespectful question for a sensible man to ask me, from the fact that a sensible man would have known that I had nothing to do with the payment of school warrants. He knew very well that I could not answer it.

Q. Was there any question asked you that was derogatory to you to have answered?

A. I don't know that there was.

Q. State a few questions that he asked you.

A. Some of them were to know how it was that the Republican party taxed the people so; what they put such heavy taxes on the people for. Of course I was no legislator, and had nothing to do with it.

Q. Still, did you think that was an unreasonable question to be asked by people who were paying taxes?

A. No, sir; not specially.

At the same time Mr. Hudnall started to get up, and Captain Rush, who was captain of a company from my county, who was a particular friend of his, got hold of him and pulled him down; and Captain Rash afterward told me that he said he was going to get up and go for me. As soon as I got through my speech Bell rejoined for a quarter of an hour, and when I got up to reply to him they commenced asking me questions again. I was to have a ten minutes' rejoinder, and I didn't get through within the ten minutes. I told them that I had said as much as I cared to, I believed, and I called my crowd. I told them that I didn't propose to bandy words with them. I says, "I have got through with my speech, and I'm going to my buggy." And I, with six or eight of my friends, walked up to my buggy; but they didn't interfere with me at all. There was no interference, except they seemed to want to get up a general talk, and see what it would amount to. I learned from other parties that they had a good many guns down there in the bushes, but that I don't know anything about. After that I had no more discussions with them at all—no more joint discussions.

I made a canvass of the county. At nearly all of my meetings they would come, from five to ten, sometimes fifteen or twenty armed men, with double barrelled shot guns, rifles, and one thing or another, from different directions; and they would say to each other that maybe they might kill a buck that day, and they would take their guns along. I made my speeches, however.

I spoke at every point that I was to speak at in the county. At some places there were no colored men turned out. They told me that they had heard so much talk in the neighborhood that there would be some trouble that they were afraid. My speeches to the colored men all the time were that I thought there would be no trouble, but if there was to just let me, and what few white men there were along with me, and the white Democrats fight it out; that it should be a straight out white man's fight. I didn't want them to have anything to do with the fighting; that if there was any fighting to do, what few white men went with me would fight; that we didn't want them to have

Q. Was there any particular disturbance at any of your meetings?

A. There was not, except on the last day that I spoke at Scooba, on Saturday before the election on Monday. On that day, after I had left De Kalb, and was about a mile from town, I was stopped by a young man named Halford —I think they called him Julius, but I am not positive now; his father was a candidate for representative on the Republican ticket, and his name is Moses J. Halford. This young man, his son, met me and threw up his hand, and hollowed for me to halt; he rode up to me—and Mr. Hopper, I believe, was in the buggy with me; I am not positive as to that, but I know there was some one with me—he rode up and said his father had started him that night to meet me; that he had heard I was coming to Scooba, and that I never would get there; that I would be killed before I got there. I told him I hated to turn back after I had started, as I usually went where I started to go to. There were four or five men with me, and they rode up and asked what was the matter, and we consulted about the matter, and I asked them to ride ahead of the buggy. I asked the young man how they were going to kill me, and he said Mr. Poole, one of the men in the Democratic club near Scooba, said that they were to be hunting right on the road; that Poole came to his father's house at midnight, and said that they were going to be hunting that day on the road, and that they were going to kill me; that they were going to pretend to be deer hunting. He belonged to the Democratic club, but came and told Halford that night, so this young man told me.

I sent these men ahead of me, and I drove on down about six miles from Scooba, and Mr. James West, who belonged to the Democratic club, came walking, as I thought, sort o' out of the woods. I got out of my buggy and took my pistol in my hand. Says he, "Judge, what is the matter? are you going to shoot me?" I said, "No, sir, I have no intention of shooting you. I am a little excited though, Jim." Says he, "I came down here to see you, but, for

God's sake, don't let anybody know I have been here! But if you are determined to go to Scooba, you must stay there all night, and not come back to night." I said, "Jim, tell me the truth about this matter." He said, "I have told you enough now, I suppose, to get myself in trouble. I don't want you to say anything about this. I am your personal friend, and I am satisfied that almost all the people in the county are your personal friends." Then I told what Halford had told me, and he said that he thought that by having the men riding on before me that we would pass by all right; but if I would go on to Scooba, he told me, not to go back from there that night. I kept my horses geared up, and ready to go back, though I didn't intend to go back, but I held out that I was going.

The negroes told me that a crowd of men had gone off from Scooba with guns, in the direction of De Kalb, leaving that day about twelve o'clock. I don't know whether that was correct or not, but at Scooba there was considerable excitement that day, and there was a man from Clark County there; I think his name was Carter. I was introduced to him that morning, and I think he was drinking right smart. He told me that he was sorry that a Southern man with the brains, and the sense, and the general intelligence that I had, would be going against his country, and his kindred, and his friends; that he thought that it was bad enough for the damned infernal Northern Yankees to be trying to destroy the South without Southern men doing it. I told him that I was conscientious in all I did; that I thought after I got whipped that I was whipped, and that I believed the best policy for the Southern people was to do what the Constitution of the United States said— give every man an equal and a fair showing to exercise his rights freely and voluntarily; and consequently, I was a Republican; but I remarked to him, "The damned carpet baggers, I have no particular love for them," (What does Wells say to this?) "got no particular use for them," but there were no carpet baggers in my crowd; it was all Southern men, and my friends were nearly all of them gallant

Confederate soldiers, and I told him that I supposed that my family had as good a record, as far as the war was concerned, as he or any other man in Kemper County; while I didn't go myself, that they had made honorable soldiers, and filled honorable graves upon battle fields.

I made my speech that day under some excitement; there was a good deal of excitement.

I will state that Mr. Duke, another gentleman at Scooba, told me that the excitement was caused by some gentlemen coming from Jackson down there, who claimed to be United States marshals. I don't know as to that. I told Mr. Duke that I didn't know that they were United States marshals. I know one of them had been a United States marshal; but I didn't know whether he was now or not. I hadn't sent for him; they said that they came there with Senator Gilmer a night or two before that. I told him that I supposed that they had a right as citizens to be there. I went to see Mr. Woods—H. Woods, jr.,—a leading man and a very quiet man. I asked him if there could not be some arrangement made whereby there could be some assurance of a fair election.

Said I, "There is a great deal of excitement here to-day, and what is the cause?"

He said he didn't know; and he remarked that he supposed that those men coming over from Jackson caused some excitement.

Said I, "Hab, I want to make some arrangement, if I can, to have a fair election; there ain't no use talking about holding an election without you let us have an election."

He said that God knew in his heart that he wanted a fair election, and no trouble. He said one difficulty might be avoided if we would agree not to let twenty negroes vote that they knew to be under age; that perhaps that would quiet them, and he said he would go over and get Mr. Duke and Mr. Miller Jones, old citizens there, and bring them over to talk the thing over in his office. They came, and I agreed with Mr. Duke and Mr. Miller Jones that these men should not vote; that I would ask them as a special favor not to vote, if that would quiet the thing.

Mr. Duke said then that that would quiet them, provided we didn't interfere with the negroes, and make them vote the radical ticket.

I said, "Duke, by God, I am a free American citizen, and I have as much right here as you have! I have as much interest in the county as you have. I will make a proposition to you. I propose now to let all hands do their own voting, and for the white men of the county to have nothing to do with it. Just let them get their tickets and vote as they damn pleased."

He says, "They won't do that."

I says, "Well, when I meet my friends, I intend to talk to them, and try to get them to vote the Republican ticket, if any of them talk of voting the Democratic ticket."

He said that if we should interfere with them, and should attempt to do that, there would be a fuss on election day.

I said, "I don't know what will be the result, but I intend to do it."

I said, "I understand there is to be an army of Alabamians over there;" and they said that they didn't know anything about that, if there was.

I made my speech, though under strong excitement. I expect I made the bitterest speech that day that I made during the canvass; but I know that I didn't advise the negroes to anything except peace, because I told them all the time that they could not fight; there was no use talking about their fighting; if they had to fight to vote, by the Eternal, they could not vote! But in my speech that day I told them every one to go to the polls and not be bluffed off; that I thought perhaps they were playing a bluff game, and go and vote and go right off immediately. Dr. Gilmer made a speech that day. He was senator at that time from that district. He stated to them that he would be there to give them their tickets, and that they intended to have a fair election.

Notwithstanding all this, it is a well known fact that no sooner did these men discover that they had sure enough lost their hold upon the negroes, whose votes they did not despair of until the last moment, than they determined at all events to prevent the holding of an election.

It is somewhat remarkable that Wells did not refer, in his work, to this sworn description of these events by Chisolm himself. He quotes, at length, Gilmer's tale of his romantic dodgings through the piny woods in endeavoring to make his way from Scooba to De Kalb, on the eve of the election; but it is plain that the language of his hero, and the facts he divulged in his testimony, did not suit the purposes of this wily biographer.

A few days before the election, Gilmer went to Jackson and procured three desperadoes, and brought them with him to Scooba, representing them to be deputy United States marshals. These men were named Davis, Eskeroll and Jeff. D. Bell, who is now in the penitentiary of the State for murder. This man represented himself also as being a Democrat, but that he intended to carry the election for the radical party, or kill every man, woman and child about Scooba. He told the radicals publicly, in a speech on Saturday previous to the election, to carry the election at all hazards, and they, at the same time, threatened to arrest, in their assumed official capacity, all the leading Democrats. This conduct created considerable alarm and indignation, in the heat of which Colonel James H. Duke, a prominent citizen and Democrat, sent a note to De Kalb, requesting help from the citizens of that place and surrounding country, should these threats be attempted to be carried into effect. The people were very naturally astounded and dismayed at this new and strange feature of Federal interference, and which was threatened to be so harshly exercised, and being at a complete loss what to do in this humiliating dilemma, they telegraphed to General J. Z. George, at Jackson, who was the chairman of the Democratic State executive committee, to know what they should do. General George at once waited on the United States marshal, at Jackson, a Mr. Lake, and was informed by him that he knew nothing of the deputies, and that no such deputies had been appointed. General George immediately apprised the people of Scooba of this fact, whereupon there was great indignation on the part of the Democrats.

The following is the testimony of James H. Neville, Esq., who conducted the inquiries about the marshals: "On Saturday before the election, three men came from Jackson, Mississippi, and represented themselves as deputy United States marshals I paid no attention to it, but supposed that if they were deputy United States marshals, they had been sent there by authority of law, until I heard of some very violent speeches that they had been making, and language that they used, tending to excite the colored people and the white people, and, probably, bring about bloodshed. I then telegraphed to General George, chairman of the Democratic executive committee of the State of Mississippi, as follows:

"'Scooba, Miss., *October* 30, 1875.

"'General J. Z. George:

"'Gilmer reached this place on Saturday, with four United States deputy marshals; says he is going to make arrests for intimidation. Would you advise us to submit to an arrest? No intimidation has been used.

"'Respectfully,

J. H. NEVILLE.'"

"'Jackson, Miss., *October* 30, 1875.

"'J. H. Neville, Scooba:

"'No such deputies have been appointed, so says the United States marshal. J. Z. GEORGE.'"

In the meantime the three impostors, so soon as they became aware of the exposure, suddenly left the village, and were seen there no more. This strategy having failed of its purpose, it was now determined to prevent an election by concealing or destroying the registration books. These books, belonging to the Scooba precinct, had been sent by the chancery clerk, who is alone their legal custodian, to the registrars, but by some means Gilmer got possession of them and locked them up in his safe in his store. After the failure of his intimidation scheme he fled to the arms of his friend Chisolm, at De Kalb, whence, in accordance with some understanding with prominent Democrats, he sent the following note:

"DE KALB, MISS., *November* 1, 1875.

"T. H. ORR, Esq., Scooba, Miss.

"*Dear Sir:* I write you as one of the managers of the election for Scooba precinct. I have talked with gentlemen of the opposite side, and in whom I have confidence, and they tell me that they will write to their friends at Scooba, and assure me there will be protection; and I am satisfied that you will not be harmed in the discharge of your duties, and that every man will be permitted to vote what he chooses. This being the case, I can see no reason why the election cannot go on. You will find the registration books in the safe: either Wood or Chancey has the combination, and will deliver them to you or Spencer, or any of the officers entitled to receive them."

The men to whom he refers here were his partners, and Spencer was the clerk in his store. So we find here the registration books locked up in the private safe of an individual far away from their legal custodian, and that individual a candidate for a seat in the State senate. These books had been unlawfully turned over to the charge of Gilmer by the registrars, to be either altered, defaced, concealed or destroyed, as he might see proper, in order to carry or prevent the election; but for some reason he concluded, as will be seen from the preceding note, to permit the election to be held. In connection with this note, and showing the temper and wishes of the people, is the following note, written by the parties with whom Gilmer made the arrangement referred to in his letter, to some leading Democrats at Scooba:

"DE KALB, MISS., *November* 1, 1875.
'J. H. DUKE, JAMES H. NEVILLE, Esq., and W. H. HALSELL.

"*Dear Sirs:* We, the undersigned, have been acting as a conference committee here between the Republicans and our Democratic friends, and have, after some excitement, agreed and determined to have a fair and peaceable election, and have arranged to have a force of good and reliable men to insure peace and good order, and a full expression of the elective franchise; and we appeal to you as representative men of your beat, to have peace and good order to-morrow, and to give the managers all the moral, and, if needed, the physical force, necessary to protect all parties and keep peace. Mr. Gilmer will write to the managers and advise them to hold the election. We will have peace and quiet here and you must do the same.

"Respectfully yours,
JAMES WATTS,
E. FOX,   } *Committee.*"
A. G. ELLIS,

These letters were given in evidence and vouched by Mr. A. G. Ellis, in his examination before the Boutwell senatorial committee, at Washington, in June, 1876, page 1,790. These registration books contained the names of every qualified voter in the county, as none were qualified who had not registered, and they were the sole evidence of the right of franchise; hence, without them no legal election could be held, and it would have been an easy matter, by a little alteration or defacement, to have changed the vote of the county. The law provided for the most considerate care of these books; they were required to be in the possession of the chancery clerk, except when needed by the board of registration for the purpose of holding an election. They were then turned over to the registrars—the clerk taking their receipt for them, and after the determination of the result of any election they were required to be returned to the chancery clerk upon his receipt.

Notwithstanding this, these books, belonging to the Scooba beat, were lodged for an unknown length of time in the private safe of John P. Gilmer, who was at that time a candidate for office.

To ascertain the fate of those belonging to the De Kalb beat, let us return to the testimony of W. W. Chisolm, Boutwell report, page 760. He says: "I went home on Sunday morning; I suppose I got home about one or two o'clock. When I got home, the chancery clerk, Mr. Poole, and the circuit clerk, Mr. Rush, came up to my house and told me that they thought there was a right smart of excitement up town; that Welsh and Watts and Allen and John Gully were in town, and they seemed to be excited about something, and they were walking over the town, and going around the court house, and walking about a great deal, and they didn't know what it meant. I told them that I didn't suppose it meant anything particular. * * * I thought things looked very bad indeed, from everything I could hear from every part of the county, and the next morning I went down town, I suppose, at about half an hour by the sun; I went to mail some letters, and was met by Mr. Charles McCrary, and he asked if I was going to be at home that day; I told him that I was; he said he heard that I was going to make a speech that day. I said, 'I have not heard of it, Charley.' I said I supposed that everybody would be gone from home to the big Democratic barbecue out at Moscow. He said he didn't know about that. I went home and ate my breakfast, about seven or eight o'clock, I suppose. I saw a great many men in town. When I got back from breakfast I saw several men from a good distance in the county coming in town. I began to inquire what the devil was on foot. Did they think to-day was the election? Phil—P. H. Gully—came into town pretty soon with some of his sons and some of the young Halfords, bringing guns with them. I sent for Phil, and I asked him what in hell and damnation all these things meant, and he told me that it meant this: that Allen and Welsh and Watts had sent runners all over he county, and that the people were all armed and coming to De Kalb for the purpose of going on to Scooba, as he understood it, from a telegram that James H. Duke had sent up there. I told him that it was very strange indeed; that I could not imagine what the devil all this thing meant. I said, 'I see you are not going to permit us to hold a fair election;' he said he hoped it would be a fair election. * * * I got a note from a man named T. H. Orr, down there, stating that it would be impossible for an election to be held at Scooba; that the whole county was in arms, and that the negroes, he reckoned, would be run off. I sent for Mr. James H. Brittain, and some others, and told them: says I, 'Gentlemen, you can take the election.' That was about four o'clock Monday evening, I suppose. I am a little ahead of my story; I will go back a little. About two o'clock that day, Mr. Lee, the president of the board of registrars of that county, came in from the western part of that county, where he lives, and came over to the court house, and seemed to be considerably excited. He said, 'Judge, I am surprised to see you here.' I says, 'By God, I am here yet! but things don't look very well, Jack.' He says, 'What are you going to do?' I says, 'Let us try and hold the election, if we possibly can, some way or other; I don't know whether we will be able to have any election or not.' * * * Just as I got the note from this man at Scooba, stating what he thought about the election there, I went over and told him. Says I, 'Mr. Brittain, you all promised this morning that these men should leave town after you found out there was no trouble at Scooba. I have got a letter from there stating that the whole county is in arms at Scooba, and that there is a regiment of Alabama men over there.' Says I, 'You can take the election, anyhow, and run it just as you damned please!' Says I, 'Gentlemen, if this is an election, I am sure that I never knew what an election was before. Here I am with ten men, and here is three hundred or five hundred men in town, with five hundred guns, perhaps, and I have got a pistol.' Says I, 'Damn you, if any ten of you will be satisfied, I will fight any ten of you, if you will only let me have a fair election!' He says, 'We don't want to have a fight.' I says, 'I know that damned well! You don't want to fight, but you don't intend to let us hold an election.' He says, 'We are going to have a fair election; but the damned niggers have ruled this county just as long as we intend to let them.' Says I, 'God damned, if I ain't as white as any of you, anyhow!' He says, 'You run with a damned black crowd!' 'I says, 'Notwithstanding that, my character is as white as yours; and I am sure that I stand as fairly with the community as you do.'" * * *

It is indeed remarkable, in view of his antecedent testimony, that Chisolm nowhere mentions the name of John W. Gully in connection with these transactions, or, indeed, with the canvass. He seems for once to have escaped his memory.

In the meantime, Chisolm had procured the registration books from the chancery clerk or the manager of the election, and locked them up in the safe of the sheriff's office. On the evening before the election, A. J. Lee, the president of the board of registration, and the other Republican managers of election, being convinced that their party would be defeated the next day, left De Kalb in order to prevent the election. On being apprised of this, the leading citizens inquired of Chisolm about the registration books. He replied that he was not their custodian, that he did not know where they were, and "damned if he cared" where they were. There are, to-day, more than a dozen gentlemen in De Kalb who would state this upon their oaths. A. G. Ellis, Esq., a prominent young lawyer, a Democrat and Christian gentleman, was one of the committee of citizens appointed to wait upon Chisolm and to ascertain where these books were. He testified, in regard to the transaction before the Boutwell investigating committee, as follows:

Q. When did those Republican managers leave?

A. They went away that night. I don't know whether they went away before or after that. One of them, the president of the board, A. J. Lee, left before night. He brought his wife with him up there, and I don't know what she came there for; it was a most unusual thing. He came up there to hold the election. He lived some twenty miles away. He said his wife became frightened. It was through him that we found out where the registration books were. We went to Chisolm and asked him where the books were, and he very tauntingly said, "I am not the custodian of those books. I expect Mr. Lee can tell you where they are;" and referred us to Mr. Lee. Mr. Lee was gone, and we sent some runners after him. They followed and overtook him some three miles from town, on his way home, and he assured them that he did not have the books.

Q. As a matter of fact, did Chisolm say that he had the books, but he was not going to give them up without Lee's order?

A. No, sir; he did not say that. He said he did not have anything to do with the books, and that he did not know where they were, and yet they were, at that time, locked up in the sheriff's office in his safe. We then told him that we were going to have those books, if we had a difficulty about it—if we had to fight; that the election had been ordered. I was spokesman of the committee, and spoke very positively, and I am free to say that we were determined to hold that election, for they had run over us in the county. I had seen white men kicked out of the court house myself at the previous election, and we were determined to hold the election. We told them that we were going to have those books, and we were going to have a lawful election; he then gave his wife the key, and he went, in company with this committee, to the sheriff's office, and unlocked the door of the safe. We hesitated about taking them out, and stated that we had no business with those books, and we would not take them out; that Mr. Poole, the chancery clerk of the county, was the proper custodian of the books, and if she saw proper she could turn them over to him. She went to him and requested him to take out the books, which he did with his own hands, and took them into his office."

This statement of Mr. Ellis, who is now deceased, is fully corroborated by the statement made to the writer by the then chancery clerk, and other gentlemen now living in De Kalb, who, with Mr. Ellis, composed the committee to ascertain where the books were. Poole said that he did not know that the books were in Chisolm's safe, or how they got there.

The conduct of the radical managers, in leaving the polls on the eve of the election, rendered it, as was intended, impossible for the citizens of that beat to hold a lawful election. The only provision, under the then registration laws of the State, for a vacancy in the board of registrars of the county, was as follows:

Revised code, 1871, section 349—" Whenever any registrar shall resign his situation, he shall give notice thereof to the president of the commissioners of the county, who, if no prior regular meeting shall be had, when the vacancy can be filled, shall, in due and sufficient time for the regular notice of registration, call a special meeting of the board of commissioners to fill such vacancy of any registrars, and any vacancy arising from such a cause, or from death, removal from the county, or refusal to accept, or act on such appointment, or to discharge the duties under the same, it shall be filled in like manner, and every person so appointed shall proceed to take oath and discharge the duties herein required."

Yet, there being no other alternative, the remaining manager, on the morning of the election at De Kalb, proceeded to appoint two associates, and opened the polls. That the election in this beat, under such circumstances, was unlawful, in view of these provisions, will not be questioned; and had the radical administration maintained itself in the State, it would doubtless have been disregarded; but the election in this beat could not alter the overwhelming majority for the Democrats in the county, and the informality being occasioned by their own wrong, the radicals never raised the question of validity. But if the refusal of the managers to act, in this instance, impaired the legality of the election, it was not the case at Scooba, where the same effort was made; for in regard to precincts of election other than at the county seat, the following provision was made by the registration laws:

Revised code, 1871, section 369—"The registrars shall appoint, at their meeting at the county seat, prior to any election, three inspectors and two clerks for each supervisor's district, and place of voting in the county, excepting that at the county seat, said registrars, with their clerks, shall preside. And if, on the day of election, any of such appointed inspectors or clerks shall fail to appear, the remaining number may elect to fill the vacancy from the qualified voters who can justly and properly take the prescribed oath. And when not more than one of the inspectors appears, or there has been some failure in the appointment, the remaining inspector and clerk, with the approval of the qualified registered voters present at the time to open the polls, may make such appointment. And if neither of the inspectors appear, then such qualified electors may make such appointment, and in such case require of the appointees the prescribed oath before any officer qualified to administer the same."

Section 373. "Registration shall in all cases be *prima facie* evidence of the right to vote; and on the day of election no person shall be challenged at the polls in his right to vote, except for identity."

The radical leaders, Chisolm and Gilmer, were very well aware of these provisions and their import, and when they were forced to give up the books containing the evidence of registration, they were in hopes that the election would yet be defeated by the withdrawal of the registrars and inspectors.

This attempt to deprive the people of their franchise, and at a time, too, when they were making every effort to throw off the intolerable yoke under which they had so long groaned, and by the very men whom they recognized as the chief agents and authors of their troubles, caused intense excitement, and engendered the most bitter feelings throughout the county against Chisolm and Gilmer. This, together with the importation of the impostors as United States marshals, and their threats and incendiary speeches to the negroes, were well calculated and sufficient to arouse the indignation of any people not utterly lost to every sense of resentment for the most outrageous wrong that could be perpetrated upon them.

They saw the very men whom they were making every legal effort to dethrone, resorting with impunity to the most high handed violation of law, availing themselves of every imposition, and resorting to every subterfuge that villany could suggest, and that, too, under color of office, to drown their voice and thwart their effort, upon the success of which hung all their hopes for an honest government, one that would give them once more peace and happiness, and preserve to them the scanty remnant of their substance. Notwithstanding these aggravating circumstances, the people proceeded to the attainment of their object quietly, but with the utmost determination, and not a threat was made, or a finger raised, against the authors of those nefarious machinations.

Yet there was one other hope left to the radical leaders, which was to invalidate the election, if possible, upon the ground of intimidation and violation of the enforcement acts of Congress. To this end, after all their other manœuvres failed, they fled when no man pursued them, and retired to the forest, where they remained until the election was over, and even until several days after.

While all these various stratagems were being attempted, they had made preparations for a collision on the day of the election. Those negroes, generally the most ignorant and vicious, who still adhered to the radical cause, or rather who were yet subject to the influence of these men, were notified to appear at the polls with their arms; in obedience to which about fifty negroes brought their guns to Scooba, and, on finding a change in the state of affairs, on account of the absence of their white leaders, deposited them in the house of a negro situated in a dense forest across the railroad, opposite to and a short distance from the village. The white people ascertained, by some means, during the day, that they were there, and took possession of them. At this, some of the negroes manifested a riotous disposition, but, finally, returned to their homes without voting, which they declined to do, as they had been instructed by their leaders, who had also designed this to be another feature of their intimidation scheme. The negroes, after the election, came in and claimed these guns as their property, and they were promptly turned over to them.

The white people were not at all surprised at the presence of these guns. They had been taught from the beginning of the canvass to expect riotous demonstrations, if not serious collisions, on the day of the election; and while they met every circumstance coolly and determinedly, they were prepared for any emergency. Chisolm had openly and frequently, during the campaign, avowed that, to use his favorite expression, "they were going to wade through blood and hell to carry that election;" and, as Mr. A. G. Ellis, in his testimony before the Boutwell committee, at Aberdeen, observed, "The white people did not know whose blood he might want to wade through." These guns were said to have been deposited on Sunday preceding the election.

The radicals had appointed a political gathering at Scooba, on Monday, the day before the election. This gathering was intended, among other purposes, to give these pseudo United States marshals an opportunity to perform their operations, which was prevented by their timely detection and flight. Indeed, it appears that the presence of these outlaws was the sole cause of all the excitement at Scooba. Their threats, their violent expressions, inflammatory speeches to the negroes, and their impudent deportment gave credence to the reports that the negroes were coming in armed for the purpose of carrying the election or killing the white people, but on their departure everything again assumed a quiet attitude.

On the exposure of his fraud and the flight of his marshals, Gilmer, in order to fashion his part of the evidence of intimidation, fled, as has been before stated, and made his way, as he says with many narrow escapes, to his friend, Chisolm, at De Kalb. This romantic hegira forms the only description Wells gives of all these transactions. It was then that Chisolm, Gilmer, Hopper and Rosenbaum, after full consultation, gathered their tents, and, in the peaceful rays of the setting sun, with suitable viands for the rustic sojourn, repaired to the forest, where their contemplation of the situation and their concoction of future plans would be disturbed by no sound, save the mournful requiems of the tall pine tops that hid them from mortal eyes. But as no one pursued them, or seemed to remember them in their forest castle, after a few days they returned, to find that the storm had calmed into a gentle breeze.

CHAPTER X.

It is charged by Chisolm and Gilmer that there was a crowd of Alabamians at Scooba on the day of the election of 1875. That there were some gentlemen there from that State is beyond question, and as to the causes of their presence, there were no doubt two.

Kemper County is situated contiguous to the County of Sumter, Alabama. The line between them runs through a densely populated district of negro voters, and it had heretofore been a notorious fact that the registration books of each of these counties contained the names of many voters in the other, and that there were many negroes who were in the habit of voting in both counties.

To avoid this, some citizens of Alabama, who resided near the line, were invited over on the day of election by the citizens of Kemper, in order that they might identify those characters living on their side of the line, so that they might be successfully challenged and prevented from voting at Scooba. For this purpose, and none other, some of them came. But there were others there who were relatives of the murdered Dawson, and who, no doubt, sought an opportunity to take revenge upon Gilmer and Chisolm for that horrible deed. Be this as it may, it is certain that none of these men were there for the purpose of interfering with the election, or intimidating any of the voters. They were merely observers, with no sinister designs, and took no part whatever in the affairs of the day, inasmuch as their presence simply was calculated to accomplish the object of their visit, which was to identify any Alabama negro who might attempt to vote. After the temporary excitement, occasioned by the acts which have been described, this election was, by the uniform testimony of every good citizen, the most peaceable and quiet ever held in the county.

The negroes were heard to express themselves generally that they had long voted the Republican ticket, that it had done them no good, and that if they voted at all at this election, they would vote with the Democrats, and give that party a trial; and when they found that Chisolm and his clan had gone to the woods, they became thoroughly indifferent and disgusted. The radicals now sought to raise the cry of intimidation in Kemper County. The governor of the State, Adelbert Ames, testified, under oath, in regard to the state of affairs in this county, as follows (Boutwell report, p. 12):

"I was speaking of counties where the men were driven away from the polls. That was true in Monroe County. It was equally true in Kemper County. I speak of those counties where there will be no controversy on the part of anybody. But you can go to the majority of the Republican counties, and you will find that the Republican voters were driven away by intimidation, which was resorted to for this effect. In Kemper County, the sheriff, Mr. Chisolm, had been an officer ever since he was twenty-one years old, and I think he must be a man of forty-five or fifty now, always a very popular man, and officially his standing was excellent. There was no complaint against him at all, except that he was a Republican. He was one of the few men who had the courage to come before the grand jury of the United States court and report the condition of affairs in that county. He was threatened with assassination, and I think I have his written statement of the facts. He said that there was no complaint except that it was really a race issue, and Democrats said to him that this was a white man's country, and white men are going to rule it. That was the charge that was made against him and his party; that the negroes were not qualified to vote, and they should not vote. He complained bitterly that men with whom he had always lived and had had all kinds of relations with (socially he stands very high), should consent that a body of men should come from Alabama to assassinate him, 'if he made an attempt to keep the peace on the day of the election.' The result was that he abandoned all attempts to keep the peace, and the election went by default.

I don't know what the returns are. I see that in Kemper County, in 1873, the vote was one thousand two hundred and twenty-nine Republican, and seven hundred and eighty-one Democratic, making a difference of four hundred and forty-eight Republican majority.

"In 1875, there were four hundred and eighteen Republican votes and one thousand three hundred and thirty-nine Democratic votes, making a difference of nine hundred and twenty-one on the other side. He will testify to your committee, as he has already testified, that it was through intimidation and violence that no election was held there."

Now let us refer to the testimony of Chisolm himself, in regard to the election of 1875, which is here introduced in refutation of this sworn statement of Governor Ames.

Question by Mr Bayard.—Mr. Chisolm, do I understand you to say that you kept all your political appointments in that canvass?

A. Yes, sir.

Q. Did you make, Mr. Chisolm, an active and vigorous canvass throughout that county up to the time of the election?

A. Yes, sir; I made a pretty active canvass up to the Saturday night before the election.

Q. And you said that your last speech on the Saturday night before the election was the bitterest of your canvass?

A. Yes, sir; I think it was. It is my opinion that I made the bitterest speech that day that I made during the canvass.

Q. Were there any threats made to you personally during the canvass?

A. Well, there was this kind of threats: stating to me that I was not to interfere with the negroes; and, when they gave them tickets, that they would be damned if we should go to them and get them to change them.

Q. Did you regard that as a threat?

A. I regarded it as this: stating to me that I should not be allowed to do what they were going to do. I did not regard it as any special threat.

Q. Did any one in the canvass specially threaten you?

A. No one that I know of.

Q. Did you witness, during the canvass, any act of violence upon any one in connection with the election?

A. No one occurred at any speaking I had.

Q. Were you armed yourself on those occasions?

A. I generally carried my pistol.

Q. How were your friends?

A. They carried their pistols in their pockets.

Q. And you generally went armed?

A. Always, sir; we had our pistols.

Q. At the time you met this young man, before you got to Scooba, you say you got out of your buggy, with your pistol in your hand. Why did you do that?

A. Because I saw him coming through the woods.

Q. Had he any arms?

A. No, sir; nothing at all.

Q. You dismounted and drew your pistol?

A. Yes, sir; I just took my pistol out of my buggy. I carried it lying on the seat.

Q. And when you were at the meeting, where did you carry your pistol?

A. Behind me, in my pocket, where I have got it now. It is a little old pistol—not very dangerous, but it is all right, you may bet (showing it).

In this conflict of sworn evidence, Wells promptly comes to the aid of Ames, and says, speaking of Chisolm, at Scooba: "His life was threatened, and pistols were drawn to carry the threat into execution. After repeated efforts to quiet the mob, he was compelled to quit the stand in order to save his life."

And so I will leave it with the reader to settle the question of veracity between the three, Ames, Chisolm and his biographer, Wells. The writer has been totally unable to learn of a single instance of intimidation in Kemper County on the part of the Democrats; that they used every method of coaxing and persuading the negroes to vote with them, and made a most energetic canvass, is beyond

dispute, but that any one was frightened by the Democrats from a voluntary exercise of his right to vote as his choice might dictate, has not the least foundation in fact. Yet, says Wells: "The Saturday before the election took place, Professor Thomas S. Gathright, for many years one of the most influential and popular educators of the youth of the State, made a speech at De Kalb, within sight of Judge Chisolm's house, in which he used words very nearly as follows. After repeating Judge Chisolm's name, he said: 'Gentlemen, if you ever expect to have peace and harmony in your county, you must get rid of this man. I will not undertake to tell you *how* to get rid of him; that you know as well as I; *but you must get rid of him!*' Then encircling his neck with a gesture, he raised his hand up and down several times in imitation of dangling some object from the end of a rope. This speech and pantomime were responded to with loud and continued cheers. On the following Monday the same language was repeated at Moscow, a cross roads store, ten miles distant from De Kalb."

From what source, if any, Wells obtained this story will, perhaps, remain unknown, save to himself and the members of the clan who concocted it. The well known character of Professor Gathright, who is at this time president of the State Agricultural College of Texas, will itself refute any such representations. There are many citizens of De Kalb who heard Professor Gathright's speech on the occasion referred to, and the writer, after conversing with many of them about this matter, is prepared to say that there is not to-day a man in the County of Kemper who would openly allege that he ever saw Professor Gathright perform any such gestures on any such occasion. He was, and is, well known to be a gentleman of mild, moral and conservative views, though a stanch Democrat and patriot, and against him the "barbed arrows" of this carpet bagger fall as harmless as they did when, on one occasion, in the town of Brandon, a negro, whom he had swindled, thrust his fist in his face and publicly proclaimed him a G—d d——d thieving scoundrel. In view of these representations of Wells, it is, indeed, strange that Chisolm, in his sworn testimony before the committee at Washington, should state (see Report, page 770), that he knew of no threat made against him during this canvass.

But there were notable instances of intimidation on the part of the radicals, of which a notorious instance occurred in Scooba, during the canvass of 1875. Dick McCall was a negro who had announced himself a Democrat. Peaceable and harmless, he bore a good character in the village among the white people. On one occasion he was sitting quietly in the store of Captain J. R. Dunlap, who was at that time the town marshal. Gilmer came in, and taking his seat in front of Dick, and pulling out a large knife, began to pitch it at Dick's bare feet, and finally thrust the knife into his foot. Dick, to avoid the difficulty, and well knowing the character of Gilmer, quietly arose and left the room. Upon this Gilmer followed him, saying that he intended to kill him, if he was the last man; but Dick by some means eluded his assailant, when Gilmer, taking his gun with him, and accompanied by his half brother, one M. Wood, proceeded to Dick's residence. Before reaching it, however, he overtook Dick, and fired two shots at him. Some one, in the meantime, had apprised Dick of his danger, and loaned him a gun, and being thus prepared for his defence, he returned the fire, firing two shots at Gilmer. This occurred just at dark, and Wood stated that the shot from Dick's gun entered the ground at Gilmer's feet.

No legal notice whatever was taken of this matter, so utterly paralyzed was every nerve and sinew of the law when in contact with these men. It can scarcely be supposed that the man who, in cold blood, had deliberately shot the dying Dawson with impunity, could be reached by the arms of the law for pitching his knife into a poor negro's foot.

To what extent this intimidation, and these threats and acts of bodily harm for affiliating with the Democrats, were practiced by these men upon the negroes, and by the negroes upon each other, in their social relations, could not be ascertained, as the very nature of the acts preserved them in secrecy; while, on the part of the Democrats, the only semblance of force brought to bear upon the negro in the exercise of his choice, was that, in some instances, they were told by their employers that, in consequence of the high rate of taxation under radical rule, and the consequent stagnation of business, which rendered their property a burden, and their agricultural operations totally unprofitable, if they voted the radical ticket and continued such a state of affairs, they could not, and would not, give them employment any longer. This policy, however, which, in view of the circumstances, should have been general, was only put in practice here and there, and it, no doubt, had its effect to some extent. In such cases these employers would say to the negroes, "Vote as you please, but remember that if you vote the Republican ticket and maintain that party in power, I cannot employ you any more." A colored preacher residing in Kemper County, on being told this by his employer, made the following demonstrative reply:

"I am a colored man, and I have to associate with my colored neighbors here, and if I do not go to the election, they won't let me go to my church. They will turn me out of the church, and they will not have anything to do with me; and I cannot associate on social terms with you white people; and I have children growing up here. I vote the Republican ticket, not from choice, but from necessity." And this same sentiment was substantially expressed by many negroes in the county. It was mostly upon their private and social relations that these men sought, in this respect, to operate.

The Republicans must have been driven to desperate straits for incidents of intimidation when they brought this charge against Southern planters and employers, when it is a public and notorious fact that the employers and owners of Northern factories and manufacturing establishments invariably control the political sentiments of their employees, and it is an established practice in the very departments of the government itself.

The platform adopted by the Democratic party of Mississippi, on the third of August, 1875, contained an invitation to the voters of both races to unite vigorously with them in the approaching canvass, to aid them in throwing off the intolerable yoke of radical rule, and to establish good government in the State, and promised them full protection in all their rights. This platform of principles contained every provision and profession that the most fastidious negro rights man could desire, and gave the Democratic speakers the opportunity of meeting their antagonists fully on all the issues they might make.

During the canvass of 1875, the candidate for Congress, Colonel Singleton, made a speech to the negroes at Scooba, in which he held up to them this platform of principles with great effect, and urged them for their own good and the welfare of the whole people, to support the Democratic ticket, and aid that party in restoring good government to the State—a government which would be honest, and dispense impartial justice to all its citizens. He arraigned the corruption, extravagance and incompetency of the radical leaders, and depicted in a clear light the ruin brought upon the whole people by radical misrule. This speech was listened to by the large negro audience with profound and anxious attention. Chisolm was present taking notes. Yet, on being invited to speak, he declined doing so. The atmosphere of the occasion was, no doubt, too hard for his style of argument. The negroes were gradually drawn to Democracy by an honest conviction, effected by the portrayal of facts of which they had a painful experience.

It has been charged that the Southern people committed a great error in not acquiescing, at first, in the policy of congressional reconstruction, in not making political friends of the negroes, recognizing all their rights, and anticipating the radicals in gaining ascendency and control over them. Yet, however plausible this policy might have been in theory, apart from the hypocrisy of such a course, it is doubtful whether it could have been practiced without dragging with it a train of troubles more permanently detrimental to society than the worst features of radical rule.

The arrogance of the negro, at that time, engendered by his sudden emancipation, and the teachings of the carpet baggers, could not have been bounded by the barriers of the most extended political horizon. He would have demanded as the price of his alliance, full social recognition; and the commingling of the two races necessary to have satisfied him, in this respect, would have degraded the white race and broken up the fountains of society. The negroes joined the Democratic party as soon as they were qualified to do so—as soon as they were capable of comprehending the difference between political and social equality.

The experience necessary for this qualification was afforded them by the corruption of the radical party, and the almost solid integrity of Southern sentiment through all the vicissitudes of reconstruction, during which period, and up to the fall of 1875, they were continually incited against the whites by Northern adventurers and vagabonds for purposes of their own, and who prowled about from church to church, school house to school house, and negro quarters to negro quarters, forming them into clubs, and binding them to their personal schemes by all sorts of oaths, and filling their ears with incendiary speeches.

But having passed through all this experience, the negro appeared at the poll box, in the fall of 1875, a much wiser being, and fully convinced that all his rights and franchises were perfectly safe in the hands of the white people of Mississippi. And the election of 1875 will ever remain a notable epoch in the history of the State as the period of the termination of the most corrupt government that ever disgraced the annals of civilization.

To show the vast increase of public expenditures in Mississippi under Radical rule, as compared with those of former and subsequent Democratic administrations, the following statistics are introduced. They were compiled from the reports of the auditor, and are perfectly reliable:

DEMOCRATIC COMPARISON OF STATE EXPENSES.

The disbursements on account of the State government were:

1848	$311,717 00
1849	270,300 00
1850	295,932 00
1851	223,637 00
1853	229,288 00
1857	315,502 00
1858	401,032 00
1859	406,015 00

The following was for the ordinary purposes of the government, for the administration immediately succeeding the war:

October 16, to May 1, 1865	$296,285 00
May 1, 1865, to May 1, 1867, 2 years	555,627 00
May 1, 1868, to May 1, 1869	502,723 00
May 1, 1869, to May 1, 1870	302,138 00

UNDER REPUBLICAN RULE.

Jan. 1, 1870, to Jan. 1, 1871	$1,061,259 00
Jan. 1, 1871, to Jan. 1, 1872	1,329,016 00
Jan. 1, 1872, to Jan. 1, 1873	1,506,828 00
Jan. 1, 1873, to Jan. 1, 1874	1,100,000 00
Jan. 1, 1874, to Jan. 1, 1875	1,319,009 00

Under radical rule the expenses of the executive department were, in 1875 — $33,971 30
Those of the legislative department were — 118,624 00
Those of the judicial department — 230,025 00

The expenditures on account of the executive department under Democratic rule were:

1848	$8,663 00
1851	8,608 00
1858	11,225 00
From May 1, 1865, to May 1, 1866	10,429 00

That was the last year of the rule of the citizens before the Republicans took charge of the State government. The expenses of the same department—the executive department—under Republican rule, were as follows:

1870	$24,200 00
1871	31,000 00
1872	32,834 00
1873	31,973 00
1874	54,900 00
1875	33,917 30

From January 1, 1870, to January 1, 1871, under Alcorn's administration, $54,000 were expended on that account and as a secret fund.

The gross amount of expenditure for the year 1875 was $1,430,192 83

For the judicial department under Democratic rule:

1848	$74,711 00
1849	83,280 00
1855	99,527 00
1858	139,821 00
1859	147,000 00
October 1, 1865, to May 1, 1866	49,775 00
May 1, 1866, to May 1, 1867	163,349 00
May 1, 1867, to May 1, 1868	191,440 00

The expenditures of the same department under radical rule were:

1870 ...$320,399 00

REPUBLICAN RULE.

1871	$328,000 00
1872	434,973 00
1873	360,221 00
1874	398,854 00
1875	230,025 00

The appropriations by the Democratic legislature, for the year 1876, for this department, were $70,000.

The following statements are taken from the annual message of his excellency James M. Stone, the present governor of Mississippi, made to the legislature at its session of 1877, and will present a very forcible comparison of the actual expenditures for the year 1875, which was the last of radical rule, and the expenditures for the year 1876, the first under Democratic rule:

Disbursements by warrants, from January 1 to December 16, 1876	$507,816 55
The disbursements for the remainder of the year will not exceed, say	10,000 00
Making total disbursements for the year 1876	$517,816 55
In 1875, from January 1 to December 31, the disbursements by warrants were, as per auditor's report	1,430,192 00
From this sum should be deducted (being interest on State debt paid in 1875)	300,000 00
Leaving the actual disbursements for the year 1875	$1,130,192 00

Showing that the disbursements in 1875 exceeded those of 1876 by the sum of $582,375.45, the excess being greater than the entire disbursements during the year 1876.

During 1876, to December 18, there was received into the State treasury the sum of	$663,259 00
To this sum must be added (taxes of 1876, not reported to December 18), say	275,000 00
Making the receipts for 1876	$938,259 00
The total acreage of the State is	23,536,799
Of which the total valuation is	$95,697,180 00
State tax on the same	623,371 00

The total valuation of personal property in 1876, four counties being omitted, the assessment rolls from which having been returned for correction and not yet re-returned to the auditor, is $35,702,040 00
On this the State tax is   232,678 00

The subjoined statement will show at a glance, and in detail, some of the substantial results accomplished by the change from Radical to Democratic rule in Mississippi. The decrease of expenditures under the administration of the latter is strikingly exemplified:

Department.	1875.	1876	Decrease, 1876
Legislature	$118,624 39	$100,854 73	$17,769 66
Judiciary	230,025 98	89 943 45	140,082 53
Executive	33,947 30	30 340 69	3,606 61
Library	4,528 87	1,888 73	2,640 14
Ex Con Fund	10,000 00	4,400 00	5,600 00
Deaf and dumb and blind institutions,	25,000 00	18,350 00	6,650 00
Penitentiary	66,616 20	19 169 75	47,476 45
Public printing	50,803 02	21,680 05	29,122 97
Lunatic asylum	97,000 00	68,730 00	28,270 00
Com immigration	5,216 65	440 13	4,776 52
Express and postage	2 559 01	1,718 42	840 59
Com for assessing	31,588 03	11,531 65	20,056 38
Militia	5 000 00	....	5,000 00
Total	$673,939 45	$262,047 60	$311,891 55

Embraced in the statement of the expenditures for 1876, there was an appropriation of three thousand four hundred and eight dollars for printing, and sixteen thousand dollars for the penitentiary, to cover deficiencies in those departments for the year 1875.

It will be observed by an inspection of the tables, that the expenditures during the year 1875 were the most economical of radical rule. The action of the tax payers in the early part of that year, together with the defectional spirit then beginning to be manifested by some of the radical leaders, forced upon their legislature for the first time even the thought of economizing.

In 1876 the Democratic legislature levied, for State purposes, a tax of six dollars and fifty cents on one thousand dollars. In 1872 the levy was thirty per cent. greater than the levy for 1876; in 1873 it was ninety-two per cent. greater; in 1874, one hundred and fifteen per cent. greater, and in 1875 it was forty-two per cent. greater. So that the expenditures for the last named year were necessarily somewhat curtailed in order to conform to the reduction of the taxes to which the radicals had been reluctantly driven. The change of administration under Democratic rule was no less beneficially operative upon the credit of the State than upon the economy of its expenditures. In January, 1875, the warrants of the State were sold on the streets of Jackson at seventy-three cents on the dollar, and sales of them were made at that rate by public officers. On the 1st of January, 1876, when the first Democratic legislature met, they were sold at from eighty to eighty-five cents, and during this session they advanced to ninety-five cents, and in the succeeding dull months of summer, when there were but few taxes to be paid, and but little occasion for financial operations, they rose to ninety-seven cents on the dollar; and in the following November they advanced to ninety-nine cents, since which time the warrants of the State have been virtually at par. Such are some of the substantial and visible fruits of " home rule " in Mississippi. From the tables it will be observed that the cost of administering the different branches of the State government was, in 1876, the first year of Democratic rule, less than one half of the public expenditures in 1875, the last year of the radical administration. The moderate tax of six dollars and fifty cents on one thousand dollars, imposed by the legislature of 1876, has been, in 1877, reduced to five dollars on one thousand dollars, while the taxes levied by the counties have been reduced in like ratio, causing a decrease of taxes on realty of one hundred and forty-eight thousand six hundred and fourteen dollars and four cents, and on personalty of one hundred and fifty-nine thousand nine hundred and forty-three dollars.

On the 1st of January, 1876, the entire indebtedness of the State proper was one million one hundred thousand two hundred and forty-two dollars and twenty-one cents. This sum, on the first day of January, 1877, had been reduced to something over six hundred thousand dollars. The indebtedness of the counties has likewise been greatly reduced, and when the indebtedness of the State and the counties incurred under radical rule shall have been discharged, the taxes in the State of Mississippi will be as low, perhaps, as in any other State in the Union; and, as seen from the preceding statement, this object is being vigorously pursued by the present administration, and will be accomplished at no distant day.

CHAPTER XI.

On the 3d day of November, 1875, the morning sun rose upon Mississippi redeemed from her long and terrible thraldom of radical rule. The angel of peace and prosperity again smiled in her skies, and all nature seemed, to the rejoicing eyes of her people, to wear a brighter aspect. Hope again beamed forth from behind the clouds of despair that had hung so long like a pall over their heads. Nearly every vestige of radical power had been swept away from the State government, save in the executive department, and the people thought that now the machinations of that party would cease forever—but not so in Kemper County. It is true that there was a lull here, but it was the pause of Apollo, sighting his arrows at the Grecian camps on the plains of Troy. Chisolm again gathered his clan, and early in the spring of 1876, appeared again upon the stage as candidate for Congress. In this canvass he was the only candidate of the clan, as the election was to be for members of Congress only. Every effort was now made in the old way to organize clubs and again band the negroes together on the Republican side, but all secret efforts of this kind failed.

The negroes had now had a taste of Democratic rule, and all the illusions with which the radicals had heretofore veiled their minds were forever dispelled. Gilmer admitted that there was no chance for his party in this campaign, and took but little part in it. And Chisolm was also well aware that his prospects were hopeless, yet there might be some chance in a contested election, should the House of Representatives remain Republican, if he could make a showing of intimidation and violation of the enforcement acts. The next effort was to gather the negroes in large crowds at public speakings, as they had been wont to do, but this plan also failed. The negroes would not turn out. The next thing, then, was to create circumstances out of which they could fashion some semblance of intimidation, which, as we shall see, was a policy vigorously pursued on every occasion where there was an opportunity. Chisolm sought to bandy words with drunken men at his appointments, for the purpose of aggravating them to use harsh expressions toward him, while the other members of the clan present would inform him of pending danger should he attempt to speak. These, with other devices, furnished the stories which they concocted for their purpose, and presented in their sworn statements before the congressional investigating committees, to which reference will be made in the progress of this narrative, and it was from those that Wells draws the inspiration of his libels. But he runs counter to the verdict of history when he seeks to fashion the following sentiment by the mould of slander. He says, quoting from the Vicksburg *Herald*, in reference to the canvass of 1875: "A few weeks preceding the election the 'great and gifted' Lamar delivered an address at Aberdeen, which the Vicksburg *Herald*, a leading Democratic paper, commented upon as follows: 'At Aberdeen, last Saturday, Colonel Lamar made an eloquent speech. A better Democratic speech we do not care to listen to; and in manly and ringing tones he declared that the contest involved 'the supremacy of the unconquered and unconquerable Saxon race.' We were glad to hear this bold and manly avowal, and it was greeted with deafening plaudits. We have never seen men more terribly in earnest, and the Democratic white line speech made to them by Colonel Lamar aroused them to white heat.' * * * In another place, the same paper makes use of the following language, which is calculated to serve well in connection with 'Lamar's great speech:' 'The wanton killing of a few poor negroes is something unworthy of our people. If the killing of anybody is necessary, we repeat what we have heretofore said: let the poor negro pass, and let the white scoundrels who have fired his heart with evil passions be the only sufferers.' The utterances quoted were repeated verbatim by Lamar,

So far from being the subject of reprobation, if the policy advised, and the principles inculcated in the preceding quotation, had been early, promptly and universally practised throughout the Southern States, it would have saved them from seas of trouble and gulfs of ruin; and would have met with the applause of all fair minded mankind. It will ever be a wonder to the historian, when he attempts to interpret the character of men, how to account for the extreme passiveness exhibited by the Southern people under the oppressive rule of radicalism. That a people who at the first alarm of war had sprung forward solidly to meet the issue, who had for four years waged the fiercest and bloodiest war of modern times, and all for the sake of a principle, should so long submit to the infamous government of ignorant and degraded negroes, led by adventurers from the slums and cesspools of a foreign society, is a question upon which history will, for all time, place her private seal; the solution of which can only be found in a rare exercise of the supreme qualities of honor. They had laid down their arms from weariness of the strife, and, for the sake of peace, had accepted the situation; and to comport themselves in good faith became as sacred to them now as were the claims of duty and chivalry and honor on the field of battle. For it cannot be denied that, notwithstanding the defeat of their two main armies, there were resources yet remaining sufficient to have prolonged indefinitely a desultory warfare; but this was spurned by the Southern soldiery. When it became impossible apparently to accomplish the establishment of the Confederacy by a grand, open and honorable means, they were willing to accept an honorable peace, and abide with honor its terms. And there is no question that much of the old affection of the Southern people for the government of their fathers would have been speedily revived had the Federal government pursued a just policy toward them. Whether or not patience is a peculiar phase of chivalry may be an open question, yet it is doubtful which is entitled to the greater admiration—the gallantry which the

Southern people displayed in the contest, or the patience with which they bore the process of radical reconstruction. So prominent was this feature of their conduct, and so aggravating the circumstances under which it was so sublimely exercised, that, in the minority report of the Senatorial committee appointed to investigate the affairs of Mississippi, in 1875, Senators Bayard and McDonald could not refrain from making the following observations, which evidently sprang from the depths of conviction, and are set forth in the spirit of candor:

"A condition of affairs which would be incredible and utterly intolerable in any of the Northern States exists in many of the black counties of Mississippi, where the property, intelligence and character of the community is trodden to the earth, insulted and ignored by the most ignorant and sometimes vicious members of the community. Things are of daily occurrence, and were proven almost daily before the committee, which, if attempted in the States of Massachusetts, Wisconsin, Minnesota, or, indeed, any of the Northern States, would be met by a popular uprising and speedy overthrow. In such a condition of affairs, the forbearance and self subordination exhibited by the white population demands and should receive the strong sympathy and high respect of every just and well regulated mind."

Yet such sympathy and respect would have been a poor condolence, coming from those who established this state of affairs, and were strenuously endeavoring still to perpetuate it, be their minds never so well regulated.

It was the reconstruction policy that the people of the South blamed for all their evils and wrongs, not so much the vile wretches who availed themselves of the opportunities it afforded them. So long as it was impossible for them to reach the cause, they spurned to vent their spleen upon the effect, otherwise than to maintain a state of ostracism and a feeling of scorn toward the carpet bagger and his degraded white allies of the South. It was the high sense of honor and self respect of the Southern people that tolerated this class. As heretofore remarked, it had been the practice of the radical speakers to play upon the ignorance and credulity of the negro. They would tell them all manner of things, such as what the President of the United States said they must do, and what the general of the army said, what Congress desired of them, and pictured to them in gloomy colors what would be the result of their non compliance. Subsidiary to this, they constantly represented the Southern whites to be hostile to every progress of the negro, and were even entertaining designs against their freedom. Such discourse had its effect upon their untutored minds; and the white people determined, during the canvass of 1876, to attend the radical meetings for the purpose of preventing the repetition of these falsehoods, and this their very presence, in most cases, effected. Where this was not the case, as it was not with Chisolm, and as they were allowed no division of time, or any chance of being heard on such occasions, they, in some instances, adopted the plan of interrupting the speaker, in the midst of such falsehoods, with questions and contradictions; but so far from this policy disconcerting the Kemper clan, they attempted, as will be seen, to turn it to advantage by moulding it into evidence of intimidation. Chisolm had made appointments to speak at many places in the congressional district, most of which he says he filled without let or hinderance, but as the canvass advanced the hopelessness of the radical cause became more apparent.

By all their devices they had failed to make any marked impression upon the negroes, who now seemed disposed to adhere as solidly to the Democratic party as they had heretofore to the radical, and it was manifest that Chisolm and his clan grew more desperate as their chances waned. Martyrdom was now his only hope, and he coveted its crown.

On the 31st of October, when the canvass was drawing to a close, Chisolm had an appointment to speak at Shuqualak, a railroad village in Noxubee County, near the border of Kemper. He appeared at that place with his *crowd*, on the day appointed. It was in a populous district, and a large audience, comprising more than a thousand negroes, headed by the radical sheriff of the county, and about one hundred whites. Under such circumstances, had the negroes been friendly and faithful to his cause, he surely would have controlled the events of the day in his own way. On his arrival in the early morning, he repaired to the hotel, shut himself up, and sent out his clan, as spies, to ascertain and report to him the prospects, and to gather whatever expression could be construed into a threat of violence. In the meantime, the sheriff, either ignorant of the gloomy prospects, or of the alternative designs which had been adopted, telegraphed to Chisolm from Macon, the county seat, to hold fast until his arrival.

While awaiting this event, the spies were active in the performance of their part of the programme. They soon ascertained that there was no possibility of making any impression upon the negroes; they saw, with dismay, the whites and blacks riding in vivaciously, side by side, with Democratic badges, and hurrahing for the Democratic party. On the arrival of the sheriff, and after taking counsel together regarding the situation, it was deemed best to refrain from speaking, and rest upon the reports of the spies. This conclusion having been reached, it was further advised that Chisolm should proceed to Macon, where, on account of the direct influence of the sheriff and other radical officers who retained positions there, it was hoped that the negroes would be more impressible; and to that place the clan, in company with the sheriff, now repaired. But in the meantime, the white people had procured the services of a Democratic negro orator, from Louisiana, named Younger, a man of uncommon talents for his race, and far the superior of Chisolm in general intelligence, as well as in the gift of oratory. The white people were, naturally, extremely anxious to hear the discussion between them, and being apprised of his refusal to speak at Shuqualak, and the reasons assigned for not doing so, they determined now to remove every imaginary obstacle from his way, and to leave him no grounds upon which to rest an excuse for failing to afford them the pleasure they anticipated in hearing the arguments between him and Younger. For this purpose they induced the sheriff to appoint one hundred deputies from both parties, whose duty should be to keep the peace. A large audience assembled to hear this discussion. The number of persons present was computed to be between five and six thousand negroes, and about three hundred white men.

The white people, although they had not the slightest apprehension of any disturbance, were so eager for the discussion that they gave Chisolm and his friends every pledge of protection and immunity from any insult or interference. Under these circumstances the discussion was begun by Chisolm, who spoke without limitation of time and without the least interruption. Younger then replied, at discretion, occupying about the same time. By prior arrangement Chisolm was to have had a half hour in which to rejoin to Younger, but so scathing and unanswerable were the arguments of the latter, so great was his superiority, and so complete was his polemical victory, that Chisolm sneaked off and declined to rejoin, as an excuse for which I will quote the language of his own sworn statement: He says, Teller's report, page 755: "I hired a hack, and went to Macon the next day. There was a division of time agreed upon there between me and a man named Younger, from Louisiana. I spoke for an hour and a half.

"Q. Did you get through?

"A. No, sir. I was to have a half hour for rejoinder to Younger; but, just about the time I was to speak, Mr. Rosenbaum, my old deputy sheriff, was there, a Southern man, born in Kemper County. He spoke to me and told me that he thought the intention was not to let me rejoin to Younger. Says I, 'Why, Charlie, have you heard anything?' 'Yes,' he said, 'I have been stirring about in the crowd a little, and they say that they have got to endure this an hour and a half, but they will go for you in the rejoinder.' That put me on my guard directly. I received a letter from Gilmer asking me to come into the circuit clerk's office. I went in there. Young Allgood was in there with him—the deputy sheriff. Mr. Gilmer said I must not attempt to rejoin to Younger. Mr. Gilmer said that he had heard some threats in the crowd; that they did not intend to let me rejoin. Young Allgood remarked to me, 'I know these people, and I know the condition they are in. The groceries are all shut up, but they have got whiskey somewhere, and are all drunk. You had better not make any speech; you had better not attempt to rejoin.' I sent for Colonel Allgood, the sheriff. He came in there. He said he thought, perhaps, I could speak. His son took him off and talked with him. A little while after he came back and said, perhaps it was well enough for me not to attempt to speak."

The superior logic of the negro, and the apparent confession of defeat, on the part of Chisolm, caused a great deal of innocent merriment among the audience, and when Chisolm failed to answer the calls made for his rejoinder, vociferous applause went up for Younger.

It is, indeed, amusing to read the excuse of Chisolm for his conduct on this occasion, when it is remembered that there were nearly twenty negroes for every white man in the audience, and then there was the radical sheriff, Allgood, who was also chairman of the county Republican executive committee, with his one hundred chosen deputies, selected from both political parties, for the purpose of keeping the peace and preventing the least disturbance; besides this, the meeting was, by an amicable and satisfactory arrangement, presided over jointly by the secretaries of the county executive committees of the two parties. The next appointment of Chisolm, subsequent to that at Macon, was at Scooba, but so great was the mortification of his defeat by Younger, that on his learning from his friend Rosenbaum that the young men intended meeting him at the depot at Scooba, with music, in celebration, as they said, of his glorious victory, he concluded to forego his appointment at that place, and proceeded directly to De Kalb.

Some time previous to this, however, Chisolm was present at a Democratic meeting, at Scooba, and was courteously invited to participate in the discussion of the questions of the day. The invitation was promptly accepted, and although he was, as usual, very aggressive and bitter in his denunciations of the Democratic party, he was listened to quietly and without the least interruption, until, in the course of his arguments, arraigning the dishonesty of leading Democrats, he took occasion to read an extract from the New York *Tribune* containing grave charges against Mr. Samuel J. Tilden, upon which some one in the audience replied that that charge was a lie. At this Mr. A. G. Ellis, a lawyer, and member of the Democratic county executive committee, arose and rebuked the interruption, upon which quiet was again maintained. But to show the acerbity of his feelings, and his constantly offensive demeanor toward the white people, I will here quote his own statement in reference to the matter. He says: "I had not spoken more than fifteen minutes before I was interrupted; at this time they had got the Democratic crowd thoroughly drunk; they were patriotic; they had patriotic whiskey in them. They were thoroughly wrought up to the point that I should not speak. I spoke about fifteen minutes, and they interrupted; said 'it was a damned lie;' said 'that I could not speak there unless I told the truth.' I pointed my remarks then to the chairman of the Democratic executive committee, and asked him if I was to speak. He said, 'Yes; go on.' I remarked then, 'If I have got to tell the truth according to this ignorant rabble, what they consider to be the truth, I certainly shall not make a speech.' Squire Ellis got up and asked them to be quiet and listen to my speaking. Of course they were not quiet. They interrupted me on divers and sundry times during my speech, but I spoke the time I was allowed to speak. I got through the hour."

In striking contrast to this sworn description, given by Chisolm himself, I will now array that of Wells. He says, page 127, speaking of this same occasion: "After the fiery eloquence of the Democracy had ceased to burn, Judge Chisolm got up and quietly intimated, that inasmuch as he had been invited there to take part in a joint discussion, he should now be permitted to speak. * * * As predicted, he had spoken but a few minutes when he was interrupted in a most violent and threatening manner, and curses loud and deep were heaped upon his head from every quarter. His life was threatened, and pistols were drawn to carry the threat into execution. After repeated efforts to quiet the mob, he was compelled to quit the stand in order to save his life."

On Friday evening preceding the election, Chisolm reached his home at De Kalb, thoroughly disgusted with the prospects and the fruits of his canvass. He had lost the shrievalty of his county the preceding year by the defection of the negroes, and he was now convinced that his efforts to regain his prestige and obtain a seat in Congress by means of the populous negro vote of the other counties of the district were in vain. Piqued at his loss of power, and the full realization of his overthrow, he now retired to his house, and wrapped himself in the grim folds of his own reflections. It was now that the desire of revenge usurped in his bosom the seat of ambition. To this he now devoted his meditation.

He had early in the canvass caused it to be posted that he would close the campaign at De Kalb on Saturday immediately before the election, on which occasion it was understood that there would be a division of time with the Democrats and a joint discussion. With this understanding, the Democratic executive committee had procured the attendance of Colonel S. M. Meek, of Columbus, a distinguished orator, to meet Chisolm on this occasion and close the canvass on the part of the Democrats. On Friday evening, quite a number of citizens from different parts of the county had gathered at De Kalb, in order to be present at the joint discussion on the next day. There were also a good many negroes present, and, in order to gratify their fondness for show and parade, a procession of Democrats was formed, in which they had a band of music and a small cannon.

There are but two roads leading into the village from the west, and at the entrance of one of these was situated Chisolm's residence, with a large common in front; so that in marching through and around the village it was necessary to pass immediately in front of his house. Being apprised of his arrival, the processionists halted on the common, in front of his house, and fired off their cannon, while the band struck up some patriotic air. This they also did at several other convenient places during their march. While here some persons in the crowd called for Chisolm to come out and acknowledge the compliment, as they said, of the serenade. In this procession were John W. Gully, chairman of the county Democratic committee, and Colonel Meek, the Democratic orator for the next day, whose participation was for the purpose of inspiring an innocent enthusiasm on the occasion, such as is always desired by all parties on the eve of an election. But if this parade and music in front of his residence was provoking under the circumstances, Chisolm did not hesitate to meet provocation with provocation; he stationed himself in his portico, with his gun at hand, and, in the words of his daughter, in a letter quoted by Wells, "cursed them in language more forcible than elegant." In this letter, which contains expressions not wont to be used by Southern ladies of refinement, and of which many of her acquaintances in De Kalb to-day doubt her authorship, she says: "But now comes the 'tug.' The wretches hired the Gainesville band to come here only to insult our family, on Friday night. Just as we were all undressed for bed, and some of the family had already lain down, they marched up to our gate with a great crowd 'serenading,' as they said, and nearly frightened me to death. You see I was then just being initiated. Others of our family had often seen the like when I was away at school. They brought the old cannon right in front of the door, and I *devoutly* prayed that it might burst and blow them all into the '*fiery furnace*,' where I am certain they will eventually land." * * * * * " Well, they left after finding how little they had accomplished, got some more men and whiskey, and came back about twelve o'clock at night and tried it over again. But all the family had to console and comfort me. I tell you, I thought I should die. I hardly slept one bit all night. By the next morning at daylight, papa's friends came in from all parts of the county, including four gentlemen from Macon. They were all at our house—about fifteen good, true, white Republicans, who swore they would die by their leader and best friend. There were hundreds of negroes in town, and nothing but papa's constant and vigilant efforts kept them from firing upon the bloodthirsty demons as they passed by on their march. They had the Democratic flag, the band playing 'Dixie' and the 'Bonnie Blue Flag,' a few ragged old negroes, and hundreds of villanous white scoundrels, half of whom were owing papa for the clothes that covered their backs. He stood on the steps, and cursed them in language more forcible than elegant. The first time, they yelled like the savages they were, and one man shot off a pistol in the air; the next time, two or three fired, and a few more each time, until the shooting became incessant, and several shots struck the wall just by the door. At this time nearly all the gentlemen who had been with us were over at Mr. Gilmer's and Captain Rush's, to get Mrs. Gilmer and her baby and Mrs. Rush and her daughter to come to our house, as all of them had been insulted and frightened nearly to death while their men folks were with us. Several of the gentlemen were worn out or crippled in the canvass, and so you see papa and brother were about the only ones who could shoot to do any good, and but for mamma's entreaties, they would have made some of the beggarly dogs bite the dust. I kept close to papa's side all day, and when he told me that if another shot was fired he intended to kill some of them, he begged me to leave him, because those who did not run would fire at him, and he feared some of the shots might hit me. I told him that I prayed the same shot which killed him might also lay my lifeless body by his side. My dear ——. I once thought that I never would tire of life; but if such is to be mine, death, if I could share it with my dear ones, would indeed be a sweet relief."

That this letter was written in the light of subsequent events, there can be but little question, and there can also be little question as to what will be the verdict of the fair minded reader against this man who introduces an innocent girl in such a character, in order to give import and authenticity to traducement. No one can read this letter, with a knowledge of the events that followed, without being convinced that portions of it, at least, were dictated to conform with those events, and no reader of refinement, should he view them as genuine, can read the expressions used by this young lady, in this letter, without entertaining at least a feeling of pity for one apparently so lost to all sense of refinement. But let us return to the letter. She says:

"Colonel Meek and John W. Gully headed the procession. At one time Meek passed by, with his arms around the neck of a ragged, filthy and degraded negro. I call him 'degraded,' not because of his black skin, but rather for being found in such company, exchanging embraces with so low and disgusting a being as Meek that day proved himself to be."

I will not follow this scurrilous jeremiad any further. But it may not be improper to observe the fact that Colonel S. M. Meek, the subject of this vituperation, be its author who it may, is too well known in Mississippi to be affected in reputation by any such foul sibilations. The attempt to impute to Colonel Meek any act not compatible with the character of a high minded Southern gentleman, is of itself sufficient to affix the seal of falsehood to any matter of which such effort forms a part. Subsidiary to and as an inducement to this letter, which seemed so well to suit his purposes, Wells indulges in the following language, a part of which he plucked from a radical paper, but which he here adopts as his own:

"Repeatedly throughout the day did this crowd of ruffians and jail birds march by Judge Chisolm's door, to the tune of 'Dixie' and the 'Bonnie Blue Flag,' firing cannon at intervals and pistols by volleys. The latter were at first discharged upward, but, as the crowd became emboldened from the excessive use of liquor, and meeting with no resistance, the shooting was directed over the house, and finally against it, when two or three shots were embedded in the pillars and weather boarding. These chivalrous gentlemen, who could thus surround, menace and assault a house occupied by women and children, breathing in their faces the fumes of the pot house, and hurling upon their heads obscene and blasphemous oaths, were headed by no greater man than Colonel S. M. Meek, of Columbus, one of Mississippi's favorite sons—a Chevalier Bayard, a man who must hide beneath the black cloth and clean linen that he wears a cowardly and craven heart. Close by the side of this *beau ideal* of Southern chivalry, walked John W. Gully, the presiding genius of the demoniac festival."

The writer has taken particular pains to discover, if possible, any indentations resembling those of bullets in any part of the Chisolm house, and there is not the least indication whatever of a bullet mark in either of the two posts that support the little porch. He has been shown only one hole in the coarse weather boarding which has the slightest resemblance to that of a bullet, and, if such, it must have proceeded from a pistol much nearer than the gate, and which was pointed downward at an angle of at least forty-five degrees. In addition to this, it is the universal testimony of every one who marched in these processions, that no shots were fired at Chisolm's house; and as to Wells' "*beau ideal of Southern chivalry,*" with a coward's heart under the folds of his black cloth and clean shirt, it is more than questionable whether that individual ever participated in any test sufficient to create *any* idea of that quality; and as to the latter part of the phrase, it applies so aptly to the character which he bore in the South, as to suggest more the offspring of consciousness than conception.

In the early morning of the day on which these hostile demonstrations are said to have occurred, John W. Gully, chairman of the Democratic county executive committee, sent a note to Chisolm over his own signature and those of the other members, politely inviting him to come out and take part in a joint discussion. This he did at the request of many gentlemen, as everybody was anxious to hear the discussion between him and Colonel Meek, who was well known to be one of the most eloquent speakers in the State. To this respectful invitation Chisolm made no answer, and as his reasons for not doing so were given by him in his testimony at Washington soon after, I will here quote them.

He says: "I suppose it was ten o'clock when I got a communication from Swanzey and J. W. Gully, and some other name—I forget the other name. They signed themselves officially, by authority of the Democratic executive committee there. I got this from the hands of a gentleman by the name of A. G. Vincent. He presented it to me. I read it, and remarked to him, says I, 'Mr. Vincent, do you think I could make a speech here to-day?' He said he did not think I could, or perhaps I could, I don't know how it was. I said: 'I understand from a hundred different sources that they will not let me speak.' Says I: 'I won't answer this note.' He says: 'Why not?' Says I: 'This carried a lie on its face. It sets out by stating that it is a Democratic meeting, when you know that such is not the fact, that it is a Republican meeting, and that the Democratic meeting was held here yesterday—that is, by appointment.' He said that he had forgot about that. Says I: 'I will not attempt to speak unless I am satisfied that I will not be interfered with.' Says I: 'I am not afraid, under ordinary circumstances, of anybody interfering with me; but when you have got such a crowd of two or three hundred men, I am afraid of what they may do.' Well, he went off, and I never saw him any more there. I made no effort to speak, and there were no Republican speeches. That was on Saturday before the election: the election was to be held on Tuesday. I did not go out of my house at all on Tuesday. They held the election, or what they said was an election."

It may be observed, as a finale to the political career of this man, that there were but three votes cast for him at De Kalb, and he ran considerably behind the Hayes ticket in Kemper County, and that he should have prosecuted the canvass to the very last, when he had long known that the whole people of the county, black and white, were almost solidly against him, shows an obstinacy and desperation rarely to be found in any man of sound mind. It can only be accounted for upon the grounds already set forth—the hopes he still cherished of successfully contesting the seat of his opponent upon the ground of intimidation. But, as this same general election for congressmen completely changed the political complexion of the House of Representatives, his hopes in that direction were likewise dislodged, and there was now nothing left him but to seek his revenge before the United States grand jury at Jackson. Thither he now hastened, carrying with him his friends, Hopper, Gilmer and Rush, and, upon the joint testimony of the three, thirty-one citizens of Kemper County were indicted, and several United States marshals sent to arrest them for violating the right of suffrage, and for intimidation, in shape of parades, serenades and the like.

In addition to this, and about this time, an event occurred which created a profound sensation throughout the county, and which was as diabolical as it was startling. On the 20th of December, while John W. Gully was returning, on horseback, from the country, where he had been on some private business, when about a mile from the village he was waylaid and shot with a double barrelled shot gun, from a little eminence, covered with a thin grove of black jacks, near the road side. Two shots were fired by the assassin, both of which took effect in Gully's breast and arms, and his horse was also severely wounded in the shoulder. The shot brought Gully to the ground, but on rising to his feet he saw and recognized his dastardly assailant, who, in the belief that his murderous work had been thoroughly accomplished, was making his way off through the forest. Gully, fearing that his assailant might make his escape, kept his identity somewhat a secret, only imparting the information to a few of his friends; and sure enough Ben Rush, whom he recognized to be the man, and who lived with his wife and children within two hundred yards of the court house, disappeared, and was, from that moment, seen publicly in the county no more. He had fled, as will be seen hereafter, to the State of Arkansas.

Rush was one of the most faithful and daring of all the Chisolm clan, and that he had been on that account deputed to take the life of Gully there is but little question. Such was, and is to-day, the general belief of the people of Kemper County. Yet, in reference to this circumstance, and in endeavoring to shift the odium of this infamous attempt from the clan, Wells has the audacity to resort to the following concoction. He says: "After the first impression upon the people in the immediate neighborhood, incident to an occurrence of the kind, there seemed to be little feeling of surprise manifested, and expressions like this were frequently heard:

"Well, the only wonder is that Gully was not killed long ago. There are scores of men living in the county who would feel warranted in taking his life in any possible way." And again, "The question, of course, arose, 'Who did do it?'" This, perhaps, might have been answered with some degree of satisfaction by propounding another: "Who, if anybody, had a right to do it?" Gully, with death and the ghosts of the victims of his own murderous hand staring him in the face, might thus have soliloquized.'

It is a fact well known in Kemper County that John W. Gully was always an advocate of peace, that he never sought a difficulty with any one, and though fearless and open in all his acts and in all his words, he always avoided personal encounters if possible. Although a man of strong passions, and quick to resent an insult, he coveted the part of peace maker between others. He was never known to use a deadly weapon but in self defence, and on but two occasions; one was when he wounded Rush, who waylaid him at the time he killed his brother, Sam Gully, and the other when he wounded McRea with bird shot, who was firing at him in his own store. Both of these circumstances have already been related.

He was one of the most popular men in the county. Besides being the chairman of the Democratic county executive committee, and the leading Democrat of the county, which position he had held from the reorganization of the party, he had long been the senior warden of the masonic lodge; and it is universally and confidently asserted that there was not a human being in Kemper County who would have done him a personal injury, save the members of the Chisolm clan, or some one instigated by them; and it was generally believed, at the time, and which subsequent events confirmed, that this attempt of Rush was the result of a conspiracy and settled plan, of which Chisolm was the chief and guide, to get rid of the leading Democrats of the county, and that Rush, because of his old personal enmity, was chosen as the most suitable person to begin the work, by taking the life of Gully, the chief of the county Democracy. But let us now return to the arrest of the thirty-one citizens, which was compassed in furtherance of this plan.

This conduct created intense indignation throughout the county. Men, whose patience and easy temper had heretofore retained the ascendancy over their feelings, and controlled their actions and expressions, now gave vent to the feelings of bitterness against Chisolm and his clan. They seemed to realize the fact that there was to be no peace in the county; no rest at all from the constant turmoil which these men had so long provoked and kept in agitation. To see thirty-one of their fellow citizens dragged off by United States marshals, at the vengeful instigation of these men, and for no other crime than that of being true Democrats, and their having endeavored to redeem the county from their ruinous control, was, it seemed, the heaviest stroke of all. It was, indeed, a most inhuman and uncalled for act of tyranny and oppression, and partook of the character and horrors of an inquisition by the government.

Mr. Money, the member of Congress from this district, on being apprised of the difficulties under which some of his constituents thus labored, nobly forwarded to them twenty dollars, with the offer of more if needed. He expressed a warm sympathy for the indicted citizens, and signified his willingness to aid them to the utmost of his ability. This prompt indignation on the part of Mr. Money, at this outrage upon his constituents, will long be remembered by the sufferers, and by the people of Kemper County.

Many of these men were poor and unable to defray their expenses to Jackson. In this extremity they called on their friends for aid. A meeting of the citizens was held at De Kalb, on the first day of January, 1877, for the purpose of raising funds by subscription for the purpose of paying the expenses of those who were unable to do so themselves.

At this demonstration of sympathy for their oppressed neighbors, Chisolm became exceedingly wroth. He collected his clan, and brought them armed with shot guns to De Kalb on the day of the meeting, and in this manner paraded the streets, at the same time comporting himself otherwise in the most hostile and defiant manner toward the people. This was now the last opportunity for a public gratification of his revenge, and he could not brook the idea of being thwarted the least in his designs. If he could provoke a difficulty on this occasion, he thought it would give strength to his proceedings. But the people were yet too patient for his purpose. No one that day came in contact with him or any of his armed clan. The object of the meeting was quietly but determinedly accomplished, and the citizens dispersed. Here, I cannot refrain from reverting to the reasons, alleged by Wells, for Chisolm's conduct on this occasion, for Chisolm nowhere makes any explanation of it himself, nor does he allude to it at all in his testimony taken soon after in Washington. Says Wells (referring to the serenaders): "But the perpetrators of these villanies in Kemper were not to escape thus easily. Some thirty or more of the gang, which had wantonly insulted Judge Chisolm and his family, were reported to the United States grand jury, comprised of men of both political parties, and indicted under that clause of the enforcement act which guarantees to every citizen who may be a candidate for office a full, free and uninterrupted canvass. Judge Chisolm, Gilmer and Hopper, in answer to a summons from the court, gave testimony before this jury. * * * *

"On the first day of January, 1877, following the arrest, a 'citizens' meeting' was called at De Kalb to give expression, in some substantial way, to the public indignation. It is not believed, as one might suppose, that this call was for the purpose of organized resistance to the Federal authorities. There was an object ahead far more significant, and one which might be realized with less trouble and expense to themselves. It was the determination of the leaders then to assemble a large crowd of ruffians at De Kalb, and take the life of Judge Chisolm and all his associates; for by so doing they hoped to destroy the last chance for a successful prosecution of their clan in the United States court. The first of January came; but, owing to a heavy fall of snow the night before—an unusual occurrence for that climate—and the bad condition of the roads, the 'meeting' was not well attended. Besides, Judge Chisolm, knowing their intent, had quietly called around him on that day a sufficient number of his friends to guard against the possibility of an attempt being made upon his life. Ten men like Chisolm, when prepared, were able at all times to hold the 'citizens' to a careful consideration of their acts."

After this gush of flummery and balderdash, it would be a matter of surprise that Chisolm, in his testimony given before the subcommittee on privileges and elections, at Washington, just six weeks after this occurrence, nowhere alludes to this instance of jeopardy, although he was called upon to relate every threat that had ever been made against him in word or deed, if the reader had not already discovered that whenever Chisolm leaves any gap down, in this respect, his consentaneous biographer has no difficulty in filling it. But there is another fact observable, and that is, that these criminal intentions have now been shifted from John W. Gully to the shoulders of the thirty-one indicted citizens. This circumstance, at least, relieves the usual monotony of his tale, and introduces variations which it will be more excursive to trace. As to Chisolm and his ten armed clansmen causing the citizens to be careful of their acts, that circumstance will doubtlessly explain their consideration manifested on another and subsequent occasion.

These thirty-one citizens, arrested purely through the malice of Chisolm and Gilmer and their clan, were all placed under a heavy bond for their appearance at the next term of the Federal court, to be held at Jackson, in the following May. In the meantime, another meeting of the people of the county was held at De Kalb, on the 19th of January, for the purpose of perfecting the arrangements for affording pecuniary aid to the persecuted citizens.

On this occasion Chisolm again summoned his armed clan. They went about the village, however, without their guns, until Gilmer, taking exceptions to some remark made by a gentleman named McWhorter, placed himself upon the door-steps of a store, and, with his pistol in his hand, began to curse and abuse him in a most violent manner. At this time Chisolm came up, and cried out, "Boys, get your guns!" Upon which the clan, fifteen in number, went straightway to Chisolm's office, and immediately returned, all armed with double barrelled shot guns, and then paraded around in a most boisterous manner. In the meantime, some of the citizens carried McWhorter off, and devoted themselves to the preservation of the peace, and the clan again failed to provoke a conflict. A few days after this occurrence, Chisolm and Gilmer proceeded to Washington, where they procured themselves to be summoned as witnesses before the committee above referred to, and there gave the testimony which the writer has quoted from on several occasions during the progress of this work. Miss Chisolm, it seems, accompanied them on this expedition, and on her return wrote a letter describing her journey, which Wells has quoted, in order to show, as he says, the refined taste of the author. From this letter I will, in turn, quote but one paragraph, to show the kind of refined taste which seems to strike him so forcibly. In this letter the young lady says: "Washington is by far the most beautiful city I saw in all my long journey. Its broad avenues, great thoroughfares, magnificent buildings, lovely parks, and, best of all, handsome gentlemen, combine to make it seem to me a perfect paradise."

While Chisolm and Gilmer were absent, perfect peace and quiet reigned in the County of Kemper. The remainder of the clan kept themselves, during this time, in retirement, and nothing occurred worthy of notice until Chisolm's and Gilmer's return, which was about the time of the March term of the circuit court. A short time prior to this an attachment had been sued out by a mercantile firm in St. Louis against the goods, wares and merchandise of M. Woods & Co., of Scooba, in which firm Gilmer was a partner, and Woods was his half brother. This attachment was returnable to this term of the court, when the trial of it was to have taken place. But on the night preceding the first day of the term, the office of the circuit clerk was entered by unknown parties and robbed, and these attachment papers, together with many others, were purloined.

Judge J. M Arnold, who presided at that term, could not do otherwise than deliver a scathing rebuke to the whole people of the county for permitting such a high handed act of lawlessness, although he was well aware that the Democrats of the county had no more to do with the robbery than with the riots in the states of Mexico.

The judge, in conformity with his duty under the circumstances, ordered the most strenuous efforts to be made to detect and bring the perpetrators to justice, and he recommended to the board of supervisors to offer a large reward for the apprehension of the guilty parties, which the board did, but in vain. The robbers had laid their plans thoroughly, and covered their tracks securely, and the deed, to-day, lies hidden beneath the veil of mystery.

No sooner had Chisolm returned than he began again to breathe vengeance against—as he called them—those damned serenaders. He declared publicly that nothing less than their hearts' blood would ever satisfy him, and that he would make the people of Kemper County feel him yet, and he invariably made use of such expressions in connection with the name of John W. Gully. He seemed to have grown more bitter from disappointment and defeat, and his expressions in regard to the leading Democrats became more violent. Yet the people hoped that he would now desist from causing any further trouble, and seemed willing that he should "curse himself down easy." But such was far from his intention. It is true, the plan inaugurated by the attempt of Rush had, for the time, failed, but now it was to be renewed under more promising auspices.

Some years before this, a negro boy, by the name of Walter Riley, who had been raised in Kemper County, shot and killed, in the streets of De Kalb, a young man by the name of Dabbs, a clerk of John W. Gully. Riley fled from justice and took refuge somewhere in Tennessee. He was a desperate character, and Chisolm and Gilmer now, no doubt, sought for and succeeded in ascertaining his whereabouts.

In the meantime Gilmer had been arrested and turned

over to the authorities of the State of Missouri for obtaining goods in St. Louis under false pretences, the particulars of which have already been related. Chisolm went up afterwards and succeeded in procuring bail for him. After this Chisolm returned, but Gilmer yet remained away. He, however, returned also in about a week afterward; and, on the night of Gilmer's return, Walter Riley was seen for the first time in the neighborhood of De Kalb. When Chisolm came back alone, he was asked why Gilmer did not return with him, to which he replied that some one in De Kalb had written a letter to the parties who were prosecuting Gilmer in St. Louis, and that Gilmer was remaining there for the purpose of ascertaining, if possible, its author, and that it would not be good for the person who wrote it should he succeed.

On the next day after Gilmer's return, and the appearance of Walter Riley, John W. Gully, while returning late in the evening to his home, about a mile and a half from his place of business in De Kalb, was shot with a load of buck shot and instantly killed, by some one who had concealed himself in a cluster of bushes immediately on the edge of the road. Gully fell dead from his horse, and the report of the gun gave the alarm to his family. Upon which, his wife seated herself at a window, and eagerly watched the road for the coming of her husband. This, she stated to the writer, she had been accustomed to do whenever she heard a gun fire in the neighborhood, since the first attempt was made to assassinate him; and when, on this occasion, she heard the report of the gun, she had a presentiment of what had occurred, and her heart sank within her bosom as heavily as if she was already standing over the cold, mangled body of her murdered husband.

When the body of the murdered man was reached it was lying in the road, and his money, hat and boots had been carried away by the assassin. So close was the muzzle of the gun that his face and neck, where the shot entered, were blackened by the powder.

The news of this terrible deed spread rapidly over the

county, carrying horror and consternation to the bosom of every citizen.

Never, perhaps, in the history of any people was there such intense excitement as in the County of Kemper at this time, and rumors of all sorts flew thick and fast. At first, all conjecture was centred upon Ben Rush, who, it was reported, had suddenly returned to the county, and had accomplished what he had before attempted.

The news flew from mouth to mouth that there was positive evidence that Chisolm and Gilmer were parties to the crime.

So great and so general was the belief that the deed was compassed by them, either directly or indirectly, that it was impossible for the minds of men to be drawn into any other channel.

They had witnessed for nine long years a persistent course of outlawry on the part of these men, perhaps never before practiced in any civilized community, and that, too, with an impunity and boldness that distanced every remedial effort. Under such circumstances, to parry the suspicion that they were, too, the authors of this deed, was out of the question. The calmest conjecture pointed at them the finger of guilt.

On Saturday, the 28th of April, John W. Gully was laid away in his final resting place, in a church yard a few miles from De Kalb. It was the wish and intention of the masons to bury him with the forms and ceremonies of that order, of which he had long been a prominent and brilliant member, but, owing to the absence of the master and other officers of the lodge, these ceremonies were postponed.

There were between two hundred and fifty and three hundred men, from all parts of the county, at the burial. Strong men were seen to weep as they looked down into that grave, and all were silent and wrapped in moody reflection. Their sympathy, their sorrow, and their tears all combined to cast a pall of gloom over the scene and depict a deep cast of anxious thought on every brow. The terrible scenes and incidents of the past wrought themselves up afresh in their memory, and then, blending with the frightful visions of the future, weighed like an incubus of horror upon their hearts. They had witnessed scenes in their county, of which these men had been the chief actors, that eclipsed, in glaring villanies, those of the Murrell and Copeland clans. They had seen robberies and forgeries in the open day light, and murders and assassinations beneath the curtains of the night. They had known the lands—the very homes of hard working and honest men and helpless women—of widows and orphans, upon which the taxes had been regularly paid, and for which they held the receipt of Chisolm, struck off to the State, and the title remain for years alienated without their knowledge, while their hard earned money had gone into the pockets of Chisolm and his associates. They had seen more than a hundred thousand acres of their lands seized, and then every means of support swept away by the enormous taxes which the dishonesty and cupidity of these men had caused to be heaped upon them.

Yet all this they had borne and might still have borne with patience. They might endure with stoic composure, while their pockets only were pierced by the fingers of dishonesty and theft, but when they saw the dagger of the assassin thrust into the hearts of their best citizens, their blood staining the altars of revenge and trickling along the path of personal ambition, it would have been less than human had they not awakened to a sense of their woes. They had witnessed the murder of Ball, in 1869, attended by circumstances the most atrocious. His house was surrounded in the dark hours of night, when he and his family were in bed, at a time when sleep is sweet to those whose necessities compel them to labor through the hours of the day. His assailants, without giving the least warning, began their assault, and fired their guns into the windows of his dwelling. His waking thoughts divined the murderous intent. No time was to be lost. It was death to remain with his family, and yet almost certain death to attempt his escape. His wife clung to him with all the strength of woman's love and woman's fear. Should he fly and leave her and his little children to the mercy of the murderers? Their loud curses told him that he alone was the victim sought. The only gleam of hope hovered around an effort to escape. He leaped from a window, and, passing his assailants, was making his way to a neighboring forest. He was discovered, pursued, and barbarously butchered. Yet he did not die immediately. He recognized the murderers to be some negroes who were well known to be warm adherents and tools of Chisolm. A short time before this, Ball had attacked Chisolm in the road, the circumstances of which have already been related.

The proof against this negro was ample, and corroborated by the dying declarations of Ball. Yet, as has been seen, one of them was aided by Chisolm to escape, and the other acquitted through his influence.

In 1870, Sam Gully was shot and killed by Ben Rush, in the streets of De Kalb. He had deliberately armed himself for the purpose, and waylaid the intended victim, who was in company with his brother Sam. For this he was acquitted through Chisolm's influence.

In 1871, Hal Dawson was enticed by Gilmer into his store, where he was shot and killed by Davis, and after he had fallen down dead, Gilmer walked up and shot two balls through his head. Chisolm, who was sheriff of the county, notoriously protected the criminals, and shielded them from the arms of the law. Gilmer, after this circumstance, became the intimate friend and companion of Chisolm, and was rewarded by a seat in the State senate. They ever afterward were joint workers in all their crimes and iniquities.

In order, however, to promote Gilmer to the State senate for his services, it was necessary to get rid of Gambril, a Northern school teacher, who now held that position, and had refused to become an accomplice in their villanies. For this reason Chisolm desired to get rid of him, and to

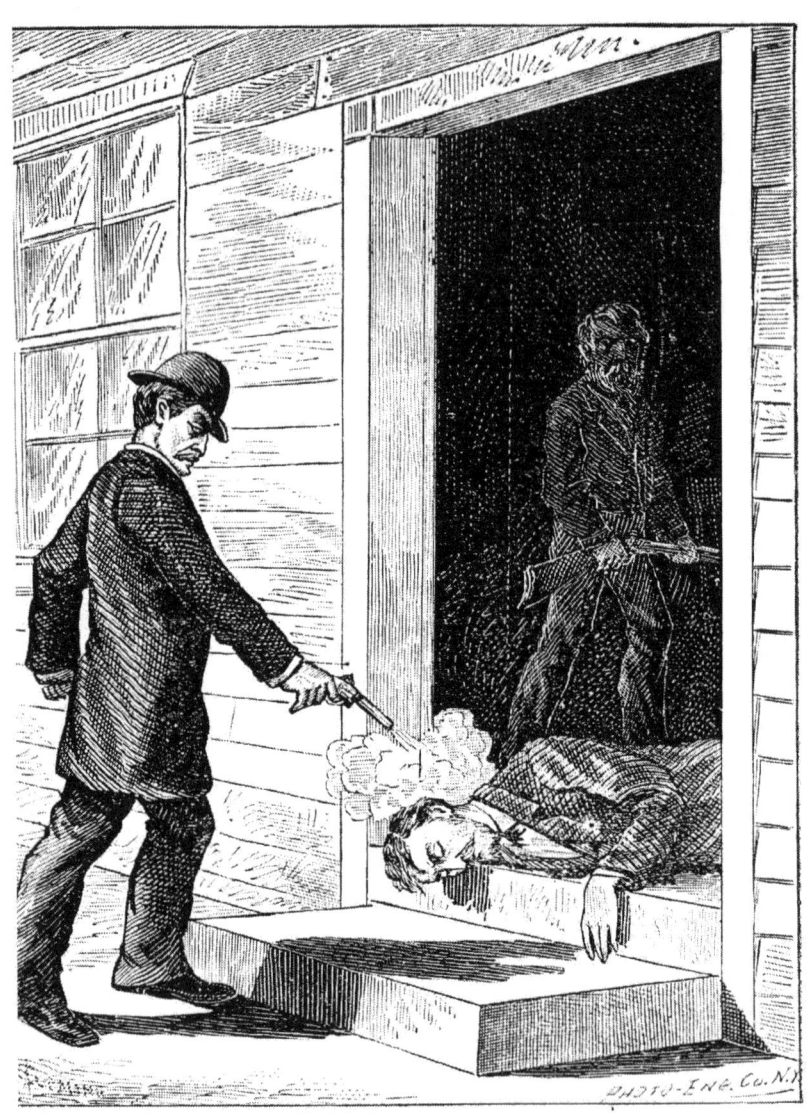

place his more obsequious and ready tool, Gilmer, in that position. To dispose of Gambril was a matter of but little moment. He was attacked and killed by a negro a short time afterward.

They had seen Floyd killed by a hired assassin in his own store, in 1871, and Chisolm, as sheriff, permit the murderer, who had been arrested, to make his escape, and even aid him in doing so. They had seen Bob Dabbs, a clerk of John W. Gully, waylaid and killed in the streets of De Kalb by a clansman of Chisolm, and the same hand that laid the corpse before them low. They had seen John W. Gully, a short time before, shot by " some one in hiding by the road side," and whom he recognized to be Chisolm's right hand man, Ben Rush, who immediately fled from the county; and now, to this list was to be added the man whose mangled body they were now committing to the tomb.

Their minds, after wandering back through all this bloody panorama of crime, returned laden with horror to the contemplation of the murder of one whom they loved, as the leader in the lodge, and the grange; their chosen leader in their efforts to throw off the oppressive yoke which these men had fastened upon them, and who was ever foremost in every enterprise for the public good. In addition to this, another thought naturally arose: if these parties were guilty, of which no one had a doubt, " could they be reached by the law?" It is true, the courts and the administration of justice are in the hands of the citizens, yet, will they not be rescued or screened by their clansmen? For ten long years Chisolm and his clan had done what they pleased with impunity; they had pursued their high handed and lawless career unchecked, and apparently beyond the reach of all human laws. He had threatened, repeatedly of late, that he would make the people of Kemper County feel him yet, and it seemed that his threat was to be made good, and to what extent was now the important question. Hence, it is no wonder the inquiry should arise in every one's mind, " Who will be the next victim?"

The writer is informed by many of the prominent men of the county that, knowing the character of Chisolm, and the threats he had publicly made, when they heard of the first attempt to assassinate Gully, they felt sincerely that they, too, would fall victims to the assassin's stroke; and their uneasiness in this respect became manifest to their families and friends, who shared in the same painful forebodings.

It was a horrible and maddening thought, and one which seemed to prey upon the minds of all who stood that day beside the grave of John W. Gully. The very repetition of the attempt demonstrated a determination and earnestness which added to the general alarm.

When the last clod had been heaped upon the body of the unfortunate man, amid the farewell sobs of the heart broken widow, the crowd slowly and silently dispersed.

In the meantime, it was rumored that Ben Rush had been seen in the neighborhood the day before the assassination, and if so, as a matter of course, suspicion would attach, first of all, to him as the perpetrator of the terrible deed.

In consequence of this, and prompted by their own belief, and the universal opinion of the citizens, some of the relatives and friends of Gully proceeded to make the following usual affidavit before Captain J. L. Spinks, who presided in another beat of the county, but who happened to be in De Kalb that day on business, T. W. Brame, Esq., the justice of that beat, being absent.

AFFIDAVIT.

"STATE OF MISSISSIPPI, }
Kemper County. }

"Before me, J. L. Spinks, a justice of the peace, in and for said county, personally came George S. Covert, who stated, upon oath, that he has good reason to believe, and does believe, that B. F. Rush did, on the night of the 26th instant, in said county, feloniously kill and murder John W.

Gully, and that W. W. Chisolm, Alexander Hopper, Newton Hopper, J. P. Gilmer, and Charlie Rosenbaum were accessories to the deed; whereupon he prays that warrants be issued for their arrest, and they be made to answer the charges brought against them.

"(Signed.) GEORGE S. COVERT.

"Sworn to and subscribed before me, April 28, 1877.

"(Signed.) J. L. SPINKS, *J. P.*

"*Witnesses.*—J. J. Griffin, S. Evans, Esq., John W. Smith, J. R. Smith, Dr. Edwards, M. Rosenbaum."

It will no doubt be amusing to those who have any knowledge of the law, to learn that Wells devotes a whole page in endeavoring to present what he considers a flagrant fact, that these witnesses afterward declared that they knew nothing about the matter, and that their names were set down as witnesses without their knowledge and consent. I dare say that it is the first instance on record where it is contended that the consent of witnesses must be obtained before they can be summoned to testify in a cause in court.

"STATE OF MISSISSIPPI, } ss.
   Kemper County.

"*To the sheriff or any constable in said county, greeting:*

"*Whereas,* George S. Covert has this day made complaint, on oath, to the undersigned, a justice of the peace in and for said county, that he has good reason to believe, and does believe, that B. F. Rush did, on the night of the 26th instant, kill and murder John W. Gully in said county, and that W. W. Chisolm, Alexander Hopper, Newton Hopper, J. P. Gilmer and Charlie Rosenbaum were accessories to the deed. Wherefore, we command you to forthwith apprehend the said B. F. Rush, W. W. Chisolm, Alexander Hopper, Newton Hopper, J. P. Gilmer and Charlie Rosenbaum, the accused, and bring them before T. W. Brame,

Esq., or some other justice of the peace of said county, at De Kalb, on Monday, the 30th day of April, 1877, to answer the above charge, and do or receive what, according to law, may be considered touching the same, and have you then and there this writ.

"Witness my hand and seal, April 28, 1877.

"(Signed.) J. L. SPINKS, J. P." [SEAL.]

This warrant was duly executed, and the parties named therein arrested according to law. It may be observed that the affiant, George S. Covert, was a nephew of John W. Gully by marriage, and seems to have been the only one of the immediate family not so overwhelmed with grief and horror stricken but that he had the presence of mind to take the above legal steps.

In the meantime the news of the murder of Gully, the reappearance of Rush, and the general belief of the guilt of Chisolm and his clan, had spread over the county; and so great was the shock and alarm that men seized their guns and hastened to De Kalb to aid, if necessary, in the arrest of the clan, and in bringing them to justice. All Saturday night and late Sunday morning, they continued to come in from different parts of the county. They well knew that the sheriff would not be able to arrest them without a strong posse, and not even then without bloodshed, should they be apprised of the warrant, and allowed time to assemble. Hence, there was a necessity for haste and caution on the part of the sheriff. To these apprehensions Wells adds what confirmation he is capable of, in the following words: "If by any means Chisolm should become apprised of their purpose before his arrest and confinement had been accomplished, they well knew he would call around him again, as in times past, a few devoted and heroic men, upon whom an assault could only be carried at a most alarming sacrifice to the assailants." This was well known throughout the county, and by noon on Sunday, the 29th of April, a large crowd of armed men had assembled at De Kalb for the purpose of preventing the *alarming sacrifice* that might otherwise attend any attempt to enforce the law against these men.

Early on Sunday morning, Alexander Hopper and his brother Newton were arrested at the residence of the former, about a mile from the village, and placed under guard. The sheriff then proceeded with his posse to Chisolm's house and arrested him, and, at his request, the sheriff permitted him to remain there, together with the two Hoppers, having placed a guard over them, composed of persons whom Chisolm himself named. But, owing to the excitement manifested by the crowd, the sheriff thought it best to remove them to the jail, which, in a short time, he did; and a deputy was dispatched to Scooba for Gilmer and Rosenbaum. Yet, notwithstanding the dispatch and caution exercised, they made an attempt to rally the clan. Hopper, on being arrested, under the pretence of finishing his breakfast, wrote a note and sent it by a negro to Chisolm, informing him of the proceedings; and Chisolm, while under guard in his house, caused a note to be conveyed to Gilmer and Rosenbaum at Scooba. Gilmer and Rosenbaum, on receiving the note sent by Chisolm, set out immediately for De Kalb. They were met on the way by the young man, Mr. John Pool, who was bearing the warrant for their arrest to the marshal of Scooba, who was deputized by the sheriff to make the arrest. They proceeded to De Kalb, where, on their arrival, and hearing the situation, they repaired to the house of Rosenbaum's father. Here they were soon arrested by a special deputy. But this attempt to gather the clan was thwarted by the prompt action of the sheriff and his deputy. In the meantime, Chisolm's horse was brought out and saddled, for the purpose of making his escape through the back way to the house; but, as the crowd had now surrounded the premises, this design, too, was frustrated.

In the Chisolm house there is a small closet, the low upper ceiling of which forms a trap door, which, on being pushed with the hand, opens into the garret above. This arrangement was, no doubt, designed by Chisolm as a means of escape in case of his being attacked.

which his many crimes, no doubt, caused him constantly to apprehend. In this closet he kept his guns and his armor. Through this aperture Chisolm's wife, according to Wells, and he doubtlessly received his information from her, persuaded her husband, prior to his being carried to jail, to take refuge, and that she would hand up his guns, with which he could play sad havoc with the heads of those who dared to intrude. This Chisolm declined doing, through fear that the house in that case might be fired. However this may have been, the writer, after a careful examination, could divine no other purpose of the construction of this trap door leading from this little closet into the low attic, than that to which his wife now desired that he should devote it.

It becomes necessary now to introduce a person to whom a casual reference has been already made, and who, at this time, becomes a prominent figure in this narrative. Angus McLelland was a Scotchman, and said to be a subject of Great Britain, but had for some time resided in De Kalb, in the capacity of a blacksmith and job worker. He is said to have been a man of very eccentric habits, and associated but little with any one in the village, and, although usually of quiet demeanor, he was known to be a desperate man when aroused.

This man, Chisolm, by some means, succeeded in enlisting in his clan, though McLelland had never before taken any interest in politics, and claiming to be yet a British subject, had never demanded even the right to vote. He was a man of silence and daring, and of unswerving fidelity. Chisolm had gained his friendship, and found him an obsequious coadjutor in all his schemes. On learning that Chisolm was arrested, this man left his mill and went to his aid, and when he was marched off to jail, McLelland seized Clay Chisolm's gun, and followed him. Mrs. Chisolm and her daughter, and her three sons, Clay and John and Willie, all went along with Chisolm and the two Hoppers to the jail, and when they reached there, notwithstanding the remonstrance of the sheriff, they all entered, and were locked up together.

CHAPTER XII.

The defiant bearing of Chisolm during all this time was not at all calculated to allay the intense and growing excitement of the people. As men recalled to each other's memory the dark days through which they had passed, the terrible crimes that had been committed in their midst, and of which they fully believed these men to have been the instigators, if not the guilty perpetrators, and the success with which they had heretofore baffled and escaped all law and justice, an ominous murmur of bitter indignation ran along the street, while the relatives and friends of the murdered men grew pale with frenzy, and became clamorous for immediate retribution.

Just at this time the deputy sheriff came along the street, having in custody Gilmer and Rosenbaum. On seeing these men, the crowd grew more furious, and a gun was fired that sent a load of shot through the body of Gilmer. He ran through a narrow alley and fell, and was then shot twice more, this time with a pistol which sent two balls through his head, and wonderful to tell, they entered in almost identically the same manner as those he had shot through the head of Hal Dawson under similar circumstances. The coincidence was indeed a striking one, but it could not relieve the horror of the deed; nothing could do that, save that deep sense of wrong which spurns all reflection and brooks no restraint. And here the writer will take occasion to state that it is not his purpose to attempt to justify or even to palliate the exercise of mob law under ordinary circumstances. Its principles he condemns; but he does contend, and the voice of history proclaims it, that there are occasions in the affairs of men when the dilatory forms and ceremonies of the written law, with its frequent uncertainties, are totally inadequate to satisfy the demands of justice. In such cases there is no other satisfactory remedy but a resort to that higher unwritten law which has its sanction in the universal sentiment of society. It is a part of the law of self defence, which belongs alike to nations, communities and individuals.

These men had long been a curse to society, not simply theoretically and sentimentally so, but actually and practically so in a woeful experience. To such extent was this the case, that every feeling of hope, every suggestion of progress, and every promise of prosperity constantly bred the aggravating thought—"If it were not for Chisolm and Gilmer." Such a state of public feeling was ill fitted to bear the shock which these terrible spectres of blood presented, and to which were now added individual fear and personal anxiety. These general sentiments, added to the feelings of grief and revenge naturally entertained by the friends and relations of the murdered men, all conspired to produce the terrible events of the 29th of April. And that no merely political animosity could penetrate or reach that intense combination of more serious considerations by which these people were that day actuated, is manifest from the fact that Rosenbaum, who was in company with Gilmer, and the Hoppers, all bitter radicals, escaped unharmed.

After Gilmer was killed, the deputy sheriff proceeded with Rosenbaum through the midst of the crowd to the jail, and there locked him up with the other prisoners. Upon this there was a seeming lull, but it was the ominous calm that precedes the storm. Men were seen in groups here and there, either wrapped in silent meditation or conversing in low and portentous tones. But, just here, Wells comes to the rescue of the chain of events, and describes the terrible beating and hanging of two negroes, of which he has, in addition, given his readers a thrilling engraving. In this connection, he says: "The two negroes, who were reported to have seen Chisolm and Rush in their mysterious nightly vigils, when concocting the scheme of murder, were to be compelled so to testify; and, now, that the confinement of Judge Chisolm and his friends prevented the possibility of interference on their part, Fox and Hampton, the pretended colored witnesses, were taken into a wood near by and hung by the neck, for the purpose of forcing them to testify to something which they never saw or heard; knowing nothing, as a matter of course they told nothing, and, after having been strangled and beaten nearly to death, were permitted to go, and the alleged proof has never yet been found." So says Wells. Now, let us see what one of these negroes (the other is not now in the county) has to say about the matter. George Fox, who is here represented to have been *beaten nearly to death* and then *hung*, now lives a few miles from De Kalb, and on hearing of the picture Wells has given of his having been hung, not long since visited the writer in his room, and desired to see the picture, which, on being shown him, with a broad contemptuous grin, and with his eyes dilated with amazement, he exclaimed with indignation: "Dat's all a lie!" He then stated to the writer that when the sheriff and his posse went to Chisolm's house to arrest him, he and Dee Hampton happened to be there, and that some one inquired of them what they were doing there at that early hour, and upon this a young man who lives in the same neighborhood with him, whom he knew well, approached with a piece of bridle rein in his hand, and, shaking it at him, or, throwing it over his shoulder, said, in a jocular manner: "If you don't tell the truth, we'll hang you;" and that this was all that occurred, and all that was said to them on the occasion, and the only beating and hanging they have ever suffered. To this he offered to make his affidavit before any officer, which the writer deemed unnecessary.

In the meantime, the old Scotchman, McLelland, had entered the jail, armed with the gun which he had brought from Chisolm's house, and volunteered to be one of the guard, and frequently remarked to Chisolm that they ought to fight it out, and proposed to the guard to fire on the crowd from the windows; and when he heard that Gilmer was killed, he went down into the hall, on the lower floor of the jail, having a large navy pistol fastened around his person, and told the guard, which was conveyed to the people, that for every one of the clan that was killed, two of them should bite the dust. The sheriff, observing the feeling which these remarks were kindling against him, approached, and advised him to go away, telling him that his language and conduct were placing him in danger, and several others did the same. He took no heed of the warning, but went outside of the jail, and into the midst of the crowd. Then, passing around to the rear of the building he was shot and killed, with his pistol half drawn from its sheath.

This circumstance caused another violent outburst of excitement, and but for which it is doubtful whether any one but Gilmer would have fallen on that day.

What it was that McLelland said or did at that moment to provoke the fatal shot, or who of the large crowd fired the gun, would, perhaps, have remained unknown had it not been for Wells, who says that Mrs. Chisolm, who had gone back to water the stock, saw two of the Gullys, from her gate, two hundred yards away, in the act of shooting him.

This was surely a difficult feat, to recognize at that distance the *two Gullys* in a dense crowd of, perhaps, more than a hundred persons, but it seems to have suited Wells best that it should have been done by some of the *Gullys*. In the meantime Miss Chisolm, according to Wells, was standing at a window above making the following taunting appeal to the multitude below: "Oh! why do you do my papa so bad? He never has harmed any one in his life, much less any of you, so many of whom have taken food from his hand!" This taunting question, however, if it did not reach the chord of mercy, gave Wells the opportunity of making the following reply: "—— —— him!" exclaimed Bill Gully, who stood below, with a gun on his back. "We'll do him worse than that!" Thus it seems that neither the visage nor the voice of a Gully could be dimmed or drowned by either distance or din. Before the killing of McLelland, Miss Chisolm had passed out of the jail and on to the house, whence she soon returned with a supply of ammunition, hidden beneath the folds of her skirts. This was, at least, a heroic act on the part of the young lady, and her filial devotion and constancy throughout the whole terrible scene entitles her to admiration, and her memory to more tender treatment than it has sometimes, as we have seen, received at the hands of Wells.

The excitement occasioned by the shooting of McLelland, caused a rush to be made toward the upper story of the jail, where the prisoners were confined, and a crowd, headed by Dr. Rosser, ascended the steps. It must be remembered that, although there was a large crowd of persons present, but few, comparatively, participated in the attack. There were a great many persons present who did not go near the jail at all, but there was a general indifference as to what the more furious might do.

In order that the reader may have a full comprehension of the event which is about to be described, it becomes necessary first to describe the construction of the jail building. It is a small, nearly square building, containing an upper and lower apartment. The cages and cells are all situated on the upper floor, in the form of a square room, so conforming to the main room as to leave a passage way around it. The ascent to this floor consists of a narrow and winding flight of steps. This stairway is entered by a strong door, and there is another door at the head of the steps, opening into the jail room proper. From the entrance of this door there is a sudden turn to the left, leading down a narrow passage, between the staircase and the inner room, containing the cages, into the open passage way on the other side, where Chisolm and the prisoners were standing. The guns left by the guard, all but two of whom retired as soon as the mob began to ascend the steps, were standing just around the corner and against the inner room. It was at the further end of this narrow passage, and near these guns, that Chisolm took his position when the attack was made. Here he stood, with gun in hand, while Rosenbaum and the Hoppers, with the remaining guards, retired to the other side of and behind the inner room.

308   KEMPER COUNTY VINDICATED.

The following diagrams show the arrangement of the floors of the rooms and the positions of the parties.

PLAN OF THE UPPER FLOOR.

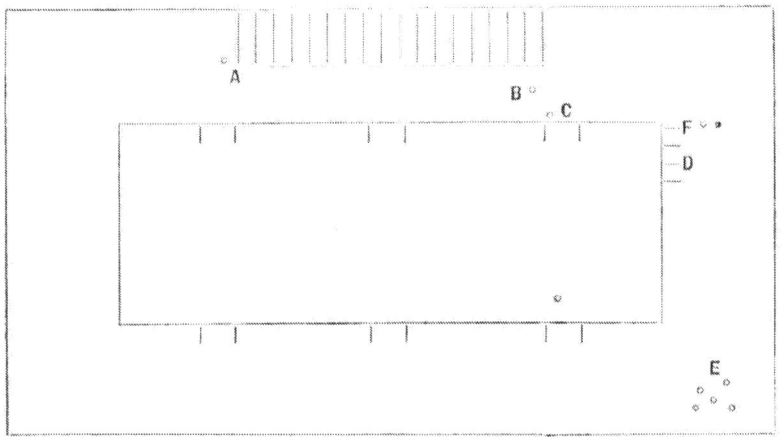

PLAN OF THE LOWER FLOOR.

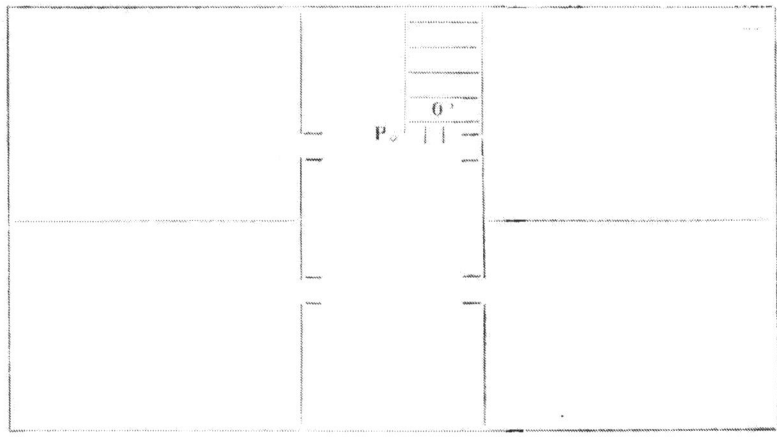

- **A** Position of Rosser when he was killed.
- **C** Position of Chisolm.
- **B** Johnnie Chisolm, killed by Rosser.
- **D** Guns of the guards, stacked against the wall.
- **E** The Hoppers, Rosenbaum and the two guards.
- **F** Mrs. and Miss Chisolm.
- **O** Position of Chisolm when shot.
- **P** Place where Chisolm fell.

When Rosser, at the van of the attacking party, entered the jail room and reached the position marked A in the diagram, he and Chisolm, who was standing at the point C, fired almost simultaneously, Chisolm's shot tearing away the fore part of Rosser's head, and Rosser's taking effect in the body of the little boy, Johnnie Chisolm, who was standing close by, and a little in front of his father, some of the shot piercing his wrist, which was extended across his breast. The dead body of Rosser was then drawn to the door and carried down the steps; on seeing which, some of the dead man's friends in the hall below cried out, "Fire the jail!" At this Chisolm seized a loaded gun and descended the steps, his wife and daughter accompanying him, the latter immediately behind, with one arm thrown around him. On reaching the lower steps leading into the hall, two more shots were fired by Chisolm, one of which lodged in the upper facing of the hall door, and the other passed through into the street. Chisolm was then shot, the same shot also striking the bracelet on the arm of the young lady, which was extended around in front of her father, shattering it and burying some of the fragments in the flesh. Chisolm now sank down on the floor of the hall, and the crowd retired from the building. Some of the mob then aided in carrying the bodies of Chisolm and the little boy home, and there was no disposition manifested to do Chisolm any further harm, but that, on some one exclaiming that Chisolm was not hurt, a few persons followed on as if led by curiosity; and on their overtaking him, Miss Chisolm, who was walking behind her father, turned and told them that they need not shoot any more, that her father was dead. The mob seemed to be satisfied, save that there was a general manifestation of horror at the unfortunate death of the little boy, and the wounding of the young lady.

That there were desperate men there, is not to be denied, and that in their maddened desperation, they were utterly reckless is too true; yet it is universally conceded that there was not an individual in all that throng who would have wilfully hurt a hair upon the head of the lady or the little boy. In his description of this sufficiently thrilling and horrifying scene, Wells could not find satisfaction without the concoction of a rigmarole about the little boy first having his wrist torn away, and in that condition attempting to bar the door against the assailants, all of which is without foundation in fact, as it is testified, unanimously, by all who witnessed those terrible scenes, and by all who examined the body, that the same shot that pierced the boy's wrist entered his breast, causing instant death. But his details of the wounding of the young lady were more truthful: "In addition to the wounds made by the shattered fragments of her bracelet, she received several shot in her leg, and her face was somewhat bruised by the splinters of the glancing shot; and the shot in her leg seems to have been of the same character. None of her wounds were considered dangerous. Indeed, it was some time before she seemed to be aware of any, except that in her arm."

When they who bore Chisolm away reached his house, they found the doors all locked, and in the confusion the keys had been mislaid. Upon this, some one entered through a back window and opened the doors. Yet Wells, in order, as he conceived, to add more horror to the circumstances, says that Chisolm was dragged into the house through a small back window. This, Doctor McClanahan, the nearest neighbor, friend and family physician of the Chisolms, and who entered the house with them, as did many others, informs the writer is utterly false, but that he was carried in at the front door, which had been thrown open as stated. If Wells' story were true, it would bespeak an unpardonable degree of criminality on the part of his wife and other personal friends who were present, especially when it was so easy to have broken the fragile locks on the batten doors of the dwelling, and it would have marred the heroic part Wells assigns her in the tragedy. While it is not to be denied that the conduct of Miss Chisolm was, throughout the whole affair, sublimely heroic, Wells again comes to the rescue of the old lady, whom he this time seeks also to cloak with the special interposition of Providence. He says: "While Mrs. Chisolm was struggling with the mob at the outside entrance, Bill Gully came up and deliberately shot at her twice; but a merciful Providence seemed to protect her, as neither load took effect. Mrs. Chisolm then seized the gun which had been brought down stairs by her husband, and discharged both barrels at Gully. The wadding struck him full in the breast and fell harmless to the ground."

This seems to have been an interposition of Providence in behalf of a terrible Gully! Yet Wells is not willing that it should be so construed, and soon finds a way out of the dilemma. He adds that the sheriff had loaded the gun with a blank cartridge. Whether it was the work of the sheriff, bad marksmanship, or Providence, if Wells desired to make her a Juan, a Judith, or an Artemisia, it is a pity that he did not choose a more plausible method.

While the writer would not add one pang to the heart of the unfortunate woman, yet, when she is thus dragged into circumstances fashioned for the twofold purpose of slander and gain, he can but remember that he has engaged in the cause of truth, and if in casting about for weapons in its defence, he indulges in conscientious reflections, all he can say is that he regrets that the biographer of her husband should have thus drawn her within the pale of his misrepresentations.

In the meantime a new light gleamed along the pall draped horizon of the Chisolm family. It was the star of martyrdom, which arose with the advent of J. M. Wells into the circle of the afflicted family. A telegram was sent to Meridian for him, and then, from the moment of his arrival, began that self ostracism which Mrs. Chisolm so strenuously maintained during all her trials. From that moment every advance of sympathy and offer of aid were contemptuously and insultingly spurned. Soon after the arrival of Wells, some ladies, who now live in De

Kalb, and who related the circumstance to the writer, went with the kindest feelings of sympathy to the Chisolm residence to tender their condolence to the family. On reaching the gate, which is but a short distance from the door, Mrs. Chisolm made her appearance on the portico, where Wells was then sitting, and cried out in a loud and angry voice, "Turn those people back. Don't let the murderers enter my gate." This treatment of these ladies deterred others from going there, and from this time the Chisolms, as a matter of course, received but little attention. They all knew the character and disposition of Mrs. Chisolm, and they were afraid to visit her. Thus it will be seen that if the ladies of De Kalb did not visit the Chisolm family during their affliction, they had every reason for their course that propriety could suggest or humanity demand; notwithstanding, Wells has the assurance to charge them with a want of common womanly sympathy. A young lady, whom the writer knows well, a bright model of nobleness, tenderness and affection, under whose mother's roof this book is being written, and who was a former schoolmate and friend of Miss Chisolm, and who, in the simplicity of her pure heart, manifested her tenderness for her memory by imploring the writer to speak of her in none but the highest terms, says that the open and violent hostility of Mrs. Chisolm to all Democratic ladies deterred her from visiting her friend during her sufferings.

One of the pastors of the churches at De Kalb, the Rev. Mr. Love, who is well known to be a man of exemplary piety and kindness of heart, in answer to a question asked by the writer, said that his reasons for not visiting them were that, on former occasions of distress in the family, he had been especially invited, and that he cheerfully rendered his services, and on his not receiving any invitation during this time, and hearing of the conduct of Mrs. Chisolm toward others, he concluded that his services were not desired and would not be agreeable.

No sooner did Wells enter the Chisolm household, where he took up his abode, than, bereft of his former occupation, every feature of martyrdom was eagerly sought for, invented and garnered up for the joint purpose of revenge and speculation, from which originated his "Chisolm Massacre."

During this time the family were attended by Dr. Kline, of Meridian, a gentleman of conscientious character, and eminent in his profession, and though he could only visit them at intervals, from such a distance, they received the best attention possible under the circumstances. Although there was not the least foundation for apprehending any further harm, the following absurd proposition was made to the governor of the State, dictated by Wells, and Shaughnessy, who had lately arrived from Jackson, returned as bearer of the appeal:

"To Hon. J. M. STONE, *Governor of Mississippi.*

"SIR: Believing you to be humane, and desirous of preventing the needless effusion of blood, I most humbly and respectfully appeal to you for aid in protecting my husband and children, until such time as I am able, with those of them whom God in his mercy may spare to me, to leave the county and their home. If you can aid me in behalf of my wounded and dying husband and daughter, I would ask that Captain M. Shaughnessy, of Jackson, be authorized to raise a body of men sufficiently large to protect and remove us to some place of safety.

"Respectfully,

MRS. W. W. CHISOLM."

This letter was carried by Shaughnessy, in person, to Jackson, and thence forwarded to Natchez, where the governor was at that time, and to which he made the following reply:

"To M. SHAUGHNESSY, Jackson, Miss.:

"I cannot consent to your proposition to go to Kemper County with a body of armed men. I will return as soon as possible.

"J. M. STONE."

This correspondence no doubt served the purpose intended. Yet prior to this the governor had visited in person Kemper County, for the purpose of ascertaining the true state of affairs there, and, if needed, of rendering such aid to the Chisolms as his presence and constitutional powers might enable him to do. He found everything quiet, and not the least indication of any further danger to that family. He, however, directed the sheriff to keep close watch and deal promptly with any demonstration of that character, which was all he could do under color of his authority. He also ordered the sheriff to appoint a special deputy to take charge of a guard to be composed of such persons as the Chisolms might name, but this offer was spurned by them; they wanted Shaughnessy and his troop of armed men to hunt down such persons as they might prescribe, and not succeeding in this, which its instigators could have had really no idea of doing, they rejected, with disdain, alike the offers of the governor and the citizens. While the administration of Governor Stone has been marked by an unswerving determination to enforce the laws, within the laws, without respect to persons or parties, he was not to be tweedled into transcending the bounds of his constitutional authority; which authority had been fixed and defined by the radical party itself.

At the time of these occurrences, the Chisolms were receiving numerous letters of condolence from their partisan friends in the North, and which Wells has triumphantly arrayed as the rewards of "outraged innocence," one of which is here inserted to show the spirit of the sympathy afforded. The letter is given in full.

"PHILADELPHIA, PA., *May* 2, 1877.

"Judge CHISOLM:

"In behalf of myself and fellow members of one of the most influential Republican clubs in this city, permit us, one and all, to offer to yourself and noble family our heartfelt, sincere sympathies in this, your hour of distress. Would to God we could offer you material protection and effective aid! Be of good cheer; keep up a stout heart, and may heaven hear our prayers for your safety. The indignation with which we received the news of the murderous attack upon your gallant little band has not yet subsided, and were the distance not so great, you should sit beneath the shadow of fifteen hundred breech loading rifles (the number of our club). Ah! for just a few minutes' *interview* with those cowardly miscreants who think it so chivalrous and brave to murder defenceless Union men. Let them remember that although " the mills of God grind slowly, yet they grind exceeding small," and that the avenging goddess will, at no distant day, blot them out. The people here at the North are beginning to talk as they did in 1861, and it is among the possible things to have " Sherman's march" repeated. If you, or any of your family, will communicate to me a full and fearless account of the events in which you have all been such prominent actors, my thanks will be of a substantial nature. A friend at my elbow has suggested that if you are in need of fire arms, be good enough to give us the name and address of a trusted friend. In the meantime, we will hope for your speedy recovery, and if there is any way in which we can serve you or yours, do us the favor to make it known at once. Pardon this disjointed epistle, for I am laboring under some excitement from having just finished the details of your martyrdom, which will account for my rambling thoughts and tremulous chirography.

" Accept again our sympathies and well wishes, while our prayers, we trust, are registered above for you all.

" Yours sincerely,

V. P."

While all these strains of sympathy for Mrs. Chisolm rent the Northern skies, not one kind word came from that quarter to soothe the bleeding heart of the widow Gully. The mangled body of her husband was now crumbling into dust, but he was only a Southern Democrat; and " the fewer of them the better" was, no doubt, a true expression of that spirit which dictated this letter.

In the meantime, both Chisolm and his daughter continued to grow weaker until the 13th of May, when Chisolm died. His death, by the advice of the attending physician, was kept a secret from the young lady, who, by this time, had grown very feeble. Although the surgeon had carefully extracted the fragments of the bracelet from her wrist, her arm was very much swollen from erysipelas, and showed symptoms of gangrene, caused by the poison of the alloy of which her bracelet was composed, in consequence of which the physician determined, on the 15th of May, two days after the death of her father, to perform a surgical operation. For this purpose, she was placed partially under the influence of chloroform, which was administered in small quantities—just enough to stupefy somewhat the sensation of pain, without perceptibly impairing her other sensibilities. The surgeon then lanced her arm, which he had done before, and which had afforded her great relief; but she had now grown so weak, and her constitution was so enfeebled, that she died before the operation could be fully performed. It was, indeed, a horrible end, and the circumstances of her death will ever awaken feelings of sorrow and regret in the bosom of every citizen of Kemper County, and which will not be lessened by the fact that it was purely an accident; and that such was the case cannot be questioned by any one acquainted with the circumstances.

She was, indeed, a model of filial affection, and possessed many qualities of mind and heart which, under more refining influences, might have constituted her a type of true womanhood. She was buried by the side of her father and brother, on the Chisolm old place—a small, barren and dilapidated farm, about twenty miles distant from De Kalb, but which Wells describes as "an oasis in the desert of Kemper County." Truly, a ludicrous sketch to the citizens of that neighborhood! After perusing this painful narrative, the reader will, no doubt, think that the facts furnish sufficient material for all the purposes of the tales of elegy, but not so with these pensioners of political animosity, whose project now was to drive a profitable trade in the mourning weeds. To add to the horror of the circumstances, they now charged that the death of the young lady was caused by the malpractice of the physician, induced by political prejudices. This charge a leading Democratic paper, the Vicksburg *Herald*, had the indiscretion to make haste to publish, for which the surgeon promptly instituted a libel suit in the circuit court at Vicksburg, and in which he has recently obtained a judgment for damages against the editor and proprietors of that paper.

This disposes of another falsehood which Wells made one of the pillars of his rickety edifice. Yet, not satisfied with his attempts to asperse the bar, the press and the people, he has the audacity to enter, with his polluted garments, the very threshold of the church, to lay hold of the sacred altars of religion, and besmear with slander the robes of the ministers of the Most High. He says that "not a minister of the gospel, or a member of the congregation with which the mother and daughter worshipped, ever visited them or offered their services at the burials." Whatever may be the custom elsewhere, it is not usual in Southern society for ministers of the gospel to perform either marriage or burial ceremonies without special invitation; and the Rev. Mr. Ellis, now the presiding elder at Meridian, who was then pastor of the Methodist church at De Kalb, of which these ladies were members, says that he did not visit them, it is true, because he was far away, but that he addressed a letter to Mrs. Chisolm, before the death of her husband and daughter, tendering them his sympathy and advice, and offering to forego his duties of ministration and all his appointments elsewhere, and go to her if she desired him to do so. To this offer he received no reply; yet he, in company with another minister, the Rev. Mr. Glann, called to see her very soon after the death of her husband and daughter. But again Wells says: "After diligent inquiry, it is yet to be learned that any clergyman preaching in De Kalb, Scooba or Meridian—all immediately adjoining towns—has publicly alluded to this in any way. What may be said of the condition of society, which so bridles the mouths of the chosen messengers of the great Prince of Peace, that they dare not lift their voices against such a crime as this, and that because of the peculiar political faith of those who are made victims of the sacrifice?" Wells surely had the opportunity of learning, during his residence in the South, if he ever visited the churches—that is, those of the white people—which is questionable, that it is not the custom here for "ministers of the great Prince of Peace" to harangue mobs from the pulpit, mingle politics, free lovism and woman suffrage with religion, and constitute themselves censors of public policy. They do not believe that the "great Prince of Peace" set any such example; but he can, no doubt, find all he desires, in this respect, in the great bloody shirt funeral sermon on the death of the Chisolms, preached by Bishop Gil. Haven, of the Methodist Church, at Washington, on the 15th of May, 1878. He will, doubtless, be pleased with the picture there drawn by this oracle of the divine mind, and with the sentiments he there proclaims as the messenger of the "great Prince of Peace." He will find there that the work begun at Bull Run should be kept up so long as a Southern man dares to raise his hand against the villanies of a carpet bagger or the outrages of a radical outlaw. He will there learn that, if by any means they should be at last overtaken by the hand of justice, wielded in the strength of despair, that they will fall "martyrs to the declaration of independence," "to equal rights," "to the purity of the polls," and for "the preservation of the American nation;" and that, like the Mahommedan, they will be transported forthwith to the "land of the blessed," where they will receive immediately the full reward of their sacred martyrdom; although, like W. W. Chisolm, they should, in the bitterest language of profanity, scout every tenet of religion and spurn every message of these "messengers of the great Prince of Peace." Yet Bishop Gil. Haven, for one, stands ready to proclaim as one of these sacred messengers, that "in Christ he lived," "for Christ he died," "with Christ he dwells." And if this glowing picture needs any further coloring of the sacrilegious, Wells stands by with brush in hand. He likens the attack upon Chisolm to that upon the Saviour of mankind, and compares the death of his daughter and son to the "slaughter of the innocents" of Bethlehem. But I will leave the bishop and the carpet bagger to hold their faith in unity of spirit, in the bonds of slander and in hypocrisy of life.

However horrifying were the details of the death of Chisolm and Gilmer, and however terrible were the circumstances, it must be confessed that all regrets were much pacified by the consideration of the great change in the state of affairs of the county—a change which left its mark upon every feature and phase of society. Men, women and children could now lie down to sleep without dread of the assassin or the incendiary; arms that had long been worn for self defence were now laid away as no longer needed, and a general feeling of confidence was restored between the two races; and in all the affairs of life men again felt that their lives and their property were their own. The county warrants, which, under the Chisolm rule, were as low as thirty cents on the dollar, now rapidly advanced to nearly par value, and every kind of business received a new impetus and new encouragement throughout the county.

CHAPTER XIII.

It now becomes necessary to again introduce the negro boy, Walter Riley. It has been already stated that, after the murder of young Dabbs, several years before, and for which he was indicted, he fled, and took refuge somewhere in Tennessee, and that, a few days after the return of Gilmer from St. Louis, and on the night previous to the assassination of John Gully, he had been seen in the neighborhood of De Kalb. It was now ascertained that he had also been seen a few days after that event about Scooba, and since then had been seen no more in the county. Upon this, a vigorous effort was made to ascertain his place of abode, which proved successful; and Henry Gully proceeded at once to Tennessee, where he succeeded in arresting and bringing him back to Kemper County. Here he was immediately taken into the custody of the sheriff and locked up in jail. At the next term of the circuit court, which was in September, he was put upon trial for the murder of Dabbs. The proof against him was positive, and he was convicted and sentenced to be hung; after which he made a full confession of this crime, and also of the assassination of John W. Gully, on the 26th of April. The circumstances of his sudden and secret return at that time, his killing of Gully and his prompt departure from the county, seemed to connect him closely with the movements of Chisolm and Gilmer. The absence of the latter, after the former's return from St. Louis, connected with other circumstances, seemed to strongly indicate the probability that Gilmer had gone after and brought him down with him. In addition to this, it was also ascertained that Chisolm, immediately on his return, a few days before Gilmer, had gone to Mobile and borrowed one thousand dollars from the firm of Dew & Kirksey, under the pretence that he wanted it for the purpose of sending his son to college. Of this money, it was said that Walter Riley had seventy-five dollars in his pocket. Be this as it may, the circumstances combined certainly afforded grounds for grave suspicion that Chisolm and Gilmer were the procurers of the crime; but no confession of that character could be obtained from Riley. All that could be elicited from him in this respect were some mysterious and guarded hints that he had accomplices.

Yet there were hopes that he would eventually make a full confession, and clear up all the mystery connected with the killing of Gully. For this purpose, when the day arrived on which he was to have been hung, a respite was granted him; still he continued obstinate and impervious to every importunity. He would frequently lead his interrogators to believe that he was about to divulge the whole matter and gratify their expectations, and then, as if in mockery of their anxiety, he would dash their hopes down, and leave them no food for their conjectures save the same mysterious hints. This inexplicable conduct he continued to the very last moment of his life. Not long before the second day fixed for his execution, a circumstance occurred which seemed calculated to add strength to the still unshaken belief in the complicity of Chisolm in the crime. By means of a file, which he said was furnished him by a friend, whose name he would never give, he succeeded in severing the chains by which he was fastened, and then in passing out of the jail. A diligent search was immediately begun, and the next day he was found in Chisolm's gin house, some miles away. The horses of Clay Chisolm and a cousin of his, named Bird, were standing in the gin house lot while they were hunting in the forest, not far distant. Riley leaped out of the house and ran, but he was pursued and captured, after having fired a nearly fatal shot at one of his pursuers with Chisolm's pistol. He also had Chisolm's double barrel gun in the gin house with him.

It was thought now that these circumstances could be used to induce him to make a full statement, but they availed nothing in that respect.

On his being recaptured, he made a written confession, it is true; but all, except his killing of Dabbs and Gully, was as vague and indefinite as ever. All he would say in reference to his accomplices was that he was persuaded to kill Gully by bad company, and that what he meant by bad company were those that encouraged him to drink and egged him on to the commission of crime.

On the 7th of December he was again led out to the gallows. He walked with a firm step, and so indifferent was his manner and heroic his bearing, that there are reasons to believe that he was not yet convinced that he was really going to be hung. His respite on the day first appointed for his execution no doubt left some hope, at least, that the same thing would be repeated, especially as he had not yet made the disclosure expected. In his bosom alone now lay hidden the secrets of John Gully's assassination; and that he yet clung to those secrets as the means of again prolonging his life, if not of saving it altogether, is still believed by many. Chisolm and Gilmer were in their graves, and the immediate cause of their deaths was the belief that they had compassed the death of John W. Gully; and while there may have been ample justification, not resting alone upon this belief, yet it was naturally a matter of great anxiety, on the part of the people, that the whole mystery should be cleared up, and relieve their consciences from the assaults of the possibility of these men being innocent of the particular charge that drew such dire retribution upon their heads. And now, when the cart halted under the gallows, and Riley leaped so impatiently and hurriedly upon the scaffold, expectation was raised to the highest degree. The crowd now gathered around the platform upon which the doomed man was standing, continued to implore him to confess, and manifested a state of anxiety which still seemed to afford him pleasure. A correspondent of the Cincinnati *Gazette* was present and made notes of the proceedings. But it is a pity for the American press that an intelligent newspaper correspondent could not describe the facts of this solemn scene without the addition of sensational expressions, and the garb of romance with which he has disguised the truth. While his statements are true as to their main features, they are warped by his efforts to produce sensation, and by the prejudice which caused him to retire from the scene with confessed feelings of triumph that Riley had refused to the last to positively implicate the Chisolm clan in the killing of Gully.

The idea of putting into the mouth of this unlettered and ignorant negro the words of a Jerome, a Latimer, or a Ridley, is so ludicrous as to almost atone for the misrepresentation. Here is this correspondent's picture of the confession and last moments of Walter Riley, published in the Cincinnati *Gazette*, December 12, 1877:

"Being asked by the sheriff if he had anything to say, the condemned man replied, 'A great deal. I want to talk about an hour.' Again there was a stretching of necks and a general murmur. Then said the sheriff, 'Men, Walter Riley will speak to you. Let all be attentive!' And the prisoner stepped to the front, and bowing gracefully, spoke as follows: 'Well, I stand here on the brink of eternity to address my old neighbors and friends for the last time. But I feel that, wicked as I have been, I am freely forgiven, and am going to a merciful God. I have been a wicked man, but now I feel no fear — no fear of the great God, and only sorrow for those I leave. For my poor old mother, whose heart is almost broken this day, and for my wife and three poor little children away up in Tennessee——' At this point the prisoner faltered a moment, but in a few seconds resumed, in a calm and dignified tone: 'I have been a bad man, and you see it has brought me to a bad end. My grave is dug in the woods as though I was a wild man, and my portion is among the despised. I am not to be laid to rest with my race, nor numbered as one among the dead of the people. But that gives me no concern, for God will raise me up even from this sand hill in the pine forest, and I will stand with you all on that awful day. I fear not the face of this congregation, for I am soon to stand before a mightier congregation than this earth ever saw. I forgive all who have injured me, and beg forgiveness of all. I bless my friends and I bless my enemies. I am guilty of these two murders, and I alone am guilty, but I have truly repented, and hope for pardon.' The prisoner here exhorted at great length, and several times repeated his confession of having killed Bob Dabbs, in 1871, the crime for which he was convicted, and John W. Gully in April last; then kneeled and offered a fervent prayer. He then confessed again and was silent.

"Sheriff: 'Would any of the people like to ask Walter a question?' Then ensued a performance, the like of which probably was never before witnessed at any legal execution. A murmur of questions rose on all sides, a dozen speaking at once, till the sheriff said: 'Let Dr. Fox talk!'

"Dr. Fox: 'Walter, you told me when we last talked that you killed John Gully, and that you were alone. Was that correct?'

"'It was.'

"'Were you hired to do it?'

"'No, sir.'

"'Remember, Walter, you are going into eternity soon, and if you can speak a word to relieve the minds of the people, do it—please do it, for your own sake and the sake of this distracted county.'

"From all sides the cry was repeated: 'Tell us, Walter, tell us why you killed John Gully; tell us who got you to do it, and relieve the minds of the people.'

"'Well' (hesitatingly), 'I might say I was persuaded to do it, but only by bad company.'

"'Walter! Walter!' almost shrieked an old man in the crowd, 'don't you know there is no hope of a heaven for you if you go into eternity with a lie in your mouth?'

"'Yes; I know that.'

"'And don't you know that if you keep back the truth it is as bad as to tell a lie?'

"Sheriff (impatiently): 'Yes, yes; Walter understands all that.'

"Old man: 'Then let him speak and relieve the people. God cannot forgive anybody who keeps back the truth.'

"And from all sides again came the appeal: 'Tell us, Walter, what led to the murder of John Gully.'

"'Well'—a long pause—'I was persuaded into it.'

"'Who, who, who persuaded you?' 'Well, only bad company.'

"'What bad company? who was it?'

"'Well, I call all that bad company that leads a man to drinking, and from that to murder.'

"'Oh, dear, dear, dear!' groaned the old man, 'he's going into the presence of God with a lie in his mouth.' * * *

"I now saw that Dr. Fox was deeply affected.

"He spoke again:

"'Walter, don't you see that these people are troubled in their minds? In your mouth lies the issue of life and death to the persons here. You may save the innocent by pointing out the guilty. You have to die. No one here can help or harm you. Tell us if you have any other knowledge, and give relief to the innocent and the troubled.'

"But the prisoner, with the same calm dignity and measured tones, without a trace of fear, replied:

"'Doctor, I know I've got to die. Man can't save me. I only am guilty.'

"A young man spoke: 'Whose gun did you kill him with?'

"'Well, it was a gun I had.'

"'But whose?'

"'Well, one I had.'

"'Did you bring it from Tennessee when you came to kill John Gully?'

"'I didn't come purpose to kill him. I was a working down this way on the railroad. That's how I came to be here.'

"'Then why did you kill him?'

"'Well, I heard he was alter me.'

"Again the blear eyed old man sung out in a sort of whining tone: 'God can't forgive anybody who keeps back part of the truth. Tell it all, Walter.' Then from all sides rose a confused shout: 'Tell it, tell it! You've got to die for it. Them that brought you here ought to be known. There's no reprieve for you this time.' (Referring to the fact that he had previously been respited when on his way to the gallows.)

"'There are too many talking,' said the sheriff, angrily.

"'Let Dr. Fox talk to him.'

"'Yes,' said the doctor; 'I believe Walter will tell me. 'Whose gun was it, Walter?'

"'I got the gun from Hezzy Jack.'

"'Ah, ah!' ran around the crowd; 'it's coming now; he'll tell about it now.'

"But he didn't. At any rate, he did not tell what they wanted to know. He said he got the gun of Hezzy Jack, and that he knew Jack worked for Judge Chisolm.

"Then Dr. Fox came to the direct question:

"'Did you see Judge Chisolm or Gilmer about it?'

"'No, sir; never.'

"'Did they send you any word?'

"'No, sir; if they did I never got it.'

"Again the blear eyed old man groaned out: 'O Walter, Walter, tell the truth, the whole truth, and nothing but the truth, or you can never enter heaven!'

"For over an hour did this sickening business go on, the poor, tortured man replying always with gentleness and dignity, that beyond what he had stated he knew nothing, and the whole crowd urging and contradicting him in half whispers. It seemed to me the most curious, irregular and illegal proceeding ever had in any civilized country. Then Mr. Brame, a magistrate, and a fair minded man, I think, from the acquaintance I have with him, said: 'Walter, let me tell you the law. What you say now can't be used against any one. You are dead in law. No one can be touched unless there is other evidence than yours. But it is to satisfy the minds of the people. There is a mystery about the death of John Gully that must be cleared up. Can't you tell who persuaded you to kill him, and give this community relief?'

"'Mr. Brame, I can't go before God with a lie in my mouth. If any white man had anything to do with it, I don't know it. Nobody ever sent me any word that I ever got, only I told Hezzy Jack, and he said, 'all right, go ahead.'

"The whole crowd then fell to questioning again, and elicited the fact that Riley took forty dollars in money, a hat, pair of boots, and a roll of cloth from Gully. In the midst of the hubbub the sheriff suddenly called out: 'William Riley, will you come up here?' and a venerable old man ascended the scaffold. The prisoner began to whisper to him, when the crowd shouted: 'Louder, louder, louder! let us all hear.'" The aged man, who was a preacher, turned to the crowd, and said: 'Brethren and friends, I have a few words with you. That man (pointing to the prisoner) was once my property. He still bears my name. He was a bad boy, as he has told you. But I have not come here to play the detective on him. I came only to exhort him to true repentance. He that confesseth his sins only shall be forgiven.' The old man then offered a fervent prayer, and said: 'Walter, in a very few minutes you are to stand before God. I believe it is the will of God you should confess to these people. Keeping back the truth is as bad as a lie. Tell it, Walter, tell it all; and may the great Searcher of hearts accept you in his everlasting kingdom.'

"Walter: 'No, no. I cannot die with a lie in my mouth, and I cannot say what this crowd wants me to say. I am guilty. I cannot bring an innocent man into this thing. O my friends, you do not believe me now! I know you do not; but the great day will come, when in the presence of a far mightier congregation than this, you will know I have told the truth, and with these words I am willing to meet my God.' For the first time he showed impatience, but the crowd persisted in questioning him about his attempt to escape from jail. He replied that the file was furnished by a friend, and he did not think a just God would require him to betray that friend. He insisted that the Chisolms knew nothing of his escape, and that Bird,

Clay Chisolm's cousin, only knew it when he went to the gin house. Again and again did the crowd urge him, and always with the phrases: 'There is trouble and sorrow among us.' 'Do speak and relieve the minds of the people,' etc. At last, when this torturing process had continued an hour and a half, the sheriff ended it by summoning a colored preacher, who offered prayer. Walter took the hymn book, and he himself gave out, two lines at a time, in the Wesleyan method, the hymn:

> "And must this feeble body fail,
>   And must it sink and die?
> And some shall quit this mournful vale
>   And soar to worlds on high."

"He led the singing in a clear voice, then sang a short hymn alone; knelt and offered a moving prayer. His brothers and a few colored people hurried up to bid him good bye. His old master came, shook hands fervently and hurried away into the forest, the tears streaming down his face. The black gown was then put on him, and the black cap drawn over his head, and the rope adjusted. Then said he, 'I want to speak last to Dr. Fox.'

"The doctor hurried forward, and such was the anxiety of the crowd for a confession that there were murmurs all around. 'Ah, he'll tell who hired him now; he didn't believe he was to die before.' But, as the doctor told me, Riley only murmured in his ear, 'One minute and I shall stand before God. All I have said here is true.' There was an awful pause. His lips moved in prayer. The sheriff severed the rope with a single blow, and though Riley fell but two feet his neck was broken, and he died almost without a struggle. From first to last he had not exhibited a tremor of fear, nothing more than a slight impatience at the persistent questioning."

Unfortunately, this is the only written description of this scene, by an eye witness, that has yet been given to the public, and that it savors strongly of the sensational and argumentative is too clear to escape observation. Yet the writer has taken the pains to read this narrative to many who were present at the hanging of Riley, including the *fair minded* man to whom this correspondent alludes, and they all concur that while there are many things truly said, there is much oversaid and much unsaid in it.

While Riley contended that what he did say was the truth, he never once said that it was the whole truth, and from his hesitations and evasions throughout the whole time of his imprisonment, and at the time of the hanging, down even to the moment of his death, leaves no question but that he died with the untold secret of Gully's murder in his breast.

The Rev. Mr. T. F. Brame, a highly respected minister of the gospel, who was sent for by Riley, while in prison, just before his death, expresses his candid opinion that although Riley made free use of expressions of penitence, he believes his heart was utterly incapable of any such sensibility. He had promised time and again during his confinement that he would tell all at the proper time, and seemed, to the very last, to take unfeigned pleasure in feeding the anxiety and curiosity of the people. He had previously said, and then denied, that he obtained the gun from Hezzy Jack, and never would he say that Chisolm and Gilmer were not his associates in the assassination. His answer was invariably that he was persuaded into it.

As to the sensational phrases with which this correspondent has interlarded his descriptions of the scene, such as "There is trouble among us." "Do speak and relieve the minds of this people," which he puts into the mouths of the interrogators of Riley, they are universally pronounced to be utterly false by all who were present, with whom the writer has conversed. Because the general belief in the complicity of Chisolm and Gilmer in the killing of Gully broke the back of patience, affords no proof that the old camel would not finally have sunk down even without this additional burden. So far as the justification of the mob was concerned, it was sufficient that the circumstances of the death of Gully, added to the former known crimes of Chisolm and Gilmer, created the indubitable belief in their guilt. Surely positive knowledge could do but little more in the way of justification. Indeed, the latter might have had the effect of preventing the mob by the certainty of legal punishment.

There is truly an unfathomable mystery connected with the whole career of Walter Riley in this matter. That he should have left his family far away in Tennessee, at that time, and hurried to Kemper County, where there was an indictment pending against him for murder, feeling his way amid the forest and beneath the shadows of the night, avoiding every eye but that of Hezzy Jack, from whom he borrowed the gun, concealing himself by the road side, killing and robbing Gully, and then making his way back to Tennessee in the same clandestine manner, without adequate inducements, is a perplexity which must find a solution outside of the known characteristics and elements of human nature. Yet all the reasons he would ever give were, "Well, I heard he was after me," and again, hesitatingly, "Well, I was persuaded to do it." Who these instigators were, is a question to which the reader must find an answer deep down the chain of events which he has followed in the progress of this work; it must be made up from the mingled voices of the many circumstances that have thronged his pathway. That the killing of Gully was closely connected with the previous attempt to assassinate him, either by the identity of actors, the identity of cause, or the identity of design, there can be no question.

There are many to-day who, notwithstanding the confession of his guilt, believe that Walter Riley had directly nothing to do with the killing of John Gully. When found guilty of the murder of Dabbs his execution became a certainty, and his confession as to the killing of Gully could not affect his fate. The total absence of every manifestation of fear, his remarkable indifference and apparent callousness to every feeling of humanity, suggest that his confessions were more the offspring of a callous heart than of a quickened conscience. There are others who believe that in consequence of his previous respite, he could not realize that he would be hung at all, and that as retention of the information sought from him by the people had been the cause of the former delay, he expected that its reservation would again have that result, and that his life would be spared so long as he retained the secret. While others, again, believe that he had entered into oaths of secrecy and fidelity with his accomplices, which he considered more binding than the obligation to betray them, even in the face of death, and in this opinion the writer, after a critical view of all the circumstances, must concur. When asked who gave him the file with which he severed his chains, at the time he escaped from the jail, he replied that it was furnished him by a friend whom he would not betray, and that he did not believe God required him to do so, and that friend remains unknown to-day.

Whatever may have been the exact arrangements for the killing of Gully, or whoever may have been the parties to the deed, it is certain that Riley acted his part of the plot with skill and life long fidelity. No martyr ever went to the stake with more calm and perfect resignation than did, apparently, this doubly dyed criminal to the gallows; exclaiming, as he stepped into eternity, that what he had said was true, but that he had not told all. That all now lies buried with him in the sand hill, there to remain ever hidden from mortal man until the great panorama of time shall pass its scenes in review, and its secret scrolls shall be deciphered to every eye.

The curtain now falls upon the last act of the bloody drama, and let us turn from these terrible scenes, bearing with us only the lessons they have taught us, and with the reflection that there is a Power that shapes the end of all things, and who can fashion the fruits of human depravity into a balm for the healing of nations.

It is to be hoped that the crimson lines in which these lessons have been written will ever be a warning to the tyrant, the assassin, and the outlaw, and continue to be a glaring menace of the terrible retribution which sooner or later will overtake him who dares to invade the sanctuary of society, and trample upon the sacred rights of the people.

CHAPTER XIV.

The feeling of perfect peace and good will to all men that has, since the death of Chisolm, reigned supreme in Kemper County, has been disturbed only by the vain, but harrassing effort to bring a large number of the citizens of the county to punishment before the courts. The Federal authorities continued their prosecution of the thirty-one citizens reported by Chisolm, Gilmer and their confederates for violating the enforcement act.

Their cause was continued from the appearance term, in May, 1877, by the consent of counsel, till the ensuing November, when it was again postponed to a special term in the following February. They were then placed upon trial for the alleged violation of the enforcement act of Congress, in intimidating Chisolm and preventing him from a free and uninterrupted canvass during his candidacy for a member of Congress. Mrs. Chisolm and the chief members of the clan appeared as witnesses for the prosecution. Their testimony was taken, and the assistant United States district attorney delivered an argument lasting two hours; but as the prosecution failed to make out any case whatever, the counsel for the defence declined to introduce their witnesses, but obtained their charges, and submitted the case to the jury, which returned in a few minutes with a verdict of "Not guilty."

Thus, before a radical United States judge, and an impartial jury, this prosecution, which had caused these citizens so much trouble and expense, proved to be without the least foundation in law or in fact. Notwithstanding this, a Cincinnati paper had the boldness to publish, in substance, the following ludicrous article: "Mrs. Chisolm has returned from Jackson, Mississippi, where she has been attending as a witness against the Kemper County rioters, for intimidating her husband during his canvass for Congress. She says that she was not permitted even to prove that her husband was a citizen of the United States." After the riddance of this trouble the citizens returned to their homes and again, in the hopes of peace, devoted themselves to their several vocations. But their hopes were not to be realized.

In the meantime, pressed on by the State authorities, who seemed anxious to gratify Northern sentiment, by a legal investigation, and by the strict injunctions contained in the charge of the presiding judge, a portion of which is given in the appendix to this work, the grand jury of Kemper County had, at the September term of the circuit court, presented indictments against six or seven persons who were present at the killing of Chisolm, and soon after their release by the Federal authorities they were arrested and placed under recognizance to answer to these indictments. That such a proceeding was dictated only by a desire to maintain the forms and ceremonies of the law, and to have a judicial investigation and interpretation of the matter, in order to appease the clamors of the radical press, is beyond question. For there were two or three hundred persons present at the riot on the 29th of April, each of whom was either a principal or an accessory to the killings, and each one was as guilty as any other, in one or the other of these capacities, and an attempt to punish six or seven men for the acts of the whole county is as absurd as would be the attempt to punish a whole county for the same act.

There is no man in Kemper County so penitent for the consequences of the riot of the 29th of April, 1877, or so lost to a sense of honor, as not to sympathize with those men whom it is sought, by these indictments, to make atone for the acts of the whole body of the assailants. And as to a judicial investigation of the matter, there is no occasion for that. No one denies but that it was a high handed exercise of mob law, and no investigation would be worth anything that did not comprehend the causes of the riot.

It was an exercise of that higher law which is beyond

the reach of all common or statute law; one of those occasions which arise in the affairs of men beyond the contemplation of all written law, to attempt to grapple with which the courts but impair their own efficiency, and bring their own power into contempt.

As an evidence of the general sympathy for the men whom these indictments seek to sacrifice as a propitiation for the crime of the county, the grand jurors who presented them soon afterward sent up the following petition to the governor:

"STATE OF MISSISSIPPI,
KEMPER COUNTY, *November*, 1877.

"To his Excellency J. M. STONE, Governor of the State of Mississippi:

"Your petitioners most respectfully represent that we were members of the grand jury of Kemper County, at the late fall term of the Circuit Court, and under our oaths we believe that we discharged our duty, and that we did it conscientiously. However we might have been inclined to spare men, we dared not, in view of the oath we had taken, and the law as given us by the court. We felt, and still feel, that the rigid duty we were constrained to perform was harsh; and we feel a great relief in understanding that, since we may have been compelled to do that which was harsh, it lies in your power, consistently with law and right, to undo it in a wise and judicious exercise of your merciful prerogative as governor.

"While we have discharged our duty fearlessly and honestly, as we claim, we think that we do nothing inconsistent with our action as grand jurors, when, in gratification of our feelings, we most respectfully and earnestly pray you to relieve all those whom we were compelled to prefer charges against concerning the riot of the 29th of April, 1877, by the interposition of your pardoning power.

"We do not enter into the reasons of the view we take of the harshness of the duty we had to perform, but assure your excellency that we honestly entertain this opinion concerning it. As old citizens of Kemper County, familiar with its trials and troubles, and knowing the actors in them, we express to your excellency our firm conviction that the granting of our petition will accomplish more toward the promotion of peace and good order in our county than the relentless prosecution of these cases, which we know will be irritating, and will produce continued excitement, running through the whole body of the county, and we fear will produce rather than quiet disorders. Executive kindness and clemency now will place our people, who long for quiet and peace, under such great and lasting obligations to be law abiding and peaceful, that we express to you our firm belief that they would not forget it. We have confidence in your wisdom and statesmanship, and hope that they will combine to favor our request.

"(Signed.)

"A. M. MOORE,   J. J. TINSLEY,
  WESLEY GRIGGS,   JAS. R. KEY,
  A. P. OVERSTREET,   C. CALVERT,
  J. C. HAMMACK,   W. J. FLAKE,
  W. H. THOMAS,   W. T. HARBOUR,
  JOHN TERRY,   T. J. CHERRY,
  P. MCCALEB,   W. K. STENNIS,
          I. M. GILLIS."

The governor declined to interpose his pardoning power, and these cases are to undergo a trial at the next term of the Circuit Court of Kemper County.

It is a pity that the governor, in view of the action of the President of the United States and the Governor of Louisiana in the forgery cases, did not comply with this petition, since "no punishment for past political offences" has become the policy of the administration, and of the radical party, the governor might have very gracefully extended the example to the prosecuted citizens of Kemper County.

Notwithstanding this, the people of the county seem to be placid, and the victims feel that if they are to be prosecuted in obedience to the law, and their sufferings are necessary for the good of the people and the interest of the State, they can but abide their fate with patience, and with the consolation that the act which brought them grief, brought peace, happiness and prosperity to their fellow citizens.

If the sufficiency of the causes of the killing of Chisolm and Gilmer is a question of which the actors were incapable of judging, neither are they competent judges who have no experience, and, therefore, no adequate conception of these causes. The question lies beyond the ken of any merely conventional interpretation of the moral code. When the beheading of Charles the First, and the execution of Mary Queen of Scots, the horrors of the French revolution, the treatment of the Indians by the Puritans, and all other popular uprisings in history, claimed to have been for the good of society, shall have been assigned a fixed place in the realms of virtue or vice, then may a true moral interpretation be given to the conduct of the people of Kemper County in the Chisolm tragedy; and until then we must leave the question to the exposition of that higher law, which derives its force and sanction from the eternal right of self preservation, too sacred to abide the delays, deficiencies and uncertainties of any fixed and formal code.

Let those who, from a deceptive standpoint, take a false or partial view of these unfortunate circumstances, and who are blinded by the mirage of barbarity which sectional or partisan prejudice and ignorance picture to their view, remember that the Southern people, notwithstanding their misfortunes, have lost no sense of their rights, and no feature of their manhood, and that the same spirit in which Mississippi laid thousands of her sons upon the crimson altars of war, is yet too vital to submit, for the sake of Puritanic heresies, to the oppression of outlaws.

But, viewed in whatsoever light, the people of Kemper County were in nowise responsible for the state of things that produced these events. If they sprang from a disregard to law and order, that condition of society was due to the demoralizing effects of radical rule. If their cause can be traced to an ungovernable popular passion, that passion had been excited and goaded by a long and intolerable series of outrages, which would have produced a popular uprising in any other State or community in the Union. No white people could have borne the oppressive rule which Chisolm exercised over this county by the aid of the negro votes.

Nor can Kemper County be made a lone target for the shafts of obloquy and reproach, however wanting in justification may have been this act of its people; but along by its side must be placed, in orbs of almost obscuring glare, the religious and Know Nothing outrages of New England, the Mormon riots of the West, the railroad and coal riots of Pennsylvania, and the destruction of the Catholic convents in Boston, in which houses of religion were entered and burned, men, women and children were murdered and mutilated, and many driven out naked upon the cold charities of the world, all in the name of religion, public policy or individual interest, and for which no man was ever punished by any human method. If the riots in Kemper County were committed with a high hand and in defiance of every law, and if the elements of barbarity entered into the act, it has its counterparts and similitudes in every Northern State. Yet the radicals of that section pretend to view the people of Kemper County as savages. Peace, Pharisees!

A late issue of the *Inter-Ocean*, a radical newspaper published in the City of Chicago, contained the following editorial:

"ILLINOIS MURDERERS.

"*Three hundred and fourteen of them sent down to Joliet in twenty years. Of these, one hundred and sixty-two escape after brief imprisonment, and walk the streets as free men. Incontrovertible figures show that three years and six months is the average punishment for Illinois assassins. Over fifty murderers, sentenced to the penitentiary for life, allowed to go free.*"

"'What shall be done with our murderers?' was the suggestive text of a minister of the gospel, of this city, two weeks ago. 'The earth is filled with violence," was another text from which a sermon was preached on the same day. These men of peace had been led to this line of thought on account of the terrible lessons of the past six months. Red handed ruffians have walked our streets, and respected citizens have been shot down in cold blood. The Almighty himself has, as it were, been smitten and insulted, and it is time the pulpit, the press, and all respectable and law abiding citizens fearlessly expressed themselves against the maudlin sentimentalism which has been conducive of such terrible results. Before the question, 'What shall be done with our murderers?' can be intelligently answered, it is necessary to ascertain *what has been done* with that large portion of the slayers of men who escape the garland of hemp which their crimes have won for them. To place these facts in a reliable manner before its readers, the *Inter-Ocean* has taken the pains to have the records of the Illinois penitentiary for the twenty years ending December 31, 1877, searched, and the disposal of every murderer that has entered the gates of that institution duly chronicled. *The list fairly bristles with terrible facts*, and while it effectually answers the question, 'What has been done with our murderers?' it certainly must prove of incalculable assistance to those who have an intelligent desire to solve the pressing question, 'What shall be done with our murderers?' For all details the reader must refer to the complete list printed below. In brief, the investigation shows that in twenty years, from January, 1858, to December 31, 1877, three hundred and fourteen murderers were found guilty of murder and sent to the State penitentiary, at Joliet.

"Of this number, *ninety were to undergo a sentence of life* in the penitentiary, and three or four long terms of imprisonment, *i. e.*, ninety nine years, sixty one years, etc., which practically means a life sentence. Twenty-three were sentenced to twenty five years and upward; twenty-one from twenty years to twenty-five, and the balance of the one hundred and seventy-nine to terms of imprisonment as low as one year, and as high, as in the case of Beede, of Winnebago County, to nineteen years. The records show, in round numbers, that *one hundred of these murderers have been deliberately pardoned* out of the penitentiary, and that sixty-two have been discharged or got out in other ways than through executive clemency; twenty-one have either died or gone to the insane asylum, and only one hundred and thirty-one are now in the penitentiary. Of those who were sentenced for life, by far the greater portion have been pardoned out, and there now remain less than forty life men in the prison. There is not now in the penitentiary a life man who was there in 1858, nor but one who was there in 1868. Eight and nine years are the longest sentences, and these are exceptions. *The average sentences of Illinois assassins is three years and a half.* Inquiry shows that there have been but few cases where executive interference was warranted."

This wail comes from the home of Wells, the slanderer of Mississippi, and the same candor would no doubt make a more terrible exposition of the state of society in some of the New England States. Yes;

"The outraged gods frown on your lewd deceit,
 To earth disgusting— and a crime to Heaven."

These references are not made in any spirit of accusation, nor are these incidents adduced as an argument of justification, but simply to show how apt men are to discover the mote from behind the beam; especially is this the case with the radical party, whose life has for years been nourished solely by tales of Southern lawlessness with which the bloody shirt has been kept aflaunt. By these arts military supremacy, which was necessary to the existence of that party in the Southern States, was for ten years exercised over these States in time of perfect peace. No sooner was civil government restored than this party ceased to exist in the South; and I, for one, would say, let its crimes be buried with it, let its memory rest in oblivion, and on its tomb be inscribed: *Lived, sinned and forgotten.*

Yet, so late as the month of October, 1876, the attorney general of the United States, who under the radical administration had also been constituted *chief of the department of justice*, attempted to meddle in the domestic affairs of Mississippi, and, if possible, find an excuse to quarter Federal troops around the voting places of the State. With this view, he opened a correspondence with the governor, who promptly replied that he had been able to execute the laws of Mississippi and conserve the public peace; that the perpetrators of wrongs were responsible to the State authorities, and that he was able to bring all such to justice, and was determined to do so. But this policy did not suit the radical press and the carpet baggers, who were yet in hopes of making profitable capital out of the Chisolm tragedy. Nothing would suit them but for Shaughnessy, with his armed troop, protected by the commission of the governor, to invade Kemper County and wreak dire vengeance on whomsoever the survivors of the Chisolm clan, Mrs. Chisolm and her flunkey, Wells, the carpet bagger, might proscribe and designate.

This allied war on the part of the governor, the carpet baggers and the remnant of the clan against the County of Kemper having failed, on account of the intractability of the governor, Wells now turned his face toward the North.

The outrage mill at Washington had ceased to grind. Yet not at all disconcerted, a thrifty scheme soon presented itself to his mind, and was immediately seized upon. The Chisolms were buried in the sand hills away down in the pine forests of Kemper, and although, as he says, "in an oasis," yet it was enough that it was unhallowed ground. So that, with the plaintive notes of compassion mingled with the howls of personal revenge and partisan prejudice, all crammed into the mouth of slander, surely here was a chance of profit not to be despised or spurned; hence, the appearance of the book entitled "The Chisolm Massacre," etc., by Wells, the falsehoods of which, so far as they are worthy of notice, are answered and exposed in this work. In this respect he will be noticed in a few more instances. The impossibility for the hand of justice to reach a member of the Chisolm clan through the courts of Kemper County during the rule of Chisolm as sheriff, has already been fully discussed and proven. If a crime was so heinous and open as to wrench an indictment from a reluctant grand jury, it was either stolen and destroyed, as we have seen in the case of the indictment against Chisolm for forgery, when the sheriff's office was robbed, and in the case of the one against Hopper, for his murderous assault upon Hezzy Jack, which was stolen from the office of the circuit clerk, on Saturday night before the March term, 1877, of the circuit court, or, if permitted to be tried, the criminals were acquitted by a petty jury selected by Chisolm for the purpose. Notwithstanding these repeated and glaring facts, Wells has the temerity to ask why these men were not brought to punishment if they were guilty of the charges against them.

The board of county supervisors, which, under the statutes of the State, selected the grand jurors, was composed altogether or mostly of radicals, from the year 1869 to 1876, who were the tools of Chisolm, who, in turn, had been elected at his dictation. But Wells endeavors to obviate and falsify this fact by giving the boards of supervisors during these years a fictitious political complexion, which will no doubt be amusing to some of the members who have never had the baseness themselves to deny their open and avowed affiliation with the radical party. The following is a list of the names of the men who composed the boards of supervisors of Kemper County from 1869 to 1876, as given by Wells, together with the politics he assigns to each:

BOARD OF 1869.

T. N. BETHANY.	Republican.
D. McNEIL	Republican.
G. E. PRIDDY.	Independent.
W. EZELL	Republican.
HEZIE FLORE.	Republican.

This is the board that levied the infamous "acre tax," an account of which has already been given, and the same which Chisolm stated upon his oath before the Congressional Investigating Committee, at Washington, February 14, 1877, page 757, to have been a Democratic board, and which statement, Wells, in his book, on page 40, adopts and reiterates; when it is a fact well known in Kemper County that every member of this board were confessed radicals, and always acted vigorously with that party.

Board of 1871.

E. Edwards	Democrat.
D. McNeil	Republican.
Wm. Hudson	Democrat.
G. E. Priddy	Independent.
T. N. Bethany	Republican.

Board of 1872.

Moses Halford	Republican.
R. Nam	Republican.
John R. Davis	Democrat.
G. E. Priddy	Independent.
W. R. Stennis	Democrat.

Board of 1874.

John R. Davis	Democrat.
E. Edwards	Democrat.
J. A. Jenkins	Democrat.
R. Nam	Republican.
T. W. Adams	Republican.

It will be observed that G. E. Priddy, a well known radical, is here assigned by Wells the status of an independent; and J. A. Jenkins, who was another staunch radical, will no doubt be surprised to find himself designated by Wells as a Democrat, in the board of 1874.

These boards chose the grand jurors of the county, and the complexion of the jury may be easily conjectured from that of the boards. The grand juries thus selected, with Chisolm as sheriff, and a radical tool as clerk, who together impanelled the petty juries, which were presided over by a radical partisan judge, who kept himself always well in harness, in order to hold his position under the Ames administration, readily answer the question of Wells, "Why were these men never brought to punishment?" and the many unsuccessful efforts to bring them to punishment, which have been laid before the reader, impart to such a question an air of folly, if not of impudence.

But again asks Wells, and with a little more plausibility, at first view, "If these charges be true, why were these 'great criminals,' Chisolm, Gilmer and others, never punished, or sought to be punished, in some legal way, after the overthrow of their power and the corrupt rule of 'radicalism' in the county?" The answer to this question will be found in the statute laws of Mississippi. The legislature, witnessing the overthrow of the radical party in other Southern States, with a view to the protection of its own members and their comrades in crime, in case of a sudden political revolution in Mississippi, made a law, which was approved by the governor, on the 5th of April, 1872, and which has already been referred to, that all prosecutions for criminal offences before that time committed, should be commenced within two years after the commission thereof, and not after.

No doubt that Gilmer, who was then in the State senate, voted for this law with great pleasure and complacency, as it relieved him from all possibility of punishment for his part in the murder of Dawson and others. The Democratic officers of the county entered upon their duties in 1876, and so great was the joy among the people at the prospect of once more having peace and quiet and good government, that but little was thought for awhile of the terrible past.

The thoughts of men were fixed upon the future, which was now, for the first time in nearly ten years, penetrated by the beams of hope. It was as if a new life had been inspired into the land, and only darkened in Kemper County by the continued operations of Chisolm and his clan.

The legislature of the State proceeded at once to tear away the coils of corruption, and put up the gaps of villany which the radical party had opened into every department of the State and county governments. The public expenditures were brought again within the bounds of necessity, and hedged against every approach of dishonesty. There were many obstructions to be removed before the ship of State could move with its wonted smoothness. The code was crammed with conflicting and unintelligible laws.

The common law had been invaded with a ruthless hand, for the purpose of protecting criminals, and every possible power had been legislated into the hands of the executive, which that functionary had, as we have seen, exercised with an arbitrary hand.

Among the first acts of the Democratic legislature of 1876 was to impeach, for high crimes and misdemeanors in office, the governor, lieutenant governor, and State superintendent of education. The proceedings in regard to the impeachment of the latter have already been discussed, in connection with the general corruption of the public school system.

It is not deemed necessary to give, in this work, a full detailed account of the impeachment of Governor Ames, or of the negro lieutenant governor. The proceedings will be found in full in the journals and reports of the legislature. A summary of the charges is here given:

First.—That he refused to take any action in regard to officials who were reported to him, on unquestionable authority, to be defaulters to the State.

Second.—That he arrogated and exercised appointing power, in violation of the constitution and laws of the State.

Third.—That he corruptly approved the official bonds of high State officers, knowing them to be worthless.

Fourth.—That he refused to remove or suspend State officers whose official bonds were declared to him, by the attorney general, to be worthless.

Fifth.—That he corruptly removed officers of the State for partisan purposes.

Sixth.—That he corruptly leased the State penitentiary to his partisan friends for a much less sum than was offered by other persons.

Seventh.—That in the exercise of his appointing power he corruptly made conditions precedent for the advancement of his own personal interest.

Eighth.—That he corruptly permitted officers of the State government to exchange offices with each other.

Ninth.—That in order to defeat the participation of the senate in the appointment of chancellors, he refused to nominate candidates to that body, as provided by the constitution, and then appointed them himself after the adjournment of the legislature.

Tenth.—That he corruptly removed judges and chancellors from office for refusing to render decisions in accordance with his wishes.

Eleventh.—That for partisan purposes he wilfully appointed persons to be judges and chancellors whom he knew to be wholly unqualified for such positions.

Twelfth.—That he sought to produce a conflict between the white and black races, and for this purpose endeavored to arm and organize the negro militia. That he did incite such a conflict at Vicksburg on the 3d day of December, 1874.

Thirteenth.—That he corruptly exercised his pardoning power.

Articles of impeachment, containing the above charges, passed the house of representatives on the 2d of March, 1876, and were, on the next day, laid before the senate. To these charges Governor Ames put in a plea of denial, to which the house of representatives replied reaffirming them.

On the 29th of March, the secretary of the senate appeared at the bar of the house and announced that the senate was organized as a court of impeachment, and was ready to proceed in the matter of the impeachment of

Adelbert Ames, governor of the State of Mississippi. On the same day the house received the following communication from the governor, through his counsel, to whom it was addressed, and which was answered by the accompanying resolution:

"EXECUTIVE MANSION,
JACKSON, *March* 28, 1876.

"*Gentlemen:* In reply to your suggestion, I beg to say that, in consequence of the election of last November, I found myself confronted with a hostile legislature, and embarrassed and baffled in my endeavors to carry out my plans for the welfare of the State, and of my party. I had resolved, therefore, to resign my office as governor of the State of Mississippi; but meanwhile proceedings of impeachment were instituted against me, and, of course, I could not, and would not retire from my position, under the imputation of any charge affecting my honor or integrity. For the reasons indicated, I still desire to escape burdens which are compensated by no possibility of public usefulness. And if the articles of impeachment presented against me were not pending, and the proceedings were dismissed, I should feel at liberty to carry out my desire and purpose of resignation.

"I am very truly yours,

"(Signed.) ADELBERT AMES.
"To Messrs. DURANT & PRYOR, Jackson, Miss."

The following resolution was immediately adopted by the house:

"*Whereas,* Assurance has been received by the House of Representatives of the State of Mississippi, that Adelbert Ames, governor of said State, but for the pendency against him of articles of impeachment exhibited by the House of Representatives, would have resigned his office of governor, and will now do so, as the managers are informed by a letter, addressed by said Governor Ames to his counsel, Messrs. Durant & Pryor, read to said house, on a resolution adopted directing its managers to dismiss said proceeding; now, therefore,

"*Be it resolved*, By the House of Representatives of the State of Mississippi, that the managers, on the part of this house, in the matter of the impeachment of Adelbert Ames, governor of said State, be and they are hereby directed to dismiss the said articles against the said Adelbert Ames, governor as aforesaid, heretofore exhibited by them against him at the bar of the Senate."

Prior to the adoption of proceedings of impeachment against the governor, a resolution was passed by the house to impeach the lieutenant governor. Why this order was adopted is as unaccountable as it is remarkable. The only charge against the lieutenant governor was the corrupt exercise of the pardoning power, while those against the governor were multifarious and equally as heinous. On the 17th of February, articles of impeachment were preferred against the lieutenant governor, charging him with having received a bribe for the pardon of Thomas H. Ballentine, for the murder of Ann Thomas, in the County of Lowndes, in August, 1874. Upon this charge issue was joined, and the trial proceeded with before the Senate, which, on the 23d of March, found the lieutenant governor guilty of high crimes and misdemeanors, and immediately pronounced sentence, removing him from office, and disqualifying him for holding any office of honor, trust or profit in the State. Whatever triumph of justice there may have been in this issue, but little credit can attach to the vigor with which this negro was pursued to expulsion in view of the fact that Ames, the guilty head of the administration, was permitted to escape through the honorable door of resignation.

This negro had always manifested, in all his conduct, the highest respect and the kindest feelings for his former owners and for the white people generally, and it was his ambition to be respected and noticed in turn by them that caused his ruin. He craved the notice and good will of prominent white men, and the very crime of which he was convicted, and for which he was expelled from office, was committed in the effort to acquire prominent notice, and was the product more of vanity that of vice.

On the downfall of Ames, the last vestige of radical power disappeared from the State. On the 29th of March, the same day on which he resigned, J. M. Stone, president *pro tem.* of the Senate, was inaugurated governor of the State of Mississippi, and entered upon the duties of that office.

A system of reform was now begun in all the departments of the State government, which was at once marked with palpable benefits to the entire community. The judiciary was purified by the appointment of judges and chancellors, with one or two exceptions, learned in the law, and of irreproachable character, and an upright administration of public justice was re-established. Crime began to rapidly decrease, and the county jails, the support of which had become an enormous burden upon the public, now became empty, and the almost daily knocks at the door of the penitentiary ceased. The certainty of punishment, always more effective than the quantity, produced a wholesome effect upon all grades of society.

The public school system was placed upon a more satisfactory and substantial basis, and every objectionable feature removed from the institution. The benefits of these measures continued to multiply, and their fruits will increase with the years.

There is not now an intelligent and honest man in the State who does not feel disgusted with the rule of corruption that afflicted the State under the radical administration.

In his annual message to the legislature on the 8th of January, 1878, the governor says:

"During the past year, general peace and quiet have prevailed. With few exceptions, confined to one or two localities, no disturbances have occurred, the laws have been enforced, and the courts have protected the citizen in his life, person and property. Local self government has been sufficient to preserve the peace and to secure to our people the blessings of good government. The wisdom of the legislation of your predecessors, enacted in the memorable session of 1876, and in the session of 1877, is seen in the prosperous and satisfactory condition of every department, and in the general content and satisfaction of the people of all classes and races."

And again, in his inaugural address, two days after, his excellency says:

"Let us be thankful that, amid our poverty and gloom, no riotous spirit of communism has raised its head in our midst; that the earnest conservatism which has ever characterized our people, has preserved us from the terrible scenes of pillage and plunder and lawlessness which, during the past summer, struck terror to the hearts of thinking men in other communities. Those who have traduced and slandered an entire State for the acts of a few maddened and infuriated men, have had to hang their heads in shame, while mobs of thousands and tens of thousands, for days and weeks together, held great cities in their grasp, and robbed, burnt, murdered and plundered with impunity."

Yet the governor did not, as he says, refer to these things in any spirit of exultation, nor in justification of mob law, anywhere or under any circumstances, but he referred to them for the same purpose for which the writer has here introduced the reference: to show what a noise may be made over an ant hill until it is lost in the shadows of the mountain. But, nothwithstanding the odium of comparing those authorities, the carpet bagger, Wells, says: "In times of comparative peace, in Mississippi, there is shown a want of respect for the laws, and a lack of energy on the part of the 'local authorities' in their execution, which, in many of the States of the Union, where a wholesome fear of the courts is maintained, would at once produce a sense of insecurity to life and property so great, as to call out at once the united voice of the people for a revision of the code or an immediate change of officers intrusted with its enforcement."

There was no " comparative peace" in Mississippi until the dethronement of the radical power in the State, and if these remarks apply to the state of affairs under the rule of the negroes and carpet baggers, then the people of Mississippi did, in 1875, just what Wells says would have been done in other States of the Union, and the people of Kemper County acted upon a similar principle on the 29th of April, 1877. Goaded by this intense feeling of " insecurity to life and property," the " united voice of the people" " called out" for an immediate change. It was wrought, and since that time a far more than " comparative peace," as the above references indicate, has dwelt in the State of Mississippi.

But, again, says this carpet bagger, " The people of the South are governed by passion and prejudice more than by reason or law." In reply to this, the writer will simply state, and this man may take the unction of its tersity to his soul, that the people of the South will in nowise accept, as a judge of what should be their ruling sentiment, an individual who stood cringing in the streets of Brandon, without the least show of resentment, while a negro man, whom he had swindled, thrust his clenched fist in his face, and called him a "damned thieving carpet bag scoundrel." This circumstance was witnessed by Col. Frantz, the well known editor of the Brandon *Republican*, and by many other gentlemen.

There is a sense of delight on the part of some persons in misrepresenting sentiment which they do not possess and cannot comprehend. It rises from a sense of inferiority, and this is evidently the case with J. M. Wells.

If a Southern man, being armed at the time, had shot this negro while committing this aggravating assault upon him, he would then, in the estimation of Wells and his class, have fallen into the category of those who have no regard for law and order. Totally destitute themselves of the sentiment of chivalry, they can recognize it only as a spirit of lawlessness. In war they characterized it as " madness of rebellion;" for a long time after it was termed "disloyalty," and then a "disregard to law and order." This quick sense of honor and fiery spirit of personal resentment, so common and so highly appreciated by the Southern people, was always a terror to the carpet baggers, and was the only thing that protected the Southern ladies from the intrusions and insults of that craven set. They might advocate with impunity their political opinions, follow their low calling without injury, and with color of politics, band the negroes together under the banners of ruin to the people without personal harm, but let them think of offering personal indignity to any white gentleman or lady, and they well knew what the consequences would be. It was a feature of ostracism which they cared not to tamper with.

But since their flight from the South, their foul tongues have not spared the ladies, who scorned them with all the power of disdain, it is true, but who otherwise did not deem them worthy even of the notice which corporeal punishment confers at the hands of a gentleman.

We have already seen Wells representing Miss Chisolm as standing on the porch of her father's house while a Democratic procession was passing along the street, and "devoutly praying that their cannon might burst and blow them all into the fiery furnace," in other words, into hell. But not satisfied with this caricature of the character of his paragon of refinement, he says that he has seen a beautiful young lady of Jackson, who was so lost to the "tender emotions of her sex," that on being questioned as to her feelings toward Governor Ames, " who with his accomplished wife and interesting family of children lived in the same town with herself," bristle up with an expression as savage as an outraged tigress and exclaim: " I could tear out his tongue and heart and burn him alive!" There are, no doubt, women in the South belonging to the only class with which Wells associated who are capable of such sentiments as he characterizes, as in the case of Miss Chisolm, as the outcrop of superior refinement; but in regard to the *beautiful young lady of Jackson*, the writer will say to him; that were he to again make his appearance on the streets of that town, which he has so often promenaded, arm in arm with cornfield negroes, while the gentlemen would scorn to notice him, the little boys of the town would cowhide him along the streets with all the deserved ignominy of a Titus Oates, while these same "*beautiful* young ladies, with dreamy eyes and drooping lashes," would wave their handkerchiefs in applause, from the windows, with all the pleasure of a "Catharine de Medici," and with hearts no less appalled. Unfortunately, as the champion and chosen historian of the family, he has the character of the amiable and unfortunate Miss Chisolm in his keeping, but if he cannot clothe her memory with more chastity than he has done, it is a pity that it cannot rest in the sand hills of her native pines.

History will ever accord the highest meed of praise to the noble women of the South. At the first sounding of the tocsin of war they buckled on the armor of their husbands, fathers, brothers and sons, and bade them go with all the exulting pride and patriotic spirit of the dames of Sparta. And amid all the vicissitudes of war, and all the trials and sufferings that fell to their lot, they maintained the same spirit of defiance, the same calm, dignified demeanor, an abiding faith and unswerving constancy unequalled by the maids and matrons of Rome in the palmiest days of heroism. If they did not lop off the head of a Holofernes, sink ships of war, or scale the frowning ramparts of an Orleans, they inspired the soldiers of the confederacy with that valor which gained the admiration of the world. Nor did their devotion slacken when the smoke of battle cleared away and the Southern flag lay trailing in the dust, but with the same lofty spirit and virtuous pride they held the rod of scorn over those of their countrymen who for one cause or another would have dragged them down to the level of that society which radicalism sought to establish. Their fidelity to the elevated principles of Democracy confined the contamination of treason to the father, and prevented the inheritance of radicalism among the youth of the South. Under such influence and restraints, no offer of honor or emolument could induce a young man, of any self respect, to ally himself with the radical party, and there are many to-day whose cheeks are mantled with the blush of shame when, in the presence of ladies, they are reminded that their fathers were radicals. All honor to the noble women of the South. The seal of their applause is stamped with more than mortal indelibility, and will blaze into a brilliant star beyond the verge of time.

But to descend from the sublime to the ridiculous, let us return to Wells, the slanderer of Mississippi. He says: "The State teems with little newspapers; for when the fact is well established that a man is utterly incapacitated for carrying on any legitimate trade or business, he is most likely to ascend the tripod, and through the agency of a 'patent inside,' and the logic of the shot gun, become a dictator of public sentiment and morals. If an editor's credit survives a dozen issues of his sheet, he is entitled by the law of a long established custom to *honors* of some kind, and there being nothing else so cheap, a 'handle' is at once affixed to his name, supposed to be commensurate with his subscription list, exclusive of 'dead heads.'" Wells speaks here in part from his own experience, for, excluding the shot gun phrase, in which feature he was incapable of sharing a part either in fact or significance, there was certainly one less of the class of papers he here describes in the State, when the filthy negro carpet bagger sheet, edited by him at Brandon, Mississippi, succumbed to the contempt of his own party, and as to the sobriquet of "captain" which he assumes, if it was acquired during his editorial career, it was but the expression of his leadership of some negro club mustered in the dark hours of the night, and organized for the purpose of hounding them on to deeds of rapine and violence. And if he obtained his title during the war, it was no doubt derived from his expertness among the bee hives and chicken coops of the South. No doubt he has a wholesome disgust for the editors of Mississippi, who so often held up his political and personal dereliction to the public gaze, and with whom he never dared to tilt the lance of debate. He sought circulation for his paper mostly among the illiterate negroes, whom, if they could not read it, he endeavored to impress with the magic effect of posting it upon the logs of their cabins.

The dignified tone, alertness and manly bearing of the Mississippi press were fatal to the operations of the carpet baggers. Its voice has always been a two edged sword, whose sharp cuts and pointed thrusts cleaved deep fissures in the radical carcass throughout the length and breadth of the land. No circumstance could thwart its aim, no distance parry its blows. And these same editors, whom Wells characterizes as "the titled gentry of the Mississippi press," have won as immortal fame and unfading glory in the great battle with radicalism as that which most of them achieved by their daring, courage and endurance on the field of battle. In the sanctum or in the camp, in the gloom of defeat, or in the brightest beams of victory, their swords and their pens, their blood and their brains, have been alike devoted to the cause of right and the interest of their people; to the great principles of constitutional law and American liberty; clinging with one hand to the doctrine of States' rights (the only hope left to the South), they grasped the hand of the people with the other, and rescued them from the shackles which vengeance and fanaticism and folly were forging and welding around their liberties; like "sentinel stars" they kept their watch in the skies, signalled the appearance of every cloud along the horizon and heralded every beam of the rising day.

No wonder that the carpet bagger looked upon the press of Mississippi as his worst enemy, and that its lashings appeared to him " the terrifying features of the hydra headed monster, which the lovers of Republican government have to confront," and that he should exclaim, with Wells: "The cardinal principles of popular government are too plebeian ever to be appreciated by the high born sons of the South." The "cardinal principles" of radicalism, which sought to convert the South into a new Africa, and by means of the negro vote, to place all the power and property of these States in the possession of thieving adventurers; to subject their white citizens to the political, social and moral code of New England thieves, mixed with so much of negro voodooism as to preserve the alliance necessary for the purpose, was indeed too plebeian to be tolerated by any people not lost to every sense of pride and every sentiment of virtue. If this state of things was alone to constitute that " domestic tranquility," in speaking of which, Wells says, " comparisons become odious," then the Southern people might well afford to welcome the chances of that " irrepressible conflict," which he says existed between the negro and his former owner.

It was upon the existence of such a conflict that J. M. Wells and his class rested all their hopes, and to the breeding of which all their aims and efforts were directed. And the fact that none such ever naturally and really existed, was the cause of their overthrow.

There was never any antagonism existing between the negroes and the white people of the South, save that kindled and fed by Wells, and others of his character; and this they did by falsehood and deceit, and by the means of every low art that vice could devise to reach the mind of ignorance.

We have seen that the leading carpet bagger of Mississippi, Adelbert Ames, rested the success of his administration, as governor of the State, upon that issue, and even proclaimed a war of races in the State, in which he declared himself to be in alliance with the blacks.

But the election of 1875 put an end to their design and broke the wings that had fanned the trouble. On the day of that election, this world proclaimed monster of antagonism shook off the unnatural garments in which radicalism had so long sought to clothe it, and disclosed an alliance of politics and interest and good will between the negroes and their old owners. It was then that the carpet bagger found himself friendless and alone. The cranes had all left the radical pasture; and the carpet bagger, his occupation being gone, and being disrobed of his disguise, sought safety behind the sheltering lights of radical rage. The legislature of 1876 was organized with a large Democratic majority in both houses, and the laws then enacted were characterized by an entire freedom from partisanship or partiality. In striking contrast with the predictions of the radical party and the representations of Wells, were the resolutions and speeches which marked the close of the session.

The colored members expressed their gratitude to the speaker and to the members of the house generally for their impartiality, kindness and courtesy which they had uniformly shown them. Young, the negro representative from Washington County, said that he came there with some doubts lingering in his mind as to the disposition of the majority to accord justice, and as to the treatment the colored members would receive. While he was a Republican, he held that if a man was pure, consistent and honest, he was the man for position, regardless of what might be his politics. He assured the members that if they would continue to keep faith with the colored people, as they had heretofore done, no foreigner, no Northern man, no Western man, no carpet bagger could ever again alienate the colored people of Mississippi from their fellow citizens of the white race. "You," said he, "have the brains, the power and the property. Only continue your kind treatment, and show my people that you will do by them what is right, and they will stand by you and with you to the last." Carter, colored, from Warren County, dwelt especially on the liberal action of the house toward the colored normal schools, and in the interest manifested in the education of the colored race. Jacobs, of Adams County, and Mallory, of Le Flore, both colored, also, in the name of their people, expressed their thanks to the speaker and to all the members for the kind treatment they had invariably received during the session, and in return expressed their kindest wishes for the white members, and for the white people generally. The resolution of thanks to the speaker was unanimously adopted by a rising vote.

This scene was truly a remarkable phase of that "irrepressible conflict" which Wells declares still exists between the negro of the South and his former owner "But," says that individual, "the friends of Republicanism meet with the same uncompromising opposition that Union men did in the South in 1860 and 1861, and the stronger the hold which is fastened upon the government, and the greater the number of 'Confederate brigadiers' who secure seats in the national Congress, the more bitter, persistent and determined seems to be the opposition to everything sought to be introduced and maintained here, that is not Democratic in name and Southern in principle." The first part of this paragraph is conceded with intensified force. The Southern people generally are far more bitterly opposed to radical rule and the carpet bagger than they ever were to the Union or to Union men. To the Union, so long as it existed or was capable of existing as it was established by its founders and interpreted by the Constitution, they were never opposed, but, on the other hand, were its stanchest supporters; but, when it was proclaimed by the radical party, when it came into power by mere accident, to be "a league with death and a covenant with hell," they thought it was time to sever their connection with such a diabolical association. And as to the significance of the presence of brigadiers in Congress, Wells misses his mark when he seeks to excite the prejudice of the Northern soldier by such an allusion. Brave men are alike everywhere, and the true soldier of the North cherishes no ill will against the "Confederate brigadiers." It is only the camp followers, sutlers, chicken thieves, women insulters, and stay at homes, and dastard politicians, who entertain feelings of bitterness toward the officers and soldiers of the Confederate army. With this class his diatribes will no doubt have the desired effect. It was often said during the war, that if the matter were left to the rank and file of the two armies, they would soon frame a treaty of a satisfactory and abiding peace; but, unfortunately, the voice of these was scarcely heard in the uproar of office seekers and non-combatants which followed the cessation of the conflict. The true soldiers of both armies, as a general thing, gladly retired to the quiet walks of life, and left the field open to the lowest grades of humanity, who, lured by cupidity and revenge, swarmed in shoals upon the surface of reconstruction.

> "The brave man seeks not popular applause,
> Nor, overpowered with arms, deserts his cause,
> Unshamed, though foiled, he does the best he can,
> Force is of brutes, but honor is of man."

These elements, when transplanted in the South, blossomed and bloomed into that queer character known as the carpet bagger, who was truly a thrifty being so long as he could flounder in the filthy slime of reconstruction. But as State after State was rescued from that sea of corruption, like the frogs of a desiccated lake, they made their way to other parts in search of congenial elements. Mississippi, unfortunately, became one of their last and favorite resting places. Here they gathered in appalling profusion, until the muddy pools of politics foamed with the struggling mass of plunderers, who finally, as we have seen, turned their thirsty jaws upon each other, and in verification of the old adage, "When thieves quarrel, honest men get their dues." This was done, and the carpet baggers fled to parts unknown, while the Southern people beheld their rapid exit with as much delight as did ravaged Greece the flight of the Persians from the plains of Marathon.

THE CARPET BAGGERS' FLIGHT.

> And do ye dream we see
> The carpet baggers flee
> From this fair Southern land,
> Where the adventurous band,
> Under the covert night,
> Gathered their savage might

> To strike the robber's blow,
> And lay all virtue low?
> Great Justice! canst thou see,
> Unmoved, the villains flee;
> Such plunderers go free,
> Unhung, with pockets packed
> From the Southern tills they sacked?
> Of curses laid on man,
> They lead the frowning van,
> Incarnate demons! Lift their name
> High up the shaft of roguery's fame.
> And when they lost their power,
> They seized the exalted dower
> Of Slander, and her frown
> Became the fitting crown
> Of their accursed renown.
> Cease, radicalism, cease,
> Your gongs of hollow peace,
> Should he again come forth,
> This pocket eating moth,
> From cesspools of the North.

Wells charges Mississippi with having been infested with " an ungovernable element, familiarly styled ' Bulldozers.' " Any radical who, in view of the forgeries of the Florida canvassers and the Louisiana returning board, can write, unblushingly, that word for the public gaze, must be too obdurate in heart, too imbecile in intellect, and too degraded in sentiment to feel the chastisement which the very mention of it should inflict upon the feelings of every patriot—of every honest man. But as he and his class were so habituated by the long exercise of such arts upon the credulous minds of the negroes, that they find themselves at a loss for other means of calumny than by charging the Southern people with using the same methods by means of which they themselves had so long flourished.

To support these charges, Wells has taken the pains to cull from the newspapers of the State every precautionary advice, every local or personal reprimand, and every flight of moral discourse he could find, however trivial the circumstances which made the suggestion and called forth the rebuke. In this connection, he again assails the governor of the State, and charges him with partisan partiality in responding favorably to a call made by the citizens of some of the lower counties of the State for the suppression of existing lawlessness, when he had declined to comply with the request of Mrs. Chisolm to send the carpet bagger, Shaughnessy, with an armed troop into Kemper County, which was then in a state of quietude. He says: "Again his excellency the governor has been forced to acknowledge the virtue found in the old adage, 'It makes a difference whose ox is gored.' Contrast his language of May, in answer to Mrs. Chisolm's appeal, when he had 'no power to do anything at all,' with that of September last, in answer to the call of his own distressed brethren." The language and the answer of the governor, to which Wells here alludes, and which he quotes, is as follows:

"EXECUTIVE DEPARTMENT,
JACKSON, MISS., *September 8, 1877.*

"Hon. A. C. McNAIR, Brookhaven, Miss.

"*Dear Sir:* I have the honor to acknowledge the receipt of your favor, detailing the condition of affairs in three of the counties of southwestern Mississippi. I am now in correspondence with leading citizens in those localities, with a view of ascertaining what the emergency demands, and then to determine what lawful means to adopt to meet that emergency. Such a state of things cannot be tolerated, and cost what it may, it must and shall be stopped.

"Yours very truly,

J. M. STONE."

The counties referred to in this letter were Amite, Pike and Franklin, in which disturbances of a local nature were then existing, and which, in some instances, had assumed proportions beyond the control of the local authorities. The cause of these troubles, which did not at all partake of a political character, can be traced only to the bad state of affairs resulting from the long radical misrule in these counties. In pursuance of the suggestions contained in the governor's message to the legislature, on the 8th of January, 1878, the house of representatives appointed a special committee of five, including the members from the distressed counties, to investigate the alleged state of lawlessness in the three southwestern counties. This committee performed its duties thoroughly and with vigor, and gave the subject the careful, deliberate and impartial consideration which its importance demanded. The testimony of many of the most intelligent and reliable citizens of those counties was taken by the committee, and a large number of affidavits made before the officers of those counties, and many private letters of prominent citizens were also submitted to the committee. These various sources of information disclosed the fact that for several months there had been more or less lawlessness existing in the counties of Amite, Pike, Franklin and Lincoln, and which had sometimes extended to the counties adjacent to these. These acts of lawlessness were generally perpetrated in the night time, by unknown persons, who posted threatening notices about the premises of prominent citizens, and who whipped and sometimes killed persons, and burnt houses.

The committee reported that they had striven diligently to ascertain the cause of this state of affairs, but were unable to arrive at any conclusion, other than that it had its origin in the general financial depression and extreme poverty of the country; that it was the work of a spirit of agrarianism, in which political considerations had no share. The long misrule and dishonesty in the management of the finances of the country, the intolerable burden of taxation to which they had long been subjected in consequence, and the failure of the system of agriculture then in use, had combined to produce a state of financial depression, as the results of which, a large number of the people saw their lands, their houses and their homes, pass away from them by tax sales, and under the execution of mortgages and deeds of trust.

In former years, and until then, the people of these

counties had been as prosperous, peaceable and law abiding as of any portion of the State, but the policy, pursued of late years, of making cotton almost exclusively, for which they obtained low prices, and of depending upon the proceeds of this crop to purchase supplies and the necessaries of life, for which they were compelled to pay exorbitant prices, in consideration of advances on credit, coupled with the onerous load of taxation imposed upon them during radical rule, caused their condition to grow continually worse, and finally culminated in disasters well calculated to produce despondency, if not desperation.

Under such circumstances, many of these people gave way to unfortunate and deplorable feelings of communism, such as have puzzled the wisest statesmen, not only in other parts of our own country, but in almost every country in the world.

The committee were emphatic in the statement that politics formed no element in the production of these acts of lawlessness, and that they sprang from no feelings of race, or animosity against the negroes. The evidence of this was obtained from the numerous disavowals of this feature found in many anonymous notes and letters which they found scattered over the country by these men for the purpose of terrifying the people. Their object seems to have been to drive away the laborers and tenants, without injuring them, in order to ruin the large land owners. It was evidently the spirit of incipient communism against which the committee urged immediate and vigorous action on the part of the authorities of the government.

The committee ascertained also that this spirit of lawlessness by no means prevailed throughout these counties, but was confined to certain localities, and that its existence was deprecated by the larger portion of the people, and by all of the better class of citizens, who were desirous that law and order should prevail, and showed a perfect willingness to co-operate with the authorities in suppressing riotousness and in bringing all violators of the law and disturbers of the peace to punishment.

On the reception of the report of this committee, the legislature promptly passed an act to suppress lawlessness, which, together with the prompt and vigorous measures adopted by the governor, caused the offenders to disperse, since which time peace and quiet have been enjoyed by the citizens of these counties.

It was the language and the action of the governor on this occasion which Wells so triumphantly contrasts with the reply he made to Mrs. Chisolm, when she petitioned him to send an armed force, under her friend Shaughnessy, to Kemper County, where he had been in person, and found everything in a state of perfect quiescence, with no obstruction of the laws, and no hindrance to the execution of the process of the courts, or to the full performance of their functions. What analogy there can be between the proper action of the executive of a State, on the occasion of existing popular disturbances, and his course when no such troubles exist, must find its development only in the logic and politics of J. Madison Wells.

And just at this point the ingenuity of that individual seems also to have been exhausted, and, in casting around to recover itself, seizes upon the names of three score citizens of Kemper County, which he thinks deserves special notice, and is "unwilling that they should be lost to posterity," as "active participants in the 'Chisolm' massacre." These names he wishes to be "hung up along all the public avenues leading into the State," there to appear as "terrifying warnings," such as that inscribed on one of the entrances of "Dante's ideal hell," to every "weary emigrant" who, in search of a home, may chance to turn his face toward the smiling gates and "genial clime of Mississippi." To all such he desires that these three score names shall read: "All hope abandoned when ye enter here," and that they should "inspire the gifted Lamar to honeyed words of reconciliation," and the honorable Mr. Money to point with "pride to the names of his constituency," and awaken a remembrance of the murdered Chisolm, his boy and sweet girl; and that they should proclaim, for all time, that four thousand negroes voted for the said Money who ought to have voted for Chisolm and the carpet baggers. Wells has heaved all these ideas into a dozen lines, and these lines, compacted into the closing paragraph of his "Chisolm massacre," which butt against its terminal bounds, like pent floods that lash the barrier shore.

As to the men whose names he wishes to illume above those of their fellows, although some of them were not even present, they have never denied, nor have they ever sought to conceal the fact that they, each and every one of them, participated either directly or indirectly, in the riot of the 29th of April, at De Kalb. This legacy they are willing to leave to posterity, even without the concurrence of Wells, and they wish their names to be painted in "letters of gold" on every guide post that points an entrance into Mississippi, as a "terrifying warning" to all outlaws, carpet baggers, and to all oppressors of the people, that there is no hope for them if they enter there, but to all honest and upright men, be they from whatever State, or from whatever clime, they wish their names to be tokens of welcome and good will; to all such, who wish to settle among them, they extend the hand of friendship, of neighborly kindness and social fellowship. And as to the honeyed words of the "gifted Lamar," or the vaunted pride of Mr. Money, the character and public services of those gentlemen are too well known to be affected by scurrility. They are too far above the reach of the spiteful shafts of a carpet bagger to discover even the random flight of his arrows.

With this feeble effort to daub with his exhausted brush the names of the United States senator from Mississippi and the member of Congress from the Kemper district, Wells, with an eye to the profits, turns with a lively faith in its merits, to the alleged object of his work as a "guarantee of the high character and responsibility" of which he quotes the opinion of his partner, Mrs. Chisolm. And we will here leave him beleaguering and bantering the young men of the country for contributions in the way of traffic for his book, which he says will be devoted to the erection of a monument over the tomb of Miss Cornelia Chisolm. If the young men of the country, or of any section, are disposed to contribute to the erection of a monument to the memory of that worthy and unfortunate young lady, the writer, so far from any disapproval, will cast his mite for the purpose, provided the management of the enterprise be placed in reliable and worthy hands, and he will undertake to say that under the auspices of honesty and sincerity a sufficient amount for that purpose could be raised in Kemper County. But perhaps there is now no such necessity, since the government of the United States has adopted the Chisolm family. In the month of December, 1877, at the special instance and request of the President, the name of Mrs. Chisolm was placed on the pay rolls of the Treasury Department of the general government, and a few months later that of Mrs. Gilmer, the widow of the infamous John Gilmer, was placed among the employees in one of the departments of the War Office. As to the personal promotion and private fortune of these ladies, the writer makes no reference; he would not pluck one sprig from their fortune's wreath; but the manifest partisan prejudice displayed in the circumstances of these appointments was unworthy of the dignity of the chief magistrate of the nation, and should incur the scorn of every fair minded citizen. It was evidently intended as an act of the highest official confirmation of the slanders perpetrated upon the people of Kemper County, and an official strike at the Democratic party on the part of the President of the United States.

But there is another, widowed by the hand of the procured assassin, whose unfading grief and quenchless anguish, veiled with meekness and Christian resignation, seeks no public ovation or governmental sanctification. Mrs. Gully, by her Christian bearing since her great misfortune, deserves all that pure and tender sympathy she has received—a woman around whose head clusters a halo of more than ordinary virtues. She has sought solace only in acts of charity, and in providing for her little children and grandchildren

She has striven to hide her grief from the world, and submits with Christian meekness to the dispensations of Heaven. Never could she for a moment entertain the idea of achieving notoriety by her misfortune, and her very soul would revolt at the thought of bartering the bullet rent and bloody garments of her husband for fortune or fame; but with the tender sympathy of her countrymen and the blessings of Heaven, she "lives on" in faith and in the firm hope that her garments of woe will be exchanged for an apparel of glory, when, with the end of her earthly troubles, shall come a reunion with her loved and lost.

CHAPTER XV.

> "What more noble,
> Than to redeem the fortunes of a state,
> And, seizing fearlessly the wayward helm,
> While the whole crew stand trembling and appalled,
> With blanchless cheek, and an undaunted eye,
> And nerved arm, framed as to rule the trident,
> To steer the shattered vessel into port,
> And, like a rock amid the troubled ocean,
> Mock at the billows and defy the storm!"

We have already noticed the great benefits which resulted from the redemption of Mississippi from the ruin of radical rule, and the advent of the Democratic party to power in the State. It now remains to show the continuation and the growth of those benefits up to the present time.

When the people of the State became again in possession of its government, the state of public affairs was truly in a deplorable condition. The State and county treasuries were, for the most part, empty, while ever accumulating loads of debt weighed down all public and private enterprise; poverty walked abroad in the land with all its train of woes, aggravated by the discontent which always attends its presence, with those who never before had felt its gripes or tasted its bitter cup.

The condition of Mississippi in June, 1876, the first year of the redemption, is truthfully described in the following extract from the minority report of Senators Bayard and McDonald, of the Mississippi Senatorial Investigating Committee. After describing their visits to Jackson and Aberdeen, where they remained from the 9th to the 29th of June, they say: "No acts of a turbulent or disorderly nature were witnessed by the committee, and no signs of enmity or incivility were exhibited, but on the contrary, courtesy and respect were, on all hands, extended to the committee. The poverty of the people was apparent in their garb, the appearance of their houses, and the marked absence of good and comfortable vehicles. The want of horses or equipages for ordinary pleasure was frankly stated to the writers by sundry gentlemen, who regretted their inability to allow us to see the surrounding country, simply because they and their families were too poor to indulge in the pleasure of a drive.

"Large numbers of ladies in Mississippi, delicately nurtured and carefully educated, are compelled to perform the drudgery of their households unaided by domestic servants.

"This great change in their mode of life and fortunes induces them to conceal their wants from a stranger's eyes, and frequently forbids that open handed hospitality once so characteristic of Southern households.

"The only exhibition of pleasure seeking witnessed was by the colored people, whose processions passed the committee room, and whose holiday excursions by railway started from the depot opposite. The only cannon sound was from their Republican ratification meeting, and theirs was the only music heard by us in Mississippi.

"The poverty of the colored people, also, was often painfully apparent in the groups of witnesses who clustered upon the long galleries, wretched in appearance and miserably clad, giving to the hotel the appearance of a county almshouse."

This picture was by no means overwrought. The negroes, taught by the carpet baggers to regard politics as the first and highest of all considerations, had for years thought of but little besides club meetings, ratification meetings, parades and public speaking. Their crops had been invariably abandoned or neglected at the most critical period, and the very means of subsistence, otherwise than by theft, was even unthought of amid the marshalling of clubs and the beating of drums. The labor of the country during all this time was utterly unreliable and worthless. No planter, when he sowed his crop, had any assurance that he would be able to have it cultivated or harvested; consequently, there could be but little credit based upon farming operations, greatly to the disadvantage of the negroes, who had no other means of obtaining the necessaries of life. Nor was this demoralizing political influence confined to the men, but the negro women also imbibed the same spirit of idleness which it engendered. They attended all the political meetings, listened with greedy ears to the tales of the carpet baggers, and entered into all their political schemes; indeed, their hostility to the white people was more manifest, if not more bitter, than that of the men. Under this state of affairs but little reliable household aid could be obtained from them. The ladies of Mississippi are worthy of all praise for the patience and resolution with which they grappled with the situation, and performed the drudgery of domestic affairs, to which they were totally unaccustomed. Their perseverance and ingenuity achieved for them a triumph over all their domestic troubles as signal as that won over political difficulties by the determination of their fathers, husbands and brothers.

The ladies of the South have indeed had a hard time, but, while the years have rolled away, and with them the causes of their troubles, while every month and day leaves a defacing mark upon the remains of radicalism, the great "clock of destiny" is summoning them back to their proper sphere, announcing the return of the epoch when intelligence, virtue and good breeding will again assume their wonted superiority over the *hoi polloi* and roughs of every race. Already the sun of prosperity has risen upon the land, and its beams shine brighter and brighter as it climbs toward the zenith. The very breezes have become more balmy, the stars twinkle more brilliantly in the canopy of heaven, and the midnight moon seems to shine with a purer and serener light, while all nature seems to clothe itself in new garments, and heaven and nature and art all combine to produce a clime

> "Where every bud that gems the vernal spray
> Swells into fruit beneath the Autumn's ray."

It was not reasonable to expect that the people of Mississippi would recover entirely, short of many years, from the utter prostration of every interest, and the extreme poverty, both public and private, to which they had been reduced by the corrupt rule of radicalism. The absolute want and destitution of a large portion of the people had first to be relieved, before any considerable avail could be made of the great political change. Yet the recuperative powers of the State have been manifested to a wonderful degree. Indeed, the convalescence has even outrun, as it were, the skill of the physician; and with many unwholesome laws upon the statute book, and sadly in need of the presence of others, the State has advanced toward a state of health even beyond the prescriptions of the legislature. And it has but one drawback, and there is but one danger of a relapse—that is demagogy. Keep back the little political poodles and conceited demagogues, who are ever ready to ride into office upon the beguilement of the people, and the State of Mississippi will soon take her firm stand among the first communities of the earth; then, and not till then, call her recovered. The great bane of unlimited franchise is its tendency to political communism; to leave the doors of office open to incompetency and demerit. A democracy presumes an intelligent, patriotic and a homogeneous people, and with the great mass of ignorance which has been incorporated in the political system of Mississippi, there is need of every restraint upon this tendency. Although it was cast upon the white people without their consent, and against their protest, yet, so great has been the political advantages of negro suffrage in a national point of view, that every effort should be made to bring it into harmony with political virtue. It cannot be parted with. Since the crown of thorns has budded into a wreath of political power, it must be cherished, and not a leaf ever suffered to be plucked away; but let it remain as the crowning arch of radicalism, the one lone pillar of its memory.

But the right of suffrage should by all means be confined to those who pay their capitation tax, for this tax is, in Mississippi, devoted exclusively to the maintenance of the public schools, and it is the only method of compelling the great mass of the negroes to contribute to their own education. In some of the States, as in Massachusetts, the condition precedent to the right to vote is twofold— the applicant must not only have paid his poll tax of two dollars, which in Mississippi should be the same, but he must also be able to read. Indeed, these two conditions are of a very compatible nature; the former requiring the voter to aid in the maintenance of the public schools, and the latter compelling him to avail himself of their privileges, prior to his full exercise of the rights of a citizen. And while the latter requisition might be inexpedient, at present, in a general application, in view of the large majority of negro voters who never had the opportunities of the proposed qualification, and who are now, perhaps, too far advanced in years to acquire it conveniently, yet both conditions should be required of the rising generation. The operation of these two laws upon the franchise, combined with the unity of interest of the two races, together with a full restoration of that mutual sympathy and kind feeling engendered by early training and old associations, would insure a lasting state of harmony and prosperity between the white people and the black in Mississippi. Notwithstanding that a large number of them were disfranchised, and therefore could do nothing, yet it is thought by many that the white people of the State committed a great error, in a politic point of view, in not forming an alliance with the negro in the early stages of reconstruction, as was done to a great extent in Virginia, and thereby preventing his complete subjection to the carpet bagger. But we have already noticed the difficulties attending the consummation and practicability of this compact at a time when the demands of the negro extended also to social equality and complete agrarianism. It may be that it was better for both races that the terrible lessons of experience should be learned, so that their natural relations, when resumed, might in consequence be better understood and more enduring. However ruinous may have been the course pursued by the negroes, they certainly deserve praise, in view of the influences brought to bear upon them, for doing no worse. It is doubtful whether any other race, under like circumstances, would have behaved better.

Although in many respects the most antagonistic races on the earth, yet there is a universal sense of inferiority on the part of the negro, in respect to the white man, which seldom rises into envy, and to this characteristic is due all possibility of harmony between them, either in politics or in private relations. So long as this natural sentiment is undisturbed by extraneous influences, so long only can they dwell together in peace. The amicable relations between the two races, resumed immediately upon the restoration of *home rule* in Mississippi, shows how disturbing, irritating and unnatural was the policy of radicalism, which for a long time so completely alienated and antagonized them.

And here, again, and for the last time, let us turn to Wells's terrible description of "Home Rule in Mississippi," under which, "*While Southern statesmen of the Kemper school are gaining admission to the highest places in the national councils, the 'bloody shirt,' by common consent of their Northern co-laborers, is sneeringly held up as a vulgar and unclean thing. Meantime Mrs. Chisolm,*" etc., etc., etc., "turns from her lonely watch by the window," and begins to pack up the old clothes of her husband, "containing blood enough to incarnadine the seas," in preparation for her journey to Washington, where she expects to barter them to the radical party for a fat little office in the United States Treasury Department, where, far away from her uncivilized and savage nativity, she can revel in that refinement which the land of her birth, her childhood and her womanhood cannot afford. This is the import, and in part the language, of Wells, in the conclusion of his picture of home rule in Mississippi. However much that individual may enjoy the flaunting of the so called "bloody shirt" at this late day, it is not believed that he ever spilt any of the fluid that gave to it its *incarnadine* hues. That was shed by gentlemen of the "Kemper school," men who knew their rights and dared to maintain them. And when "the onward tide of thought" shall have kept yet "more pace," and yet more of the "highest places in the national councils" shall be filled by true and upright statesmen, be they Northern or Southern, the government of the United States, freed from the perjury of "joint high commissions," with the "bloody shirt" no longer waving from the dome of the national capitol, and fraud no longer sitting in the presidential chair, will cease to be a by word of scorn and contempt in all the world. The national government will then join in the promotion of that tranquillity which home rule has produced unaided in Mississippi, the restoration of which has been so beneficial to the entire community.

The effects of this home rule, or, more properly speaking, of white rule in Mississippi, cannot be hidden beneath the spiteful misrepresentations of a loafing carpet bagger. Its advantages are felt and acknowledged by every honest citizen, and its fruits are apparent to every observer. It has established peace throughout the State, and if it has not produced a millennium of good feeling, it is because there yet lingers some of the poison disseminated by radical rule.

The State has again inaugurated the development of the resources in which it so plenteously abounds. Every interest has received a new impetus, and its social condition is fast assuming its wonted purity. Negro supremacy, the most infamous feature of radicalism, and which will form the darkest page in the annals of this, or any other age, has been buried forever beneath the scornful indignation of virtue and intelligence. The dethronement of ignorance and vice, or, as it has been more aptly called, the taking of the "bottom rail" from the top and replacing it where it belongs, has wrought a reaction which will not fail to produce that state of prosperity which the rule of intelligence promotes, and the natural condition of things always favors. The way of the pursuit of happiness has been cleared up and reopened to all classes and to every citizen of the State, and the possibility of wealth and political preferment, under the ordinary conditions, made equal in respect to all.

The enormous burden of taxation under radical rule has been greatly lightened, and its limits fixed far short of what they had heretofore been, and what they are in many other States of the Union. The rate of the levy for State purposes has been reduced from fifteen mills on the dollar, upon an arbitrary and excessive valuation of property, to three and a half mills, upon a just and equitable valuation, which has brought the State levy to less than one seventh of what it was under Republican administration. The taxes levied by the county boards of supervisors have also been reduced to less than one half, and fifteen mills on the dollar has been made by law the utmost limit to which the combined taxation can be extended. This rate of taxation will certainly compare favorably with that of most of the other States, and is far below that of many of the States of the Union. In Kemper County, under the radical *régime*, the county levy reached as high as seventeen mills on the dollar, yet, notwithstanding this outrageous rate of taxation, a county debt of thirty thousand dollars was accumulated between the years 1870 and 1875. This debt was bonded when the white people obtained possession of the county government, in 1876, and immediately placed in process of liquidation. The rate of county taxes was then reduced to ten and three quarter mills, which has not only met the current expenses of the county, but has paid the interest on and largely reduced the principal of this debt.

Similar circumstances existed in many other counties of the State, and in all of which similar results have been achieved, and this in the face of the fact that several heavy burdens were, in 1875, the last year of radical rule, transferred from the shoulders of the State to the several counties. In order to make a show of economy in the State expenditures, that party shifted the cost of prosecuting criminals and the maintenance of prisoners upon the counties. These burdens the Democratic party has very wrongfully allowed to remain upon them. The argument that peaceable counties should not, through the channels of the State government, pay in part for the suppression of crime in more disorderly counties, is false in principle, and subversive of that armed unity which the whole State should exhibit against the violation of its laws in any of its parts. It is to the interest of every county that the sword of justice and the dignity of the law should be upheld in every other county of the State. But in addition to these new burdens upon the counties, there was an imperfection in the law which imposed them. These expenses were transferred to the counties, while the revenues heretofore appropriated to them were retained by the State. Such, for instance, was the jury tax, which was an assessment of three dollars for every jury empanelled in a State case. This had always been appropriated to the criminal expenses of the judiciary department of the State government, and it is still retained by the State, although the object of the appropriation has been shifted to the counties. And, as these additional expenses should be considered in regarding the county levies, they should be noted also in computing the reduction of the State expenditures, or in comparing them with the expenditures under radical rule, except those of 1875, which were the lowest under that regime, and were made so by these same transfers.

The expenses of the State government are also less than one half of what they were under the radical administration. From the tabular statements already given we have seen that in 1875 the disbursements on account of the State government were about $1,500,000. In 1876 the whole cost of running the State government, including the expenses of the charitable institutions, was only $518,709.03. At the beginning of the year 1877 the total indebtedness of the State was $3,197,036.47; and during that year $305,659 of this debt was paid, besides the interest, which amounted to $105,868. And certificates of indebtedness to the amount of $22,785 were cancelled. The receipts into the treasury, from all sources, during the year 1877, were $865,327.17, and the entire disbursements during the year were $662,034.69, leaving a balance in the State treasury of $203,292.78. Nor has this great reduction of expenditure been attended by any impairment of the efficiency of the State government. If, under Democratic and home rule, economy has superseded extravagance, so have honesty and competency taken the place of ignorance and corruption. Every function of government has received new strength and vigor from the great change. Intelligent and responsible citizens now fill the offices formerly held by ignorant, incompetent, irresponsible and vicious negroes and adventurers, who floated upon the surface of reconstruction, and were foisted into office by the strength of negro majorities.

Under radical rule the people had no confidence in or respect for, first, the officers, and then for the functions of the offices themselves. They despised alike the legislature and its enactments. They scorned the judges and the judgments of the courts, and submitted to them only from necessity and for the sake of peace and order. But as the administration of the law became more honest, it became also more efficient, and produced a feeling of personal security almost unknown during radical rule. The result has been, also, to destroy all feelings of distrust and bitterness, engendered by radicalism, between the races, and to bring them together upon terms of amity and mutual confidence. Since this natural state of things has been established, and the two races have taken the positions naturally belonging to each, there are no longer grounds of discord between them.

And the negroes no sooner found that their prospects were enhanced and brightened equally with those of the white people, than they cheerfully acquiesced in the change, and a great majority of them would as bitterly oppose the restoration of the old order of things as the whites themselves. The consciousness of the kind disposition of the whites toward them has produced a feeling of security and contentment to which they were strangers during the alienation of the races under radical rule. Consequently, they pay but little attention to politics, and seem disposed, by common consent, to leave the conduct of public affairs to the superior race, while they devote themselves more to their material improvement. Their crops are better cultivated, and their improved condition is manifested in the better garb they wear, and in the number and appearance of their stock. They have laid aside the grum and silent aspect many of them were accustomed to maintain toward the whites, and have put on the air of cheerfulness so natural and peculiar to their race. The sound of the banjo and the old songs of the harvest are again heard in the land, while their children are no longer taught to look upon the white people as objects to be hated, and the time is fast drawing near when it may be said that the color line is entirely eliminated from the politics of the State, and with it the last lingering vestige of radicalism will have passed away.

A far greater interest is felt in the public schools, and more money is appropriated directly to their maintenance, and appropriated more guardedly and wisely.

When the Democratic legislature began to withdraw the school appropriations from the corrupt channels through which they were passed by the radical party, a howl was raised in the North that the public school system was about to be abolished in Mississippi. Yet, so far from this being the case, the State distribution among the counties, together with their aid, has enabled the public schools, in many of the counties, to be maintained six months in the year, instead of two months, the period of their annual existence under the radical administration. The people of Mississippi never objected to the public school system upon principle, but on account of its corrupt management by the radicals, and the social equality which that party sought to force, through it, upon the white people of the State. This feature caused it, at first, to be an object of peculiar disgust and contempt; but since its purification, if there is any inordinate lack of interest felt in the public schools, it is on the part of the blacks, who, in many instances, since its novelty has passed away, manifest but little interest in the cause of education. But there is one difficulty frequently in the way of the establishment of public schools in some localities. It arises from the sparseness of the population. There being no such thing as mixed schools, which, though not prohibited by any special legislation, are made impossible by public sentiment, it often happens that there are not a sufficient number of white children in a district to form a white school, while in other communities there are not negro children enough to form a school having the number of pupils required by law. This is an evil which, like many others of a local nature, can only be regretted.

This obstacle, together with other discouraging local conditions, such as creeks, swamps and bayous, which abound in many sections of the State, renders it almost impossible to maintain a thorough system of education in Mississippi. Yet everything is being done that can be for the education of both races.

The legislature that came in on the reactionary tide of 1875, many members of which were totally incompetent to grapple with the measures which the situation demanded, and many were not the choice of the intelligent portion of the people, except so far as they were the opponents of the radicals in what was, in many instances, deemed a hopeless contest, is entitled to great praise for the action it took in regard to the public school system. The two negro universities and the State normal school for the benefit of the blacks received liberal appropriations, and fully commensurate with those made to the white university of the State, and to the charitable institutions. Surely these appropriations for the maintenance of the colored high schools does not evince much hostility on the part of the white people of Mississippi to the common school education of the blacks. Mississippi fell into the possession of the Democratic party burdened with more contrivances for taxation, for the depletion of the pockets of the citizens and for partisan perpetuation than with public debt! With the exception of the infamous Pearl River navigation scheme, there were no gigantic swindles under color of internal improvements, as in some of the Southern States; the constitution of Mississippi, by a wise and fortunate provision, forbidding the assumption by the State of railroad bonds, and prohibiting all grants to corporations, thus relieving the State in a measure from the thieving rings that preyed upon the treasuries of all the other Southern States. This constitutional restraint enabled Mississippi to emerge from negro carpet bagger rule in a much better condition financially than her less fortunate sisters.

The State debt, on the first day of January, 1876, amounted, as we have already seen, to only about three million dollars, and one half of this sum was due to the school fund, the interest only of which is payable annually, the principal never falling due. The total debt proper of the State, on the first day of January, 1878, had been reduced to less than six hundred thousand dollars. This rate of reduction, running through the present year, will place the public debt proper of Mississippi at a sum below the reach of anxiety and beneath all consideration in comparison with the resources of the State.

Thus, with a pure political atmosphere, and an honest and competent administration of the government, a healthy financial condition, and a greatly improved social and moral state, the future of Mississippi under home or white rule is all that her citizens can desire or her friends wish for. The resources and recuperative genius of the State have been exemplified in a wonderful degree, and have raised it rapidly from its utter prostration under negro radical rule; and it is for its citizens to push the process of elevation to the level of the highest degree of prosperity. To accomplish this, they must first of all thoroughly adapt themselves to the necessary conditions of progress, cut loose from all the drawbacks of old customs, shape their course to fit the circumstances of their situation, and present a solid front to every foe.

From o'er the land and o'er the sea
Comes the loud voice of history,
In solid phalanx lies the strength
That gives to freedom breadth and length,
As the tall oak that towering shoots,
Needs the support of all its roots
To give it beauty, height and form,
And strength to weather out the storm;
So concord must sustain the tree
That bears the fruit of liberty
"Divide and conquer!" was the cry
That often veiled proud Freedom's sky
Then let us, friends, close ranks preserve,
And from our progress never swerve;
And then prosperity will sweep
Across the land from deep to deep,
And hope and happiness will shower
Their beams of gold from Freedom's tower.
Let every breeze that fans the day
Afflate the admonitory lay·
Put on the new, pull off the old,
And all the past forever fold,
Pull off the old, put on the new,
And on the future fix the view;
Let all dispute and bickering cease,
Stilled by the lethic waves of peace.

CHAPTER XVI.

The citizens of Mississippi are and have been the peers of any people in morality, intelligence and bravery. The four leading Protestant denominations have dotted the State with churches, while the Catholics and the denomination called Christians have made considerable progress. Religious services are generally well attended, and there are comparatively but few adults who are not members of some church.

The ministers are noted for their retired and circumspect life, and the gospel is preached in its purity, free from politics and all the whining isms that characterize some of the denominations in the Northern States. Children, generally, are early trained to religious habits, and are taught to view spiritual advancement as the highest aim in life. Profanity is generally looked upon as an evidence of low breeding, and is often a bar to the entrance of good society, while an oath uttered in the presence of a lady is considered a disgrace and a violation of decency, that demands and generally receives punishment, as an insult, at the hands of her relatives or friends. The laws throw every protection around property devoted to religious uses, and are fierce against those who, in any way, disturb the exercise of public worship.

The Baptist and Methodist denominations are the most numerous and prevalent, the Presbyterians and Episcopalians being confined mostly to the towns and villages, where they generally have thriving churches. Great interest is generally manifested in Sabbath schools, the denominations vie with each other in promoting their thrift; and in every town and village, and in many a rural neighborhood, where the population is sufficient, the Sabbath bell sets the feet of the little ones in motion, who, with clean and smiling faces, and clad in their best garb, trip their way to the church of God to learn the lessons of Christianity. It is here that all the distinctions of class are battered down, and the rich and the poor, the glossy silk and the dingy calico mingle in hallowed communion. It is here, too, that holy associations are formed, and here are learned those lessons of charity which cling to the heart through life, and which have always rendered the Southern people the most hospitable and generous on earth. These Sabbath schools, like the churches, are not merely places for the inculcation of peculiar doctrines. The children of parents of every denomination can mingle here and learn nothing but the pure precepts of Christianity untainted with any sectarian dogma. Here is caught that liberality of religious sentiment which characterizes the people of all sects in the South.

Drunkenness is considered a terrible disgrace, and nothing short of the most heinous crime, so surely causes a young man to lose caste, both in society and in business. Indeed, from its promptness and certainty, the social ruin caused by habitual drunkenness is even more to be dreaded than the material adversity which generally overtakes the habit. The consequence is that there is but little dissipation prevalent among the better classes of young men in Mississippi.

The condition of the common school system in the State has already been noticed. There are three public universities in the State, and one State normal school. The latter, with two of the universities, is devoted exclusively to the education of the blacks. The university proper of the State, situated at Oxford, has always held a high rank among the learned institutions of the country, and is very deservedly the object of the pride of the State. It is the fountain from which many of her most distinguished men have drunk the deep draughts of wisdom which made them conspicuous in the councils of the State and of the nation. In this respect the rolls of its alumni society will compare favorably with the escutcheons of any institution of learning in the land, and under its present able management, this institution bids fair to become one of wide celebrity.

Gen. A. P. Stewart, a distinguished officer in the Confederate army, and one of the best scholars in America, is now the president of the university; and his administration has clothed it with a renown which is fully sustained by its other advantages. A prosperous future is assured to this institution by the thriving present.

During the last session three hundred and ninety-one students were matriculated into the university; of these, thirty-one were students of law. There are now a chancellor, eight professors, a principal of the preparatory school connected with the college, and eight tutors employed in the institution. This institution enjoys no private endowments, yet the necessary appropriations, made by the State, including repairs, were, during the year 1877, only $39,000, and there is every prospect that it will, in a few years, become entirely self-sustaining.

The negro university of Alcorn bids fair to be of great benefit to that race and a credit to the State. Its career, however, has been checkered. Under radical rule its mismanagement and corrupt government became so disgusting to the negroes that many of them withdrew their sons from the institution. The discipline, so far from restraining them from evil practices, was so lax and pernicious that it encouraged the worst traits and propensities of the race. The classes had become so badly deranged as to be almost incapable of being identified, and, in some instances, were entirely broken up. Valuable property was allowed to be defaced or destroyed, and the furniture of the institution was stolen and carried away. Such was the condition of the university when the Democratic party assumed the management of affairs, in 1876. Early in that year the governor appointed to the presidency of the institution the Rev. H. R. Revels, a negro, who had been a senator of the United States from Mississippi, and who was, in morality and intelligence, far in advance of his race. His wise and economic government was soon felt, and the university, from that time, entered upon a career of prosperity which has continued to characterize it. The succeeding term opened with fifty students, and the expenses of each were reduced to one dollar and thirty-five cents per week, thus placing it in the power of every industrious negro to send his son to the institution. Regard is now paid to the cultivation of good morals and honest habits, and the president, evidently mortified at the predictions which its former decline seemed to justify, is doing all in his power to prove that his race is capable of enjoying and profiting by the advantages which the higher institutions of learning afford. The students, instead of being a nuisance to the neighborhood, as formerly, have so deported themselves, under the new administration, as to receive the commendations of the citizens.

The appropriations made by the legislature to this institution were, for the year 1877, $10,000, which was managed and applied with economy and honesty. At the beginning of the present year, the number of students had been increased to eighty-three, the price of board reduced to one dollar per week, and only the salaries of the president and the three professors are now drawn from the State appropriations. The other expenses are all paid by the products of the agricultural department of the institution.

Tougaloo University, also for the education of the colored youths of the State, was established, and is chiefly maintained by the American Missionary Society; but a normal department was added by the State, and a State board of trustees was appointed by the legislature to act in conjunction with the society in supervising the application of the appropriations made by the State. This appropriation for the year 1877 was $2,500, but since that time the missionary society has entirely ignored all participation, on the part of the State board, in the management and control of the normal department, and in consequence of which the State legislature has declined to make any further appropriations to the institution. It is, however, in a thriving condition, and at the beginning of the present year numbered one hundred and six students. This is the institution of which the notorious Cardoza was treasurer, and who, while acting in that capacity, stole $2,500 of the State appropriations for the year 1874, and who, notwithstanding, continued to be the radical State superintendent of education, until he was impeached and deposed by the Democratic legislature, in 1875.

There is, also, a thriving normal school for the use of negroes, situated at Holly Springs, which, at the beginning of the present year, numbered eighty-eight pupils This school was established by the State for the purpose of educating colored teachers, and last year the legislature appropriated $3,000 to its use, which the governor, in his subsequent message, recommended to be enlarged. Besides these State schools, there are many other institutions of learning in Mississippi of a high order.

The Baptists have quite a flourishing college at Clinton, in which many young ministers are educated for that church. The university of Columbus, established in that town by Mr. T. C. Belcher, a distinguished educator, is well patronized, and the institution is endowed with the power of conferring all the literary degrees.

The Cooper Institute, situated near Lauderdale Springs, and established by the Rev. J. L. Cooper, is a thriving school, and reflects great credit on its founder. Prof. T. S. Gathwright, late superintendent of education, of Mississippi, and now president of the Texas Agricultural College, for many years conducted a most thriving and popular school at Summerville, in Noxubee County. At this school many young men of the State, who occupy prominent positions, were educated, and his successor will, no doubt, keep it up to its high standard of efficiency and popularity.

The Mississippi Military Academy, established by Col. E. D. Murphey, first at Aberdeen, and lately removed to Pass Christian, also bids fair to become an institute of note. Besides these, there are many female colleges of high character in the State. Most of the religious denominations have female schools, under the especial auspices of their several sects.

The Methodists have a popular college at Verona and Meridian, and the Baptists also have a thriving college at Meridian

The Catholics have a flourishing female school at Holly Springs; they also have a largely patronized and well sustained orphans' home, at Natchez.

The public charitable institutions of Mississippi will compare favorably with those of any other State. These alone the corrupt hand of radical rule never dared to pollute That the appropriations for their use were extravagant, and that the salaries of their officers and attendants were excessive, is true; but that they were left in good hands and were generally well managed, is also true. The arm of Omnipotence seems to have thrown its protection around these institutions through all the dark days of reconstruction and the radical *regime*, and they stand to-day the monuments of the best features of human nature—of charity, which the voice of heaven proclaims a veil for many sins; of sympathy, one of the hinges upon which hang all the law and the prophets.

The asylum for the insane, situated at Jackson, is in a prosperous condition. At the beginning of the year 1877, there were three hundred and thirty-six patients in the institution; during that year one hundred and eight were admitted and thirty-five were restored and discharged, and seventeen died, mostly from old chronic affections. The health of the institution has been remarkably good, there having been but few cases of acute disease.

The capacity of the asylum will accommodate four hundred and ten patients, and the number of inmates at the commencement of the present year was three hundred and ninety-one. The expenditures for the support of the asylum were, for 1877, $58,900, or about $168 for each inmate, which included the cost of board, clothing, medicine, fuel and the wages of the officers, nurses and servants. This was a great reduction from the cost of the asylum under radical rule, the disbursements on account of which were, in 1875, as per treasurer's report, $153,550. This result has been accomplished by the practice of economy and the judicious use of the appropriations in the purchase of supplies. The deaf and dumb institute, and the institute for the blind, both situated at the capital of the State, are noble State charities. During the year 1877, the average number of inmates of the deaf and dumb institute was thirty-nine. In the beginning of the present year there were about fifty. The only drawback to this institution is a lack of room; it has every other advantage that could be desired. It is already filled to its utmost capacity for that comfort to the unfortunate inmates commensurate with the great sympathy and interest which the State manifests in their welfare.

The institute for the blind numbered, on the first day of January, 1879, twenty-nine pupils. In consequence of a remarkable oversight no provision existed, prior to the last session of the legislature, for the admission of colored females. This provision will largely increase the number of pupils.

Both of these institutions are in a flourishing state, and a knowledge of their advantages should be widely disseminated. The deaf and dumb and blind of the State have in them a comfortable and sure support, and every facility for securing an education and learning useful trades, at the public expense, calculated to make them independent and useful citizens. There is no excuse to the rich or the poor for not availing themselves of these advantages, which the State urgently invites them to do. The spirit and conduct of these institutions are beyond the level of any grounds of false pride on the one hand, and within the reach of the humblest citizen on the other. Whatever may be the situation in life of the unfortunate individuals for whose benefit these institutions were established, the State claims the opportunity they afford of extending to them that public sympathy which misfortune should awaken in the bosom of all intelligent humanity—a touchstone—the soul of states as well as the heart of individuals. Between the first of October, 1877, and the first of January succeeding, twenty-one pupils were received in the institute for the blind, and the amount appropriated for the support of the institution during that year was $9,300. The appropriation, under radical rule, for the year 1875, with a sparser attendance, was $15,200, and that for the deaf and dumb asylum, for the same year, was $27,250. The disbursements on account of this institution, for 1877, with a large increase of attendance, were, as per auditor's report, $16,516.12. Dr. Carter, who, for many years, managed the affairs of this institution with success, resigned his position during the summer of 1876, and Professor Charles H. Tolburt was chosen by the board of trustees to fill the vacancy. Professor Tolburt is a gentleman of experience, and under his management the institution has every indication of pushing forward in the same path of prosperity it has steadily pursued under his predecessor.

The rapid increase in the number of convicts in the State penitentiary is much to be regretted, as evidencing a prevalence of crime unknown to the State before the demoralization of radical rule.

On the 1st day of January, 1870, the whole number of prisoners in the penitentiary was two hundred and forty-four, of whom sixty-five were white and one hundred and seventy-nine colored. On the 1st day of January, 1877, there were seven hundred and eleven, of whom six hundred and twenty-eight were negroes; and on January 1st, 1878, there were in the penitentiary one thousand and twelve convicts, of whom nine hundred were colored. Yet with this largely increased number the expenditures on account of the institution have been greatly diminished. The disbursements on account of the penitentiary under radical rule, for the year 1875, amounted to the sum of $132,825.84, and there were then four hundred and ninety-four convicts in the prison. For the year 1876, under Democratic rule, the prison cost the State $23,497.88, and during 1877 the amount disbursed on account of the penitentiary was

The learned professions, in Mississippi, have been adorned by many distinguished members, and her statesmen have ever held a prominent place in the councils of the nation. It would be inapt and inefficacious, in a work of this character, to attempt to mention all whose names glitter in the galaxy of fame, and are interwoven with all that is bright and pure in the annals of the State. At some future day the writer may make these the subject of another work, in which he will allot himself time and space to do justice to their character. Her Prentisses and Davises, and Sharkeys and Yergers, Georges, Barksdales, Browns, Gholsons, Lamars, and a host of others, living and dead, enjoy a renown whose scope is far beyond the reach of this work.

The governors of the State have generally been distinguished for their purity and simplicity of life, and for their patriotism. With the exception of the radical *regime*, no State can show a brighter list of its chief executives than Mississippi. The judges of the supreme court have also been distinguished for their learning and exalted character, and their decisions are noted for lucidness and sound judgment. Nor has the State been wanting in a comparable supply of poetic genius; the streams of Parnassus have gushed from many a hill and meandered through many a valley of the State. Prominent among those who have drunk of its waters are S. Newton Berryhill, of Columbus; W. W. Hoskins, of Corinth; W. S. Kernan, of Okolona; William Ward, of Macon; and Emmet L. Ross, of Canton. Major Jonas, of the Aberdeen *Examiner*, has also written some fine pieces. Nor have the ladies been callous to the sweet inspiration. Among the poetesses may be mentioned Mrs. A. J. Frantz, of Brandon; Miss Hunt, of Vicksburg, who wrote under the *nom de plume* of Madge; Miss Sallie Ada Malone, of Courtland, and many others too numerous to mention, among whom discrimination would be unjust.

The citizens of Mississippi are and have ever been noted for bravery. In the council and in the field, in the storm of battle and the night of persecution they have borne themselves with the same intrepid spirit, and with a valiantness that has awakened the admiration of friend and foe. Her soldiery have been conspicuous in every battle in which they were engaged. Their arms shone with brilliant lustre at New Orleans, on the memorable 8th of January, 1815, where the steady and deadly aim of the Mississippi rifles poured death into the face of the British columns; and at the battle of Buena Vista the Mississippi regiment, led by the gallant Jefferson Davis, received the congratulations of the commanding general for saving the day to the American arms.

Mississippians played a prominent part in the late war. From the Mississippi to the Potomac, from the bloody ravines of Shiloh to the iron clad crests of Gettysburg, wherever they fought, they piled their dead in the foreground of every battle. At the first tocsin of war, they rushed to the front, opened their defiles on the plains of Manassas, and never faltered until they rested beneath the shade trees of Appomattox.

Their promptness and constancy caused them to incur the peculiar spite of the radical party, and drew upon their heads the most rigorous features of reconstruction, which they met in the same undaunted manner, and with the same spirit of defiance and endurance that had characterized them upon the field of battle. They scorned the craven strokes of revenge, and while they renewed in good faith their allegiance to the old government, they indulged in no pinings of regret; and will forever cherish the memory of their dead, and glory in the cause in which they fell.

> The rebel dead, the glorious rebel dead!
> No brand of hate can bow their country's head
> Beyond the shafts of death or hatred's ban,
> Their names are safe, their deeds ennobled man;
> They fell with honor in their country's fight,
> With conscience basking in the beams of right,
> Whatever be their cause, or right or wrong,
> They live in heaven, in history and in song.

APPENDIX.

PETITION AND APPEAL

OF THE

TAX PAYERS TO THE LEGISLATURE.

To the Legislature of Mississippi:

The tax payers of Mississippi, assembled by delegates in convention, respectfully show:

That by reason of the general poverty of the people, and the greatly depressed values of all property, and especially of our great staple, the present rate of taxation is an intolerable burden, and much beyond their ability to pay.

To say nothing of the very large expenditures of common schools, the present rates of public expenditure greatly exceed the amounts deemed sufficient in former days of abounding wealth.

To-day the masses of our people are very poor, and they naturally feel, as they may well demand, that all public expenditures should be greatly reduced, and limited by the strictest rules of economy to the plain Republican system made necessary by their impoverished condition.

It was hoped by many that a period of great prosperity would follow the reorganization of the State, and provision was accordingly made for a costly government, but that hope has given place to despair. Every day the people have grown poorer; lands have diminished in value; wages have grown less, and all industries have become more and more paralyzed. It is daily harder and harder for the people even to live; and many hearts are saddened to-day, burdened with dread lest the little home, only shelter for wife and children, should be sold by the tax gatherer.

These terrible truths show that the present rate of exorbitant expenditures must cease, or the means of the people to pay will soon be utterly exhausted, and their government will be disorganized. A wise statesman will be careful to consider the wants of the people, and studious to devise and prompt to apply needful remedies; and this is what we respectfully ask from the representatives of the people. We are satisfied that public expenditures can be very largely reduced without impairing the efficiency of the public service. It should not be forgotten that the Southern people, in their poverty, have now to bear many burdens unknown here in former times. The public debt of the United States is enormous, and we all contribute, indirectly it may be, to pay the increased Federal expenditures. We may never see the tax gatherer, but we pay the taxes—they make part of the price of the goods we buy. In addition to this, we have the large expense of our common school system. These large items may doubtless be greatly diminished by a wise economy, and the people may bear them, thus limited, as necessary burdens; but the fact that, with strict economy, such burdens may continue to be great, is a strong reason for rigid economy of administration wherever possible. It must be remembered that the people of Mississippi suffer not only from the enormous burdens of needless State expenditures, but also from gross waste and extravagance of boards of supervisors. Added to these are the heavy local burdens that fall upon the inhabitants of cities and towns and the unhappy people of the levee districts.

In September last, Senator Sherman said to the people of Ohio: "The first requisite of a party to administer the government now is *economy*. The most difficult to practice, especially after a period of great expenditure. What we most need is a very large reduction in local taxes; and, still more, a very great limitation of the power of local taxation. Now, in

numerable local authorities, counties, towns, cities, etc., have authority to levy taxes until this amounts, in many instances, to *confiscation.* * * *
Upon this question of local taxation we ought to have no party, or soon incomes will be absorbed by taxes." Apt words these, and wise, even when addressed to the people of rich and prosperous Ohio. With what added force do they apply to us who suffer under greater " local burdens," with the additional weight of enormous State expenditures?

To show the extraordinary and rapid increase of taxation imposed on this impoverished people, we will cite these particulars, viz: In 1869, the State levy was ten cents on the hundred dollars of assessed value of lands. For the year 1871 it was *four* times as great; for 1872, it was *eight and a half* times as great; for the year 1873 it was *twelve and a half* times as great; for the year 1874, it was *fourteen* times as great as it was in the year 1869. The tax levy of 1874 was the largest State tax ever levied in Mississippi, and to-day the people are poorer than ever.

It is true that now, because of diminished property and depressed values, the percentage of taxation must be increased to the amount of revenues levied in former times; but what we complain of is, that the aggregate amount of taxes levied on us in our poverty greatly exceeds the amount levied in prosperous days. The enormity of this great increase in the percentage will become plainer if we consider the fact that our present assessments very greatly exceed the market value of the property assessed. Thus as the people become poorer are their tax burdens increased. In many cases the increase in the county levies, in the same period, has been still greater. But this is not all. A careful estimate shows that during those years of increasing and most extravagant tax levies, the public debt was increased on an average annually over six hundred and sixty-four thousand dollars—a sum of itself sufficient to defray the entire expenses of the government, economically administered. That is, the State spent on an average this large sum each year over and above the amount collected on those monstrous tax levies. What may be the excess for the year 1874 is not revealed. All that we know is, that many of the very large appropriations for the year were some time since exhausted. The like extraordinary results have followed the operations of the boards of supervisors, at least, in many of the counties. Whether these facts prove a lack of economy in administration, or are to be regarded as sad proofs of the rapid exhaustion of the means of the people and their consequent inability to pay, they are painful to contemplate. This excessive rate of expenditure would constrain even a prosperous people to cry aloud for retrenchment and reform. It is corrupting in effect, and altogether evil in results. But if none of these things existed, we should be constrained by still other facts to make this appeal to your honorable body. The present year has been most disastrous to all engaged in agriculture, and consequently to all other pursuits. If all the crops raised in the State this year were sold at present market value, the proceeds of the sales thereof would not, as many estimate, pay the cost of production and the taxes. In many counties the result was still more disastrous, the crops being almost a total failure. It is a sad truth, that in some parts of the State many of our people are beginning to suffer for want of food, and very many are restricted in their poverty to a very few of the necessaries of life. These afflictions fall heaviest at present on the very large class of our poor citizens, but all classes suffer more or less from this common calamity, and the year of their probation of want and suffering is but just begun.

Presented in these several views of the sad condition of the people of Mississippi, our present appeal amounts to this: Shall the few officials, the mere servants of the people, be permitted to fatten and grow richer, while the people grow poorer and starve? Shall these public servants be privileged to enjoy an extravagant waste of the money of the people to the destruction of the property of the State, or will the legislature interpose immediately, and by a vigorous system of wise reform enforce rigid economy of expenditure in all departments of the government, legislative, executive and judicial, and in counties, cities, towns and districts? Let all superfluities be abolished; let every supernumerary be discharged; let every dollar, as far as possible, be saved to the suffering people. For the present, and until the State has become rich and prosperous, let all salaries and public expenditures be graded, not according to the merits and capacities of officials, but be reduced and graded to the lowest possible scale compatible with the efficiency of most rigid economy of administering suited to the extreme poverty of the people.

Throughout the whole State the outcry against this oppression of excessive taxation, and still greater waste of expenditure, becomes louder and deeper every day, and it comes increasing in volume and significant emphasis of tone and expression from citizens of all classes and conditions. All fear the approaching ruin, and all suffer from this common oppression, the difference being only in degree.

With regard to possibilities for retrenchment and reform, we quote and commend to the careful consideration of all the official opinion of Governor Ames, as follows: "There are opportunities for curtailment in every branch of the government" (message on finance, session 1874, page 3). We ask the earnest attention of your honorable body to the following particulars, in which, by proper legislation, very large sums may be saved.

The public printing, by the grossness of its excesses,

amounts to public robbery. We submit that such is the practical result, whatever may be the motive on which the extraordinary system is tolerated. Let examples be cited in evidence: For the five years next preceding the 1st of January, 1861, the average cost of printing for the State did not exceed eight thousand dollars per annum. For the five years commencing with the fiscal year 1870, the average cost of the printing for the State has exceeded seventy-three thousand dollars each year, being an average excess each year on the former of sixty-five thousand dollars. This enormous increase in the cost of public printing cannot be attributed to increased expense of performing the public work, nor to the large increase in the number of our citizens, for the like conditions exist in Mississippi and Georgia; and yet the recent report of the controller general of Georgia shows that the average cost of the public printing in that State for the years 1872 and 1873 did not exceed ten thousand dollars. Mark the contrast, according to the above average. The cost of the public printing for impoverished Mississippi for those two years was over eight times greater than the cost of the same work done in the same year for the State of Georgia. The journals of the two houses of our legislature contain a vast amount of matter utterly worthless to the public; and their enormous bulk, with supplements added, might well cause the inquiry, why were they gotten up in that bulky form if not to swell the profits of the public printer? We cite for the contrast two examples, and one may verify the figures in our State library. In the year 1856, the journals of the two houses contained together one thousand one hundred and sixty-three pages. In the year 1873 the journals contained together six thousand three hundred and ninety-three pages—that is, more than five times the number of pages contained in those two journals for the year 1856. Those journals contain in full every little report that a certain bill do pass, and thus they are swelled with a mass of useless matter. Doubtless the enormous difference in the cost for public printing in Mississippi and Georgia arises from the fact that our journals are thus bloated with useless matter, and also that official reports are printed and charged for more than once, and in part because of exorbitant rates allowed our State printer.

The remedy for these gross abuses and waste of expenditure is plain. Let the journals be greatly reduced in bulk, so as to contain no matter not useful to the public in a legislative journal. Require the official reports to be so reduced in bulk as to contain only essential matters, and those to be stated in briefest intelligible terms. Diminish both numbers and quantities. Let no documents be printed and paid for more than once, and reduce to moderate rates the prices for public printing. Apply like rules of economy and justice to the people—to the public printing of counties, cities and towns.

In this connection, it is proper to call special attention to the district printing bill, which was publicly advocated upon the plea, most extraordinary in a free government, that it is both just and proper to tax the general public to sustain party newspapers. In case of public sales, and in many others, the chief value of a newspaper publication consists in the fact that it gives notice to the people of the particular county in which the sale, etc., is to be made. It seems a mere mockery, under a pretence of fairness, to advertise the property of a citizen for sale under execution or for taxes in a distant part of the judicial district, and at a point remote from the county in which the sale is to be made. The same is true of many other notices required to be published. In very many cases of publication required to be made under the law, the seeming notice can be of no possible use, and yet the poor citizen is taxed with the cost of such useless publication.

The number of circuit judges and chancellors is far greater than the needs of the public service require.

Before the present constitution went into effect, there were but ten circuit judges in the State, who not only discharged all the duties imposed on the thirteen circuit judges now provided for, but also performed nearly all the duties now imposed on twenty chancellors, and there was no complaint that this number was insufficient. By the present system (and we believe in that respect it is a good one) most of the business formerly done by the probate judges is now transacted by the chancery clerks. The chancellors are almost exclusively occupied in what is strictly chancery or equity business, which, as before stated, was formerly within the jurisdiction of the circuit judges. The litigation in the circuit and chancery courts is now far less in amount and value than it was when we had only ten circuit judges. The constitutional amendment, by which the jurisdiction of justices of the peace has been made to include all civil cases not exceeding in amount $150, and the poverty of our people, by which business transactions are very much limited in value, have taken away at least one third of the civil business of the circuit and chancery courts.

The expenses of the legislative department have grown recently into enormous proportions. The sessions are now annual, and have been greatly prolonged, and there has been a great, and, as we respectfully insist, an unnecessary increase in the number of its employés, clerks, doorkeepers, sergeants at arms, porters and pages. Formerly, all the clerical force needed was furnished to the House of Representatives at $1,500, and to the Senate at $1,200 for a session.

We do not wish to be understood as stating that the services of the members of your honorable body are not worth all that is now charged, viz.: five hundred dollars per annum. There is no price within our means to pay which could possibly be too high for the inestimable blessing of an intelligent, working and honest body of men, who consecrate their lives and devote their talents to the study of political economy, and those arts which make a people great, prosperous and happy, and who bring to the great work of enacting laws for the State the rich results of a ripe and varied experience in court affairs. But in our present impoverished condition we respectfully, but earnestly represent, that retrenchment in all parts of the administration is absolutely necessary, and we cannot doubt that the members of your body will initiate this reform by fixing their salaries at the sum paid before the war, which amounted generally to about two hundred and fifty dollars for two years, there being but one session in that time. This sum would be greater than is realized on the average by citizens in private life, and greater also than the average paid members of the legislature by the other States in the Union.

The governor's salary might be, without detriment to the public service, fixed at $4,000 per annum, which is far larger than is paid by other States in the Union having no more wealth than Mississippi. The lieutenant governor's salary might also be fixed at the price usually paid to the presiding officer of the Senate, viz., double the salary of a senator. The salaries of the treasurer, secretary of state, auditor and attorney general we ask may be fixed as they were under the code of 1857; and the clerks and assistance allowed these officers reduced to the number and compensation with the salaries fixed by that code; and the salary and expenditures of the State superintendent of education should be reduced to a very moderate sum. His office should be a room in the capital. And we respectfully ask that the salaries of all other State and district officers should be fixed at the rate paid before the war. The salaries then allowed were sufficient to procure the services of able and competent men, and we feel sure they will be sufficient now. The truth is, that all private pursuits are so depressed, and all official positions so highly remunerative, that the difference begets a wide-spread greed for office, and encourages that bane of all free governments, the growth of a large class whose sole interest in the State consists in their reception of the emoluments of official position.

The cost of assessing and collecting the revenue of the State is out of all proportion to the necessary labor and responsibility required in the discharge of those duties. The gain to these officers is enormous. Under the code of 1857 the maximum which an assessor could receive in any one year was five hundred dollars, and the commissions of the collector were graduated according to the amount collected, so that it rarely happened that a collector received as much as one thousand dollars per annum, and he seldom, if ever, received as much as one thousand five hundred dollars in one year. We respectfully ask that the compensation paid to these officers should be so regulated as in no case to exceed the sums above mentioned. The compensation of the county treasurer should be fixed so as not to exceed in any instance the sum of five hundred dollars per annum. His duties are light, and his responsibility will be small if the county levies are restrained as hereinafter asked for. The fees of the chancery and circuit clerks and sheriffs are too high, and, we are sorry to add, in many instances are very much increased by exorbitant and illegal charges. We ask that this subject be carefully looked into by the legislature, and the rates so fixed, that while a fair and just compensation is allowed for these services, the burdens of the suitor shall not be so great as they now are; and we suggest that the State, like the United States, will fix a point in compensation of county officers beyond which the fees shall go into the State treasury.

In many counties this point might be fixed at $600

in others at $1,000 or $1,200, but in no instance should it be fixed beyond $2,000 for clerks and $2,500 for sheriffs, including their gains as tax collectors. The jail fees are a great burden on the people. They are now too high, and yet, in many instances, extra compensation is allowed by the board of supervisors. They should be fixed at the costs of a plain and healthy support of the prisoners. Imprisonment in the county jail, as a punishment, should be made less frequent. Unfortunately, many who are guilty of petty misdemeanors feel neither the burden nor the disgrace of imprisonment in the county jail. We leave it to the wisdom of the legislature to devise some other mode of punishment which, without inflicting corporeal pain, or bringing forward any badge of slavery, may yet prove more efficacious in reforming offenders, and be less expensive to the tax payers.

The law, also, should require the convicts sentenced to the penitentiary to be immediately removed to the State prison. They are now, in many instances, left in the county jails for many months, to the great cost of the several counties. The jail fees for a day should not exceed thirty cents. The salaries of inspectors of the penitentiary ought to be saved to the State by imposing the very light duties of these offices on other State officers, or on competent citizens, without salaries.

The trustees of the insane, deaf and dumb, and blind asylums should be prohibited from using any of the funds appropriated to these institutions in the way of salaries or fees to themselves.

The appropriations to the State universities are beyond the means of the State to pay, and beyond the necessities of these institutions. The salaries and mileage paid to the trustees of those institutions ought to be prohibited. The duties of these officers are extremely light and highly honorable; like services of all other institutions of learning, in the State, and throughout the Union, are rendered by the best citizens without compensation.

Again, the expenditure of the State's money, poor as the people are, and laboring under the most crushing taxation, for the board and support of certain students, is wrong. The State is under no obligation to furnish these favored few with what is denied to the children of the State at large. The State supposes she discharges her duty to the great mass of her children when she furnishes schools free of tuition for four months in the year. These schools are for the people at large; the colleges and universities are for the more favored few. Not more than one in a thousand, even in the most favored countries, ever go to college. It is wrong that nine hundred and ninety-nine should be burdened with a taxation so crushing that they are deprived of the means, in many instances, of even going to a private school, in order that one fortunate person shall have extraordinary benefits denied to the others. We therefore ask that the scholarships in the two universities be abolished. These remarks apply also to the normal schools.

While we cordially indorse the wisdom of that policy which extends to the children of the State the advantages of a free common school education, we respectfully submit that our present legislation in that respect is radically defective in theory, and in its practical workings is a great wrong, rather than of benefit to her citizens. The present rate of taxation for the purposes of education, and the appropriation made for that purpose, amounts to the enormous sum of $675,000 annually; greatly more than is necessary for carrying on the State government. We suggest that the mistake in this matter has been this:

The attempt has been made on an impoverished State, with all its industrial pursuits in a deranged and constantly changing condition, and all of its property values greatly depreciated, to suddenly inaugurate a complete system of common schools, fully adequate to the wants of the whole people of the State, and to extend this even to a collegiate education. While this would be well enough, perhaps, in a great, prosperous and wealthy commonwealth, yet the attempt in our State, in its present condition, has been productive of such an enormous taxation as to bring ruin to the doors of the parent in the attempt to educate the child, and to produce in the public mind a growing and annually increasing hostility to the policy of free education itself. We therefore respectfully suggest a thorough change of the law in this respect; that the present tax for educational purposes be greatly reduced; that free education be restricted simply to elementary grammar schools; that the pay of county superintendents be reduced, as herein recommended, and that the effort be directed to the gradual and economical building up of a common school system which shall not, by its enormous exactions, excite the hostility of the citizen, but will rather attract to itself his support and affection. } PERCY.

The commissioner of immigration is an unnecessary officer. His duties are nothing; his services of no value. We suggest that his salary might be abolished, or be made merely nominal, and all appropriations subject to his control be repealed. The salaries of county superintendents of education might be saved by uniting that office, having such light duties, with that of sheriff, with an extra compensation of fifty dollars per annum, except when the services of a competent citizen can be got for that sum. The salaries of teachers in common schools are far greater than is necessary to secure the services of the persons employed. For second class schools, $25 per month would be ample, and for first class, $50. On this subject we suggest that a constitutional amendment is necessary in order to give to the present common schools the benefits of fines, forfeitures, and licenses } GEORGE.

now required to be funded. The sessions of the legislature should be biennial. It is within the power of the legislature to fix by law that it should meet only once in two years. This is the plain meaning of section six, article eleven, of the constitution. We ask, however, that biennial sessions be not left to the discretion of the legislature, but that the rule be adopted by constitutional amendment. The constitution should also be amended so as to prohibit all special legislation. A great portion of the time of the legislature is now spent in making that kind of legislation, when the same end would be attainable by general laws. One of the evils of the times is excessive legislation. Statutes are passed and then modified or repealed in whole or in part, without due deliberation, and the result is that the statute laws of the State are becoming more and more intricate and confused at every succeeding session of the legislature. The laws should be plain and simple, so that the citizen may, without danger or mistake, conform his action to them.

There are many other abuses in the administration besides those we have referred to. We leave these to the wisdom and patriotism of the legislature to correct. But, probably, the most flagrant evil of which the tax payers complain, and the greatest outrages perpetrated on their rights, arise from the action of the board of supervisors. This court is really the most important of any in the State, and should be composed of the best men in the several counties. As a general rule, we are sorry to say, the members of this board are wholly unfit to discharge their duties, and are without responsibility or accountability. This, however, is not the fault of the legislature of the State, except in so far as it encourages such men to seek for that position. The county levies, in a large majority of the counties, are extravagant and oppressive beyond all endurance. The contracts for public work are made without economy or care, and with a reckless indifference to the interest of the public. These boards, in some instances, employ their own members to do the work not authorized by law, merely for the purpose of making them extravagant allowances. In many instances these members are wholly ignorant, and are completely under the control of the clerks and sheriffs of these counties, to whom they make extravagant allowances. This is a great evil, and we suggest that remedy which alone seems adequate. Legislation should be immediately enacted, fixing the maximum rate of taxation at fifty per cent. on the State, beyond which they shall not go in any instance. These boards should also be prohibited from making any contracts, or allowances, or appropriations, except when there is money in the treasury to pay them. And every such order or warrant so made and ordered, when there is not money in the treasury sufficient to pay it, should be declared utterly null and void, and all persons concurring in making or issuing them be declared guilty of a misdemeanor in office, and punished for such, as provided by law.

There is another fruitful source of peculation and wrong in the power assumed by the board to allow for stationery, fuel, etc., to the county officers. Under this head large and unnecessary sums are allowed for ink, paper, envelopes, sealing wax, gold pens, pencils and printed blanks. The actual cost of these things is very little, and the actual wants of the office very small, as compared with the amounts furnished. It is the habit of these officers to furnish their friends and favorites with stationery at the public's expense. The remedy for this is to return to the old rule, by which each officer was required to furnish his own stationery, wood, lights, etc., at his expense, except alone where bound volumes of record books were required. There remains another remedy to which we earnestly but respectfully call the attention of the legislature. It is confidently believed that either of the following would tend greatly to the character and responsibility of the board of supervisors. To repeal all laws allowing the members thereof any compensation for their services. The services required of a competent and faithful board would not exceed ten days annually, and the work would be done within that time, if there were no inducements in the shape of a per diem to prolong the sessions. The services would not be more burdensome than the liability to work on the public roads and streets, and the members of the board might be exempted from the latter duty, as well as from jury service. It is believed that if no compensation were allowed, no citizen would seek the office, but that the people could find, without difficulty, a sufficient number of the very best men to discharge the highly honorable and responsible duties of members of the board of supervisors.

But if this be deemed wrong, then we suggest that the compensation of the members of the board be reduced to twenty-five dollars per annum, and that each member be required to give bond and security in the penalty of two thousand dollars, at least, by which he shall be bound to a faithful performance of the duties of his office, and in which he shall be liable for all illegal allowances for which he may have voted. And it shall be provided that in every instance where an allowance or appropriation of money is made, the names of the members voting for and against should be recorded, and that such names voting for such appropriation be embraced in every warrant issued on such appropriations. And in case the alternative of a salary is adopted, then it should be provided that no warrant for such salary should be issued in any case, except where there is money in the treasury sufficient to pay it, after first paying all prior warrants ordered by the board.

The necessities of the people demand further time within which to pay their taxes for the year 1874. A delay of sixty or ninety days would afford great and needful relief; and if, then, the lands of delinquents have to be sold, the period of redemption should be two years, and the damages twenty-five per cent. for each year. We feel constrained to call your attention to the many thousand acres of land now held by the State under sales for taxes in arrears and unpaid. Practically, these lands are a burden to the State, and useless for all purposes of revenue. Many of them were sold during the last war, and some in 1848. If the titles could be depended upon at all, it would be wise to husband the resources thus provided and await the developments of the future; but the tax titles, we may fairly assume, are all worthless. The great object to be secured is, to make these lands available for purposes of revenue, and we suggest that the owners, or parties interested therein, be allowed to redeem them on payment of the State tax for 1874, and if not redeemed by the 1st of July next, that they may be sold to any one upon the same terms. Nor would we restrict any one as to the right to purchase; and would allow any man to buy any quantity he may desire. This policy would defeat the purpose of those who suffer their lands to be held by the State because of the invalidity of her tax titles.

In conclusion, we beg to assure your honorable bodies, that in thus exercising the sacred right of petition we have not intended to cast any reflection upon this or any former legislature. Nor have we been influenced by any motive of gaining a party advantage. The members of the convention which presents this petition belong to all parties. We regard the great interests of the State and her people, so much impoverished by the abuses we complain of, as too high and sacred to be made the subject of party contests. Mississippi has a soil unequalled in fertility and in the variety of its products. Our climate is genial and healthy. Every element of high prosperity and of material and moral advancement exists. But, notwithstanding all this, every business is depressed, the people discontented and paralyzed. We have the benumbing influence of despair and threatened ruin in lieu of the healthy and vigorous activity and energy of hopeful progress. And there yet remains the saddest truth of all. There is distrust and a want of mutual confidence between the different classes of our population, and a deep and wide gulf separating the rulers and the ruled. The tax payers do not desire this, and they now make this respectful petition and appeal to the legislature in the hope that that body may receive it in the spirit in which it is made, and that such action may result as will speedily put Mississippi on the high road to prosperity, which shall bless all classes and conditions, and extend to every section of the State.

EXTRACT FROM THE CHARGE DELIVERED BY HON. J. S. HAMM, JUDGE OF THE SEVENTH JUDICIAL DISTRICT OF MISSISSIPPI, TO THE GRAND JURY OF KEMPER COUNTY, AT SEPTEMBER TERM, 1877, OF THE CIRCUIT COURT.

This extract is introduced to show the spirit of the courts, and the strict enforcement of the law on the resumption by the white people of Mississippi of the control of the affairs of the State.

" The circumstances under which you have come together to discharge your duties are peculiar, and impose upon you a grave responsibility. Since the last term of this court, extraordinary events have marked the history of the County of Kemper. The assassination of one citizen was followed by the deaths, by violence, of several others. The laws were set at naught, the public officers resisted and defied, the jail broken into, and six persons shot to death; some of these persons being at the time in the custody of the officers of the law, under accusations of crime, and the others not being even suspected of any offence. All these acts, except that of assassination, were done openly, and the actors must be known. These things were widely published in the newspapers of the country, and made the subject of acrimonious controversy and discussion—one side attempting to show that the homicides were excusable, and the other seeking to make the impression that they were prompted by political hatred. With the opinions of the newspapers, however, we, as persons charged with public duties, have no concern: on the one hand, they can relieve us from no obligation; on the other, they can impose upon us no duty. For the rule of our duty, and for the extent of our authority, we must look to the constitution and laws of the State, as they have been ordained and enacted, in the appointed ways—through constitutional conventions and legislative bodies. We are not permitted to refer to that mysterious, indefinite, undefined and undefinable thing called the 'higher law;' a law which finds no place either in the code of any civilized State or in the creed of any good citizen.

"The Constitution provides that no person shall be deprived of life, liberty or property, except by due process of law; it also provides that the right of trial by jury shall remain inviolate; and it further provides that in all criminal prosecutions the accused shall have a right to be heard by himself or counsel, or both; to demand the nature and cause of the accusation; to be confronted by the witnesses against him; and to have compulsory process for obtaining witnesses in his favor; and that in all prosecutions by indictment or information, he shall have a speedy and public trial, by an impartial jury of the county where the offence was committed; and that he shall not be compelled to give evidence against himself.

"These great and essential rights of the citizen were not left by the framers of the Constitution to be secured by legislative enactments. They were placed in the bill of rights—in the very front of the Constitution. The legislature cannot take them away. They are fixed in the serene firmament of the Constitution, high above the reach of legislative caprice and popular frenzy.

"Has any person in the County of Kemper been denied these great and essential rights? Has any person been deprived of life without due process of law—without indictment by a grand jury, and a fair and impartial trial by a petit jury? And if yea, who has presumed to set at naught these great, cardinal provisions of the Constitution, designed for the protection of every person? These are inquiries for you to make—these are questions for you to answer. And it behooves you to address yourselves diligently and earnestly to these inquiries. You owe it to the County of Kemper, whose good name has been seriously compromised, by the acts of blood and death of which it has been the theatre, and by the oft-repeated assertion, that the whole people of the county approve those acts; you owe it to the State, the majesty of whose laws has been contemned and set at naught, and the authority of whose officers has been resisted and defied; you owe it to the humane, the just, and the good, everywhere, particularly in your own State, to whose opinion you cannot be indifferent. There is yet another tribunal of which you should not be unmindful. That tribunal is posterity—the men who will succeed you. When the mists of prejudice which pervert the judgment of the actors in the scenes passing before us shall vanish; when these scenes shall be divested of the adventitious importance imparted to them by transient excitement, and be viewed in their true character; when you, who are now required to sit in judgment upon the acts of others, and they whose acts are to become the subject of your inquiries, shall alike repose in the silence of the grave—then will come the faithful historian, who will record the proceedings of this day; then will come a just posterity who will review your decision. And I trust that then your action may be noted in terms of commendation, and that this day may be remembered in the history of the State as honorable to her character for calm, dignified and impartial justice.

"There are still higher considerations which must constrain you to a faithful performance of your duties. You are ministers, sworn ministers of justice. You have taken a solemn oath, and you have called the great Searcher of hearts to witness that you will present no person through malice, hatred or ill will, and that you will leave no person unpresented through fear, favor or affection, or for any reward, or hope or promise of reward, but that in all your presentments you will present the truth, the whole truth, and nothing but the truth. We stand in the presence of that awful Being whose all-seeing eye views with especial concern the temples dedicated to justice and religion. In a little while we shall appear at the bar of our final Judge, where the secrets of all hearts shall be made known, and where every human being shall account for his deeds done in the body. To our final Judge, at that supreme hour, may we all be able to appeal for the purity of our motives and the rectitude of our conduct, and may our appeal not be answered by the blood of innocence, or by the mute anguish of the widow, or by the moaning cry of the orphan, bearing witness against us, as recreant to the high trust reposed in us.

"When a great crime has been committed, it is the duty of every good citizen to aid the public authorities to bring the perpetrator to the bar of justice, in order that he may be indicted, and tried, and convicted and punished according to law, and by his punishment an impressive example set to deter others from the commission of crime. But in no case does the law authorize persons to take the life of a fellow creature, though they may suspect or believe, or even know him to be guilty of crime.

"If men may take the law into their own hands; if they may with impunity slay others, because they suspect or believe, or even know them to be guilty of crimes; if they may arrogate to themselves the right of revenge; then there is an end of all law, and of all lawful authority, and of all government. There will be no safety for the rights of persons, and no security for the rights of property; for there will be no rule of reason or justice, and no power to enforce such a rule. The law of the mob and the rule of revenge will be the only law and the only rule. Terror will paralyze every heart and render valueless every right; and a mournful scene of anarchy and violence, and rapine and spoliation, and bloodshed and death will be the inevitable and melancholy result.

"The true question, then, is, whether criminal justice shall be administered with the forms and solemnities prescribed and by the officers and agents appointed by the law, or by irresponsible mobs, acting not only without the authority and forms of the law, but in direct contravention of all its rules; whether the rights of the citizen shall be determined by known and fixed laws, enacted and promulgated according to the constitutional requirements, or by mob law— a law brutal in its instincts, blind in its decisions, and cruel and unrelenting in its punishments. The one eyed monster of heathen antiquity is its fit personification, for in its darkened rage it rends alike friends and foes, the innocent as well as the guilty. It sways a bloody sceptre over the ruins of social and political order, and wherever its dominion is fixed, there we behold the disintegration of all the bonds of society. This is an important question, for it involves not only the lives, the liberty and the property of the individuals who compose society, but the very existence of society itself. And the solution of this question depends, to a great extent, upon you; for the initiatory and preparatory steps in the punishment of crime can be taken only by you. The law is not self acting, or self enforcing, or self executing. It can only speak through its ministers and agents: and you are the appointed organ to give formal expression to its accusations against all who have disobeyed its precepts. Then let the potent voice of the law be heard through you, and heard in tones neither to be misunderstood nor disregarded by those who have violated its mandates. As good citizens, you must loathe and detest crime. Then do not make yourselves responsible for crime by conniving at it; for in your case connivance will be interpreted to be approbation.

"You are engaged in the service of no party; you are enlisted in the cause of no faction; you owe no allegiance but to the State: and the State now calls upon you to perform your duty, your whole duty to her, fearlessly as men, conscientiously as jurors. She requires you to administer the high public trust with which she has clothed you, with exclusive reference to the public welfare, regardless of all consequences to individuals. She commands you to rebuke the spirit of licentiousness now so mournfully prevalent, to stay the arm of violence so often uplifted for the shedding of blood, and to point out the guilty heads upon which the sword of justice should descend. It is not for you to absolve men from the legal consequences of their own voluntary acts. You possess no such dispensing power. As grand jurors, acting under the solemnities of an oath, you must know no man. Like the law, whose servants you are, you must be no respecters of persons. All whose acts become matters of inquiry before you, must be subjected to the same ordeal. It is not for you to inquire whether those who are accused of crime, be high or low, rich or poor, but whether they be guilty or innocent. You know it is a popular belief, that if a culprit possesses wealth or has influential friends, the law is powerless to reach and punish him, however atrocious may be the crime with which he is charged, and however clear may be the proof of his guilt; and to the reproach of criminal justice, candor constrains the admission that facts go very far to justify this belief.

"Perform the grave and important duties with which you are charged as the solemn oath you have taken requires you to perform them, and you will furnish no ground for such an imputation upon the criminal justice of the State. Inquire diligently into all violations of the criminal laws, and make such presentment in each case as the very truth of the matter requires. Present no persons through malice, hatred, or ill will; leave no person unpresented through fear, favor, or affection, or for any reward, or hope or promise of reward. In all your presentments, present the truth, the whole truth, and nothing but the truth. In this way, and in this only, can you acquit yourselves of your duty to the State; in this way, and in this only, can you merit the applause of the just, the good and the wise; in this way, and in this only, can you secure what is preferable even to the applause of the just, the good and the wise—the approbation of your own hearts and consciences."

Lightning Source UK Ltd.
Milton Keynes UK
UKHW022037220321
380813UK00003B/356